FARM EQUIPMENT
And How to Use It

Other Classic Farming Titles Available from The Lyons Press:

Farm Appliances and How to Make Them

Farm Blacksmithing

Farm Conveniences and How to Use Them

Farm Machinery

Farm Motors

Handy Farm Devices and How to Make Them

Operation, Care and Repair of Farm Machinery

FARM EQUIPMENT
And How to Use It

HARRY C. RAMSOWER

THE LYONS PRESS

Guilford, Connecticut
An imprint of The Globe Pequot Press

The Lyons Press is an imprint of The Globe Pequot Press

Originally published by The Athenæum Press, 1917

Printed in Canada

2 4 6 8 10 9 7 5 3 1

The Library of Congress Cataloging-in-Publication Data
is available on file.

CONTENTS

ACKNOWLEDGMENTS

The author desires to acknowledge his obligation to the following firms for their hearty coöperation in furnishing illustrative material: Acme Harvesting Machine Company, Peoria, Ill.; Advance-Rumley Thresher Company Inc., Laporte, Ind.; The Akron Cultivator Company, Akron, Ohio; S. L. Allen & Company, Philadelphia, Pa.; The American Seeding-Machine Company, Springfield, Ohio; Angle Manufacturing Company, New York, N. Y.; Appleton Manufacturing Company, Batavia, Ill.; Aspinwall Manufacturing Company, Jackson, Mich.; Baker Manufacturing Company, Evansville, Wis.; Bateman Manufacturing Company, Grenloch, N. J.; The Bauer Bros. Company, Springfield, Ohio; H. L. Bennet & Company, Westerville, Ohio; The N. P. Bowsher Company, South Bend, Ind.; The Brown Manufacturing Company, Zanesville, Ohio; Challenge Company, Batavia, Ill.; Champion Potato Machinery Company, Hammond, Ind.; The Cook Motor Company, Delaware, Ohio; Deere & Company, Moline, Ill.; The Joseph Dick Manufacturing Company, Canton, Ohio; The Domestic Engineering Company, Dayton, Ohio; The Duplex Mill & Manufacturing Company, Springfield, Ohio; Edison Storage Battery Company, Orange, N. J.; The Electric Storage Battery Company, Philadelphia, Pa.; Fairbanks, Morse & Company, Chicago, Ill.; Farm and Fireside, Springfield, Ohio; The Fitz Water Wheel Company, Hanover, Pa.; The Foos Gas Engine Company, Springfield, Ohio; Gale Manufacturing Company, Albion, Mich.; Goodell Company, Antrim, N. H.; The Hardie Manufacturing Company, Hudson, Mich.; The Hercules Electric Company, Indianapolis, Ind.; The Hoover Manufacturing Company, Avery, Ohio; International Gas Engine Company, Cudahy, Wis.; International Harvester Company of America, Chicago, Ill.; The Janesville Machine Company, Janesville, Wis.; The Johnston Harvester Company, Batavia, N. Y.; The James Leffel & Company, Springfield, Ohio; The Litchfield Manufacturing Company, Waterloo, Iowa; The Mantle Lamp Company of America, Chicago, Ill.; Moline Plow Company, Moline, Ill.; New Idea Spreader Company, Coldwater, Ohio; The "New-Way"

Motor Company, Lansing, Mich.; The Ohio Rake Company, Dayton, Ohio; Oliver Chilled Plow Works, South Bend, Ind.; Oxweld Acetylene Company, Newark, N. J.; Parlin & Orendorff Company, Canton, Ill.; Parrett Tractor Company, Chicago, Ill.; The Reliable Engine Company, Portsmouth, Ohio; Robinson Spreader Company, Vinton, Iowa; Rock Island Plow Company, Rock Island, Ill.; Roderick Lean Manufacturing Company, Mansfield, Ohio; The E. W. Ross Company, Springfield, Ohio; Root & Van Dervoort Engineering Company, East Moline, Ill.; Rude Manufacturing Company, Liberty, Ind.; The Silver Manufacturing Company, Salem, Ohio; Stoughton Wagon Company, Stoughton, Wis.; The Stover Manufacturing Company, Freeport, Ill.; Charles A. Stickney Company, St. Paul, Minn.; Strickler Hay Tool Company, Janesville, Wis.; Superior Manufacturing Company, Ann Arbor, Mich.; Van Gleckland Company, New York, N. Y.; The Webster Electric Company, Racine, Wis.; The Whitman & Barnes Manufacturing Company, Akron, Ohio; Wilder-Strong Implement Company, Monroe, Mich.; Windhorst Light Company, St. Louis, Mo.; Walter A. Wood Mowing and Reaping Machine Company, Hoosick Falls, N. Y.; The Youngstown Sheet and Tube Company, Youngstown, Ohio; The Ypsilanti Hay Press Company, Ypsilanti, Mich.

PREFACE

This book, as suggested by its title, contains a discussion of the general problem of equipping the farm and the farmstead. The material herein presented has been collected from various sources during the author's service as a teacher. An effort has been made to bring together and to present in a readable and teachable form such facts and principles as the modern farmer demands and must understand for the successful practice of his profession.

It is only in very recent years that questions such as those discussed in this book have been given the consideration which they deserve. Colleges, experiment stations, institute speakers, and lecturers generally, have given their full time and effort during the past quarter of a century to the discussion of larger crop yields and better live stock. It is well perhaps that it should have been so, for profitable crop and live-stock production are the foundation of agricultural prosperity. On the other hand, when one reflects that about one fifth of the total value of farms in the corn belt is wrapped up in buildings and machinery, the wonder is that the subject has not been given adequate discussion long before. But times have changed and the remarkable interest which is now being taken in such questions as farm buildings, water supply, sewage-disposal, farm lighting etc. proves beyond question that information on these and kindred subjects is being eagerly sought.

The point of view taken in this book has been, first, that of the farmer of the present who is seeking information as to ways and means of making his work easier and his burdens lighter — to whom it is hoped the book will make a strong appeal and in the solution of whose problems it is believed he may find practical help; second, that of the student who is to become the farmer of the future. In the student's interest an attempt has been made to arrange the subject matter in pedagogic form, though it is probably true that the formal rules of pedagogy have frequently been violated, for in the presentation of a subject so new, and on which there is so little available material, the chief problem has been what to present rather than in what manner it should be presented. An effort has also been made to approach each subject in such a way as to emphasize the practical application of the principles involved and studiously to avoid academic discussion of detail having little or no practical value.

The author wishes to express his deep obligation to the many commercial firms through whose hearty coöperation the use of many of the illustrations herein found was made possible, and especially would he commend his publishers for their painstaking care in the preparation of illustrative material. Thanks are due also to Mr. F. W. Ives, for generous assistance in the preparation of drawings. It is hoped that the many errors which are sure to occur, together with the possible shortcomings of the book, will be given charitable consideration.

H. C. RAMSOWER

EQUIPMENT FOR THE FARM AND THE FARMSTEAD

CHAPTER I

SOME PRINCIPLES OF MECHANICS

In a study of farm engineering and, in particular, of that phase of the subject dealing with farm mechanics, we are constantly considering the matter of forces, their application, their transformation, their effects, as embodied in even the simplest farm tools. A certain force is required to draw a plow, to drive a wedge, to lift a load, to make an engine run, to tie a knot in a grain-binder, each task requiring a different method of utilizing the same thing — force; and it is only through a knowledge of some of the simple principles of mechanics that we can come to a clear understanding of these things.

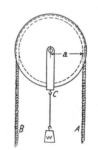

Fig. 1. Illustrating the principle of moment and moment arm

Force. A *force* is an action exerted by one body upon another, which tends to change the state of motion of the body acted upon. Thus, a loaded wagon is drawn by a team. The team (one body) exerts a force upon the wagon (the other body) and changes its state of motion. A man picks up a bucket of water. His hand changes the state of motion of the bucket and therefore exerts a force. A small boy endeavors to lift the same bucket but does not move it. The definition of a force, however, still holds true, since he tends to change its state of motion.

Moment of a force. If a rope AB is directed over a pulley as shown in Fig. 1, and another rope is attached to the axle of the pulley as at C and a weight W suspended from this rope, there will obviously be no rotation of the pulley. If the weight be transferred to *A*, however, the pulley will begin to rotate toward the right. The force exerted by the weight in this posi-

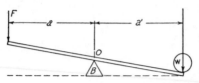

tion is said to have a moment arm *a*, which is the perpendicular distance from the line along which the force acts to the axle of the pulley, or, more generally speaking, to the axis of rotation. This tendency of a force to produce

FIG. 2. Another method of illustrating the principle of moment and moment arm

rotation about a given axis is called the *moment of the force* in respect to that axis; hence,

The moment of a force = the force × the moment arm.

In Fig. 2 the force *F* applied to the end of the lever working over the fulcrum *B* tends to lift the weight *W*. In other words, it tends to produce rotation about the axis *O* because it has a moment arm *a*.

The moment of the force $= F \times a$.

Line representation of forces. Any force acting on a body is completely described if three things are stated: (1) its point of application, (2) its direction, and (3) its magnitude. Since a line may begin at any point, may be drawn in any direction, and may be of any length, it may be used to represent a force. Any convenient scale may be assumed, as 10 lb. to the inch, 20 lb. to the inch, etc. Thus, two boys each have a rope tied to a post at approximately the same point, as shown in Fig. 3.

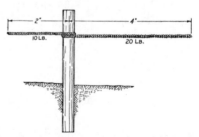

FIG. 3. Line representation of forces

One of the boys exerts a pull of 10 lb. in one direction, the other a pull of 20 lb. in the opposite direction. If two lines are drawn, one 2 in. long representing the 10-pound force, and the other extending 4 in. in the opposite direction, we have a representation of the magnitude and direction of each of the forces in question. Plainly, the sum, or *resultant*, of these is represented by the difference in length of the two lines,

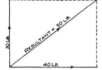

a difference which represents a force of 10 lb. acting in the direction of the greater force.

Composition of forces. In Fig. 4 let it be assumed that two ropes are attached to a weight. A force of 40 lb. is applied at the end of one rope and a force of 30 lb. at the end of the other, which is at an angle of 90° to the first, both ropes being in the same plane. The tendency of the two forces will be to move the object in a direction represented by

FIG. 4. Resultant of two forces acting at a 90° angle

The resultant produces the same effect as the two original forces

the diagonal of the parallelogram as constructed on the two force lines. Since the two lines as drawn completely specify the two forces acting on the body, the diagonal will specify in magnitude and direction a single force which could supplant the two forces and produce the same effect on the body. Plotting the forces to a scale of 10 lb. to the inch and completing the parallelogram, we find that the length of the diagonal represents the resultant of the two forces.

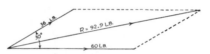

FIG. 5. Resultant of two forces acting at a 30° angle

The parallelogram method applies even though the forces are not acting at an angle of 90° with each other

The same relation exists between the two forces and their resultant, even though the forces act at angles other than 90°. If, for example, a horizontal force of 60 lb. acts at an angle of 30° with another force of 36 lb., the diagonal of the parallelogram, completed as before, will show the resultant to represent a force of 92.9 lb. (Fig. 5).

It may be concluded, therefore, that if two forces act at the same point and in different directions in the same plane, the resultant may be found from the parallelogram of forces and will be represented in magnitude by the diagonal of the parallelogram.

If more than two forces act at a point, the resultant of the system may be found by determining the resultant of any two, then the resultant of this resultant and a third force, etc. through all the forces, the last resultant being that of the system (Fig. 6).

Resolution of forces. Just as two or more forces acting upon a body may be combined into one force having the same effect on the body, so may a single force be resolved into two or more component forces having the same effect upon the body as the original force. Such a process is called the resolution of forces, and the solution of such cases is through the parallelogram, as before. In Fig. 7, for example, a force of 100 lb. is acting at an angle of 30° with the horizontal. This force may be resolved into its horizontal and vertical components by completing a parallelogram of which the given force is the diagonal, one side being vertical, the other horizontal. Constructing

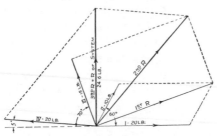

FIG. 6. Showing method of finding the resultant of three or more forces

A system of three or more forces may be reduced to a single resultant by the parallelogram method

to scale, the horizontal force is found to be 86.6 lb. ; the vertical force, 50 lb.

It should be clearly understood that the result of the solution shows that when the force of 100 lb. acts on the body at an angle of 30°, as shown, there is a tendency to lift the body vertically as well as a tendency to draw the body in a horizontal direction. To find the values of these two tendencies is the object of the solution.

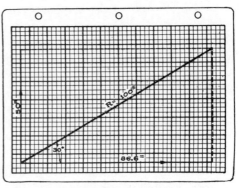

FIG. 7. Showing the use of coördinate paper in plotting curves

The use of coördinate paper. The solution of simple problems in the composition and resolution of forces is readily accomplished on coördinate paper. A sample of eight-division paper with a problem solved is shown in Fig. 7.

Work. When a force acts upon a body and causes it to change its state of motion, work is done upon that body. For example, a team draws a loaded wagon. The state of motion of the wagon is changed, and hence work is done. *Work*, therefore, is equal to the product of the *force* exerted and the *distance* passed over in the direction in which the force acts; or,

$$\text{Work} = \text{force} \times \text{distance},$$
or $$W = Fs.$$

If the displacement is not in the direction in which the force acts, the work done is equal to the product of the force and the component of the distance in the direction in which the force acts, or the product of the distance and the component of the force in the direction of displacement. Thus, a barrel of salt is rolled up a plank twelve feet long into a wagon four feet high, the force acting in a line parallel to the ground. The work done is equal to the horizontal component of the distance over which the force acts (which is the distance on the ground from the end of the plank to the wagon) × the force.

The significance of the factor s should be noted. The load above referred to might be so heavy that the team could not move it. No matter how hard they strain, no matter how much force they exert, no work is done until the wagon is moved.

Measure of work. Since work is the product of force × distance, if, as is the custom, force is measured in pounds and distance in feet, the unit of work becomes the *foot-pound* (ft.-lb.); that is, a foot-pound of work is done when a force of 1 lb. acts through a distance of 1 ft. In the case of the barrel of salt, if the barrel weighs 180 lb. and is lifted through a vertical distance of 4 ft., the work done is equal to $180 \times 4 = 720$ ft.-lb.

Power. A mason's helper carries a pile of bricks from the ground to the second story of a building. The same amount of work is done whether he performs the task in one hour or in ten. If the work is done in one hour, however, more energy is consumed, more effort is put forth, more power is required. Hence *power is the rate of doing work*, the element of time entering into consideration.

Unit of power. The customary unit of power is the *horse power* (H. P.). When coal was raised from the mines in England, it was found that the average horse could lift a certain number of pounds through a certain height in one day. From this practical approximation the value of the unit for horse power was determined. It represents work done at the rate of *33,000 ft.-lb. per minute*,

or $\qquad$ H.P. = 33,000 ft.-lb. per minute.

Energy. Energy may be defined as the *power to do work*. Thus, water flowing over a dam possesses energy which may be used to turn a water-wheel. A storage battery possesses energy, since it may furnish the current to run a motor, ignite the charge in a gasoline engine, etc. A sledge hammer possesses energy when poised in the air.

Energy is of two kinds. *Potential* energy is defined as energy due to *position*, such as that possessed by water flowing over a dam. It may be measured by ascertaining the amount falling and the distance through which it falls. Thus, if the dam is 10 ft. high, each cubic foot of water has a potential energy of 62.4 × 10 = 624 ft.-lb. Therefore,

$$\text{Potential energy} = W \times h,$$

where $\qquad W = $ weight in pounds
and $\qquad h = $ height in feet.

Kinetic energy is energy possessed by a body because of its *motion*. Thus, after water begins to fall it possesses energy because of its motion, and the common expression for this condition is

$$\text{Kinetic energy} = \frac{MV^2}{2},$$

where $\qquad M = $ mass (weight ÷ gravity)
and $\qquad V = $ velocity in feet per second.

Machines. When the word "machine" is mentioned we think at once of corn-planters, grain-binders, gasoline engines — tools with which we are familiar. These are machines, indeed, but each one, being rather complex, is made up of simpler elements which are machines just as truly as are the more complex structures. A machine is a device which receives energy from some outside source and transmits and delivers it, in part, to some other point for the purpose of doing work. The object in using machines is to perform work which could not be performed so easily or so quickly without them, and at the same time to secure certain mechanical advantages.

The lever and the inclined plane are the two basic machines. All other simple machines, such as the screw, the wheel and axle, the wedge, etc. — of which more complex machines are composed — are different forms of the lever and the inclined plane.

The lever. The lever is used in three different forms, or classes — the class used depending upon the kind of work to be done, since each class has its particular advantage. The three classes are shown in Fig. 8. The distinguishing feature in the classes is found to be in the point at which the force is applied in relation to the weight and the fulcrum. In the *first* class the force must move over a much longer distance than the weight; hence power is gained at the expense of distance, and the force moves in a direction opposite to that of the weight. In the *second* class the same advantage is had as in the first class, but in this case the force and the weight move in the same direction. In the *third* class the force moves through a shorter distance than the weight, velocity being secured at the expense of force.

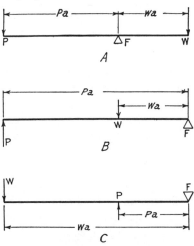

FIG. 8. Three classes of levers

A, first class; *B*, second class; *C*, third class

The solution of problems involving any one of the three classes depends upon the equation

Power × power arm = weight × weight arm,

or $P \times Pa = W \times Wa.$

No matter what the shape of the lever, the power arm is measured as the *perpendicular distance* from the fulcrum to the line in which the power acts.

8

The inclined plane. The inclined plane is another simple machine, and is frequently used in rolling barrels up a plank, in the tread power, etc. The mechanical advantage depends upon the direction in which the power is applied. In Fig. 9, W might represent a barrel being rolled up an inclined plane. The weight of the barrel is represented by the vertical line WD. Resolving this into its two components, WE and WF, we find that WE represents the force that tends to pull the barrel down the plane. From the similar triangles DEW and ABC,

$$EW: DW :: BC: AC,$$
or
$$P: W :: BC: AC,$$
or   Power × power's distance = weight × weight's distance.

When the power, therefore, acts in a line parallel to the plane, the power's distance is the length of the plane. When the action is parallel to the base of the

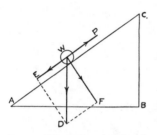

FIG. 9. Illustrating the principle of the inclined plane

plane, the power's distance is the length of the base — the weight's distance being the same in either case and being equal to the height of the plane.

The jackscrew. The screw is a modification of the inclined plane. The pitch of a screw designates the distance in inches between threads. Therefore a screw of $\frac{1}{8}$ pitch (sometimes designated as 8 pitch) has eight threads per inch, and in order that the screw may be moved through one inch it must be turned eight times around. The jackscrew is a screw built on a large scale and so constructed as to use the principle of the inclined plane in a peculiar way. The mechanical advantage is determined in the same way as for the inclined plane. This calculation is based upon the condition that the power moves through a distance equal to the circumference of a circle whose radius is the length of the jackscrew bar, while the weight is being moved through a distance equal to the pitch of the screw.

The wheel and axle. The wheel and axle is an application of a lever of the first or the second class — usually of the second class. In most cases, as in the common windlass, the radius of the wheel (in this case the crank) is the power arm, while the radius of the axle is the weight arm. Problems involving the wheel and axle are solved most easily by means of the lever formula.

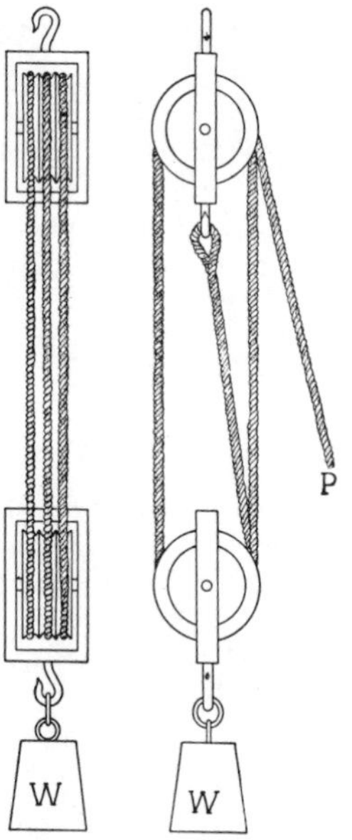

The pulley. The pulley is a lever of the first or second class having equal arms. A single pulley has no mechanical advantage, but serves simply to change the direction of the rope. When pulleys are used in combination, however, as in a tackle, the mechanical advantage varies directly as the number of cords supporting the weight.

In the tackle shown in Fig. 10 there are three sheaves in both the upper and the lower block. If the lower block is raised one foot, the power applied at P will move through six feet. Hence, neglecting friction, a given power at P will raise a weight W six times greater than itself.

FIG. 10. Front and side view of a tackle

Each block has three sheaves or pulleys. The rope to which the power is applied is the fall rope, and the block from which this rope passes is the fall block

The differential pulley. The differential pulley is a modified block and tackle used in lifting great weights, as in machine shops, where the load must be held by the pulleys for some time. Fig. 11 illustrates the construction, and its operation may be explained, with the help of Fig. 12, as follows : The upper block has two sheaves differing slightly in diameter ; the lower block has but one sheave. The pulleys are usually threaded with a cable chain. If a force, applied at P, moves downward until the upper sheaves turn once around, it will have moved through a distance equal to $2\pi R$, and rope AA' will be raised the same distance. At the same time the smaller sheave will turn

FIG. 11. The differential pulley

once around, and rope BB' will have been lowered a distance equal to $2\pi r$. The rope $AA'B'B$ will be shortened a distance equal to $2\pi R - 2\pi r$, or $2\pi (R - r)$, and the weight will be moved up one half this distance. The ratio between the distance through which the power moves and the distance through which the weight moves, which is the mechanical advantage of the pulley, becomes $\dfrac{2\pi R}{\pi (R - r)} = \dfrac{2R}{R - r}$. The question might arise as to why the weight does not travel downward when the power is removed.

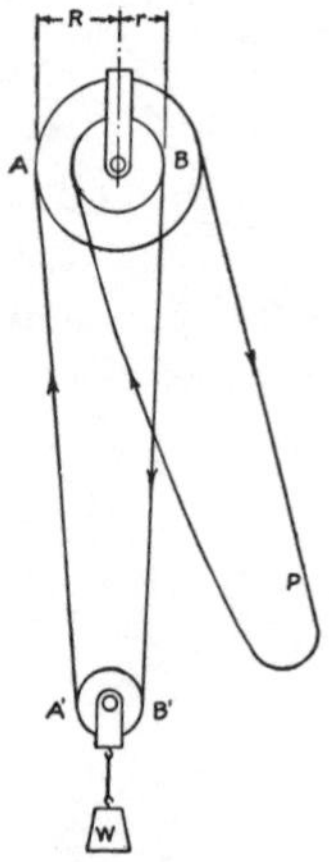

FIG. 12. Illustrating the principle of the differential pulley

The moment tending to turn the sheaves in a clockwise direction is equal to $\dfrac{W}{2} \times r$; the counterclockwise moment is $\dfrac{W}{2} \times R$. Since R is greater than r, the tendency to a counterclockwise rotation is $\dfrac{W}{2}(R - r)$. Friction in the pulley must equal this amount or the weight will move downward if the power is removed.

Friction. Friction is the resistance encountered when an effort is made to slide one body along another. If a loaded sled is standing on snow, quite a force is required to start it; but once started, it is kept moving by the application of a very small force. Here, then, are two kinds of friction : (1) *static* friction, or friction encountered when a body is started from rest, and (2) *sliding* friction, or friction encountered when a body is kept in motion.

The *coefficient* of friction is the ratio between the force necessary to start or draw one body along another and the pressure normal to the surface in contact ; that is,

$$\text{Coefficient of friction} = \frac{\text{friction}}{\text{pressure}}.$$

It is very evident that friction is an extremely variable factor depending upon many variable conditions. Experimental evidence goes to show, however, that certain general statements, which are known as the laws of friction, may be made.

1. Friction is independent of the area in contact.

2. Friction is proportional to the pressure between the surfaces in contact.

3. Friction does not vary greatly with velocity, but is greatest at low speeds.

4. Friction depends upon the nature of the surfaces in contact.

Friction in machines. Since all machines, no matter how simple, have surfaces rubbing on other surfaces, the element of friction must be considered. The amount of friction, with other losses, determines the *efficiency* of a machine; by efficiency is meant the ratio between the amount of energy delivered by a machine as useful work and the amount put into the machine. For example, a certain amount of gasoline is consumed in operating an engine for a given length of time. This fuel in the process of combustion exerts a certain definite force against the piston head. If, now, a break is applied to the belt pulley, and the useful work which the engine is capable of delivering is measured, it will be found to be less than that delivered to the piston head. Friction and other losses consume the difference. The efficiency, then, may be stated thus:

$$\text{Efficiency} = \frac{\text{output}}{\text{input}}.$$

As a concrete illustration, a jackscrew having $\frac{1}{4}$ pitch is placed under a load of 4 tons. To lift the load it is necessary to exert a force of 50 lb. on the end of the jackscrew bar, the bar being 18 in. from its end to the center of the screw. Theoretically the force required if the jackscrew were a frictionless machine would be as follows:

$$8000 \times \frac{1}{48} = x \times 9.42 ;$$

whence
$$x = 17.6 \,\text{lb.}$$

In this case the output, or the work actually delivered, is 17.6 lb., while the input is 50 lb.; hence,

$$\text{Efficiency of jackscrew} = \frac{17.6}{50} \times 100 = 35.2 \text{ per cent.}$$

It is not possible to eliminate all of the friction in farm machines, but their efficiency may be generally increased by giving attention to their proper care and adjustment. Dull knives will greatly decrease the output of the mower, the grain-binder, the ensilage-cutter, etc. A little rust on the plow, the cultivator shovels, or the binder knotter materially increases friction. Lack of grease and oil on the bearings of the wagon, the manure-spreader, the binder, etc. increases not only friction but the wear on the bearings.

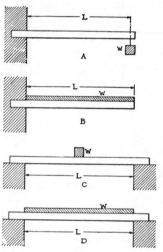

FIG. 13. Four different ways in which beams may be loaded

Strength of materials. All materials used in the construction of farm implements and farm structures are subjected to certain stresses and strains. They must therefore be so designed as to meet the demands made upon them without breaking. In determining the load which a timber — for example, a floor joist — will carry, two things must be taken into consideration, namely, the size and shape of the joist and the manner in which it is loaded.

The load which a timber submitted to a bending stress will carry, varies as the breadth, as the square of the depth, and as the length between supports. A timber may be loaded in at least four different ways: it may be (1) supported at one end and loaded at the other, (2) supported at one end and uniformly loaded, (3) supported at both ends and loaded in the middle, (4) supported at both ends and uniformly loaded.

A *factor of safety* is used, also, in the design of timbers subjected to stress. This factor recognizes the fact that the safe load is very much less than the breaking load, the amount by which it is less depending on the strains to which it is likely to be subjected. The safe load may vary from one third to one twelfth of the breaking load, but as a rule it is taken to be about one sixth, in which case the factor of safety is said to be six. Taking these factors into consideration, certain formulas are presented to fit the cases above mentioned, by means of which it is possible to determine the proper size of timbers to use in places where a load is supported (as on floor joists) or to determine the safe load which timbers will carry.

Naturally the load will vary with the kind of timber used. To allow for this a *constant, A,* is included in the formulas, and the value given this constant provides for a reasonable factor of safety. The values of *A* are as follows for the materials mentioned :

Yellow pine, 100   White oak, 75   Chestnut, 55   Steel, 889
White pine, 60   Hemlock, 50   Cast iron, 167   Limestone, 8

CASE I. *Beam supported at one end and loaded at the other.* (Fig. 13, A.)

$$S = \frac{bd^2 A}{4L},$$

$$b = \frac{4\,SL}{d^2 A},$$

when
S = safe load in pounds,
b = breadth in inches,
d = depth in inches,
L = span in feet,
A = constant.

CASE II. *Beam supported at one end and uniformly loaded.* (Fig. 13, B.)

$$S = \frac{bd^2 A}{2L},$$

$$b = \frac{2\,SL}{d^2 A}.$$

CASE III. *Beam supported at both ends and loaded in the middle.* (Fig.13, C.)

$$S = \frac{bd^2 A}{L},$$

$$b = \frac{SL}{d^2 A}.$$

CASE IV. *Beam supported at both ends and uniformly loaded.* (Fig. 13, D.)

$$S = \frac{2\,bd^2 A}{L},$$

$$b = \frac{SL}{2\,d^2 A}.$$

As an illustration of how the formulas are handled, the following problem is assumed : A yellow-pine timber 2 in. in width

14

supports a hay fork and carrier at the end of a barn. How deep must the timber be to carry safely a load of 1500 lb. when applied 3 ft. from the support?

The problem falls under Case I, in which $b = 2''$ and $L = 3'$.

Substituting,
$$1500 = \frac{2\,d^2 \times 100}{4 \times 3},$$
$$18{,}000 = 200\,d^2,$$
$$d^2 = 90,$$
$$d = 9.4.$$

Hence a $2'' \times 10''$ piece would be used.

Eveners. Fig. 14 illustrates the principle underlying the construction of the common two-horse evener, or doubletree. In the

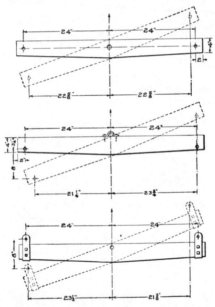

upper figure the three holes are on the same straight line. No matter in what position the horses are in relation to each other, the load will be evenly divided between the two, because the lever arms, as shown in the figure, will always be of the same length.

In the middle figure the end holes are placed to the rear of the middle hole, a construction which is very common in farm eveners. One end is shown in a position 8 in. to the rear of the normal. In such a position the lever arm of the rear horse is seen

FIG. 14. The principle of the two-horse evener
The upper figure is the only one which will equalize the load with the horses in any position

to be $21\frac{1}{4}$ in. while that of the other horse is $23\frac{3}{4}$ in., this arrangement giving the horse in the rear a much greater portion of the total load. If the total pull is 400 lb., in the position shown

the load would be divided between the two horses as follows:
The sum of the two lever arms, $21\frac{1}{4}$ in. $+ 23\frac{3}{4}$ in., is equal to
45 in., which represents the effective length of the evener.
Then, if x represents the pull of the rear horse, and since the
load is in inverse proportion to the lever arms,

$$45 : 400 :: 23\tfrac{3}{4} : x;$$
hence, $\qquad 45\,x = 400 \times 23\tfrac{3}{4},$
$$x = 211.2 \text{ lb.}$$
$$400 - 211.2 = 188.8 \text{ lb., pull of other horse.}$$

From this solution it is found that the rear horse, though usually
the weaker of the two, is forced to pull 11.8 per cent more than
his mate when the former is in a position 8 in. back of normal.
The farther he gets behind, the heavier does his load become.

The lowest figure shows a common construction for wagon
doubletrees. The end clevis is firmly bolted to the evener, in
which case the point of application of the pull is in front of the
middle hole. As one horse forges ahead, his lever arm becomes
shorter, and consequently his load becomes heavier, while the
load of the horse which is behind becomes lighter.

Although it is not practicable to make eveners with the three
holes on the same straight line, this condition should be approxi-
mated as closely as possible. The further lesson taught by these
figures is that the driver should at all times keep the two horses
abreast if he would have each pull one half the load.

An *advantage* may be given either horse by lengthening his
end of the evener or by shortening the other end. The amount
of advantage given may be easily figured. Suppose one arm in
a 48-inch evener were shortened 2 in. This would make one
arm 22 in. and the other 24 in., with a total length of 46 in.
If the total pull is 500 lb., then

$$46 : 500 :: 22 : x;$$
hence, $\qquad 46\,x = 11,000,$
$$x = 239.1 \text{ lb., the smaller load.}$$

The other horse will then pull $500 - 239.1 = 261.9$ lb. The horse
given the advantage pulls 8.7 per cent less than the other horse.

CHAPTER II

TRANSMISSION OF POWER

As gasoline engines, electric generators and motors, and various forms of water power are finding wide use on farms, a knowledge of the simple principles of power transmission is necessary. Only those principles a knowledge of which is likely to be useful upon the farm will be considered. Power is usually transmitted by means of belts, pulleys, and shafting; by chains and sprockets; and by gears. Rope transmission is only occasionally used in rural districts.

Belts. There are three kinds of belts as regards material in common use — leather, rubber, and canvas. *Leather* belts are cut from the main body of a hide after the neck, belly, and tail portions are removed. The best belting is cut from the center, or the backbone portion, of the hide; the poorer qualities come from the edges. Leather belts are made in single-ply or double-ply. The latter costs twice as much as the former, but it is said to last more than twice as long. A double-ply belt cannot be used on pulleys smaller than ten or twelve inches in diameter. The leather belt should always be worked with the hair side next to the pulley, for this is the smoother side and so clings more closely to the pulley. Leather belts must be protected from moisture, steam, and oil. They should be cleaned and dressed occasionally. There are many belt-dressings on the market, but neat's-foot oil is probably as good as any of them.

Rubber belts are made by cementing together alternate layers of rubber and canvas, coating the whole with rubber, and then vulcanizing the rubber under high pressure. In thickness they vary from 2-ply to 8-ply. A 4-ply rubber belt is considered the equal of a single-ply leather belt. A rubber belt withstands heat and moisture better than leather, though under ordinary conditions it will not last so long as leather. A rubber belt must be carefully protected from oil and grease.

16

Canvas belts are used a great deal on agricultural machinery, where they are exposed to the weather. They wear well, but are not quite so desirable for pulleys at fixed distances apart. To give an idea of the relative prices of the three kinds of belts, the retail prices in effect at the present time are quoted: 4-inch, 4-ply rubber, 15 cents per foot; 4-inch, 4-ply canvas, 13 cents per foot; 4-inch single-ply leather, 48 cents per foot. The *gandy* belt is a special form of canvas belt made by combining the canvas layers with waterproofing material and then stitching and coating the whole again with the same material. This belting is very durable and withstands hard usage well.

Horse power of leather belts. Power is transmitted by a belt by the aid of friction between belt

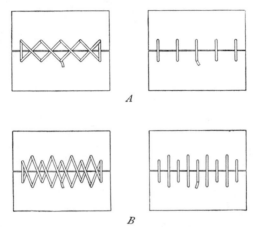

FIG. 15. Two methods for lacing belts

The lacing is begun at the middle of the belt

and pulleys. The horse power which a belt is transmitting at any time depends upon the pull, or tension, in the belt and upon the rate of travel. Kent gives the following formula for the horse power of a single-ply leather belt working under a tension of thirty-three pounds per inch of width:

$$\text{Horse power} = \frac{vw}{1000},$$

where v = velocity in feet per minute
and w = width in inches.

The *length* of the belt required for two pulleys may be secured by a rule given by Kent: "Add the diameter of the two pulleys, divide the sum by 2, multiply the quotient by $3\frac{1}{4}$, and add the product to twice the distance between the centers of the shafts."

Pulleys. Pulleys are made of iron or wood. The split-wood pulley is well adapted to all kinds of line-shaft work, though for permanent positions, as on grinders, shellers, etc., the iron pulley is perhaps to be preferred. The face of the pulley should be crowned, so that the belt will run to the center. A leather covering is frequently used to secure a better grip between belt and pulley, but, except under heavy loads, it is not necessary. In case of pulleys so placed that the belt is horizontal, the lower side of the belt should be the tight, or driving, side. Such an arrangement permits the slack upper side to settle upon the pulleys, thus adding to the friction and tending to prevent slippage.

The speed and size of pulleys. A convenient rule for determining either the speed or size of pulleys connected by a belt is the following:

R. P. M. of driver × its diameter = R. P. M. of driven × its diameter.

If any three of these factors are given, the fourth may be found. If, for example, a gasoline engine having a pulley 10 in. in diameter is belted to an electric generator having a 4-inch pulley and running at 1700 revolutions per minute, the speed may be found as follows. If x be the R. P. M. of the engine, then

$$x \times 10 = 1700 \times 4; \quad \text{whence} \quad x = 280.$$

If the speed or size of *toothed* gears is to be determined, it is only necessary to substitute the number of teeth for the diameter of the pulley, as given above.

Shafting. Shafting is very frequently used where more than one machine is to be operated by the same engine. Cold-rolled steel shafting is the kind most generally used, it being supported upon hangers which are fastened to the floor, the wall, or the ceiling. The distance apart of the hangers depends on the size of the shafting. Kent gives the following formula for determining the proper distance between hangers:

$$L = \sqrt[3]{140\,d^2}, \quad \text{or} \quad d = \sqrt{\frac{L^3}{140}},$$

when L = distance between hangers, in feet,
and d = diameter of shaft, in inches.

As a general rule the hangers should be about eight feet apart.

The *horse power* which shafting will transmit depends upon the diameter and upon the number of revolutions per minute. The usual formula is as follows, and assumes that the shaft is well supported, with pulleys close to bearings :

$$\text{Horse power} = \frac{d^3 R}{50},$$

when $d =$ diameter of shaft, in inches,
and $R =$ revolutions per minute.

Sprockets and chains versus gears. In the construction of grain-binders, mowers, manure-spreaders, and other farm machinery both sprockets and chains, and gears, are used. Chain transmission is suitable where the speed is not great and where a positive drive is desired, if lost motion is not a consideration. It has this very decided advantage over the gear drive — it is cheaper to break a link in a chain than a tooth in a gear. In spur gears and bevel gears two teeth take almost the entire strain of the load, whereas in chain transmission a chain wraps around both sprockets, thus engaging a large number of teeth. Gears, however, afford a more compact and substantial construction, and though lost motion is always found, proper adjustment reduces it to a minimum. *Chain links* are made of steel or of malleable iron. The latter is more generally used, though either gives satisfaction. It is claimed that steel links wear the sprockets more than do the malleable links.

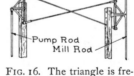

Triangles. Triangles are frequently used to transmit power from a windmill to a pump some distance away, which distance should not exceed one hundred and fifty feet. As shown in Fig. 16, the wires should be crossed so that the mill rod and the pump plunger will work in unison and the windmill will do the heavy work on the upstroke.

FIG. 16. The triangle is frequently used to transmit power from the windmill to a pump some distance away

CHAPTER III

MATERIALS OF CONSTRUCTION

In the chapters relating to various farm implements and machines, certain terms will be used in describing the materials from which such implements and machines are made. It is desirable that some space be given to a discussion of these materials, in order that the student may better understand their properties.

Wood. Wood enters to a greater or less extent into the construction of nearly all farm machines. It is far superior to iron or steel for those parts where a certain degree of resiliency is desirable, as in wagon wheels and in pitman rods for mowers. Since the weight of woods varies greatly, wood of light weight can be selected where lightness rather than strength is desirable. Wood lends itself, moreover, to neat construction and to artistic decoration with paint.

Where strength and durability are required, the harder woods, such as hickory, oak, ash, and maple, are used. Such woods are found in bed rails for manure-spreaders and in wagon gears, tongues, eveners, etc. Where lightness is desired, pine and poplar are greatly used. Wagon beds, for example, are largely made of poplar. The wood entering into the construction of farm machinery, since it must endure hard usage and must often stand out in the weather the year round, must be of the best quality, well seasoned, and thoroughly coated with paint.

The increasing scarcity of timber has been largely responsible for the wide use of iron as material for farm machines. Iron is used in many common forms, such as cast iron, chilled iron, malleable iron, and steel.

Cast iron. In the manufacture of cast iron the crude iron ore is charged into a blast furnace with alternate layers of limestone, or flux, and coke. A fire is kindled at the bottom of the furnace, and an intense heat is maintained by means of a forced air blast.

The melted iron drops to the bottom of the furnace. Some of the impurities pass off in gas, some combine with the flux, and still others remain in the iron. The melted iron, when not taken directly through other processes, is drawn off and cooled, forming pig iron. The pig iron is then remelted and cast into various forms which are known as cast-iron castings.

Cast iron is of a coarse crystalline structure and is extremely hard and brittle. The carbon content is high, ranging from 2 to $4\frac{1}{2}$ per cent, and exists in two forms, known as combined carbon and graphitic carbon. *White* iron contains carbon in the former state and is extremely hard and brittle. *Gray* iron contains carbon in the graphitic form and is much softer than white iron, though of course it still possesses the characteristics of cast iron.

Cast iron finds its greatest use in machine-construction. It can be readily cast into various shapes, and for the making of large castings, as engine foundations and mower frames, and for smaller castings where its physical properties meet the requirements, it has no competitor. Gray iron is used extensively for gears, pulleys, and other parts which must be turned to shape in a lathe.

Chilled iron. In certain parts of some farm implements and machines, as in some types of plow bottoms and bearings for disk harrows, a material is wanted that will take a good polish and wear well. Chilled iron meets these requirements in a very satisfactory way. In the making of chilled castings the usual method of making cast-iron castings is followed, except that the sand mold, or certain parts of it, is lined with iron, such part being called a chill. The result is that the casting cools rapidly and the carbon consequently remains in chemical combination and makes the casting extremely hard. The chill extends to a depth of from a quarter to three quarters of an inch, the depth depending upon the nature and effectiveness of the mold; the exterior surface, consequently, has the appearance of white iron, while the interior remains a gray iron. Chilled castings, such as those for bearings and plow bottoms, since, because of their hardness, they cannot be worked in a lathe, are ground and polished to the desired shape and smoothness.

Malleable iron. Malleable-iron castings are manufactured by first making white-iron castings of the desired shape and size. These castings are then thoroughly cleaned of sand and put through an annealing process. This process consists in packing the castings in large iron boxes, surrounded by some packing-material, and heating them to redness for from four to six days. The packing-material is generally a decarbonizing agent such as iron oxide, though sand or clay will do. As a result of this process the carbon disappears from the surface of the castings, leaving a layer resembling steel and from about a sixteenth to a quarter of an inch thick, which covers the body of the castings, while the inner portion is softened to some extent. A malleable-iron casting, therefore, is tough ; it will stand a heavy blow, and will bend before it will break.

Malleable-iron castings find a wide use in the manufacture of farm machines, for such parts as the packers and needles of binders, the gears of binders and spreaders, and for innumerable other small parts which are subjected to great strains or sudden shocks. Malleable-iron castings are never large, but since they combine the advantages of cast iron (in that they can be molded to any desired shape) with the toughness and ductility of steel, they occupy an unusual place in the field of farm-machinery construction. Other things being equal, a considerable number of malleable-iron castings in a machine is an almost certain indication of superior quality.

Wrought iron. Wrought iron is a very pure form of iron made by melting pig iron in the hearth of a furnace until, on the removal of a large percentage of the impurities, the mass becomes pasty. It is then worked up into a ball and is removed from the furnace and rolled into large bars. Wrought iron is remarkably tough and ductile and is the iron most commonly used by blacksmiths for forging purposes. It is largely used in the manufacture of rolled rods and bars, pipes, pipe-fittings, etc.

Steel. Steel is a form of iron which, in composition and properties, stands between cast iron and wrought iron. It is low in carbon content in comparison with cast iron, ranging from about 0.1 to 1.5 per cent of carbon. There are several kinds of steel, the kind depending upon the process by which it is made.

Bessemer steel is manufactured by charging molten pig iron into a large Bessemer converter and forcing blasts of air through the mass until the impurities are largely eliminated, the boiling temperature being maintained by the oxidation of the impurities. A recarburizer, chiefly ferromanganese, is then added to secure the proper carbon content and to assist in eliminating air bubbles from the boiling mass. The metal is then poured into large molds and carried to the rolling-mills, where the ingots are reduced to smaller blocks, or billets, preparatory to being rolled or shaped into commercial products.

In the acid Bessemer process the converter is lined with sandstone, in which case the phosphorus of the pig iron remains in the steel. In the basic Bessemer process the converter is lined with limestone, in which case the phosphorus of the iron combines with the limestone, forming basic slag, which is used as a fertilizer.

Open-hearth steel is manufactured by melting a charge of pig iron and steel scrap on the hearth of an open-hearth furnace; a flame from the fire-box of the furnace is passed over the molten mass, being reflected back upon it by the arched roof above the hearth. The decarbonizing agent is added in the form of ferromanganese, as in the Bessemer process, either before pouring or as the metal is poured. Open-hearth steel, like Bessemer steel, may be made by either the basic or the acid process.

In 1912 about 33 per cent of all the steel produced was made by the Bessemer process, while 66 per cent was made by the open-hearth process, the remaining 1 per cent being largely crucible steel.

Soft-center steel. Soft-center steel is now rather generally used in the manufacture of steel plow bottoms and cultivator shovels. It is made by welding together three sheets of steel. The two outer layers are made of high-carbon steel and hence are extremely hard. The inner layer is made of a softer grade of steel. The outer layers take a good polish and withstand the wearing action of the soil, while the inner softer layer seems to prevent the parts from breaking when subjected to sharp blows or sudden strains.

Babbitt metal. Babbitt metal is an alloy of tin, copper, and antimony, in the proportion of about 85 parts tin, 6 parts copper, and 9 parts antimony. This metal, which is used chiefly for bearings, is sufficiently hard to resist wear, and yet soft enough to be easily shaped to a bearing. Moreover it adjusts itself to the shaft and so gives a minimum of friction.

Bronze. This metal is an alloy of copper and tin, containing about 80 per cent copper and 20 per cent tin. It is used as a bearing metal, and for stuffing-boxes, piston rings, cut gears, etc. *Phosphor* bronze is made from ordinary bronze by adding a small amount of phosphorus. This addition, which increases the tensile strength and produces a harder metal, makes phosphor bronze especially valuable for gears and bearings, for which use it excels almost any other class of bearing metals, since it offers great resistance to wear and has a low coefficient of friction.

CHAPTER IV

CEMENT AND CONCRETE

Concrete is now used in such a great variety of ways about the farm that everyone should study its possibilities and learn how to use this important and valuable building-material. Its successful use depends upon the care and judgment exercised in the choice and handling of the materials. Crumbling walks, broken posts, and leaking watering-troughs, too frequently seen, testify to the fact that great care and judgment are required.

MATERIALS USED

Cement. Cement is the foundation of all concrete work. There are two kinds to be found upon the market — natural cement and Portland cement.

Natural cement is made from a rock containing varying quantities of lime and clay. The rock is first ground into fine particles and then burned. The resulting clinker is then reground into a very fine powder known as natural cement. Inasmuch as the rocks from which natural cement is made vary greatly in their composition, the cement varies in its quality. Natural cement, although it begins its initial set more quickly than Portland cement, never attains the ultimate strength that the latter does. It is somewhat cheaper in first cost, but Portland cement should be given the preference for all kinds of concrete work.

Portland cement takes its name from the Portland rocks near Leeds, England, from which it was first made, in 1829. In the United States it was first manufactured in 1870, at Copley, Pennsylvania. Its use has increased so rapidly that now the output amounts to about 100,000,000 bbl. per year.

Portland cement is made from an artificial mixture of comparatively pure limestone or chalk, and clay or shale, the active ingredients being lime, silica, and alumina. The raw materials

25

are first mixed in the proper proportions and ground to a rather fine powder. The mixture is then fed into large rotary kilns and heated to an extremely high temperature, the powder partially fusing and forming clinkers. These clinkers are then ground into a very fine powder known as Portland cement.

Inasmuch as the quality and chemical composition of the raw materials, as well as the proportions in which they are mixed, are accurately controlled, the resulting cement is of uniform composition. There are many brands of Portland cement, one differing but little from the others in general desirability. The consumer can and should judge of the physical condition of the brand or brands available. If the bags are exposed to dampness, the cement becomes lumpy. If the lumps are hard, the cement is practically worthless and should not be used. It will keep indefinitely if stored in a dry place. The bags should not be piled on or very near an earth floor.

Sand. In all concrete work some coarse material, or aggregate, is used. A fence post made of pure cement and water would be very strong indeed, but its cost would be prohibitive. The aggregate is used solely to cheapen the cost of the object made. Sand is sometimes called the fine aggregate. That portion of the aggregate the particles of which are one-quarter inch in diameter or under is called sand. For good concrete work, sand must possess several characteristics. *It must be clean* ; that is to say, it must be free from fine clay and from loam. Either of these impurities will completely cover the quartz grains of which sand is composed and prevent a proper bond, or union, between the cement and the sand grains. The presence of these impurities in damaging quantities can be detected by a few simple tests : If a small quantity of the sand is picked up in the hand and then thrown away, fine particles will be seen clinging to the palm of the hand. If these particles are soft to the touch, and if the coating on the hand is rather thick, it may be suspected that clay is present in too large quantities.

If this simple test discloses the presence of a considerable amount of clay or loam, a small quantity of the sand should then be thrown into a small glass jar filled with water. If the water remains very roily for a considerable time, it is likely that there is too much clay in the sand to allow its being good aggregate material. If the jar is allowed to stand until the particles have completely settled, and if, when the water is poured off, the surface of the jar is found to be covered with clay, it may be concluded that the sand is not of the best and should not be used without being tested in an actual mixture. The test may be carried out by making a small block of the concrete and testing its strength after setting.

The sand should be *well graded* from fine to medium-coarse particles. A great deal of the sand usually available is too fine for the best work. A fine sand, as will be seen when the question of proportion is considered, requires more cement than a well-graded, or even a coarse, sand. With fine sand a little more cement than the proportion calls for should be used.

It was formerly considered necessary that the sand grains should be sharp and angular, thus giving opportunity for a better bond between the cement and sand; this is no longer considered a necessity, however. If the sand particles are clean, the cement will form such a perfect bond with them that if a rupture occurs the particles will frequently break through the middle instead of cleaving from the cement.

Coarse aggregate. *Gravel* is the most common coarse aggregate used in concrete construction on the farm. There is no better material if it is clean and properly graded. To be *clean*, it, like sand, must be free from clay, loam, or other foreign matter. Bank gravel frequently has a considerable amount of clay mixed with it. If this occurs in rather coarse and separate lumps, a small quantity will do no harm. If, however, the clay is very fine and covers and adheres to the pebbles or gravel, good concrete work is impossible. If such gravel must be used, it should be thoroughly washed by dashing water over it after spreading it out in a thin layer.

The gravel should be *well graded*; that is, the pebbles should grade from fine to coarse. The size of the largest pebbles should be determined by the kind of work to be done. If the concrete is to be used for heavy foundations, rocks up to several inches in diameter may be used. If fence posts or other small reënforced objects are being made, the largest pebbles should not be more than three quarters of an inch in diameter; if larger, they interfere with the placing of the reënforcing rods.

Crushed limestone, where available, makes excellent coarse aggregate. It is usually clean and well graded and can be secured in almost any size desired.

Cinders, brickbats, sandstones, and other similar materials may be used in unimportant work, but inasmuch as concrete is no stronger than the weakest material put into it, the use of such aggregate cannot be expected to result in good work. If such materials are to be had in large quantities, they may be used to good advantage as a foundation for the concrete.

Proportioning the Mixture

Theory of proportions. In all concrete work it is desirable to secure the densest possible mixture. To do this in an ideal way, just enough sand must be taken to fill the voids, or air spaces, in the coarse aggregate and, in turn, just enough cement must be used to fill the voids in the sand. Such a proportion would, in theory, give a mixture free from air spaces and consequently as dense as the materials used in making it.

Proportioning in practice. Obviously it is not possible in practice to obtain a mixture in accordance with the theory just outlined. It is very essential, however, that every effort be made to secure a mixture that will correspond as closely as possible to the theoretical.

If the percentage of voids in the material used were known, it would be possible so to proportion the cement and aggregate as to approach very closely to the best possible mixture. A rough approximation may be secured by filling with water a bucket of known volume into which has been placed as much as possible of the material to be tested. Then the volume of water used, divided by the volume of the bucket, will give the percentage of voids in the material. This crude method will give a fair idea of how much sand to use with the coarse aggregate at hand or of how much cement to use with the sand in question. Such a test as this, if it does nothing more, enables one to see some reason for the proportions usually given for standard mixtures.

It is readily understood that, no matter how accurately the voids are determined, when the materials are actually mixed the theoretical conditions are changed, and the proportions so accurately determined no longer obtain. This is true because in mixing the sand and coarse aggregate, for example, the sand particles will not accurately fill the voids in the stone or gravel, but will tend to fit in between the larger pieces, separate them, and thus increase the space to be filled by sand. There is then only one correct method for determining the proper mixture to use, and that is to make up blocks of concrete, using different proportions of the materials. Then, after the blocks have been allowed to set for a period of from two to four weeks, that proportion which is best adapted to the work at hand may be determined by means of appropriate tests.

Standard proportions. Long experience with concreting-materials and with such concrete work as is done about the farm has suggested several standard proportions. A standard proportion has reference to a certain mixture of cement, sand, and gravel that is deemed best for a particular kind of work. For example, a 1–2–3 mixture, that is, one in which the materials are mixed in the proportion of 1 part (by volume) of cement, 2 parts of sand, and 3 parts of screened gravel or rock, is standard for watering-troughs. That is to say, without going to the trouble of determining the best possible mixture for the material at hand, if this material is of average grade, it may be expected to make a good watering-trough if mixed in the above proportions.

The following table of standard mixtures with the purposes to which each is best adapted will be found helpful in choosing the proper proportions for the work at hand :

1. *A 1–2–3 mixture.* This represents a very rich mixture and is used where exceptional water-tightness is desired, for reenforced beams carrying great weight, or where unusual stress is to be withstood.

2. *A 1–2–4 mixture.* This is a rich mixture and is commonly used for reënforced beams and columns, floors, walks, tanks, troughs, fence posts, etc.

3. *A 1–2½–5 mixture.* This is a medium mixture and is used for ordinary floors, feeding-floors, retaining-walls, foundations, etc.

4. *A 1–3–6 mixture*. This is a lean mixture and is used for subfoundations and heavy walls, where the concrete is placed in great masses.

It will be noticed that in most of the standard mixtures the volume of cement used is one half that of the sand, and the sand one half that of the coarse aggregate. Such a proportion is based on the assumption that one half the volume of the coarse aggregate and sand is made up of voids. Though this corresponds very closely to the fact, the voids will frequently be found to compose much less than half of the volume of the aggregate.

Proportioning cement and gravel. In most concrete work done on the farm, bank or creek gravel is used. This is commonly mixed with cement in such proportions as 1–4, 1–5, 1–6, etc. These proportions are all based upon the assumption that the proper amount of sand is already to be found in the gravel; hence the sand factor is simply eliminated from the standard proportions given above, and where unscreened gravel is used a 1–4, a 1–5, or a 1–6 mixture corresponds respectively to a 1–2–4, a 1–2½–5, or a 1–3–6 mixture when the sand and coarse aggregate are separately provided. The idea frequently obtains that a 1–6 mixture where unscreened gravel is used is the same as a 1–2–4 mixture in which the three materials are separate. That such an idea is erroneous will be seen when the question of the proper quantity of materials necessary for a given structure is discussed.

Fig. 17. A good type of screen

The wires are ¼ in. apart

Gravel seldom contains the proper amount of sand. Almost all bank and creek gravel contains too much sand, often from two to three times as much as the standard mixtures demand. Consequently, for the best results, the gravel should be screened by throwing it upon a No. 4 screen (Fig. 17), that is, one whose meshes are one-quarter inch in size. That part of the gravel which passes through is used as sand, and the remainder as the coarse aggregate. After the fine and the coarse aggregate are separated they may be remixed in the proper portion. When such a procedure is followed, it will usually be found that at least as much sand is left over as was used in the standard mixture.

If it is not practicable to screen the gravel when more than the required amount of sand is present, it is well to use a little more cement than the amount indicated by the proportion it was intended to follow. This is necessary because in the final mixing it is the aim to have every particle of sand coated with cement. If extra sand is added to any one of the standard mixtures, it will be necessary to increase the quantity of cement used if the resulting work is to be of the quality reasonably to be expected from the mixture used.

Measuring, Mixing, and Placing the Materials

No matter how good the materials used or how rich the mixture, if the materials are not properly mixed and placed, poor work is bound to result. Too much attention cannot be given to this important step in the making of concrete.

Quantity of materials required. It is necessary that one know how to determine the amount of the various materials that will be required to construct the object or complete the piece of work at hand. Such problems as the following, for example, are constantly presenting themselves to the farmer: If a floor 20 ft. wide by 30 ft. long and 4 in. thick is to be laid in a hog house, how much cement, sand, and screened gravel or crushed rock will be required to complete the job if a standard $1-2\frac{1}{2}-5$ mixture is to be used?

If the sand and coarse aggregate are graded according to the assumption underlying the proportions given in all of the standard mixtures, the sand is intended exactly to fill the voids in the coarse aggregate, and the cement in turn is supposed to fill the voids in the sand. Under average conditions this will be very close to the fact, as previously explained. This could be very easily demonstrated by filling a box holding 5 cu. ft. with the coarse aggregate and then pouring in $2\frac{1}{2}$ cu. ft. of sand. With a little shaking, the sand will disappear and fill the voids in the coarse material. If, now, 1 cu. ft. of cement is added, it too will disappear, since it fills the voids in the sand. Thus, $8\frac{1}{2}$ cu. ft. of materials have been poured into the box, with a total volume of slightly more than 5 cu. ft. resulting. The slight increase in volume represents the difference between theory and practice and should be taken into consideration when the quantity of the various materials required is determined. This increase is fairly constant, and, in order to allow for it, a good rule is to take as the volume of the coarse aggregate 0.9 of the total volume of the mold. The sand and cement will then be such portions of this volume as the mixture specifies.

Thus, in the floor mentioned above, the total volume of the mold to be filled is equal to

$$20 \times 30 \times \tfrac{1}{3} = 200 \text{ cu. ft.,}$$
$$0.9 \text{ of } 200 = 180 \text{ cu. ft.}$$

Therefore there will be required

180 cu. ft., or 6.66 cu. yd., of coarse aggregate,
90 cu. ft., or 3.33 cu. yd., of sand,
36 cu. ft., or 36 bags, of cement.

Mixing the materials. If the materials are to be mixed by hand, a mixing-platform (Fig. 18) at least 12 ft. square should be provided in case the work is not being done near a barn floor where a smooth surface is available. The platform should be practically watertight, since water which runs away from the mixture after mixing has begun carries with it a great deal of cement. There are at least two methods followed in regard to the order in which the materials are placed upon the platform, but the one generally accepted as the best will be given first.

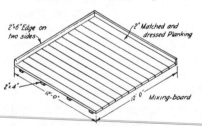

Fig. 18. A mixing-platform

The mixing-platform should be of liberal size, and be smooth and tight

Assuming that a 1–2–4 mixture is to be used, a bottomless box (Fig. 19) 2 ft. long, 1 ft. 6 in. wide, and 8 in. deep, holding 2 cu. ft., would make a convenient size for mixing. The box should be placed upon the mixing-platform and filled with sand. The sand should then be spread out, and one bag of cement poured over it. The sand and cement should then be turned with a shovel, the operator starting at one end of the pile and working systematically toward the other end, taking care that all parts of the pile are stirred. The shovel should be given a spreading motion as it is turned over. Two men can perform the work to the best advantage, and can best work directly opposite each other. Two or three turnings are necessary to secure an even

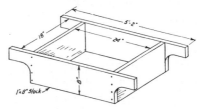

FIG. 19. A measuring-box of convenient size and shape

mixture. If gray streaks are to be seen after the shovel has been run over the surface of the pile, one more turning should be given. As a rule three turnings are required.

The mixture should then be spread out and two boxfuls of coarse aggregate measured out upon the pile. The pile should then be turned at least twice. If the coarse aggregate is very dry, it is well to sprinkle it shortly before it is used. The materials should then be thrown together in a round pile, a good-sized crater formed, and water poured in. The edges should then be gradually spaded into the water, more water being added as needed. To secure the proper amount of water it is best to begin the final turnings while the mixture is rather dry, applying water by means of a sprinkling-pot while the material is being turned. The water should not be thrown upon the mixture with much force, as the cement will be washed from the sand or gravel and a faulty mixture will result. Two or three complete turnings are necessary after the water is added. This last mixing is important and should not be slighted.

A wet, a medium, or a dry mixture may be used, the mixture depending upon the kind of work to be done. A *wet mixture*, which is made so thin that it will run from a shovel or pour readily from a bucket, is used in making foundation walls where perfectly tight forms are provided. A *medium mixture* is that most commonly used; that is, one in which just enough water is used to give a mixture that will run slightly when piled up — a " quaking mixture " so called. When placed in the forms it is usually tamped until water rises to the surface. This kind of a mixture finishes well both on the surface, as in a feeding-floor, and on the sides next the forms, as in a watering-trough. A *dry mixture* is used in making building-blocks, drain tile, and, frequently, fence posts — in short, when rather expensive molds are required, and when it is desirable to make one piece after another as fast as the mold can be filled and removed. The resulting work will be porous, will not harden properly, and will not attain the most desirable ultimate strength.

As was said at the beginning of this chapter, Portland cement will begin to set within thirty minutes after the water is added. Consequently, the size of the batch should not be larger than can be used within thirty minutes.

Instead of first mixing the cement and sand together and then adding the coarse aggregate, some follow the plan of first measuring out the coarse aggregate, next placing the sand on top of it and the cement on top of the sand, and finally mixing the three together at the same time. While this seems to result in first-class work, the first method, as a rule, is to be preferred, since it undoubtedly secures a more intimate mixture of the sand and the cement. Inasmuch as it is the object to coat each particle of sand with cement and in turn to cover each particle of the coarse aggregate with a layer of the mortar, the first method, it seems, would result in a more uniform mixture.

Machine mixing. Mixing concrete by hand is extremely hard work, and if one has much to mix, it pays to engage a machine for the purpose. In almost every village in the country there is someone who is engaged in the business of laying cement walks and doing other kinds of concrete work. Such men can usually be hired by the day, and it will be found economical to engage them for such work as putting in foundations, laying floors, etc., if the material to be mixed exceeds, say, a volume of fifteen cubic yards.

There are some inexpensive but satisfactory hand and small power mixing-machines now on the market, and if one contemplates doing much concrete work it will be advisable to investigate them and see whether the labor which it would be possible to save would not pay a good rate of interest on the investment. It is frequently possible to interest several neighbors in concrete work and buy a power mixer in partnership. Such a plan is especially practicable if one of them already owns an engine which might be used for such work. Fig. 20 shows an excellent type of machine

FIG. 20. A good hand or power batch mixer

This machine will mix 3 cu. ft. at a time, will last a lifetime, and costs about $50

mixer. It has a capacity of three cubic feet and may be turned by hand or by power. Such a mixer costs about fifty dollars.

FORMS FOR CONCRETE WORK

It is essential that forms for such concrete work as watering-troughs, foundation walls for barns, etc. be rigidly braced. Concrete of itself is very heavy, and in addition it is frequently tamped as it is being placed, so that the strain on the forms is great. If inch boards are used in such straight work as foundation walls, they should be supported by uprights every two or three feet. As shown in the illustrations, the outer and inner forms may be wired together for wall work, spacers being placed between the forms to maintain the proper thickness of wall. This method is particularly useful where it is convenient to brace but one of the forms. There are several different ways in which this bracing can be accomplished, one common method being shown in Fig. 21.

Material. Material for the forms must vary with the kind of work. In rough work, as that for foundations, almost any kind of rough, unfinished lumber will do, provided it is strong enough. A few knot-holes are not objectionable, it being possible to fill many of them with clay. If, however, a smooth finish is desired, as in a watering-trough, good lumber must be chosen. It is not essential that it be dressed lumber, though a perfectly smooth wall cannot be secured otherwise. If the forms are to be used several times for the same work, more expensive material can be used. For watering-troughs it is advisable to use one-and-one-half-inch lumber. If the boards are matched it is all the better.

For more particular work, where a good finish, inside and out, is desired and where the forms are to be removed while the concrete is still green, in order that the surface may be properly dressed, it is well to paint the forms with linseed oil just before erecting them. This not only keeps the form boards from absorbing water from the concrete and thus interfering with the setting of the cement, but it also makes it easier to remove the forms, since cement will not stick to an oiled surface.

CONSTRUCTION DETAILS

It will be quite impossible in a work of this kind to give the details of construction for the scores of things which might be made of concrete. However, the average farmer's activities in this direction are confined to relatively few lines of work, and these will be covered in some detail. A working familiarity with concrete, obtained through the making of the simpler objects, will suggest ways and means for the construction of more complex things.

Foundations. In the construction of foundations for various farm buildings, concrete finds one of its best uses. The importance of a good foundation, properly constructed, is too frequently overlooked. In most of the older farm buildings (and the same thing is true of many of the newer ones) good-sized stones were buried in the ground at the corners and the sills placed upon them. The siding was then carried down to the surface of the ground. In a few years the lower ends rotted off, presenting a very untidy appearance and permitting cold winds and rain to blow up under the barn floor. If concrete is used for a foundation it is a very simple task to carry the wall above the surface of the ground, thus keeping out wind, rain, and snow and at the same time enabling one to keep the siding up where it will not be stained and rotted by spattering rains.

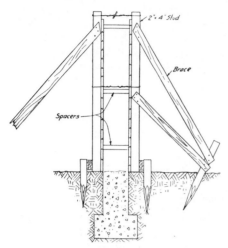

FIG. 21. A method of supporting forms for a foundation wall

Note the extra width of wall at the bottom

A foundation should extend below reasonable frost depth. This means that the trench should be about 20 in. deep for small buildings, though for large barns and silos it should be at least 2 ft. deep; and if the soil is not firm at this depth, even 3 ft. is none too much. The base of the wall proper should be widened as shown in Fig. 21, and for large buildings where the soil is not very firm this should be made at least 2 ft. wide. In general, for small buildings, the foundation walls should be 6 in. thick; for large buildings, from 8 to 10 in. thick; and for silos made of concrete or clay blocks, from 14 to 18 in. thick, the thickness depending upon the height of the silo.

Fig. 21 illustrates a common method of erecting and bracing foundation-wall forms. The outer

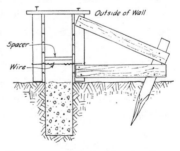

FIG. 22. A method of bracing forms where the inner form cannot be braced from the outside

and inner forms may be braced from their respective sides; or if it is not convenient to get at the inner form it may be fastened to the outer form by wiring the two together, as shown in Fig. 22, and nailing stays across the top.

The concrete should be mixed in the proportion of $1-2\frac{1}{2}-5$ and made wet enough to pour well. As the forms are being filled that part of the wall which is to appear above the surface of the ground should be well "spaded"; that is, as the concrete is being tamped a straight spade or even a thin board should be worked up and down between the forms and the concrete. This forces all large pieces of the coarse aggregate back from the surface and allows the finer particles to form the face of the wall. A very smooth finish can be obtained in this way if the spading is thoroughly done. The forms should not be removed for at least one week, and the superstructure should not be started for from ten days or two weeks after the concrete is placed.

If the wall is carried much more than one foot above the surface of the ground, it should be reënforced at the corners by No. 9 fencing-wire placed near its center. Two $\frac{1}{2}$-inch steel bars should be placed across the top of all windows in foundation walls. In very windy sections it is deemed advisable to embed long bolts, with the threaded end up, in the concrete before it sets. Holes are then bored in the sills and the superstructure thus anchored to the foundation.

Walks. In the construction of walks the first step is to excavate to a depth of from 12 to 18 in. and to tamp the bottom of the trench thoroughly if it is not already solid. The trench should then be filled to within 5 in. of the top with gravel or cinders, tamped into place as the filling proceeds. If the soil is not well drained naturally, it is well to lay a string of tile at the bottom of the trench, to prevent water from collecting beneath the walk. This precaution will in such cases prevent walks from heaving because of freezing. Ordinarily the tile will not be needed.

Next, 2×5 pieces laid edgewise should be placed along the edge of the walk and held in place by stakes driven on either side, as shown in Fig. 23. If the walk is along the side of a building, the outer form strip should be lower than the one next to the building in order that water may not stand on the walk. A slope outward of $\frac{1}{8}$ in. for each foot of width is sufficient.

The outer edge of the walk should be well above the level of the ground. While it is not absolutely necessary, it is a good plan to place cross strips at intervals of from 4 to 6 ft., as shown in Fig. 24, marking their position on the outer form. These cross strips, which may be removed, as described later, divide the walk into blocks, and thus provide for expansion and for easy repair should a section prove faulty.

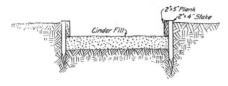

FIG. 23. Showing method of erecting and bracing forms for walks

The materials should be mixed in the proportion of $1-2\frac{1}{2}-5$, or if bank-run gravel is used, $1-4$. The mixture should be made medium wet and thoroughly tamped, the form finally being filled to within about one inch of the top. If the walk is not too long, the entire first coat can be laid before the surface coat is started. The latter should be laid, however, within three hours or so after the first course in order to secure a proper bond between the two courses.

The crosspieces should now be taken out, and if tarred paper is at hand a strip should be put in, the crack being filled in with concrete. This very effectively prevents the adjacent slabs from bonding together and provides for expansion during extreme changes in temperature. If nothing of this kind is available, the cracks may be filled in with some of the first-course mixture.

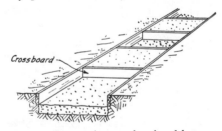

FIG. 24. Cross strips may be placed between the side forms, and the walk laid in sections

The surface coat should be mixed in the proportion of one part of cement to one and one-half parts of good sand. It should be made just wet enough to trowel well, the danger being in getting it too wet. When it is placed, a straightedge should be run across the top to level it and give the surface the proper slope. If the work is not along a building, the straightedge — or the template, as it is in this case — can be hollowed out on the under

40

side, this procedure giving the walk a good crown. After the surface has begun to harden it should be gone over with a

FIG. 25. A steel trowel (on the left) and a wood float

The use of the wood float gives a rougher finish

wood float or a steel trowel (Fig. 25). The latter is used if a very smooth surface is desired; the float finish, however, is generally preferred. The surface should not be troweled too much, especially if it is very wet, as there is a tendency to separate the cement from the sand.

If a jointer (Fig. 26) is at hand it should be used to crease the blocks at the expansion joints, the side forms having been marked so that the joints can be easily located. The sides of the walk may be smoothed with the edger (Fig. 27), thus adding a finishing touch to the job.

The finished walk should be protected from the sun and the wind for three or four days — straw, grass, old sacks, etc., being used for the purpose. It should not be used to any extent for five or six days.

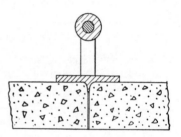

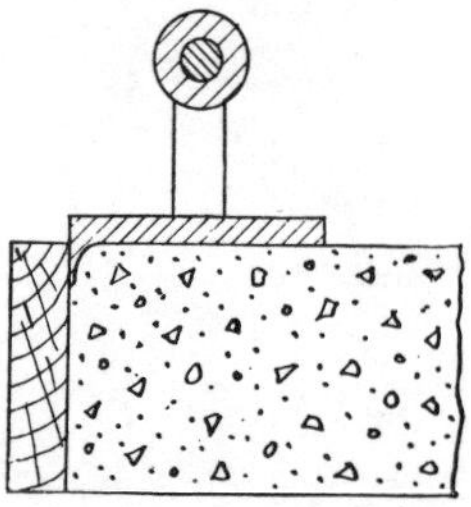

FIG. 26. Illustrating the use of a jointer

FIG. 27. Illustrating the use of the edger to round off the corners of walls

If a walk about the barn is desired, where utility rather than appearance is the chief aim, the surface coat can be omitted. With a little extra care in tamping and troweling the first coat, a fairly smooth and perfectly satisfactory job, so far as lasting quality is concerned, may be secured. In such case a 1–2–4 mixture should be used.

Floors. Floors are laid according to the directions given for walks. They should not be laid in blocks larger than 6 ft. square. The usual custom is to lay the floor in strips 6 ft. wide, blocking off the strips to the desired size. For stable or hog-house floors, where a slope is necessary, particular care should be taken that

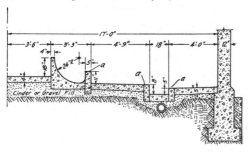

FIG. 28. Showing a good method for laying out the floor, manger, and foundation for a dairy barn

the forms are properly set to give the desired slope. The slope towards gutters and drains should be about $\frac{1}{8}$ in. per foot. Nothing more than a wood-float finish is necessary. In many cases the surface is scored, or creased, to give the animals a better footing. The standard thickness for floors is 4 in.; for driveways, 6 in.

The concrete floor is frequently criticized as being cold and damp for stock. The criticism is undoubtedly a just one, since the simple experiment of sitting in cold

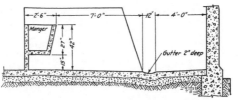

FIG. 29. Illustrating the spacing and arrangement for a horse-stable

weather first on a plank and then on a concrete slab will quickly

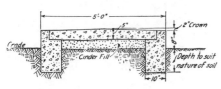

FIG. 30. Showing a good way to lay the foundation and floor for a corncrib

prove to anyone that the slab is much the colder. If, however, when the floor is laid, a two-inch course is first put down, then a layer of tarred paper spread on top of this, and then the top layer of concrete put on, moisture from below will be cut off

and much of the dampness and coldness prevented.

FIG. 31. A suggestion for a feeding-floor

42

Fence posts. The scarcity of timber for fence posts has served to direct the attention of farmers to concrete as a possible substitute. As a result concrete posts have been made and used in large quantities during the last few years. Success with this material has been rather indifferent, however. Undoubtedly in the early history of the industry the posts were not properly reenforced; and, further, since many farmers who attempted to make their own posts were not sufficiently informed as to the

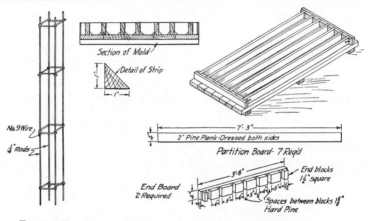

FIG. 32. Showing the details of a good mold for making concrete posts

At the left is shown one way of preparing the reënforcing rods

materials, mixing, etc., poor work frequently resulted. To make satisfactory posts, good materials, plenty of reënforcement, and a great deal of care are required.

Forms. In Fig. 32 is shown a simple, easily made gang mold. This is constructed to make a post 4 by 5 in. at the bottom, 3 by 4 in. at the top, and 7 ft. long. The forms are made of $1\frac{1}{2}$-inch yellow pine, the end pieces being held in place by screen-door hooks, as shown in the figure. It is seen that the posts alternate bottom with top at each end of the form. It is desirable to place triangular strips having 1-inch faces in the bottom of each mold to cut off the sharp corners. It is not so convenient to do this at the top, though if the top is used as the face of the post, it is not so necessary that the corners be cut off.

Materials and proportions. Fence posts are usually made from a 1–2–4 mixture. A 1–2½–5 mixture is frequently recommended, but failures are likely to result, and the extra cost of the richer mixture is very small when compared to the probable life of the finished post. If bank-run gravel is used, it should first be run over a ¾-inch screen to remove the large pebbles and then over a ¼-inch screen to separate the sand from the coarse aggregate. If crushed limestone is purchased for coarse aggregate, the grade known as "three-quarter" should be used; that is, the grade in which no particles are larger than ¾ in. in diameter.

Reënforcement. A concrete post without reënforcing material is almost worthless. In fact the post is just about as strong as this material makes it, since the concrete itself will stand but a very small bending stress.

The reënforcing rods or wires should be so distributed in the post that they will be put under a tensile stress when the post is subjected to a bending stress. This simply means, in the case of a rectangular post, that they be put as near the corners as possible, being not nearer than one inch to the surface. Fig. 32 shows one way of preparing the rods for placing in the mold.

Various materials may be used for reënforcing posts. Ordinary No. 8 or No. 9 fencing-wire is very good. Two No. 12 fence wires twisted together make excellent material, for the twist does away with the danger of the concrete's slipping on the wires. One-quarter-inch round iron rods, which in 7-foot lengths cost from about 1½ cents to 2 cents apiece, make perhaps the best material that it is possible to secure.

Mixing and placing. The materials should be mixed according to rules already given, a medium-wet mixture being best. After the forms have been thoroughly oiled, about 1 in. of concrete should be placed in the molds, leveled, and tamped. Two reënforcing wires should then be put in, about 1 in. from the sides, and the molds filled to within 1 in. of the top, the mixture being thoroughly tamped while it is being placed, or until water comes to the surface. The remaining rods should then be placed and the filling completed. The sides of the posts should be thoroughly spaded with a trowel or other tool to make them as smooth as possible, and a trowel should be used also to finish the surface of the posts.

44

The forms may be removed on the second or third day if the work is carefully done, but the posts should not be disturbed for at least one week. If in a dry place, they should be sprinkled daily while curing. They should not be set for at least one month after being made. There is a tendency to move the posts within a few days after they have been made, because they seem to be thoroughly hard. This is a mistake, however, as the posts may be greatly injured by being handled too soon.

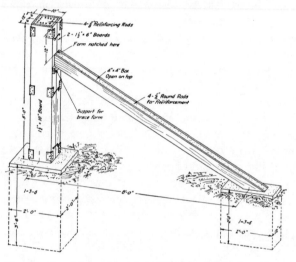

Fig. 33. Showing the construction of a mold for a concrete corner post with a concrete brace made in place

The mold may be easily taken down and used elsewhere

End and corner posts. End and corner posts are usually made 8 by 8 in. or 10 by 10 in. square. They may be made in molds and then set as line posts are, or they may be molded in place. The reënforcing of an end post is even more important than that of the line posts. At least ten wires or rods should be used, evenly distributed near the four sides. Gas-pipe, if less than 3 in. in diameter, placed in the center of the post does not constitute adequate reënforcing.

Fig. 33 shows a form that has been used for molding end posts in place. The concrete brace is molded with the post.

This is not essential, however, since the brace may be separately molded and then used as an ordinary timber brace; in this case a block should be nailed to the inside of the post form at the proper height to make a hole to take the end of the brace. The same thing should be done with the brace post. Other forms and other methods of bracing will suggest themselves as one becomes used to working with concrete. Gate hinges and gate latches may be set in the posts as they are being molded.

Patent molds. There are a number of patent molds on the market. They are usually made of sheet iron and make posts of all shapes — trian-gular, square, and of various odd shapes. Each has some good points to recom-mend it, but few of them are better than the homemade mold described, if as good, and they cost five or six times as much.

Provision for fas-tening fence. In most concrete fence posts the only method used for fastening the fence to the posts

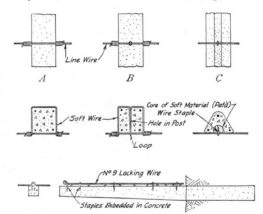

FIG. 34. Showing different methods of fastening fence to concrete posts

Front and sectional views are shown at *A*, *B*, and *C*

is that of wrapping a small soft-iron wire about the post and around the line wires, as shown in Fig. 34, *A*. This method, in the main, is satisfactory, though there is sometimes a tendency for the fastening wires to slip on the post. If, while the post is being molded, short three-eighths-inch greased rods are inserted in the concrete at the proper distances (the distance depending upon the spacing of the wires in the fence) and then removed after the post has hardened, one of the very best means for fastening the fence is provided. This method is illustrated in Fig. 34, *B*.

One patent post on the market (Fig. 34, *C*) places down the middle of the face of the post a strip of composition material about two inches deep which is soft enough to allow a staple to be driven into it and yet hard enough to hold the staple well. This works very satisfactorily, though it has been found that the parts harden with age so that it is difficult to drive staples into some of the posts.

FIG. 35. Showing a massive trough that developed a crack (on the right side) in one year

Probably the reënforcing was faulty at this point

Watering-troughs. It is possible to make a first-class watering-trough of concrete, though it is very easy to make a miserable failure. Success is assured only when good materials and plenty of reënforcement are used, with extreme care in mixing and placing.

Forms. Fig. 36 illustrates one way of constructing forms. The sides must be rigidly braced and the inner form thoroughly secured so that it cannot move as the concrete is placed. The walls should ordinarily be about 4 in. thick at the top and 6 in. thick at the bottom, the inner form being given the desired slope. When the proper slope is given, there is not much danger

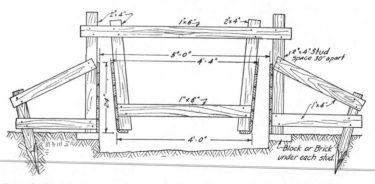

FIG. 36. Showing one method of erecting forms for a concrete watering-trough

from the walls' bursting should the water freeze to a considerable depth. The inner form should be so constructed that it may be easily taken down without injuring the trough. It is well to put a 4-inch board on the bottom of this form as shown in the figure to prevent the concrete from being forced up above the lower edge of the form as the walls are placed and tamped.

Foundation. In most soils it is necessary to prepare a foundation by excavating a hole at least one foot in depth and somewhat larger than the finished trough is to be. Gravel or cinders should then be filled in, sprinkled, and thoroughly tamped. If the soil is not well drained naturally, a string of tile should be laid beneath the filling. The outer form may then be set in place

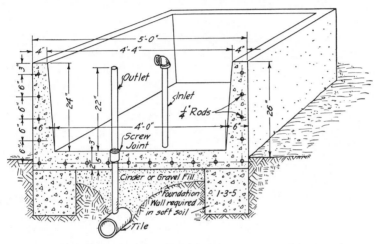

Fig. 37. Showing a section of a well-made concrete watering-trough

Note the method of emptying the trough

and well braced, as shown in Fig. 36. The inlet pipe and the overflow pipe should be put in while the foundation is being made.

For a very large trough, say 5 by 15 ft., it is best to dig a trench from 20 to 24 in. deep and 10 in. wide, under the sides of the trough (Fig. 37), in addition to the excavation above mentioned. This trench may be filled to the bottom of the trough with a 1–3–5 mixture. This additional foundation is a safeguard against the cracking due to uneven settling. It is a good plan to lay a floor, or apron, some three feet wide around the trough, which prevents the mudhole so frequently seen about watering-troughs.

Reënforcing. The reënforcing rods or wires should now be prepared. If round steel rods are to be used, they should as the filling proceeds, be bent and placed as shown in Fig. 37. The rods are placed 1 ft. apart in both directions over the bottom, extending well up into the sides of the trough. The horizontal rods should be placed 6 in. apart, beginning about 2 in. above the level of the bottom of the trough. Woven-wire fencing, preferably of No. 9 wire, makes excellent reënforcing material for a trough.

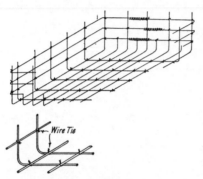

This should be cut and bent, as shown in Fig. 38. It is not a bad plan to double the reënforcing around corners.

Mixing and placing. A 1–2–3 proportion should be used and at least enough mixed at first to lay the bottom of the trough, the mixture being medium dry. The outer form should then be filled to a depth of 2 or 3 in., and after this has been thoroughly tamped, the bottom reënforcing rods should be put in and 4 in. more of concrete placed. This should be thoroughly tamped and the surface finished with a trowel.

FIG. 38. Showing a satisfactory method of bending and fastening reënforcing wires for a watering-trough

The inner form should next be put in place, the lower edge just touching the concrete. As shown in Fig. 36, this form must be held in place by cross ties and fastened so that it cannot be moved as the walls are filled in. Two or three inches of concrete should then be put in and the first horizontal rods placed. Filling should then proceed as rapidly as possible, the reënforcement having been placed as shown, and the sides tamped and spaded. With careful spading, the sides of the trough can be made very smooth.

The inner form may be removed in two or three days, and while the concrete is still green the inner walls should be finished by the application of a thick wash of pure cement and water, with a whitewash brush. This fills all small holes, leaves a smooth surface, and adds to the water-tightness of the trough.

The outer forms should not be removed for several days, and in the meantime the trough should be protected from the hot sun and from drying winds. The trough should not be filled for two or three weeks at least.

Cement drain tile. Cement tile are made in a special mold, from a mixture of cement and coarse, well-graded sand, in the proportion of 1–3. The mixture must of course be a dry mixture, since the mold must be removed immediately. Because of this fact the proper curing of the tile after they are removed from

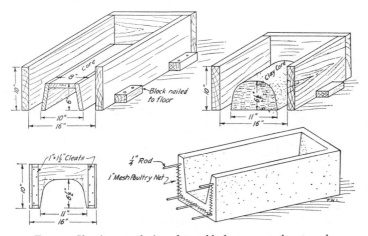

Fig. 39. Showing two designs for molds for concrete hog-troughs

the mold is an important feature in their manufacture. It is doubtful whether a farmer is justified in attempting to make his own tile. Under ordinary drainage conditions cement tile have no advantage over hard-burned clay tile; in fact, the advantage is with the clay tile, since there is usually considerable breakage in handling cement tile. If one has good sand on the farm it may be profitable to attempt the manufacture of cement tile; but ordinarily it is not to be recommended.

Complex work. Such work as building reënforced driveways and reënforced beams, and constructing elevated tanks and towers, monolithic silos, etc., should not be undertaken without the advice of a competent engineer in regard to proper sizes and the amount and size of reënforcement required.

CHAPTER V

LAYING OUT THE FARM

Laying out the farm includes the location of the buildings with reference to each other and to the fields, the division of the land into fields of the proper size, the location of the orchard, of the garden, of tile drains — in short, the proper setting of the entire plant. Quite naturally many of these questions will be determined by the topography of the land, and inasmuch as there are never two farms with identically the same surface contour, the question of laying out the farm must in its final analysis vary with each individual farm. There are certain principles, however, which apply to farms in general, and it is with these principles that this chapter is concerned.

Usually the plan of the farm has already been fixed by previous owners. The buildings have been located, the number and size of the fields determined, the orchard planted, the permanent pasture well established; and to change these matters is not the work of one or even five years, if a change is at all possible. It frequently happens, however, that changes for the better can be made without much inconvenience and without involving any great outlay of time or money, if the owner fixes in his mind a general scheme according to which he can develop his problem. He must have an ideal, in other words; and the task before him is to bring his farm arrangement as close to that ideal as all conditions will permit.

Location of the buildings. Every farm should be regarded as a manufacturing establishment, in which the buildings represent the central plant, and the fields branch houses where the raw materials are produced. The proper location of the buildings with respect to the fields and the highway is worthy of careful thought. With respect to the public highway, the buildings may be located close to or at some distance from it; the former location is understood to mean not less than one hundred nor more than three hundred feet from the road.

If the chief concern is to develop a manufacturing plant to the highest degree of economy as measured in dollars and cents, a location *near the center of the farm* is without doubt the proper one. In such a position all fields are accessible from the central plant, and little or no time is lost in going to and from the fields. The teams may go directly from the barnyard into any one of several fields. The crops are harvested and brought to the barns at a minimum expense of time and labor. The farmer is always near the barns in case the stock should need his attention during the day. Fig. 40, which is a plan of an actual plant in central Ohio, illustrates these points. It will be seen that four fields in this instance adjoin the barnyard, and stock from any one of these may have the run of the yards. On this farm, where the pasture is rotated in common with other crops and where the water is found in the barnyard and nowhere else, this is a matter of first importance. Again, there are no expensive lane fences to keep up, since the two fields at the east end of the farm are never pastured.

A location *close to the highway* sacrifices the merits of a central position, but in the minds of many possesses advantages which more than offset its disadvantages. Such a location affords ready communication with the school, the church, and the town. Neighbors do not seem so far away; and friendly visits and roadside chats are all factors in a contented rural life. City folk who seek the country as a place to rest prefer a more secluded location, but the permanent country dweller chooses, and perhaps wisely, to locate his buildings near the highway.

The *house* should if possible be set on a slight elevation, not merely for the better outlook which it is nearly always possible to secure, but for better drainage facilities, a feature so essential to the health of the family. It should seldom be closer than 100 ft. to the highway, and 150 ft. or 200 ft. away is better. There should be an open expanse of lawn between house and road, with shrubs and vines tastefully decorating the border. The approach to the house should, if possible, be by a winding road and where convenient the road to the barns should not approach too closely to the house.

The *barns*, as a rule, should be placed back of the house — never between the house and the road, and never on the side of the road opposite the house except for some unusual reasons. The main barn should be at least one hundred feet from the house and not much farther away, and in a direction opposite to that of the prevailing winds, which in the Central West would be north or east of the house. This direction is desirable in order that the odors from the barn and the stables may be carried away from the house, and that the danger to the house in case of fire at the barns, where fires seem most likely to occur, may be lessened.

The barn should be on a site slightly lower than that of the house, although none of the buildings should be in a depression, or hollow, as such locations are damp and the soil is difficult to drain. The drainage of the barnyards should be carefully looked to. A little slope is desirable, though too much is likely to lead to loss of manure by leaching. A dry footing for animals in winter, however, is of vastly more importance than the loss of a little manure if one or the other must be sacrificed, which is seldom the case.

The various barns and outbuildings, including the main barn and the corncrib, implement-shed, hog-house, poultry-house, etc., should be grouped close together and placed each in such a position that it will serve best the purpose for which it is intended. In this matter the saving of time in choring should be kept constantly in view. The corncrib, for example, should be but a few steps from the main barn, and close to the hog-house. In Fig. 40 the corncrib is adjacent to the feeding-floor, where nearly all of the corn is fed, and at the same time, very close to the stable door. The second barn in Fig. 40 is in the back barnyard, and is used chiefly for the storage of rough feed which is fed in the yard. The poultry-house is frequently best located near the house, since the farmer's wife usually takes care of the poultry, and house scraps may then be conveniently thrown to the chickens. It is very desirable to be able to confine the poultry, at least during certain seasons, to keep them out of barns and other buildings.

The danger from fire is, of course, an objection to the close arrangement of buildings, and to avoid it many farmers are inclined to locate their buildings several rods apart. That there is merit in the objection cannot be denied, but it would seem that

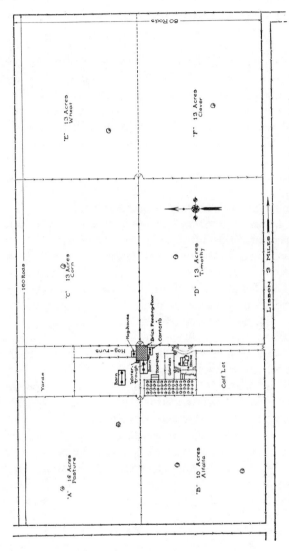

FIG. 40. An eighty-acre-farm plan in which four fields adjoin the barnyard

The house is necessarily at a considerable distance from the road

53

with insurance, which is inexpensive, together with reasonable fire protection, especially lightning-rods, the risk involved where buildings are closely grouped is small when compared with the total saving of time and labor through a lifetime. It might be mentioned, at this point, that small chemical fire-extinguishers which may be purchased for seven dollars and a half make a valuable addition to fire-protection equipment.

Location and size of fields. The location and size of the fields will be determined chiefly by the topography, the shape, and the size of the farm. So far as topography is concerned, each farm represents an individual problem and must be dealt with accordingly. In the interest of tillage and of harvesting-operations an effort should be made to avoid having widely different soil types in the same field. Hills should, where possible, be so included in the various fields as to make field operations as easy as possible. This is particularly true of plowing, as it is essential that lands be so laid out that furrows may be turned downhill. A single hill had better be near the center of a field. Streams should be included in fields intended for pasture, and if two or more fields can be so laid out as to include a small portion of such a stream, a valuable source of water is easily provided.

It is always advisable to have the entrance of as many of the fields as possible near the barn. Fig. 40 shows an admirable plan in this respect, the advantages of which have already been discussed. Fig. 41 shows what is perhaps the nearest approach to the central-location plan. In this plan all fields are fairly close to the barn, and only a short lane is necessary.

A long rectangular field, say two, three, or four times as long as it is wide, is much to be preferred to a square one. In such a field some of the field operations, such as cultivating the short way, are carried on at a disadvantage, but on the whole a great saving of time is effected. For example, in plowing, say, a 10-acre field laid out in the form of a square 40 rd. on each side, if a 14-inch furrow were cut, there would be required 282 rounds, necessitating 1128 turns. If the same area were in the form of a rectangle 20 rd. by 80 rd., just one half as many turns, or 564, would be necessary. The distance traveled, neglecting turns, would be the same in either case, a little over 7 mi., but if only one minute were allowed for each turn, one day would be saved in plowing the rectangular field. The saving of time is perhaps sufficient to overcome all other objections.

On the other hand, the amount of fencing required is affected by the shape of the fields. The most economical shape for a field,

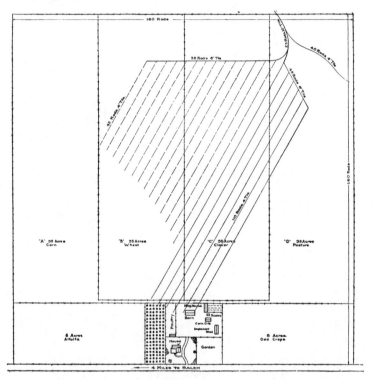

FIG. 41. A one-hundred-and-sixty-acre-farm plan

The buildings are close to the highway, yet all fields are reasonably accessible. Only a short lane is necessary

so far as fencing is concerned, is a circular one. For example, to inclose 10 A. would require (1) in a round field, 141.7 rd.; (2) in a square field, 160 rd.; (3) in a field $26\frac{3}{4}$ rd. by 60 rd., $173\frac{1}{3}$ rd.; (4) in a field 80 rd. by 20 rd., 200 rd. The extra cost of fencing, however, when compared to the saving of labor in the longer fields, is slight. By way of comparison, the last

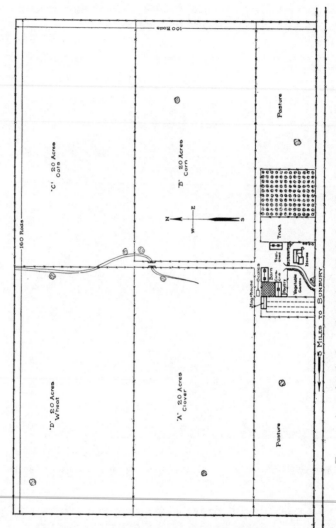

FIG. 42. A one-hundred-acre farm plan with the long side adjacent to the highway

Only a short lane is required

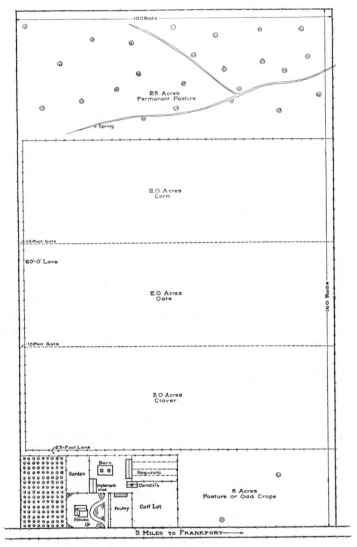

FIG. 43. A one-hundred-acre-farm plan with the short side adjacent to the highway

The long lane is objectionable

57

field mentioned requires 40 rd. more fence than the square one, which, at 75 cents per rod, would cost $30. If the fence lasts ten years, the annual cost, including interest at 6 per cent, would be $5.40, which amount would be easily saved in labor during one season.

Figs. 42 and 43 show one-hundred-acre farms, the one with the long side next to the road, the other with the short side adjoining the highway. In Fig. 42 the buildings are most advantageously located in the middle of the long side. None of the fields is very far from the barns, and the shape of each is very desirable. In Fig. 43 the long lane is objectionable, but there is no other method if the buildings must be near the road. It very frequently happens that the scattering woodland is on the back end of the farm and the stock must have access to it. The cultivated fields could well be run the other way if the topography permitted.

The size of the fields will be determined by the size of the farm and the type of farming practiced. The one-hundred-acre farm in Fig. 42 is conveniently divided for a four-year rotation, while in Fig. 43 a farm of the same size is divided for a three-year rotation. The fields should be of the same size so far as possible, though it is well to have a small field for odd crops, as for soiling purposes.

CHAPTER VI

FARM FENCES

One of the most serious questions that confronts the present-day farmer is that of what kind of fence to build. As an illustration of its magnitude, attention may be called to the fact that there are 272,000 farms in Ohio, according to the census of 1910, averaging 88 A. each. According to figures compiled by the United States Department of Agriculture, Ohio farms of 100 A. or less require an average of 7 rd. of fence per acre. This would mean 700 rd. of fence per farm, which, at 75 cents per rod, would cost $525. For the state as a whole there would be required an investment of $142,800,000 to fence the farms at the average rate, an amount almost equal to the total value of the live stock as shown by the same census. In a consideration of fences the question divides itself into two parts — fence posts and fencing proper.

FENCE POSTS

By far the greater part of all farm fence is made of wire, and for this reason the selection of the proper post material is of much importance ; in fact any fence using posts is just about what the posts make it. The choice of posts, so far as material is concerned, is confined to wood, steel, and concrete.

Wood posts. Wood in the past has been, and will for some time continue to be, the most widely used post material. The kind of timber used depends upon local conditions. If oak or chestnut is abundant, posts of those timbers are likely to be the most common. In the corn-belt region nearly all post timber is shipped in, and the choice becomes largely a matter of cost per post and of probable durability, as frequently two or more timbers are represented in the local market. In an extended investigation of the fence problem, covering the states of the Middle West, the United States Department of Agriculture collected information

59

concerning the kinds of timber most commonly used for posts, their length of life, and the cost. Table I shows a summary of the results. The investigation was carried on in different areas, these areas being specified by number. Area No. 1 included Ohio, Indiana, and Michigan; No. 2, Wisconsin and Illinois; No. 3, Iowa, Missouri, southern Minnesota, eastern Kansas, and eastern Nebraska; No. 4, northern Minnesota, the Dakotas, western Kansas, and western Nebraska. The investigation, while not exhaustive, is thought to be a fair index of common practice.

TABLE I. AVERAGE LIFE AND COST OF DIFFERENT KINDS OF FENCE POSTS AS USED IN THE STATES OF THE MIDDLE WEST[1]

| Kind of Post | Average Life | | Average Cost in All Areas | | Average Cost in Each Area | | | | | | | |
| | Number estimated | Years | Number estimated | Cents | Area No. 1 | | Area No. 2 | | Area No. 3 | | Area No. 4 | |
					Number estimated	Cents	Number estimated	Cents	Number estimated	Cents	Number estimated	Cents
Osage orange : . .	789	29.9	774	22	105	25	326	24	320	17	23	18
Locust	464	23.8	465	24	501	26	21	22	29	18	14	18
Red cedar	557	20.5	574	29	346	29	97	31	104	27	27	21
Mulberry	88	17.4	82	19	45	20	25	17	12	15		
Catalpa	48	15.5	45	17	15	17	17	17	13	18	10	18
Bur oak	97	15.3	90	15	10	10	54	15	26	15		
Chestnut	94	14.8	91	15	91	15						
White cedar	1749	14.3	1709	18	642	18	459	18	374	19	274	16
Walnut	60	11.5	56	13	6	15	11	13	39	12		
White oak	1242	11.4	1218	12	333	14	389	11	421	12	75	13
Pine	41	11.2	37	18	12	23	7	22	3	11	15	12
Tamarack	67	10.5	64	9	6	16	26	8	7	9	25	9
Cherry	9	10.3	9	8	7	8	2	8				
Hemlock	10	9.1	9	12	3	20	6	8				
Sassafras	19	8.9	17	14	11	15	6	10				
Elm	15	8.8	15	12	6	10	5	9	4	15		
Ash	69	8.6	58	10	17	11	2	10	15	10	24	10
Red oak	22	7.0	24	7	6	7	10	8	8	4		
Willow	41	6.2	33	7	1	12	2	7	25	7	5	9
Concrete (estimated)	42	48.0	121	30	53	30	48	29	19	31	1	35
Stone	11	36.3	15	35					4	38	11	35
Steel (estimated) . .	131	29.9	219	30	82	30	71	29	54	30	3	30

[1] *Bulletin No. 321*, United States Department of Agriculture, 1916.

The table shows that *white cedar* is the leading post timber of all the areas studied but one, and that it is estimated to have an average life of 14.3 years; white *oak* follows for the area as a whole, with an average life of 11.4 years. The next most common timber used is *osage orange*, which, with an average life of almost thirty years, stands at the top in regard to durability. *Catalpa*, which is being talked of a great deal as a promising post timber, has not as yet, according to this report, become widely used. Its lasting quality, 15.5 years, compares very favorably with that of other common timbers.

As bearing upon the question of durability, the Ohio Agricultural Experiment Station[1] carried on a personal investigation of over 30,000 fence posts found in 292 different fences, and in its findings rated the timbers encountered in the order of their durability as follows: osage orange, locust, red cedar, mulberry, white cedar, catalpa, chestnut, oak, and black ash. As regards the first four kinds of timber, the two investigations agree, while in the others there is but a slight difference in the ratings given.

It will be noticed that so far as *cost* is concerned there is a wide variation in the different areas, largely due to the presence or absence of the timber as a local product. Red cedar heads the list with an average cost, for the whole area, of 29 cents per post; white cedar and white oak, the two most common timbers, being rated at 18 cents and 12 cents respectively.

In the Ohio bulletin are found some general conclusions based on the results of the investigation, which are interesting.

1. There is no difference which end of the post is put in the ground except that the larger end should have preference.

2. From data collected so far, seasoning does not seem to have any marked effect on durability. It is hoped that the matter will be investigated further.

3. Timber that grows rapidly in the open is not so good as the same variety that grows in the woods.

4. There is some evidence that it is not a good time to cut posts just as the tree begins to grow in early spring.

5. The wood at the center of the tree is not so good as that just inside the sap wood.

[1] *Bulletin No. 219*, Ohio Agricultural Experiment Station, Wooster, 1910.

Preservative treatment. The rapidly increasing cost of the more durable woods for fence posts has led to the investigation of certain treatments designed to prolong the life of the cheaper woods when used for posts. Some of these are feasible and worthy of consideration, while others are worth but little.

Rotting is caused by the growth of fungi, or low forms of plant life which feed upon the tissues of the wood. The fungi require *heat, light, moisture,* and *food* for their development. These requisites are all supplied near the surface of the ground, and hence posts rot off at this point. A post rots but little beneath the surface of the ground, because the lack of air prevents the growth of fungi, while aboveground the lack of moisture prevents their growth. It is not possible to control the moisture, the heat, nor the air supply, but if the food supply can be controlled the fungi cannot develop. The most feasible method of destroying the food supply is to impregnate the wood with *creosote*, a coal-tar product.

This method is best carried out by heating the creosote in a large kettle and setting well-seasoned posts into it, leaving them there for an hour or so. They are then removed and set into a kettle of cold creosote and left for several hours, during which time the liquid soaks into the posts to a considerable depth, the depth depending upon the nature of the wood. The hot bath is of itself fairly effective, but the cold bath following is essential to a thorough impregnation. This method, to be successfully carried on, requires an equipment specially arranged for the purpose. Painting the lower portions of the posts with hot creosote will probably prolong the life of the post long enough to pay for the treatment. The estimated cost of treatment is about 15 cents per post; and when the cheaper timbers are used it may reasonably be expected that the life of the post will be doubled or even trebled. It probably will not pay to treat the better classes of hardwood posts, since the denseness of the wood prevents the absorption of the creosote in beneficial quantities.

Charring the post is a very effective method of preventing decay. That portion of the post which is to go into the ground is placed in a bed of hot coals and left until thoroughly charred. This process destroys the food supply of the fungi and prevents their getting a start.

Painting the lower portion of the post with an oil paint is effective as long as the paint lasts, but it soon scales off. The beneficial effects are probably not worth the time and trouble taken to apply the paint.

Zinc chloride has sometimes been recommended as a preservative. It is usually applied by boring holes in the posts and filling the holes with the solution, which is slowly absorbed by the wood. Zinc chloride is easily soluble, and as a consequence the solution next the surface of the post soon loses its effectiveness. This method is used but little if at all.

Steel posts. Steel posts are now being widely used in many sections of the country. They are generally so made that they may be driven, thus materially decreasing the labor cost of the fence, a fact which makes a strong appeal to the farmer. Furthermore, they do not heave so badly as wood or concrete posts. A steel post, too, forms a ground connection for the wire fence, thus lessening the danger to stock from lightning.

It is impossible to say which form of steel post is best. The heavy angular post made of soft steel has not proved satisfactory, since it is too easily bent by stock crowding against the fence, and once bent, even though straightened, it never possesses its former strength. Moreover such posts frequently rust off in five years' time. The galvanized-iron posts, either round or irregular in shape, are so easily bent as to make one hesitate to use them. The lighter forms of high-carbon steel posts are meeting with considerable favor. They have the decided advantage of springing back into place when bent out of shape, though they are not easily bent.

The lasting quality of steel posts seems to be somewhat variable. They have been known to last for fifteen or twenty years, while, as above mentioned, they may rust off, or be broken off because of rusting, in a few years. Manufacturers have evidently not yet discovered the best material for fence posts, though the posts of the future must be largely made of steel in some form.

Concrete posts. A discussion of the making of concrete fence posts will be found in the chapter on concrete. It need only be said, at this time, that though the durability of concrete recommends it as a post material, unusual care and the best of materials and reënforcement are necessary if a good post is secured. Numerous failures have resulted when farmers have attempted to make their own posts, largely because of a lack of attention to one or more of the above requisites. Beyond a doubt concrete posts will find a wide use in the future, and where good materials are available at moderate prices it may pay to make the posts on the farm, utilizing labor at spare times.

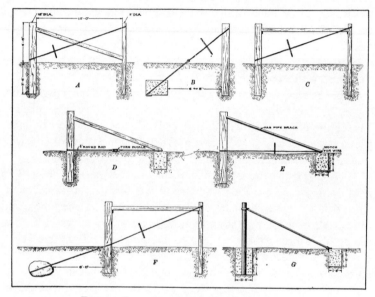

Fig. 44. Several methods of bracing end posts

At *A* is shown the most common method, though it is not so satisfactory as the method shown at *C*. The brace shown at *B* is frequently used if the wire is not in the way. Excellent braces are shown at *D* and *E*; *G* shows a commendable patent brace for steel posts

The cement post is not cheap in first cost, as many are led to believe. The cement alone, in a well-made post, will cost from 8 to 10 cents, and the reënforcing rods from 5 to 10 cents — the amount depending upon the material used; so that even if the sand, gravel, and labor are thrown in, the total cost will be from 15 to 20 cents per post. There is no intention in this discussion to discourage the use of concrete posts, but the idea that they can be hurriedly and cheaply made is a mistaken one — a fact which should be now widely known.

Setting the posts. End posts, of whatever kind, must be of good size and thoroughly anchored and braced. It is utterly useless to hang a good fence on small end posts poorly set. Fig. 44 shows several common methods for bracing end posts. These posts may well be of concrete or heavy-steel construction, even though wooden line posts are most frequently used. If steel posts are used, they should be set in liberal portions of concrete, though some of the manufacturers of spring-steel posts do not so recommend. Wood posts have been set in concrete with varying

FIG. 45. Neat and substantial corner-post construction

Note that the braces are horizontal; they could well have been placed a little higher

degrees of success. There is a tendency for the post to swell and rupture the concrete, and water seeping down the sides of the post causes decay to set in. It is doubtful whether the concrete prolongs the life of the post, though it undoubtedly secures a more substantial setting.

End posts are required at least every 40 or 50 rd. Line posts should not be set more than 20 ft. apart, and it probably pays to put them not more than 1 rod apart. Though the cost for post material is of course more if the distance between posts is short, the stock will usually not bear down the fence so badly, a circumstance which effects a saving that more than offsets the added expense for posts.

FENCING

While almost every conceivable kind of fence can be found in any section of the country, there are only three materials of wide importance; namely, wire, wood, and hedge. Wire fences consist chiefly of some form of woven wire or barbed wire. Wood fences may be of the worm rail or the post-and-rail type, or of boards or pickets. Hedge fence may be entirely of hedge or of hedge and woven wire. Table II shows the distribution of the leading types of fence in the areas shown, as taken from *Bulletin No. 321* of the United States Department of Agriculture. A woven-wire fence over forty-two inches high is classed as a high fence; one under forty-two inches, as a low fence.

TABLE II. PERCENTAGE OF DIFFERENT TYPES OF FENCE USED
IN THE AREAS NOTED

AREA	HIGH WOVEN WIRE	LOW WOVEN WIRE WITH BARBED WIRES	BARBED AND SMOOTH WIRE	HEDGE	WOOD	STONE
	Per cent	*Per cent*	*Per cent*	*Per cent*	*Per cent*	*Per cent*
Western Dakota, western Kansas, western Nebraska, and northern Minnesota	5.5	10.2	84.0	0.03	0.3	0.0
Eastern Dakota, eastern Kansas, eastern Nebraska, and southern Minnesota	8.8	20.0	63.0	6.4	0.6	0.6
Iowa	8.0	45.5	43.5	2.1	0.9	0.0
Missouri	13.8	49.4	27.2	5.6	3.8	0.04
Wisconsin	13.5	33.4	49.8	0.04	2.3	0.8
Illinois	11.4	41.7	29.0	12.4	5.5	0.0
Michigan	55.9	11.8	11.9	0.6	19.7	0.0
Indiana	53.3	18.0	12.9	1.6	14.1	0.05
Ohio	59.8	3.8	7.0	1.2	27.9	0.05

The table shows that *woven wire* is the most common type of fence in the Middle West. Ohio shows 27.9 per cent of wooden fences, while barbed wire finds its greatest use in the range sections.

Although there is a wide variation in the size of wire used in woven-wire fences, the modern tendency is to use a fence made of No. 9 wires throughout. This makes a more expensive fence and one that is harder to erect, but the increased length of life more than offsets the difference. The use of stay wires so small as No. 12 or No. 14 is to be discouraged.

The *rapid rusting* of modern fencing-wire is a phenomenon observed by all users of woven-wire fence. Scientists have long been searching for the cause of this rapid rusting, but as yet no satisfactory explanation has been offered, though there seems to be some evidence which tends to attribute the difficulty to the modern method of making the steel from which the wire is manufactured. Years ago nearly all the steel used in making fencing-wire was manufactured by the puddled-iron process, in which the metal was carefully and thoroughly worked by hand. However, it was only after the introduction of the Bessemer and open-hearth processes for the manufacture of steel that woven-wire fencing came into prominent use, and it did so largely because these processes made possible cheaper steel.

After the steel is taken from the Bessemer converter or from the open-hearth furnace, it is poured into large molds, forming ingots of solid steel. It is then carried to the rolling-mills and reduced by constant rolling to a size approaching that of a lead pencil; finally it is drawn through a die and formed into a round wire of a size equal to No. 5 or No. 6. After it has been properly heated and tempered, this stock is drawn cold through appropriate dies and gradually reduced to wires of the desired size.

To *galvanize* steel fence wire is to coat it with a layer of zinc. The wire to be galvanized is first drawn through an oven, in which it is properly annealed. On leaving this oven it is taken into a tank of weak acid to clean it properly, and to provide a soldering-solution. It is then drawn through a tank of molten zinc, and a portion of the material clings to the wire. On emerging from the tank the wire is drawn through asbestos wipers to secure a uniform coating. Undoubtedly the thickness of the zinc coating is a factor in the lasting quality of the wire.

In spite of the zinc coating, however, the wire rusts, and investigations carried on by the United States Department of

Agriculture in 1905 and reported in *Bulletin No. 239* seem to indicate that the element manganese, which is added to the steel just before it is poured from the furnace, whether it is made by the Bessemer or by the open-hearth process, is at the bottom of the trouble. When a wire rusts it pits, and the explanation, as frequently given, is that the pitting is due to electrolytic action set up because of the unequal distribution of manganese in the wire. It seems that this explanation is not yet regarded as an established fact.

It is generally claimed by manufacturers that wire made from open-hearth steel is superior to that made from Bessemer steel. This statement cannot be made with absolute certainty, however, though evidence seems to point to such a conclusion. Nevertheless the fact remains that modern fence wire does rust out rapidly, though it is believed that manufacturers are doing everything in their power to improve the quality of their product. The farmers' chief protection lies in buying a fence made of nothing smaller than No. 9 wires, and even larger sizes may be advisable.

The height of woven-wire fence varies considerably. What is known to the trade as a 10–47 fence, that is, a fence having 10 wires and measuring 47 in. in height, is the most common type in Ohio, Indiana, and Michigan. A fence of this height, if intended for horses, is not complete without a barbed wire on top. The low fence, with 2 or more barbed wires, is most common in Iowa, Wisconsin, Missouri, and Illinois. This makes a good cattle fence, but where it is used to fence in horses it is somewhat more dangerous than the 47-inch fence with but one barbed wire on top.

Barbed wire should be used with the utmost care. The practice of placing it on old fences, and, especially, near the ground, when horses are to be pastured or inclosed, cannot be too severely condemned. Horses maimed and ruined for sale if not for service are to be found in every community where barbed wire is used. It has, to be sure, a real place on top of a well-constructed fence 42 or 47 in. high, but if it is placed lower than this there is an element of danger that is likely to result in serious accidents.

Homemade woven-wire fences are constructed in a variety of ways by machines especially designed for the purpose. Good fences may be made in this way, and at a cost below that of ready-made fence, but, as a rule, they are not equal in general desirability, appearance, or tightness to a factory-made fence.

Stretching the wire fence. When erecting the fence, one should remember that it is to be in place for a number of years, and that the degree of tightness will determine in no small measure the length of life of the fence. In view of this fact every effort should be made to secure it properly at both ends after stretching it as tightly as possible.

FIG. 46. Illustrating one of the best types of fence-stretchers

Chains at both top and bottom are very desirable

Fig. 46 shows one of the best types of stretchers. The chains are fastened to the top and the bottom of the clamp-bar, each chain being controlled by a separate windlass. This makes it possible to keep the fence plumb, a thing which is not possible where there is but one windlass. The clamp-bar should be so placed that it will stand about three feet from the end post when the fence is finally stretched. The fence should then be cut off and the wires tightened by means of an individual wire-stretcher as each is stapled to the post. The wires should be bent around the post and wrapped around themselves, as the staples are usually not sufficient to hold the fence. If steel or concrete posts are used, the wires must be wrapped around the post and fastened

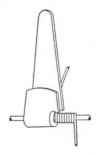

FIG. 47. A simple tool for splicing wires

by twisting about themselves. This is a rather difficult task, but it may be accomplished in such a way (Fig. 48) that there is but little slack in the fence after it is released.

One should never lose sight of the fact that the wire fence is put up to last for at least ten years, and in the majority of cases for

FIG. 48. Fastening wire fence to a steel post

The single-chain stretcher used here is not so good as the one shown in Fig. 46

fifteen years, and no effort should be spared to secure a first-class job. The need of first-class workmanship is especially important in view of the fact that a properly erected fence will invariably last longer than one poorly stretched and supported.

Wood fences are used as general farm fences only in those regions where timber is plentiful. The old-fashioned worm rail fence is rapidly disappearing. This type of fence has served an excellent purpose, but in comparison with the woven-wire fence it has but few things to recommend it. It occupies too much space on the ground, it harbors weeds, trash, and insects, it blows down frequently, and it is easily pushed over by horses; these disadvantages are sufficient to eliminate it from the field of available

FIG. 49. A woven-wire fence on concrete posts

Note the concrete brace post and brace. The fence is stapled to the line posts

fences even if timber were sufficiently abundant to afford a supply of rails. The post-and-rail fence and the board fence are likewise only occasionally seen. Picket fences, although used for yard purposes, do not play an important part in the fencing of fields. Such fences are erected by nailing pickets to wood rails or by weaving the pickets into horizontal wires usually arranged in three pairs at the top, bottom, and middle of the pickets. A neat and substantial yard or garden fence may be made by bolting wood rails to steel posts set in concrete and nailing the pickets on. If pine pickets are used, it is a good plan to paint them before they are put on.

Hedge fences grown from osage-orange plants are very much in favor in certain parts of the country. Properly trained and

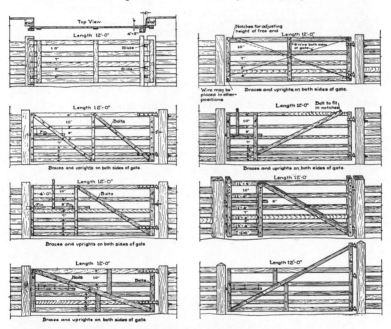

FIG. 50. Illustrating the construction of eight types of farm gates

Substantial, properly hung, well-painted gates add much to the appearance of a farm

cared for, hedge makes a very desirable fence. A common way of making hedge fences is to set the plants 8 in. apart where the hedge is to be and, after they have grown to a height of about 3 ft. (which generally means a growth of two years), to erect a 24-inch or 30-inch fence on short posts driven in the line of the fence. Two smooth wires may then be stretched on the opposite side of the hedge row for the purpose of holding the plants erect and close to the wire fence. The hedge should then

be kept trimmed to a height of 4 ft. and the width should not
exceed 10 or 12 in. Such a fence may be kept in proper shape
by trimming twice each year. If a hedge fence is permitted to
grow to a height of several feet, it shades the land, draws heavily
on the soil for food and water, and usually stands for poor farming
and faulty management. If it is properly cared for, however, none

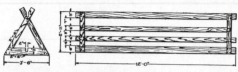

of these objections can
be urged against it.

Movable, or tempo-
rary, fences are fre-
quently desired, as for
pasturing sheep and
hogs or in arranging

FIG. 51. A good method of making movable
fence panels

yards. When hogs are turned in on corn and only a portion of
the field is used at one time, a twenty-four-inch wire fence may
be tied to hills of corn, where it will stand until moved to another
position. With a few well-made stakes, a narrow wire fence may
be made to serve many purposes as a temporary fence. Fig. 51
shows a common method of constructing movable panels.

CHAPTER VII

FARM BUILDINGS

A work on farm equipment is scarcely complete without some reference to farm buildings, but the subject covers so wide a field that it can be given only the briefest consideration in this text. Plans of those farm buildings which are of interest to the general farmer are presented, with the idea that in this way details of plan and construction can best be presented.

HOG-HOUSES

The individual cot. Figs. 52, 53, and 54 illustrate one method of constructing the individual type of hog-house. This type of house is in great favor among many swine-breeders and is recommended for a number of reasons. It is possible to isolate the sow at farrowing-time and for some time thereafter from the remainder of the herd. The cots may be moved about and placed in pastures or other desirable places. The sows and pigs are forced to take a certain amount of exercise in going to and from their feed, since the cots are usually at some distance from the feeding-place.

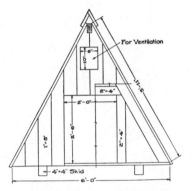

FIG. 52. Front view of the A-frame, individual type of hog-house

From the standpoint of sanitation the individual cot offers an unusual advantage. The hogs are not permitted to bunch together, and since it is frequently moved, there is less likelihood of contamination than where the location is fixed for all time, as in the colony house. The chief objection to this type of house is that the herd is usually very

73

much scattered, a condition which makes necessary the expenditure of much time in feeding and in other required attention.

The cot is usually built on runners and may or may not be provided with a floor, though for use at all seasons of the

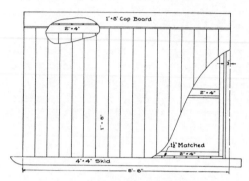

FIG. 53. Side view of the A-frame hog-house

year a floor is very much to be desired. The door may or may not be provided. In some instances a canvas or a gunny sack weighted at the bottom is hung at the door. It keeps out cold winds, and the hogs soon learn to raise it on leaving or entering the cot.

The colony house. There are very many designs which may be used for the colony type of hog-house. Fig. 56 shows a standard plan. The colony house is in great favor because it centralizes the herd and greatly lessens the time required to feed and care for the hogs. Further, it is possible to warm the house at farrowing-time if desirable. Provision may be made, too, for storing feed in the house so that all operations are carried on under one roof. Good construction and a great deal of care and attention are required to keep such a house clean and free from disease; but this is quite possible under proper management.

FIG. 54. Perspective of the A-frame hog-house

The *pens* in this plan are 8 × 8, though many consider a 6 × 8 pen amply large for a sow and her litter. The partitions may be constructed so as to be readily removed, thus making it possible to use the entire house, if necessary, as a feeding-floor for fattening hogs.

The *floors* for hog-houses are now rather generally made of concrete. Such a floor is very easily cleaned and never wears out. Inasmuch as it is somewhat cold and damp for sows at farrowing-time, a wood mat should be provided in one corner of the pen, as a nesting-place. This mat may be hinged to the wall so that it may be turned up out of the way when not needed.

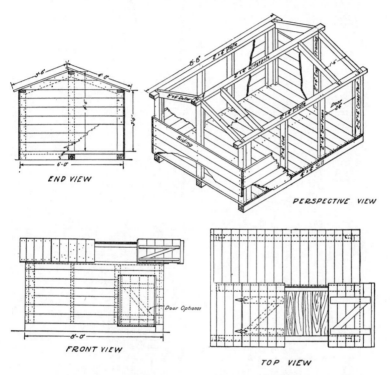

FIG. 55. Showing the construction of the gable-roofed individual hog-house

The end elevation (Fig. 56) shows the half-monitor roof-construction. Since it is highly desirable to have as much sunlight as possible in every pen, this type of construction is especially to be recommended. With such a house facing the south, sunlight strikes all of the pens for a considerable portion of the day. The height of the windows is determined by the latitude in which the house is built.

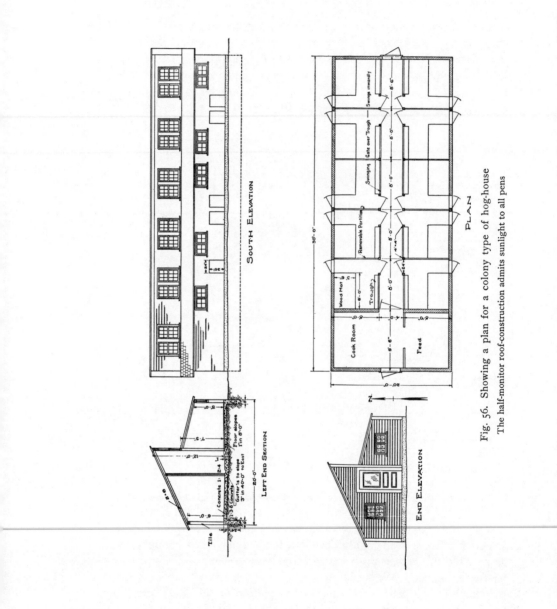

Fig. 56. Showing a plan for a colony type of hog-house

The half-monitor roof-construction admits sunlight to all pens

76

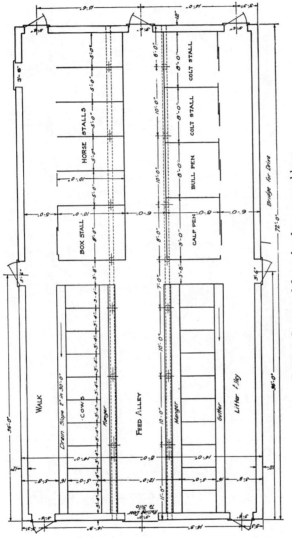

FIG. 57. Suggested floor plan for a general barn
Note stall dimensions, alley widths, etc.

77

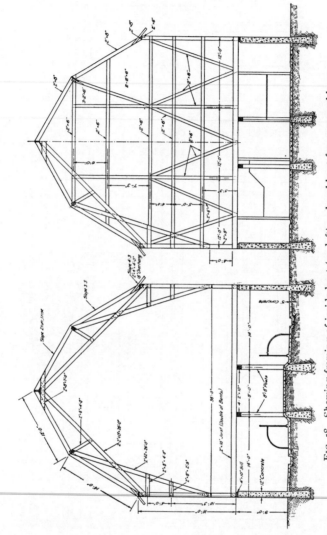

Fig. 58. Showing framing of inside bent (on left) and end bent for a general barn
Plank-frame construction is used throughout

78

A great many farmers prefer a two-story house with ample room above for the storage of feed, baled straw, etc. With a liberal area of windows there is no objection to this construction, and it is very convenient and economical.

The General Barn

The general barn as it is found on the average farm has been built with but little thought given to the interior plan. The usual procedure has been to erect the barn and then to make the

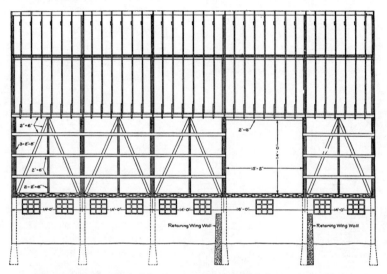

FIG. 59. A side view of the framework of a plank-frame general barn

best of the inside arrangement, although just the opposite plan is the more logical one to follow. The general barn usually provides room for the horses and for the milk-cows, with box stalls for calves, colts, brood mares, etc.

Figs. 57, 58, and 59 are presented as a type of the general barn more for the purpose of showing certain principles of arrangement and construction than of presenting an ideal design. The interior arrangement (Fig. 57) could be changed to that of a dairy barn or that of a horse barn, or the space allotted to horses and cows may be divided in any suitable manner.

The *framing* details shown in Figs. 58 and 59 are of the plank-frame type, as opposed to pin-frame construction, so common, particularly in older barns. This type of construction is comparatively new, and consequently has not as yet come into extended use. It has, however, so many advantages over the pin-frame type that it will undoubtedly be the barn of the future. In its construction all beams, posts, etc., are built up from two-inch plank. Some of its advantages are the following: (1) the interior space above the second floor is not cut up

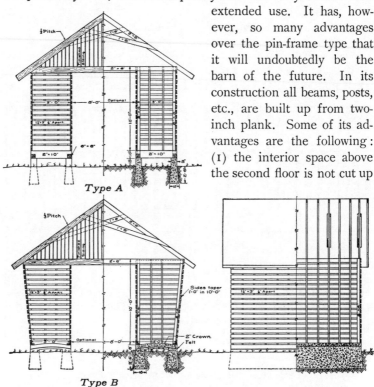

FIG. 60. Showing plans for a double corncrib

Type *A* has straight sides and a plank floor. Type *B* has flaring sides and a concrete floor

by posts and cross ties; (2) there is a saving in the amount of lumber required; (3) there is a great saving in the time and labor required; (4) timber can be used that would probably find no place in a pin frame; (5) the self-supporting roof is used to advantage.

The chief objection to this type of construction is that the sides are not securely tied together and that the ends are not sufficiently supported against the inward pressure, a condition which results in bulging sides. This, no doubt, has been true in many barns of this type where a sufficiently strong truss was not used for the roof. With care in this regard, there is little danger from spreading.

The barn may be built with or without a basement structure. In sections where the bank barn is possible, the basement plan is perhaps to be advised. Sometimes, however, in level sections an elevated driveway is built up and the basement structure provided. One or two driveways may be included, the number depending upon the length of the barn. The gambrel roof shown is well adapted to this type of construction and increases the mow room materially.

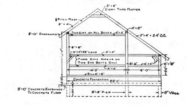

CORNCRIBS

Fig. 60 shows two types of a double corn-crib, which is, undoubtedly, more commonly used than any other form. The dimensions may be varied to suit the size of the farm, though the width of the cribs should not exceed six feet. Storage space for seed corn may be provided above,

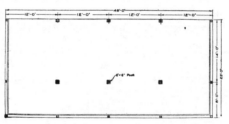

FIG. 61. Floor plan and end view of a simple implement-shed

if desired. The width between cribs may be varied as indicated in the drawings, with ten feet, perhaps, as a standard width.

THE IMPLEMENT-SHED

Fig. 61 shows a simple and inexpensive plan for an implement-shed. This plan may be varied to suit local conditions. For example, the height of the posts can be increased so as to provide a limited amount of storage above. One bent may be made higher than the rest, for housing machinery that will not enter a ten-foot door, or one bent may be constructed so as to be used for manure storage.

The Poultry-house

Plans for a 100-fowl poultry-house are shown in Figs. 64, 65, and 66. The type is that now generally recommended by poultry-

raisers. The floor plan (Fig. 64) provides ample roosting space. The perches are spaced 15 in. apart, and an allowance of about 8 in. of perch room is made for each fowl. The dropping-board is hinged to the wall and supported in a horizontal position just beneath the roosts. Both roosts and dropping-board should be made removable for ease in cleaning. Almost the entire floor of the house is available for scratching room. Nesting-boxes may be placed in either end of the house or under the dropping-board.

FIG. 62. Perspective of the implement-shed shown in the plan in Fig. 61

In the front elevation (Fig. 66) the size and location of windows are shown. About 1 sq. ft. of glass is allowed for each 15 sq. ft. of floor space. If much more glass than this is used the house will be hot in summer and cold at nights in winter, since heat will

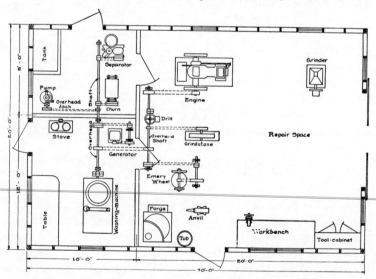

FIG. 63. Floor plan for a farm shop, designed by G. W. McCuen

readily pass out through the windows. The tops of the windows should be about 6 ft. from the floor for a house of this width, in order that the sun may shine into the back part of the pen. They should also extend nearly to the floor, for a similar reason. The muslin-covered sash permits the passage of air for purposes of ventilation without draft, which is an essential feature, and, when open, provides for free circulation of air in warm weather.

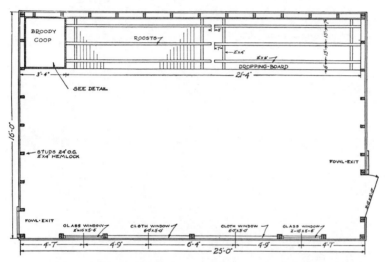

FIG. 64. Floor plan for a one-hundred-fowl poultry-house

The floor and foundation of the house should be made of concrete. Earth makes a fairly satisfactory floor, but is usually damp at certain seasons of the year, and it cannot be kept clean. A concrete floor is easily cleaned, is dry, and, if kept covered with litter, is sufficiently warm.

If a layer of tarred roofing-paper is placed in the floor about two inches from the bottom while the concrete is being placed, it will aid in keeping the floor warm and dry. Its function is to prevent the passage of moisture up through the concrete and thus to prevent evaporation from the surface of the floor, which in itself is a cooling process. Though, even with this precaution, the concrete floor is rather cold, its evident advantages greatly outweigh this one disadvantage.

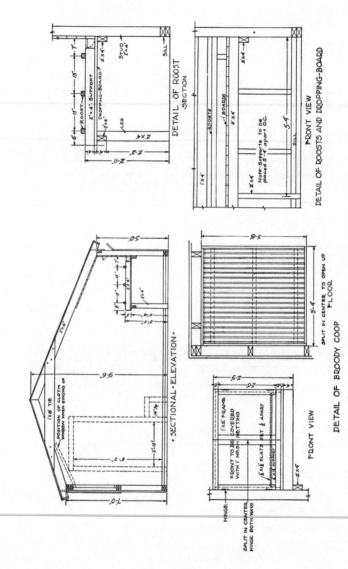

FIG. 65. End view and details of a one-hundred-fowl poultry house

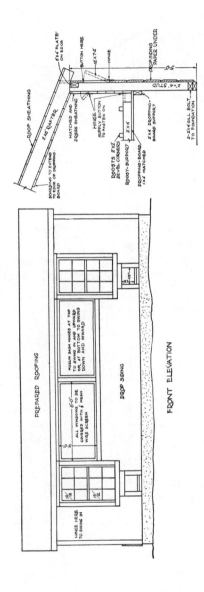

FIG. 66. Front elevation and ventilation details of a one-hundred-fowl poultry-house

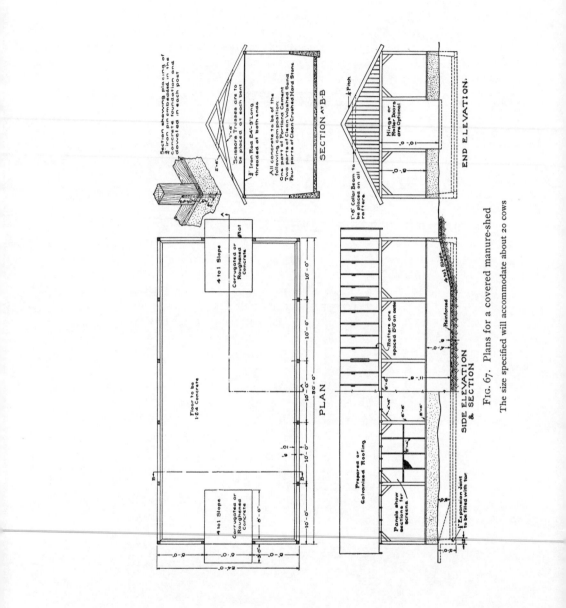

FIG. 67. Plans for a covered manure-shed

The size specified will accommodate about 20 cows

86

Silos

Storing feed in a silo has beyond question demonstrated itself to be an economical and satisfactory method, and anyone who keeps ten or more head of cattle should seriously consider the advisability of purchasing a silo. The chief questions which face a prospective purchaser relate to the kind and size of silo best suited to his conditions. There are so many types of silos on the market that it becomes a difficult question to determine which kind to buy.

What constitutes a good silo? The purpose of a silo is to preserve the green food placed in it. To do this the walls must be tight enough to keep out air and to retain the moisture, and they must be strong enough to withstand the pressure from within. Further, they must be smooth so that the ensilage will settle evenly around the edges. Any material which meets these requisites will keep ensilage. In addition to these chief essentials, a silo should be reasonably permanent and durable.

Kinds of silos. The *stave* silo is by far the most common silo in use. If properly constructed it will keep ensilage as well as any other type, or possibly better than others, and if properly cared for it will last for from ten to twenty years. The best of staves should be purchased. The joints should be leaded when the silo is put up, and when finished it should be painted on the inside with creosote or some other wood preservative and on the outside with a good oil paint. If the hoops are kept tight in the summer and if the silo is anchored to a good foundation, satisfactory service will result from its use. This type of silo is quickly and easily erected and may, if occasion demands, be taken down and erected elsewhere, though not without considerable damage. The stave silo sometimes blows down and twists out of shape, but such things do not happen often if proper precautions are taken.

The *wooden-hoop* silo is only a modification of the stave silo, wooden hoops being used in place of the iron ones, and the staves nailed to them. There is no way of tightening such hoops, but they should expand and contract with the staves, so that adjustment is not so necessary. A well-constructed wooden-hoop silo is a good investment, but this type has been so cheaply put up and so unsatisfactory in many cases that it is not in good favor.

The *monolithic concrete* silo has been constructed with success and used with satisfaction in large numbers. When made of good materials, with a four-inch to six-inch wall, and well reënforced, it will serve its purpose well. The concrete must be rich in cement (a 1–2–4 mixture is none too good), to prevent the absorption of juices by the walls. If the inner surface is painted with asphalt paint or a similar preparation, absorption is reduced to a minimum. The objection is frequently raised against a concrete silo that the juices of the silage soften the concrete. Experience seems to show that there is little foundation for such a statement. The concrete silo costs a little more than the stave silo, but its longer life more than makes up for the extra cost. Of course there is always danger that the silo will crack because of poor construction in walls or foundation, and if the cracking is severe the loss is great. This one thing militates against the wider use of this type of silo. Another objection is that expensive forms are required, and the labor cost of erecting it is heavy.

The *cement-block* silo is now used quite extensively. The ease with which it is erected, when compared to the monolithic type, recommends it. The blocks must be made with extreme care. Too frequently the blocks are made with a mixture so dry that it is impossible to procure an impervious block. When the silo is plastered on the inside with a thick coating of cement, it is made sufficiently impervious, but this must be carefully done to secure a lasting job. The silo must, of course, be well reënforced, this being accomplished by laying reënforcing wires in the mortar joints. The success of this silo depends upon the quality of the blocks used and the manner of erection. Many are giving unqualified success.

The *vitrified-clay-block* silo is growing in favor every year. Vitrified clay blocks represent a material that is almost ideal for the construction of silos. They are impervious to moisture and air and are strong, smooth, and durable. They furnish a hollow wall that has some advantages in freezing weather, and they are easily built into a silo, with a minimum requirement of time and labor. When laid with good cement mortar and well reënforced, they make a silo that is sure to keep the ensilage well and that is practically indestructible.

Relative cost of silos. The following statement as to the relative cost of different types of silos represents average costs as collected from a large number of Ohio farmers, the figures representing cost per ton capacity of the silo: wood-stave, $2.75; homemade wooden-hoop, $1.70; monolithic-concrete, $3.93; concrete-block, $4.20; vitrified-tile, $4.75; metal, $4.

The size of the silo. The question of the size of the silo is a very important one for the farmer, and of course has to do with the diameter and the height. The diameter will be determined by the number of cattle to be fed, while the height will be determined largely by the number of days the herd will be fed from the silo. It is necessary to feed from $1\frac{1}{2}$ in. to 2 in. in depth from a silo each day to prevent molding. Hence the proper diameter can be determined by figuring the quantity of ensilage in pounds to be used daily; then by reducing the quantity to cubic feet a diameter can be determined that will cause at least the minimum amount to be used from the silo each day. The average weight of a cubic foot of ensilage is taken as 40 lb.

The following table gives the amount of ensilage ordinarily consumed by live stock.

TABLE III. ENSILAGE CONSUMED DAILY BY LIVE STOCK [1]

KIND OF STOCK	DAILY RATION IN POUNDS
Beef cattle	
Wintering calves, 8 months old	15–25
Wintering breeding cows	30–50
Fattening beef cattle, 18–22 months old	
First stage of fattening	20–30
Latter stage of fattening	12–20
Dairy cattle	30–50
Sheep	
Wintering breeding sheep	3–5
Fattening lambs	2–3
Fattening sheep	3–4

[1] *Bulletin No. 141*, Iowa State College, Ames, 1913.

As an illustration of the method used to determine the proper diameter of a silo, let it be assumed that 15 cows are to be fed 40 lb. per day each, that a cubic foot of ensilage weighs 40 lb., and that 2 in. are to be fed from the silo each day. If d be the diameter of the silo, then,

$$15 \times 40 = 600 \text{ lb. fed each day,}$$
$$600 \div 40 = 15 \text{ cu. ft. fed each day,}$$
$$d^2 \times 0.7854 \times \tfrac{1}{6} = 15,$$
$$d^2 = \frac{90}{0.7854},$$
$$= 114.6,$$
$$d = 10.7.$$

The result shows that a silo 11 ft. in diameter will be required if 2 in. are to be removed each day.

The height of the silo is to be determined by the number of feeding-days and by the quantity to be fed daily. If the 2-inch-per-day plan is followed, a silo whose height is equal to one sixth the total number of feeding-days will be required. Thus, to feed for one hundred and eighty days, a silo 30 ft. high would be

TABLE IV. DIAMETER AND HEIGHT OF SILO REQUIRED FOR
HERDS OF DIFFERENT SIZES[1]

Number of Cows in Herd	Feed for 180 Days			Feed for 240 Days		
	Silage consumed (tons)	Size of silo		Silage consumed (tons)	Size of silo	
		Diameter (feet)	Height (feet)		Diameter (feet)	Height (feet)
10	36	10	25	48	10	31
12	43	10	28	57	10	35
15	54	11	29	72	11	36
20	72	12	32	96	12	39
25	90	13	33	120	13	40
30	108	14	34	144	15	37
35	126	15	34	168	16	38
40	144	16	35	192	17	39
45	162	16	37	216	18	39
50	180	17	37	240	19	39

[1] *Bulletin No. 103*, Agricultural Experiment Station, Columbia, Mo.

required. Of course ensilage settles, and a 30-foot silo would not have 30 ft. of ensilage in it; but the lower part is packed so much that considerably less than 2 in. would give the required amount per day, and in the winter-time less than 2 in. may be fed without trouble from molding.

Table IV gives the proper size of silo for different sizes of herds for feeding-periods of one hundred and eighty days and of two hundred and forty days.

CHAPTER VIII

THE FARMHOUSE

By F. W. Ives

The farmhouse has many functions to fulfill and should be designed to perform these functions with economy, harmony, and convenience. Durability and beauty of construction may, in a measure, be secondary, but are of no less importance in promoting happiness and permanent comfort.

The function. The chief function of the house is to shelter the occupants and the equipment. In our climate, where the extremes of temperature may vary 120° F. within the short space of two or three months, and where varying conditions of rainfall and drought must be faced; where there are long and short periods of daylight and where there are rodents and insect pests, the shelter must be weather resisting, waterproof and damp-proof, well lighted, and sanitary. Further, the house is the social center and nearly always the business center of the farm. Family and neighborhood gatherings are held in it; visitors and callers are entertained in it; dinners are served and business is transacted in it. It is also a laboratory for the preparation of food.

The site. As the farmhouse is the center of human activity on the farm, its site must be determined somewhat by the fact that the house should be accessible to barns, garden, and highway. For the most part, the barns are the first permanent structures on a farm, and the farmhouse follows. It is necessary, therefore, to fit the house site to existing roads and buildings. With this in view, the house should be placed so that the prevailing winds shall not blow toward it from the yards and barns. The ground should, if possible, slope from the house to the barn rather than the other way about, and the water supply should be in a place free from contamination from barns, yards, and outbuildings.

A hill affords an ideal site from the standpoint of air, but it may be very bleak and cold in the winter. On the other hand, a low site may be excellent for plants and trees and shrubs for beautiful surroundings, but may be subject to damp air and poor drainage, and hence be unhealthful. The happy medium would be the side of a slope, where all conditions would seem to be in better balance.

The design. It would be difficult indeed to build an ideal house, but if care and thought are given to its planning, one may be built that will suit a given family in most respects. The habits of the family, its size, and the manner of living, as well as the site and surroundings, will all influence the design. In general it may be said that one should secure the services of a competent architect when he is building a house, for the architect's experience and knowledge of materials and methods will save many mistakes; he will also plan the building to fit the site and will make it pleasing in appearance.

It is not always possible to incorporate into one house all the desirable features that one would wish, since one idea may conflict with another. It is evident that it is hardly possible to give every room a south or an east exposure, although such exposures are very desirable in a room. Planning, then, resolves itself into putting together the most desirable rooms, and the most desirable features into rooms, the whole to make a harmonious unit.

The materials. Permanent and sanitary construction are easily attained with our modern materials. Brick, hollow tile, and concrete are the materials best suited for this construction. These materials are fireproof and weatherproof, and while the first cost may run from 5 per cent to 15 per cent more than that of other types, there is a saving in the long run. No material is more beautiful or more easily worked than wood. Its main objection, of course, is its comparatively high degree of inflammability. Many wooden structures are now covered with stucco, which is a plaster applied to lath, either of wood or metal, but preferably of metal.

Roof coverings are diverse and are easily obtainable in one form or another. Wood shingles are beautiful, and are durable if properly taken care of. Shingles of asphalt and of felt are procurable also, as well as of asbestos and of tile. Slate and tile are good, but require heavier roof framing than the others. Sheet-metal roofings of tin plate, galvanized iron, or copper are satisfactory when properly laid. There are also on the market many good patented prepared roll roofings. On the whole, the fire-resisting materials are to be preferred.

The plan. To fulfill the functions of the house as a home some rooms may be listed as necessary and some as desirable. The necessary rooms are a kitchen (which may also serve as a dining-room), a living-room, and sleeping-rooms. These may be on one or on two floors. Additional rooms to make the house more pleasant and more comfortable are a dining-room, a wash-room, a pantry, a library or office, and an inclosed porch.

With the one-story bungalow type it is possible to have all the rooms on one floor. When there are two floors a stair hall, a bathroom, and a sleeping-porch should be added. Plans for a second floor should never be drawn without careful comparison with the first floor, so that stairways, halls, chimneys, and plumbing can be properly taken care of. Windows on the second floor should correspond in location to those on the first floor as far as convenience will allow. Chimneys should be straight from cellar to roof, and must not be supported partially or wholly upon a wood structure. Winders in stairways should be avoided, since they are dangerous. Outside light and ventilation in all rooms should be carefully prepared for. Spindles and brackets are costly and are difficult to maintain and repair; simple beauty is best. The square house is the most economical to construct, and it is easily divided into shapely rooms.

The *kitchen* is one of the most important rooms in a house, and should be given first thought in planning the house. The housewife spends more time and does more work in the kitchen than in any other room. A particular effort should be made to design this room so that the distance between sink and stove, stove and worktable, worktable and sink, will be cut to a minimum. Light and ventilation are next in consideration, and to make these satisfactory there should be windows on two sides of the room if possible. These windows should be not less than thirty-four inches above the floor, so as not to interfere with tables or sinks beneath them. A rear porch, screened in the summer

and fitted with sash in the winter, will add much to the comfort
of the workers. Useful adjuncts to the kitchen would be a storage
pantry and a room in which the men coming from the fields or

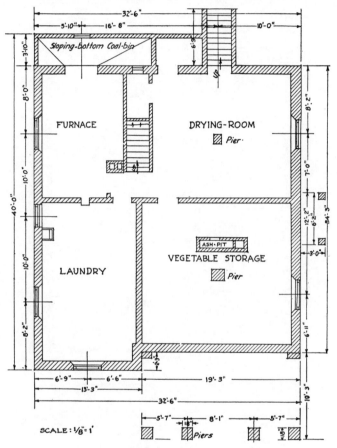

FIG. 68.[1] Basement plan for a farmhouse

The laundry room may be used for storage

stables may wash themselves and change their garments. Access
to the cellar stairway and front door should be easy. The dining-
room door should be double swung and provided with a small

[1] Courtesy of French & Ives, "Agricultural Drafting." McGraw-Hill Book Co.

glass panel. Kitchen sinks should not be less than thirty-four inches from the floor, and some may prefer to have them higher. Walls and woodwork should be plain, while floors should be either of hard wood or of pine covered with linoleum.

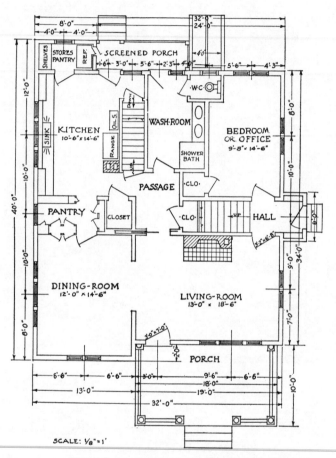

FIG. 69.[1] First-floor plan for a farmhouse
Notice the wash-room for the men

The *dining-room* should be cheery and well lighted. Its shape should be rectangular, and the smallest dimension consistent with

[1] Courtesy of French & Ives, "Agricultural Drafting." McGraw-Hill Book Co.

convenience is twelve feet. The living-room, being the place of family and other gatherings, should be large and roomy. If possible a fireplace and group windows should be built in. This room takes the place of the old-fashioned conventional parlor and should be easy of access from all rooms, so that it will be used.

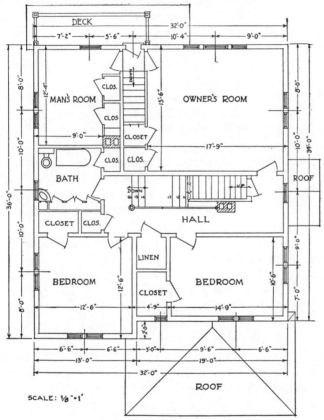

FIG. 70.[1] Second-floor plan for a farmhouse
Notice that the room for the hired man is shut off from the rest of the house

Provision for an *office* or *library* in a quiet corner of the house is desirable for the business farmer. In times of sickness such a room saves many steps up and down stairs if it is used for a

[1] Courtesy of French & Ives, "Agricultural Drafting." McGraw-Hill Book Co.

bedroom. A living-porch of ample size is almost a necessity in the summer. A porch, to be comfortable, should be not less than eight feet in width.

Although the *bedrooms* may be built on the first floor, economy of construction will result in utilizing the second floor. As far as possible all rooms used for sleeping should have cross ventilation. Access should be provided direct from a hall so that it will not be necessary to pass through one room to enter another. The bathroom should be accessible and not too small. If care is taken to place the bathroom nearly above the kitchen, some saving in plumbing will result.

Ample *closet space* should be provided upstairs and downstairs. A closet to each bedroom, with additional closets for bedding, linen, and cleaning-apparatus will make a considerable addition to the value of the house.

Sleeping-porches are becoming popular. They are not necessarily expensive, and add much to comfort. Provision should be made for closing the openings in stormy weather. Glass sash, canvas curtains, or shutters may be used. Screens are of course essential during the warmer months.

The *cellar* should be accessible from both the exterior and the interior of the house; the former to aid in taking in vegetables, fruits, and fuel, and in taking out ashes and refuse, and the latter for the convenience of the housewife. The cellar should extend under the whole house and should be provided with light, ventilation, and drainage. These three things will keep the cellar sanitary and make it less likely to harbor rats and mice. If the heating plant is in the basement, it should be in a room by itself; otherwise the vegetables and fruits must be provided with means of storage cut off from the rest of the room. It is well to have the laundry in the cellar or basement, and a drying-room is a great convenience on rainy days.

Heating. No house is complete without some means of heating and of ventilation. Good ventilation is easy to secure where a warm-air furnace is used or where there are fireplaces. Window ventilators may also be used. The common types of heaters, aside from stoves and grates, are the warm-air furnace, and the steam, the hot-water, and the vapor systems.

The *warm-air furnace*, which may be quite cheaply installed, draws part of its air from out of doors and part through cold-air ducts from the first and second floors, and discharges the warm air through pipes to registers in the floors or walls of the various rooms. It is a fairly satisfactory method of heating if a means of adding moisture to the air is provided. However, difficulty in heating rooms at a distance from the furnace or on the windward side of the house is sometimes experienced.

Steam heats by means of radiators placed in the rooms or in air ducts leading to the rooms. A boiler is provided. It is somewhat more expensive to install than a warm-air plant. Since the water must boil, heat cannot be obtained immediately; but with good piping it will heat the whole house. Vapor heating is not unlike steam, but will heat the room for some time after the fire has died down. The cost of installation is higher than that of steam, but the cost of operation is somewhat lower.

Hot-water heating is steady and reliable and is economical of fuel. Its cost of installation is higher than that of warm-air or steam heating, it requires larger radiators than the steam or vapor systems, and, unless properly installed, it may give trouble from leakage. This last disadvantage can be eliminated by hiring good workmen.

The advantages and disadvantages of all the above systems should be carefully weighed before any type is installed. In many cases individual taste should decide the question.

CHAPTER IX

LIGHTING THE FARM HOME

It is a matter of common observation that places of business such as saloons and moving-picture houses, designed to attract persons who are looking for some place to while away the time, are usually dazzlingly illuminated, the owners realizing that money spent for this purpose will bring its sure return. All who are interested in the making of a good home should take the lesson to heart. The absence of a good light makes work difficult of accomplishment, deadens companionship, and drives cheer away. Modern developments in the art of illumination have made it possible for every farm home to be cheaply and adequately lighted.

The tallow candle was the only means possessed by our forefathers of but a few generations ago for the lighting of their humble homes. It served its purpose until a better method became available, and just as our fathers and even our grandfathers would have considered it a great hardship to have been forced to depend upon a candle for light, so we, in a very short time, shall consider it almost out of the question to get along without electricity or acetylene or some other completely installed system of lighting.

The present generation should have a better lighting system than was in vogue three generations ago. To-day the farm home is abundantly supplied with magazines, books, and daily and weekly papers, and we must read and study if we would keep up with the march of progress; so the demand for a better method of lighting the farm home is not due to pride alone, but is a matter of economic necessity. There are four sources of light that may be used in country homes, — kerosene, gasoline, acetylene, and electricity. These will be discussed in the order named and in connection with the equipment designed for their utilization.

KEROSENE AND KEROSENE LAMPS

Although kerosene had been known and, in a limited way, used for purposes of illumination for several centuries, it was not until 1859, when Drake made his petroleum discoveries in Pennsylvania, that it became a commercial possibility. In that year the first American patent for a petroleum lamp was granted; before the year was ended forty other applications had been presented, and for the following twenty years eighty applications a year were made, on an average.

Crude petroleum is a liquid varying in color from pale yellow to black, and has a disagreeable odor. Its specific gravity ranges from 0.8 to 0.9. It is made up chiefly of carbon and hydrogen, being on an average about 85 per cent carbon and 15 per cent hydrogen. It is composed of a variety of the so-called " hydrocarbon " compounds, which are separated the one from the other by means of fractional distillation. On being subjected to heat, naturally the lighter and more volatile compounds pass off first. Among the first of the distillates to pass off is gasoline, with a density of about 0.65, followed by the naphthas (including benzine), with a density of 0.68 to 0.74, and kerosene, with a density varying from 0.78 to 0.84. These lighter compounds are then followed by the various grades of lubricating-oils, with densities from 0.87 to 0.93, after which come the heavier oils, or greases, as vaseline.

Kerosene should be nearly colorless (though it sometimes approaches a yellow color), and it should not give off inflammable vapor below 120° F. It is much better if inflammable vapors are not given off below 150° F., since frequent lamp explosions are due to the fact that the heat of the flame causes the oil in the fount to vaporize, a condition which, if the wick-holder is taken off or the filling-cap removed, is likely to result in the explosion of the vapor.

The kerosene lamp in its typical form consists of the bowl, or fount for carrying the oil, the wick-holder, the wick, and the chimney.

The wick-holder, or burner, consists of a device for raising or lowering the wick, of a perforated platform, or gallery, which supports the chimney, and of the dome which surrounds the upper portion of the wick. The perforations in the platform of the burner are for the purpose of breaking up air currents in order that the air may be evenly distributed as it passes up around the flame. The dome assists in directing the air currents against the flame at the points where the most air is required, and steadies the flame.

The operation of the lamp may be explained as follows: by the force of capillary attraction the oil is drawn up through the wick to the flame, where it is volatilized by the heat of the flame, and where the carbon and the hydrogen of the oil vapor, uniting with the oxygen of the air, yield carbon dioxide and water, the usual products of combustion. The luminosity of the flame is due to the fact that, since some of the carbon is not completely consumed, the free carbon particles floating about in the flame are heated to incandescence.

Just the proper amount of oil must be supplied — not too much and not too little. If there is an excess of oil, or, rather, a deficiency in the air supply, products of incomplete combustion will result, such as carbon monoxide and petroleum vapor — the former injurious to the health, even poisonous, in fact, and the latter very disagreeable. These conditions will also result in the deposit of carbon, or soot.

To control these two factors, the oil and the air, the fount must be kept well filled with oil, and the wick must not be allowed to become too short. There is a tendency to use a wick as long as it touches the oil, but a wick just dipping into the oil will not feed freely — it should extend well down to the bottom of the fount. Some authorities claim that a new wick should trail the bottom at least two inches and should be discarded when the trail is used up; the statement is perhaps true for maximum efficiency. The wick should not be unduly compressed in the wick-holder, as this tends to break the capillarity. The air supply is frequently interfered with if the gallery perforations become clogged.

There are several types of kerosene lamps, the types differing mainly in the construction of the burner and the wick. The principle of operation as explained above applies to nearly all types, though there are slight differences arising from construction details which will be pointed out in the following paragraphs.

The flat-wick lamp. This was the first form of kerosene lamp to come into prominent use. There is a wide variation as to size and shape of fount and width of wick. The latter varies from $\frac{1}{2}$ in. to $1\frac{1}{2}$ in. in width. This type of lamp when supplied with a wick $1\frac{1}{2}$ in. wide will develop about 12 candle power and will burn from fifty to sixty hours on 1 gal. of fuel.

The round-wick lamp. The round-wick kerosene lamp was the result of an effort to secure a more even distribution of air around the flame, thus bringing about more complete combustion. The principle of this type of lamp is illustrated in the cross section shown in Fig. 71. The central draft-tube extends from the base of the lamp to the top of the burner. The flame is thus supplied with air from both sides. The flame-spreader diverts the flame from the vertical path which it would naturally take in following the draft currents.

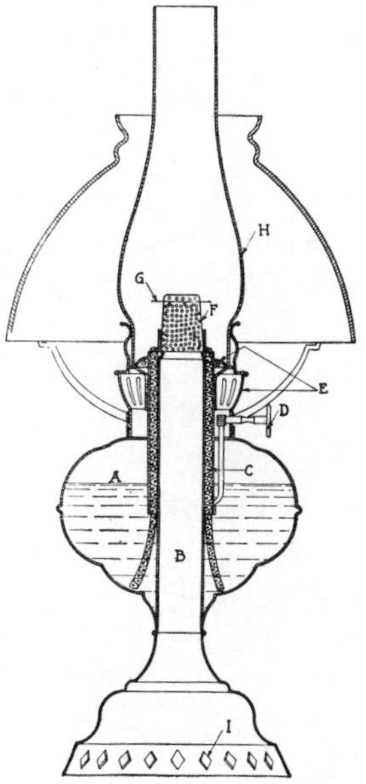

This type of burner is generally known as an *Argand* burner, from the name of its inventor. A lamp equipped with such a burner $1\frac{1}{2}$ in. in diameter will develop about 18 candle power and will burn from twenty-five to thirty hours on 1 gal. of fuel. Its efficiency

FIG. 71. Cross section of a round-wick lamp

A, fount; *B*, draft-tube; *C*, wick; *D*, device to raise and lower the wick; *E*, gallery; *F*, dome; *G*, flame-spreader; *H*, chimney; *I*, air-vents

is not greatly superior to the flat-wick lamp, its increased candle power being chiefly due to the increased wick surface.

The mantle lamp. Fig. 72 shows a kerosene mantle lamp. This is a lamp of the round-wick type, with a mantle suspended above the flame. Its construction and operation are essentially the same as the round-wick lamp, though for highest efficiency it requires greater care in its manipulation.

The *mantle* is responsible for the higher efficiency of the lamp and is at the same time the source of the difficulty encountered in the actual use of the lamp. The mantle is made of a small cylinder of cotton net soaked in a solution of the nitrates of some of the rare earths (chiefly thoria and ceria), after which the net is burned. During the process of burning, the nitrates are changed to oxides, only the framework of the net remaining. This is then soaked in collodion (guncotton in ether and castor

FIG. 72. A kerosene mantle lamp

A shade, not shown here, is ordinarily used with this lamp

oil), to give a firm set to the structure. This material is burned off when the mantle is put in place on the lamp. The materials of which the mantle is made reach a high degree of incandescence when properly heated, and the lamp in consequence yields an unusually soft and pleasing white light.

The *difficulty* in the operation of a kerosene lamp equipped with a mantle comes from the fact that the mantle must be heated to a high degree, and, to attain the proper temperature, the fuel must be burned with a blue flame ; that is, combustion must be complete, so that no carbon particles, or soot, will be deposited upon the mantle. This requires careful trimming and regulation of the wick. A special wick-trimmer is usually furnished with the lamp, and this should be regularly and carefully used. No attempt should be made to trim the wick with scissors or with a match stem, as is sometimes done. If the wick becomes uneven or if a thread is loosened and not cut off, the flame will be uneven and soot will collect on the mantle. Only the charred portion of the wick should be removed, and the trimming should cease just before the unburned part of the wick is reached.

When the lamp is lighted the wick should not be turned high. As the flame becomes even and the burner heats through, the wick should be gradually turned up until the full brilliancy of the flame is reached. This is an important matter, and its neglect often leads users of this lamp to become dissatisfied with it, when the fault is all their own. Should any portion of the mantle become coated with soot, it is only necessary to turn the wick down a little, when the soot will disappear.

The mantle costs 25 cents and with reasonable care will last from two to five months. Many times it will last a full year. If the lamp is carried about from one room to another, it must be set down with care or the mantle will be jarred from its support.

The wick is supported in a special framework, and when it is burned short a new wick and frame should be supplied. No attempt should be made to put a new wick into the old frame, because it is impossible to get the wick perfectly even.

The best makes of mantle lamps cost about $6. They will develop from 50 to 60 candle power, and by numerous tests on at least one make it has been shown that they may be expected to burn about fifty hours on 1 gal. of fuel.

The quality of the light is of the very best. Its clear, white, soft rays are unusually pleasing, and when it is placed beside the common round-wick lamp the contrast between the white light of the former and the yellow light of the latter is very great. Attention will be called later to the healthful qualities of this lamp in comparison with other forms of illumination.

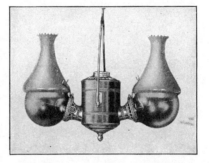

FIG. 73. A two-burner angle lamp

This is essentially a flat-wick lamp with the wick supported in a nearly horizontal position

The pressure lamp. There are mantle lamps designed to burn kerosene, the fuel being supplied under pressure, without the use of a wick. This type of lamp will be discussed more fully under the subject of gasoline, since in such a lamp gasoline seems to give better satisfaction than kerosene.

The angle lamp. An illustration of an angle lamp is shown in Fig. 73. This is a flat-wick lamp with the burner placed at an angle, the wick being almost horizontal. It may be provided in the form of a single-burner wall lamp or as a 1-burner, 2-burner, or 3-burner hanging lamp.

The chief merit of this lamp is found in the fact that the flame is directed downward from the flat surface of the wick, rather than upward as in the common wick lamp. The oil is supplied to the wick by a double-chambered fount, the oil in the outer chamber being kept always at exactly the same level. This feature undoubtedly secures a more uniform flow of oil through the wick than would ordinarily be secured in the common wick lamp. No tests are available to prove the performance of the lamp, but the manufacturers claim that it will burn about sixty hours on one gallon of fuel and give 50 per cent more light than the common round-wick lamp.

Gasoline and Gasoline Lamps

Gasoline, as before mentioned, is one of the lighter and more volatile hydrocarbon compounds derived from crude petroleum by distillation. It has a density of about 0.65 and is so volatile that it gives off inflammable vapors at ordinary temperatures. It is thus much more dangerous to handle than kerosene, which fact has prevented its wider use for lighting purposes. The increased demand for gasoline has led to a material increase in the price, with the tendency to include in the so-called "gasoline" product a part of the distillate from petroleum formerly included in kerosene. In other words, the density of gasoline approaches more closely to that of kerosene, with a consequent decrease in volatility — a characteristic which renders it less desirable for the uses to which it has been considered best adapted. For lighting purposes it is used in tightly inclosed founts and in connection with incandescent burners.

The gasoline mantle lamp. The individual gasoline lamp is found in two forms, which differ in the manner in which the fuel is supplied to the burner, one form using gravity pressure by suspending the fuel-container a few inches above the burner, the other form using air pressure to lift the fuel up to the burner. The gravity-pressure type is the older, and is being rapidly replaced by the air-pressure type, which overcomes the very real danger of leakage always present where the fuel supply is above the burner.

Fig. 74 shows a common form of air-pressure lamp. The fount forms the base of the lamp, and from this a small tube leads up to the burner. A small needle valve controls the opening at the upper end of this tube. By means of a small hand pump, air is forced into the fount (which is filled about three-fourths full of gasoline) until the fuel is under a pressure of several pounds. One charging with air is intended to last until the entire fount of fuel is consumed. The light will gradually grow dimmer as the pressure decreases, but if the proper initial pressure is obtained, it will usually burn with satisfactory brilliancy until the oil is consumed. By referring to Fig. 75, which is a sectional view of a similar lamp, one may trace the path of the fuel from the fount to the burner.

In all types there is a pinhole opening in the upper end of the fuel-tube (Fig. 74, *A*). If the needle valve *B* is opened, the fuel under pressure will be forced into the burner and mantle through tube *C*. Before it can be burned in such a way as to heat the mantle to incandescence, however, it must be volatilized. In the particular lamp shown this is done by soaking an asbestos torch in alcohol and hanging it under the tube, just to the right of point *A*, for a minute or two. When the needle valve is opened, the fuel is vaporized as it crosses this hot tube, and is consumed as a gas in the burner. Before the vapor reaches the burner it is properly mixed with air as the vapor emerges from the pinhole, so that combustion is complete and there is almost no sooting of the mantle.

FIG. 74. A common type of gasoline pressure lamp

A, mixer; *B*, valve; *C*, fuel-tube; *D*, cleaning-lever

The chief difficulty encountered with this type of lamp is keeping the pinhole in the feed tube free from impurities found in the oil. The lamp shown is provided with a cleaner, which consists of a finely pointed wire placed in the fuel-tube and controlled by a convenient lever *D*. When the hole becomes clogged, or at frequent intervals whether the clogging is noticeable or not, the wire is forced through the hole, which is thus kept free from all obstructions. This may be done while the lamp is in operation if done quickly. The best lamps of this type are provided with some sort of convenient cleaner.

Lamps of a similar kind are designed for the use of kerosene. Many of them are giving satisfaction, but owing to the higher percentage of impurities in this fuel it does not give the same satisfaction as gasoline. The pinholes frequently become clogged, and it is difficult to keep them clean.

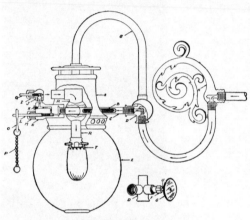

FIG. 75. Section of a gasoline pressure lamp, showing the path of the fuel to the burner

A, gallery shell; *B*, asbestos packing; *C*, packing-tube; *D*, shut-off valve; *E*, globe; *F*, packing-nut; *G*, valve handle; *H*, brass scroll; *I*, packing-nut; *J*, tip; *K*, removable plug; *L*, valve needle; *M*, valve packing-nut; *N*, generator; *O*, cross-arm valve lever; *P*, chains for cross arm; *Q*, cleaning-needle; *R*, induction tube; *S*, dead-arm gallery-support; *T*, mantle; *U*, valve stem

Lamps of this type cost about ten dollars and under favorable conditions will deliver as high as three hundred candle power. The efficiency of this light will be discussed under the next system.

The hollow-wire gasoline system. As soon as it was proved that gasoline could be successfully used in incandescent burners there came a desire to design a system in which it could be used to light a residence, a store, or a church with the fuel supplied from a single source and piped to various parts of the building after the manner of natural or artificial gas. The modern hollow-wire system, which is the result of this desire, affords a method of lighting farm homes that is inexpensive both in

first cost of installation and in operation, and that is reasonably safe. The plant consists of a pressure tank or tanks, a hand air pump, the necessary length of hollow wire, and burners with the desired fixtures properly placed.

A compound *tank* is shown in Fig. 76. For a house of average size each tank holds from four to eight gallons. A single tank is sufficient, though a compound tank is sometimes installed, the chief advantage of the latter being that it is possible to charge the tanks with more fuel without permitting the pressure in the pipe to run down; in fact the charging can be

FIG. 76. A compound tank for use with the hollow-wire system

A single tank is ordinarily used

done while the lamps are in operation. The tank must be well made and must be provided with good valves and connections. An

ordinary hand bicycle pump will serve to charge the tank with air. The tank may be placed in the basement or at any other convenient location, preferably in a room where there is no fire, in order to eliminate any possible danger from explosion while filling the tank. It is highly important, too, that the tank should never be filled when a flame of any kind is in the room.

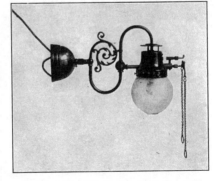

FIG. 77. A wall light for the hollow-wire system

The *burners* for this system are similar to the one described above, in both construction and operation. Fig. 77 shows a wall fixture; Figs. 78 and 79, chandeliers. These may be had in many styles and prices.

The tank is filled about three-fourths full and then charged with air to a pressure of from twenty to thirty pounds. Then, after the valve leading from the tank to the piping system is opened, any of the lights may be lighted. Of course it is necessary to generate each individual light, as was explained under the individual lamp above. As is shown in the illustrations of the various fixtures, they may

FIG. 78. A two-light chandelier as used with the hollow-wire system

be provided with convenient cut-off valves for turning the light low instead of putting it out. The pendent chains shown are for this purpose. In this way the fuel-tube is kept warm, so that it is not necessary to generate the lamp each time it is lighted. So small an amount of fuel is consumed with the light turned low that the cost is negligible, and as a usual thing mantles and globes will last longer if kept warm.

The Iowa Agricultural Experiment Station has reported a series of tests[1] in which alcohol and gasoline as fuels for lighting were compared. In this test, gasoline was

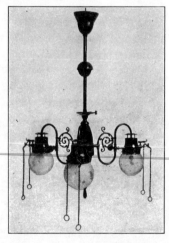

[1] Comparative Values of Alcohol and Gasoline for Light and Power, *Bulletin No. 93*, Iowa Agricultural Experiment Station, Ames.

FIG. 79. A three-light chandelier

used in a hollow-wire gasoline system. With the fuel under a pressure of 16 lb. the lamp developed 147 candle power, while at a pressure of 34 lb. it developed 300 candle power. In the first instance the lamp would burn for twenty-three hours on 1 gal. of fuel, while in the second case 1 gal. would last for fifteen hours.

FIG. 80. A gasoline pressure lantern
Such a lantern gives a brilliant light and is being widely used

The question of safety is always raised when the use of gasoline for lighting purposes is considered. It cannot be denied that there is an element of danger present when gas of any kind is piped into a house, and the fact that gasoline is such a volatile liquid adds to the danger. However, in the hollow-wire system, with the pipes thoroughly tested, as should be the case with any gas system, and with reasonable care exercised in the operation of the plant, there is no more ground for fear than when the house is piped with natural gas or artificial coal gas, both of which are used with almost no thought of danger.

The cost of installation for this system may be enumerated as follows :

1 pressure tank, 6 gal. capacity	$15.00
1 air pump	1.50
100 feet hollow wire @ 6¢	6.00
2 three-light chandeliers @ $10	20.00
2 two-light chandeliers @ $8	16.00
8 pendant fixtures @ $4	32.00
Labor (estimated)	15.00
Total	$105.50

ACETYLENE AND ACETYLENE SYSTEMS

Although the gas product known as acetylene has been familiar to the chemist for many years, it having been produced from calcium carbide in 1862 by Wöhler, a famous chemist, its commercial use is of very recent origin. Thomas L. Willson,[1] an electrical engineer of Spray, North Carolina, in 1892, while attempting to prepare metallic calcium by fusing a mixture of lime and coal tar in the heat of an electric furnace was disappointed in his search and threw the product which he secured into a near-by stream. It was observed that a large quantity of gas was liberated, which on being ignited burned with a bright but smoky flame. Further investigation proved the product to be acetylene, and to Willson belongs the honor of discovering a commercial method for the manufacture of calcium carbide, from which acetylene is made.

Calcium carbide. Calcium carbide is now manufactured by combining ground coke and lime in the heat of the electric furnace, the two uniting to form calcium carbide and carbon monoxide.

$$CaO + 3C = CaC_2 + CO$$

Quicklime and coke form calcium carbide and carbon monoxide.

In this reaction 56 lb. of lime (CaO) combine with 36 lb. of coke (C) to form 64 lb. of calcium carbide (CaC_2) and 28 lb. of the gas carbon monoxide (CO).

Calcium carbide is a dark-gray, extremely hard crystalline compound. It is not affected by heat or cold, but it must be kept absolutely dry, exposure even to air causing it to disintegrate. It is packed for shipment in air-tight steel drums containing 100 lb. each. Five-pound and 10-pound cans are available for certain uses. It is prepared in five different grades (the grade depending upon the size of the pieces); namely, lump, egg, nut, quarter, and granulated, the pieces ranging in size from that of coarse gunpowder in the granulated grade to 2 or 3 in. in diameter for the lump grade. The size purchased depends upon the use to which it is to be put.

[1] George Gilbert Pond, Calcium Carbide and Acetylene, Bulletin of the Pennsylvania State College, State College.

Acetylene. Acetylene is the gas evolved when calcium carbide and water are brought together.

$$CaC_2 + 2 H_2O = C_2H_2 + Ca(OH)_2$$

Calcium carbide and water yield acetylene and slaked lime.

In other words, 64 lb. of calcium carbide (CaC_2) combine with 36 lb. of water (H_2O) to form 74 lb. of slaked lime ($Ca(OH)_2$) and 26 lb. of acetylene (C_2H_2). The materials always combine in this proportion and yield products in the same proportion. One pound of pure carbide will yield between $5\frac{1}{2}$ and 6 cu. ft. of acetylene, but the commercial product may be expected to yield only from $4\frac{1}{2}$ to 5 cu. ft.

From its chemical formula it is seen that acetylene is one of the hydrocarbons, being composed of 92.3 per cent carbon and 7.7 per cent hydrogen. It is a colorless, tasteless gas having an extremely pungent odor. It has a density of 0.91, being thus lighter than air but much heavier than natural gas, the latter having a density of 0.56. When ignited in the presence of air, acetylene burns with a bright but smoky flame. When it is consumed in a proper type of burner, however, the flame is almost pure white, yielding a light that approaches daylight more closely than any other artificial light available for common use. The combustion reaction may be shown as follows:

$$2 C_2H_2 + 5 O_2 = 4 CO_2 + 2 H_2O$$

Acetylene and oxygen yield carbon dioxide and water.

From this reaction it is seen that $2\frac{1}{2}$ cu. ft. of oxygen (O_2) combine with 1 cu. ft. of acetylene (C_2H_2) to form 2 cu. ft. of carbon dioxide (CO_2) and 1 cu. ft. of water (H_2O).

As compared with other illuminants, acetylene deprives the air of much less of its oxygen and adds very much less carbon dioxide, as a later table will show.

A great deal of misinformation is abroad in regard to the danger accompanying the use of acetylene as an illuminant or for cooking purposes. The gas in its pure state will not explode, and it will ignite only when a certain quantity of air is supplied. To secure an explosive mixture it must be combined with air until it forms from about 3 per cent to 50 per cent of the mixture. Experiments indicate that a mixture leaner or richer than the limits stated above will not explode.[1] It is therefore next to an impossibility that enough gas should escape from an ordinary burner to create an explosive mixture. The common burner discharges $\frac{1}{2}$ cu. ft. of gas per hour. If such a burner were to discharge gas continuously into a sleeping-room 10 by 12 by 8, with all openings tightly closed, it would take fifty-seven hours to reach the lowest limit of explosibility.

Asphyxiation by acetylene has never been known to occur. Not only is the gas much less poisonous than coal gas or natural gas, but the odor of the gas is so disagreeable that escaping gas is quickly noticed, and it would be next to impossible for one to sleep with the gas escaping into the room.

There is no desire, however, to underestimate the danger that is likely to occur from the careless use of the gas. No fire, not even a lighted cigar, should be permitted in the room when the generator is being filled. If the odor of gas is noticed, the leak should be found, but a candle should not be used in searching for it. Quoting from Dr. Pond's bulletin before referred to, "the use of acetylene for the illumination of rural homes, provided it is generated from good carbide in a first class apparatus, and all reasonable regulations followed, is no more fraught with danger at the present day than any available method of illumination by gas or by electricity and less so than the usual employment of petroleum."

Generators. The essential part of an acetylene-lighting system is the generator. There are two general classes known as (1) carbide-feed generators, in which the carbide is fed into the water, and (2) water-feed generators, in which water is fed into the carbide.

In Fig. 81 is shown a sectional view of a typical *carbide-feed* generator. The portion to the left constitutes the generating-chamber, the portion to the right the storage chamber. The carbide is placed in the chamber A, at the bottom of which is a rotating disk B. This disk is rotated by means of the clockwork C. The clockwork, or motor, is operated by the weight D. As the disk B is rotated, the carbide which it carries comes in contact with shoes on the collar which are supported by chains,

[1] Burrell and Oberfell, The Explosibility of Acetylene, *Paper No. 112*, Bureau of Mines.

and a portion of the carbide is forced off and falls into the water in the chamber E. As soon as the carbide strikes the water the gas is formed, and, bubbling up through the water, it passes through the pipe F into the base of the collecting-chamber, thence upward through pipe G into the gasometer chamber H. The gasometer bell I is an inverted bucket fitting into the larger chamber J, which is filled with water, the level being shown at K.

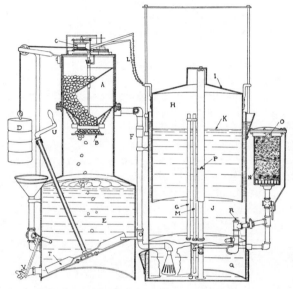

FIG. 81. Sectional view of a carbide-feed acetylene-generator

As the gas collects in chamber H the bell rises until through the chains L the motor is stopped and the formation of gas ceases.

From chamber H the gas passes down through pipe M and up into the filter N. This is a chamber filled with felt, through which all the gas must pass before it enters the service pipes, the purpose of the filter being to remove any particles of lime dust or other dirt that may be carried in with the gas. The service pipes are connected at point O. As soon as any gas is consumed the pressure in H is lowered, the bell I drops by its own weight, and the motor starts the carbide-feed, causing the generation of a new supply of gas to take the place of that used.

Safety devices are provided to meet certain possible conditions. For example, if for any reason the pressure in the gasometer should rise to an unusual degree, the bell would be lifted higher than is ordinarily done. The excess gas would at once enter the holes at P in the outer section of this telescopic tube and would pass down into the sealed chamber Q, which connects with the open air through pipe R. Again, should the bell become fastened or caught for any reason and the motor continue to feed carbide into the water, the excess pressure would force the gas to bubble through the lower end of pipe M at S and escape at R. Since the chamber Q contains only a few inches of water, it is seen how small is the pressure in any part of the pipe line.

This type of generator must have capacity for 1 gal. of water in the generating-chamber for each pound of carbide charged into it at one time. Thus, a 50-pound generator must hold 50 gal. of water. This necessitates some convenient device for cleaning. The slaked lime collects in the bottom of chamber E. When it is necessary to clean the chamber, the contents are stirred up by the agitator T worked by the crank U, and the material is drawn off through the valve at V.

All carbide-feed generators work on a similar plan. They differ only in the means provided for the accomplishment of the steps outlined. The chief advantages of the carbide-feed generator over the water-feed generator are that the carbide is dropped piece by piece into a large volume of water, thus insuring complete chemical action and preventing an undue rise in temperature, there being a large amount of heat liberated as the gas is generated. Besides, the gas is thoroughly washed as it passes through the water. An objection to this type is that much labor is required to supply the large amount of water necessary, as well as to clean out the generator.

The *water-feed* generator, which is the older type, is now largely displaced by the carbide-feed generator, though several companies are still making excellent forms of this machine. The water is fed into the carbide, which is charged usually into several small compartments, the water being forced to enter and consume all of the carbide in one compartment before it can get into the next. These compartments hold from one and one-half to two pounds, the amount depending upon the size of the machine.

The objections urged against the water-feed generator are that since the water is fed into the carbide the temperature is likely to rise higher than is desirable; and, further, the reaction will probably not be so complete. Various cooling-devices are provided by manufacturers of this type of generator, so that the danger from high temperatures is virtually eliminated. This type has one decided advantage over the carbide-feed in that it requires but little water, and hence less labor is necessary for its operation. While the carbide-feed seems to be the most approved form of generator and is preferred by experts on acetylene generation, the water-feed is giving satisfaction in many homes.

The following *requisites* for a good generator are specified by Dr. Pond in his bulletin previously mentioned:

1. It must allow no possibility of the existence of an explosive mixture in any of its parts at any time. It is not enough to argue that a mixture, even if it exists, cannot be exploded unless kindled. It is necessary to demand that a dangerous mixture can at no time be formed even if the machine is tampered with by an ignorant person. The perfect machine must be so constructed that it shall be impossible at any time, under any circumstances, to blow it up. It must be " fool-proof."

2. It must insure cool generation. Since this is a relative term, all machines being heated somewhat during the generation of gas, this amounts to saying that a machine must heat but little. A pound of carbide decomposed by water develops the same amount of heat under all circumstances, but that heat can be allowed to increase locally to a high point, or it can be equalized by water so that no part of the material becomes heated enough to do damage.

3. It must be well constructed. A good generator does not need, perhaps, to be " built like a watch," but it should be solid, substantial, of good material. No light-weight, half-price metal, likely to rust through and cause leakage and resultant gas mixtures, should be tolerated. It should be built of the best material adapted to the purpose. It should be built for service — to last and not simply to sell; anything short of this is to be avoided as unsafe and unreliable.

4. It must be simple. The more complicated the machine the sooner it will get out of order. Understand your generator. Know what is inside of it and beware of an apparatus, however attractive its exterior, whose interior is filled with pipes and tubes, valves and diaphragms, whose functions you do not perfectly understand. If a complicated mechanism is employed to perform what seems to you a simple duty, rely upon your own common sense and look further till you find a perfectly simple but strong mechanism to perform the work of automatically making gas. There are plenty of them and you can afford to meet the price of the machine which is least likely to call for repair next season.

5. It should create no considerable pressure in any of its parts. More than a pound of pressure at any point may be a source of danger; more than a few ounces is wholly unnecessary, and not to be tolerated.

6. It should be capable of being cleaned and recharged and of receiving all other necessary attention without loss of gas, both for economy's sake, and more particularly to avoid filling the house with a disagreeable odor. There is no need of any perceptible odor about the machine or in the house, and the better machines successfully guard against this nuisance.

7. It should require little attention. All machines have to be emptied and recharged periodically; but the more this process is simplified and the more quickly this can be accomplished, the better.

8. It should be provided with a suitable indicator to designate how the charge is in order that the refilling may be done in good season. A generator which can by any reasonable possibility leave the household, without warning, plunged in darkness, is not to be tolerated.

9. It should completely use up the carbide, generating the maximum amount of gas.

Location of the generator. The National Board of Fire Underwriters has adopted a code of rules and regulations concerning not only the location but the manufacture of generators. As to the location, they specify, among other things, that generators should preferably be placed outside the residence, though basement locations are not prohibited. They must be so located that they may be filled without the use of artificial light and must be at least 15 ft. from a furnace. They must be placed where water will not freeze. They must have sufficient capacity to make charging at night unnecessary and must supply at least 1 lb. of carbide for each burner, the $\frac{1}{2}$-foot burner being the standard. The piping must be done according to standard specifications and be thoroughly tested by competent persons.

Neither the generator nor the piping should ever be tested for leaks with a flame. A lighted match, lamp, candle, or other flame should never be brought near the machine. There are generators made in such a way that they may be buried in the ground, a possibility which results in a safe and satisfactory installation. In this case the sludge is pumped out of the generator.

Piping. The average house is piped with one-half-inch and three-eighths-inch pipe, there being specified sizes for regulation distances and for a certain number of lights. If the house has been piped for natural gas, it is only necessary to connect the generator with the piping, though the pipe is probably larger than necessary.

Burners and fixtures. Fig. 82 shows the typical acetylene burner. The gas emerges from the two angles of the Y, the two jets meeting and forming a flat flame. There are four common sizes specified, — the $\frac{1}{4}$-foot, $\frac{1}{2}$-foot, $\frac{3}{4}$-foot, and 1-foot burner, the figures meaning that the burners consume this amount of gas in one hour and generate respectively, 12, 25, 37, and 50 candle power. The $\frac{1}{2}$-foot burner is the size most commonly used. Of course no mantles are required and globes need not be supplied. The latter, however, are to be preferred as well for appearance' sake as for the better distribution of the light. It is possible to equip all burners with a *lighting-device* operated by dry-cell batteries or by friction, which makes it possible to light the burners by simply pulling a chain. This is especially desirable for barn lights since the use of matches is always dangerous. These devices cost from one to two dollars per light.

Fig. 82. A typical acetylene burner

No mantle is used, and globes are not necessary

Cost of installation. Table V shows the cost of installation of an average plant as furnished by a reputable company and includes fixtures, piping, and labor, complete. Several items included in this installation might well be omitted if it is desirable to lower the first cost. The plant is given as a first-class installation with good fixtures.

TABLE V. COST OF INSTALLATION OF AN ACETYLENE PLANT

1 generator (carbide-feed; capacity, fifty $\frac{1}{2}$-foot burners) .	$150.00
2 two-light chandeliers (burnished brass) @ $6	12.00
1 dining-room dome	12.00
1 hall light	4.00
1 two-burner kitchen light	4.90
1 pantry light	.50
4 bedroom lights @ $1.50	6.00
1 bathroom bracket light	1.65
1 basement bracket light	.50
1 porch lantern	7.50
1 porch lantern	3.00
3 barn lanterns @ $3	9.00
17 lighters	17.00
Plumbing (labor and pipe), 18 openings @ $2.50 . . .	45.00
Total cost of installation	$273.05

Cost of operation. The cost of operation should include not only the annual cost of the carbide, but interest on the original investment, and allowance for depreciation, repairs, and taxes. Assuming that the plant completely installed will cost $200, and figuring interest at 5 per cent and allowing 10 per cent for depreciation, taxes, and repairs, we have the following figures:

Interest on $200 @ 5 per cent	$10
Depreciation, etc. ($200 @ 5 per cent)	10
Carbide, 500 lb. @ 4¢	20
Total annual cost	$40

A small acetylene plant. There is on the market at present a small semiportable generator having a capacity of twelve lights.

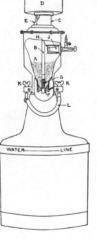

FIG. 83. A semiportable carbide-feed acetylene-generator

The maximum capacity is 12 lights

This system is different from all others, in that mantles are used instead of the openflame burners.

Fig. 83 shows a sectional view of the generator. The lower part contains the water, the capacity being 5 gal. The carbide, granulated in form, is charged into the hopper A, which has a capacity of 5 lb. The plunger rod B is fastened to the plunger top C, on top of which is the removable weight D. In the position shown, the plunger is locked up by the spring lock E, the plunger shaft closing the hopper-feed opening at F. The generator is started by unlocking the plunger by simply pushing the lock E in. The weight then forces the plunger down, a position which allows some of the carbide to pass out, since the corrugated portion G does not completely close the feed opening. As soon as a sufficient amount of gas is formed, the pressure on the plunger above the carbide raises the weight and so prevents the further passage of carbide into the water.

The gas enters the service-pipe connection at H and passes through the muslin filter J, through the coil connection, into the service pipe. As soon as the pressure in the hopper is lowered, the weight forces the plunger down, permitting more carbide to feed into the water when the process just described is repeated.

To recharge the generator it is necessary to loosen the thumb-screws K, remove the hopper, unscrew the cap at F, and refill. The lower chamber is easily picked up by the handle L, carried out, and emptied.

The generator may be placed in the basement or in any convenient place where it will not freeze. It may be placed in the house, though there is an objectionable odor when it is being recharged.

The pipe used is three-sixteenths-inch nickeled brass tubing. It is soft and pliable and may be bent around corners, placed under picture-molding, etc. Convenient unions are supplied for making the necessary connections, and it is a comparatively easy task to pipe a house.

The burners are different from the common open-flame type, since a mantle is used. They are rated as $\frac{1}{4}$-foot burners, and the company claims that each will develop from 40 to 50 candle power.

Fig. 84. An acetylene table lamp

The construction of this lamp is similar to the construction of the generator shown in Fig. 83

The mantle is, of course, very fragile and is subjected to a strain each time the burner is lighted, because of a slight explosion, or pop, that occurs when the gas is ignited. Under reasonable care, and barring breaks caused from drafts, jars, etc., the mantle should last from one to two months, the company stating that from two hundred to three hundred hours of service may be expected.

The maximum capacity of the system is twelve $\frac{1}{4}$-foot burners Since 5 lb. of carbide are put in at one charging, a total of 20 cu. ft of gas should be generated. If the burners are not underrated, this would run the 12 burners for six hours or 6 burners in continuous service for twelve hours. Reasonable service would demand the equivalent of eighteen hours of light from 1 burner, at which rate the generator would burn four days on one charging. Experience indicates that two chargings per week are usually necessary. It is not safe to count on operating the 12 lights at one time, as this maximum capacity is virtually an overload.

The *cost of installation* of this system may be figured as follows :

1 generator	$60.00
100 feet nickeled brass tubing @ 12½¢	12.50
3 two-light chandeliers @ $8.10	24.30
2 pendants @ $4.10	8.20
7 wall lamps @ $3.05	21.35
Connections	8.00
Labor (estimated)	15.00
Total, plant complete	$149.35

Comparative tests of lamps. *Bulletin No. 103* of the Pennsylvania State College of Agriculture reports a series of tests made on lamps of different kinds using different fuels. The lamps used are specified by number in part as follows :

1. A common flat-wick kerosene lamp, wick 1½ in. wide.

2. A round-wick kerosene lamp, wick 1½ in. in diameter, Argand burner.

3. A round-wick kerosene lamp with mantle.

4. A gasoline lamp with mantle, 16 in. fluid pressure.

5. An acetylene lamp, carbide-to-water feed, ½-foot burner.

TABLE VI. EFFECT OF LAMPS ON ATMOSPHERE OF ROOM

Lamp	Fuel used	Heat produced, in Calories	Oxygen consumed, in Cubic Feet	Carbon Dioxide given off, in Cubic Feet
No. 1	kerosene	4937	35.7	23.9
No. 2	kerosene	7325	51.9	33.3
No. 3	kerosene	2508	17.8	11.4
No. 4	gasoline	1634	11.7	7.9
No. 5	acetylene	1342	10.1	8.0

The lamps were first compared in regard to their effect on the atmosphere of the room in which they were burning. Table VI shows the heat produced in calories, the oxygen consumed, and the carbon dioxide given off per 100-candle-power hours.

The table shows a remarkable variation in the amount of heat produced and in the extent to which the air was vitiated. For example, comparing lamps No. 2 and No. 3, both of the round-wick type, but the latter using a mantle, it is seen that No. 2 produces about three times as much heat, consumes three times as much oxygen, and gives off three times as much carbon dioxide. In Table VII, it will be shown that in this test, lamp No. 2 developed only about eighteen candle power, while No. 3 developed about twenty-nine candle power. The favorable record, by comparison, of acetylene in lamp No. 5 should also be noted. It stands virtually at the head of the list.

TABLE VII. CANDLE POWER AND COST OF OPERATION OF LAMPS

LAMPS AND MATERIAL	CANDLE POWER DEVELOPED	HOURS TO CONSUME 1 GAL. OF FLUID	HOURS OPERATED BY 10 CENTS' WORTH OF FUEL	COST IN CENTS, PER CANDLE-POWER HOUR
No. 1. Kerosene, flat wick 1½ in. wide	12	58.3	48.6	0.0170
No. 2. Kerosene, round wick 1½ in. in diameter	18	26.7	22.2	0.0240
No. 3. Kerosene, round wick ⅞ in. in diameter, with mantle	29	48.4	40.3	0.0080
No. A.[1] Kerosene, round wick 1 in. in diameter, with mantle	60	52.0	43.3	0.0038
No. 4. Gasoline, liquid pressure, with mantle	37	51.7	34.5	0.0080
No. 5. Acetylene lamp, ½-foot burner	23		15.0	0.0290
No. B.[2] Gasoline mantle lamp, air pressure at 16 lb. . . .	147	23.0	15.0	0.0044
No. C.[2] Gasoline mantle lamp, air pressure at 34 lb. . . .	300	15.0	10.0	0.0033

[1] Results of tests made by several universities.
[2] *Bulletin No. 93*, Iowa Experiment Station, Ames.

Table VII is adapted from the same bulletin and compares the candle power of the lamps tested, together with the cost of operation. The cost is figured on the basis of 12 cents per gallon for kerosene, 15 cents for gasoline, and 4 cents per pound for carbide.

By comparing lamps No. 1 and No. 2 it is seen that No. 2 gives one half more light than No. 1, while the cost of operation for a given period of time is just about doubled. Comparing No. 2 and No. A, the latter representing probably the best type of mantle lamp available, one finds that the candle power is more than trebled by the use of the mantle, while the cost of operation is less than half as great. Acetylene is the most expensive light of all when cost per candle-power hour is considered. Gasoline burns most efficiently in the air-pressure lamp at thirty-four pounds. It would not be possible to maintain this pressure, but from the standpoint of operation even at a pressure of sixteen pounds, it is the cheapest source of light shown.

ELECTRIC-LIGHTING SYSTEMS

Until recent years electricity has never been seriously considered as a source of illumination for isolated country homes, but the advent of the low-voltage generator with the storage battery made possible by the introduction of the tungsten lamp, has made it a possibility, and the first cost of installation has been sufficiently lowered to bring it within the means of large numbers of farmers in every community. As compared with kerosene, gasoline, or acetylene, for illumination purposes, it has the advantage of affording a light that is noiseless, dirtless, odorless, and nonexplosive, and the danger from fire is reduced to a minimum.

Terms defined. In the discussion of electric-lighting plants certain technical terms will be used which should be well understood. The *ampere* is the unit used to measure the flow of current through a wire, just as the gallon is the unit used to measure the flow of water in pipes. The *volt* is the unit used to measure the pressure at the source which causes the flow of current, just as the pound is used to measure the pressure which causes the water to flow from a pneumatic or elevated tank. The *ohm* is the unit used to measure the resistance which the current meets in flowing through a wire. There is no definite unit used to measure the corresponding factor in the flow of water in pipes, which is called friction, though it is estimated as requiring so many pounds of pressure, or feet of head, to overcome it. These three factors form this familiar equation:

$$\text{Amperes} = \frac{\text{volts}}{\text{ohms}}.$$

The *watt* is the unit used to measure the power of a current, just as the horse power is used to measure the power of a flowing stream. The power of a stream flowing at the rate of so many gallons or pounds per minute, and under a head, or pressure, of so many feet, is determined by multiplying the flow in pounds per minute by the head in feet, a process which gives the power expressed in foot-pounds per minute. To reduce to horse power, this product is divided by 33,000; as

$$\text{Horse power} = \frac{\text{pounds per minute} \times \text{head in feet}}{33000}.$$

So the power of an electric current is the product of the flow in amperes by the pressure in volts. The power is usually measured in kilowatts, or 1000 watts, this being a larger and more convenient unit; as

$$\text{Watts} = \text{amperes} \times \text{volts},$$

or

$$\text{Kilowatts} = \frac{\text{amperes} \times \text{volts}}{1000}.$$

$$1 \text{ H.P.} = 746 \text{ watts.}$$
$$1 \text{ kilowatt} = 1.34 \text{ H.P.}$$

Electric-lighting systems may be purchased in low-voltage or high-voltage plants, the fundamental difference being in the generator, which may be constructed to furnish current under either low or high pressure, as desired. In common lighting plants, low voltage means from 30 to 45 volts, while high voltage means 110 volts. The low-voltage system, which is the most common, will be discussed first. The essential parts of a lighting plant are the generator, the storage battery (which with a 32-volt plant consists of 16 cells), and the switchboard, with some form of motor (usually a gasoline engine) to drive the generator.

The generator. The generation of electrical current by mechanical means is discussed under gas-engine ignition, and generators for electric-lighting plants are built on exactly the same principle.

There are, however, complex variations which cannot be discussed here. Suffice it to say that a direct-current generator, usually one of the shunt-wound type, is always used with storage batteries. The capacity depends upon the size of the plant and will be discussed later. The care of the generator consists in using a little oil at regular intervals, and in seeing that the brushes are kept clean. They should be wiped off with a dry cloth

FIG. 85. A common type of generator ready for service

or with cotton waste when dirt and oil collect. The brushes wear out slowly and should be replaced when the contact becomes poor, a condition which will be indicated by faulty and irregular amperage in charging.

The storage battery. If two plates, one of copper and one of zinc, are immersed in a weak solution of sulphuric acid and connected by a wire, a current of electricity will flow from the copper plate to the zinc plate. During this action the zinc plate is attacked by the acid, zinc sulphate being formed, and the zinc is gradually consumed. If a current from some outside source is now passed through the cell, entering at the pole of the copper plate, the zinc in the solution will be deposited upon the remains of the zinc plate, thus restoring it to something like its original condition. When the cell is so constructed that it may be recharged and

FIG. 86. A type of positive plate used in a storage battery

This plate is reddish in color

caused to return to its former state after having been partially or wholly discharged, it is known as a secondary, or storage, cell. Several cells together constitute a battery.

The *plates* in the common storage cell are made up of a metal framework consisting of an alloy of antimony and tin which gives the plates stiffness and rigidity. Moreover these materials are not acted upon by the acid in the cell. Pure, spongy lead (Pb) is pressed into holes punched in one of the frames to form the negative plate, which is gray in color. Lead peroxide (PbO_2) is pressed into the other frame to form the positive plate, which is reddish in color. The lead and the lead peroxide constitute the active parts of the plates. The plate is sometimes called a grid. Fig. 86 shows one type of positive and Fig. 87 one type of negative plate. There are many other ways of forming these plates.

FIG. 87. A type of negative plate used in a storage battery

This negative plate is gray in color

When the cell is being discharged the sulphuric acid (H_2SO_4), as before stated, attacks the lead of the negative plate, forming lead sulphate ($PbSO_4$). At the same time the acid attacks the lead peroxide, forming lead sulphate at the positive plate, both plates being reduced to lead sulphate. The cell will continue to deliver current until either the lead or the lead peroxide is consumed. The action within the cell may be shown as follows :[1]

$$PbO_2 \quad + \text{ Pb } + \quad 2\,H_2SO_4 \quad = \quad 2\,PbSO_4 \; + 2\,H_2O$$

Lead peroxide and lead and sulphuric acid form lead sulphate and water.

The reaction in charging the cell would be just the opposite of that given above for the discharge, the lead sulphate being broken up and the lead and the lead peroxide restored to their original condition.

The *size* of the cell, or what is usually referred to as " type " in commercial catalogues, depends upon the size of the individual plates and the number included in each cell. In the usual farm lighting plant there are 3, 5, 7, or 9 plates to a cell. Where there are 2 or more of either the positive or the negative plates,

[1] Timbie, Elements of Electricity, p. 341.

they are joined together in parallel. There is always one more negative than positive plate in a cell, the idea being to have both sides of each positive plate covered by a negative plate, an arrangement which makes an odd number of plates in each cell. The size, as well as the number, of the individual plates is varied to suit the capacity desired. The plates are separated by a thin sheet of wood or other nonconductor.

The *capacity* is rated in ampere-hours; that is, to suit the demand for current which is to be made upon the cell, the size and number of plates must be such as to deliver so many amperes for a given length of time. Eight hours is the period for which cells are usually rated, and to say that a cell has a capacity of 80 ampere-hours means that it will deliver current for eight hours at the rate of 10 amperes. Manufacturers allow a capacity of about 50 ampere-hours for each square foot of positive-plate area, counting both sides of the plate.

Table VIII shows the normal charging-rate and discharging-rate for two different sizes of plates and for a varying number of plates as given by a leading company which manufactures storage cells.

TABLE VIII. CHARGING-RATE AND DISCHARGING-RATE FOR STORAGE
CELLS OF DIFFERENT SIZES

Size of plates	$6'' \times 6''$				$7\frac{3}{4}'' \times 7\frac{3}{4}''$			
Number of plates per cell	3	5	7	9	5	7	9	11
Discharge in amperes for eight hours	$2\frac{1}{2}$	5	$7\frac{1}{2}$	10	10	15	20	25
Discharge in amperes for five hours	$3\frac{1}{2}$	7	$10\frac{1}{2}$	14	14	21	28	35
Discharge in amperes for three hours	5	10	15	20	20	20	40	50
Normal charging-rate in amperes	$2\frac{1}{2}$	5	$7\frac{1}{2}$	10	10	15	20	25

It will be noticed that the *normal charging-rate* in amperes, meaning the rate at which current may be forced into the cell, is the same as the eight-hour discharging-rate.

The jar used as a container for the electrolyte and the plates is usually of glass or rubber. The *glass* jars are made in open or closed types. In the *open* type (Fig. 88) the elements of the cell are shipped separately, and the jars are filled with the electrolyte and the plates put in at the place of installation. This means that the cells are not charged and must be given the initial charge when assembled. This requires from fifty to sixty hours of constant charging and should be done by one who thoroughly understands the work. It means, in fact, that an expert must assemble the plant. The *sealed glass* jar (Fig. 93) is shipped completely assembled and charged ready for use. The *rubber* jar (Fig. 92) is always completely sealed and charged when shipped. It has the

advantage over the glass jar of not being so easily broken in shipment, but the contents of the cell are completely hidden from view so that it is impossible to see the internal action of the cell, a thing to be desired in charging. Further, the electrolyte evaporates, and the level frequently falls below the upper surface of the plates. With the glass jar this condition is easily seen and more electrolyte may be added. The only way of observing this with the rubber jar is to screw off the small cap and look down on the top of the plates. The tendency seems to be toward the use of the sealed glass jar.

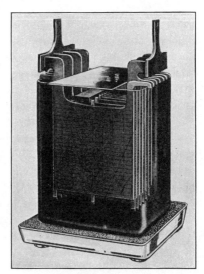

FIG. 88. An open-glass-jar storage cell

Note the parallel connection of the plates and that the negative plate is on the outside

The operation and care of the storage cell. The operation and care of the storage cell should be carefully studied. The operation is relatively simple and the time required small, but a little neglect may injure, if not ruin, the entire battery. The first cost of a cell is high, and the depreciation is rather rapid under the best of care and very rapid under poor care.

The chief ways in which cells may be injured are (1) by the use of an impure electrolyte or by the failure to keep the electrolyte at the proper density; (2) by being too rapidly charged or discharged ; (3) by being overcharged or overdischarged, the latter, especially, being a frequent cause of injury.

Injury by the use of an impure electrolyte or by failure to keep the electrolyte at the proper density. The electrolyte is made up of a weak solution of sulphuric acid. The density at the beginning of the charging is usually 1.2 ; when fully charged it is about 1.28 ; on discharge it should not fall below 1.25. The relative values of these densities differ in different types of cells, making it necessary to follow the manufacturer's specifications. A hydrometer is furnished with every battery, and it should be frequently used in order that the electrolyte may be kept at the proper density. The water evaporates from the cells even though they are tightly closed. The solution should always stand about one-half inch above the top of the plates, and if it drops below this, more water must be supplied. Pure rain water or distilled water should be used for this purpose. Well water should never be used ; it is likely to contain minerals that would injure the plates in the cells.

Injury by being too rapidly charged or discharged. As has been noted in Table VIII, every cell has its normal rate of charge and discharge. For example, the cell having five plates, each $7\frac{3}{4}'' \times 7\frac{3}{4}''$, has a normal discharging-rate of 10 amperes. If the cell is discharged too rapidly, chemical action does not keep apace, and the sulphate will collect on the plates in such quantities as to cause them to buckle and twist out of shape, possibly resulting in a short circuit within the cell. Moreover too heavy a collection of sulphate will interfere with the proper chemical action on the metals beneath. If the cell is charged too rapidly, the electrolyte will bubble and froth, showing a disturbed condition which interferes with normal chemical action and frequently results in a deposit in the bottom of the jar. The ammeter should be carefully observed and the normal rate of charge or discharge not exceeded.

Injury by being overcharged or overdischarged. Not much harm is likely to come from overcharging ; in fact it is often advised that cells be given an overcharge occasionally. One should be sure that chemical changes are complete. However, when all of the lead sulphate has been reduced to lead or to lead peroxide, it is useless to continue charging further. When the cells are fully charged they will bubble freely, or boil. Another indication of complete charging is to be found in the change in the specific gravity of the electrolyte. According to the chemical action which takes place during charging, the lead sulphate and water are broken up and sulphuric acid formed. This increases the density of the electrolyte, which should not rise above 1.28. Further, when the voltage at normal charging has reached 2.5, charging should cease.

Overdischarging is the greatest danger that the battery-user must guard against. It is so easy to neglect to charge the batteries until the lights begin to get dim, that a great deal of damage is thoughtlessly done. Overdischarging gives rise to several troubles — lead sulphate is formed in excessive quantities and, being deposited upon the plates, causes buckling; an excess of lead sulphate also increases the internal resistance of the cell and greatly weakens the action and renders it sluggish.

FIG. 89. A nickel-iron storage cell

Note the small size in comparison with the lead cell in Fig. 88

When the cell is discharging at the normal rate, the voltage drops from 2 or 2.3 to 1.8 volts per cell. A cell should never be further discharged after the voltage has dropped to 1.8. Furthermore, the specific gravity of the electrolyte, which gradually falls on discharge, should not be allowed to drop below 1.25 or the minimum figure fixed by the maker of the cells. A battery should never be discharged so completely that the lights begin to grow dim.

The nickel-iron battery. There has recently been designed and put upon the market a storage battery in which the positive element is nickel oxide and the negative element pure iron. The electrolyte is a solution of caustic potash. The container is made of nickel-plated steel. The average discharge voltage is 1.2. The reaction in charging, according to Timbie, is as follows:

$$Fe + NiO_2 + KOH + H_2O = FeO + Ni_2O_3 + KOH + H_2O$$

Iron + $\begin{Bmatrix} \text{nickel} \\ \text{oxide} \end{Bmatrix}$ + $\begin{Bmatrix} \text{caustic} \\ \text{potash} \end{Bmatrix}$ + water = $\begin{Bmatrix} \text{iron} \\ \text{oxide} \end{Bmatrix}$ + $\begin{Bmatrix} \text{nickel} \\ \text{oxide} \end{Bmatrix}$ + $\begin{Bmatrix} \text{caustic} \\ \text{potash} \end{Bmatrix}$ + water.

Some of the advantages claimed for this cell are that it is light in weight and therefore suited for traction purposes. The great difficulty, encountered with lead cells, of sulphating the plates is

FIG. 90. A positive and a negative plate as used in the nickel-iron cell

entirely overcome. It is claimed that the cell will stand a great deal of abuse in over-charging and overdischarging, and that it will stand idle in any condition for a long time without injury. It is a little more expensive than the lead cell and has not as yet been used widely for farm lighting plants.

The switchboard. The switchboard carries the apparatus which makes it possible to control the current. The chief instruments found upon it are the *voltmeter* and the *ammeter*. By means of the former the voltage of the current at the time of charging the batteries may be tested, as well as the voltage of the batteries after they are charged. The ammeter is for the purpose of determining the amperage of the current while charging the batteries and the rate at which the current is being discharged from the battery when the lights are on.

FIG. 91. A complete battery of nickel-iron cells

The board should be so wired and provided with the necessary switches that the lights may be run (1) from the battery alone, and at the same time that it is being charged, (2) from the generator and battery combined, which virtually doubles the capacity of the plant, or (3) from the generator alone.

An *automatic circuit-breaker* should be provided and so regulated that should anything happen to the engine to stop it, the circuit from the generator to the battery will be broken and the current prevented from flowing back through the generator.

A *rheostat* is usually provided for the purpose of throwing the necessary resistance into the path of the current, that the battery may be charged at the desired rate. This rate is usually the specified normal rate of charge. However, if the engine were being used for other work, it may be convenient to charge for a longer time at a lower rate. Again, it is sometimes deemed advisable to charge at a rate slightly above the normal, to render complete the chemical action within the cell.

An *ampere-hour meter* is regarded as a valuable addition to a switchboard. The purpose of such an instrument is to indicate to the operator (1) when the battery needs to be charged; (2) when the battery has been fully charged; (3) how fast the batteries are discharging; and (4) how fast they are being charged. A dial with a moving hand indicates the above conditions at a glance. Furthermore, this instrument may be set so that the circuit will be broken and the engine stopped when the batteries are completely charged.

FIG. 92. The generator, switchboard, and storage battery of a low-voltage plant

A, ampere-hour meter; *B*, voltmeter; *C*, automatic circuit-breaker; *D*, rheostat. Note the rubber cells

Counter, or end, cells. When it is necessary to operate the lights while the battery is being charged, a voltage higher than normal will be thrown upon the lighting circuit, with the result that the lamps will burn with unusual brilliancy. To overcome this difficulty, counter, or end, cells are frequently provided, usually three in number, and an extra switch attached to the switchboard, so that they may be thrown into the circuit and made to absorb the extra voltage resulting from the fact that the generator as well as the battery is in the circuit. Many companies do not include end cells, maintaining that with the improved tungsten lamp they are not necessary.

The size and capacity of the plant. The *size* of the plant is determined by the demand that is to be made upon it. For lighting purposes only, this depends upon the number of lights, the size of the lights, and the length of time they are to be operated.

FIG. 93. A complete low-voltage plant

The switchboard is mounted on the engine, and the generator is connected directly to the engine shaft. Note the sealed glass jars

The tungsten lamp is the form most commonly used with low-voltage plants. It has an efficiency greatly in excess of the carbon-filament lamp, since it requires but $1\frac{1}{4}$ watts per candle power, whereas the carbon-filament lamp requires from 3 to 4 watts per candle power. In addition to having such a low rate of current-consumption, it gives a whiter light and maintains its rated candle power better than the carbon-filament lamp. The latter requires so high a voltage for its operation that it is not used in low-voltage plants.

TABLE IX. COMMON SIZES OF THIRTY-TWO-VOLT TUNGSTEN LAMPS, WITH WATTAGE AND AMPERAGE

Candle power	Watts	Amperes
8	10	0.313
12	15	0.469
16	20	0.625
20	25	0.781

Table IX gives the most common sizes for thirty-two-volt tungsten lamps, together with the power required, in watts, and the current-consumption, in amperes.

The *capacity of the storage battery* is to be determined by the number and size of the lights on the circuit. There are several ways of figuring the requirements of a circuit, and in order thoroughly to comprehend the problem it will be well for the computer to assume an actual installation, determining the probable number of lights and the size of each, and estimating the probable service in hours per day. In Table X is found such an installation. In column A is shown the location of the lights; in column B, the number in each location; in column C, the probable number of hours the lamps will be in service; in column D, the number of lamp-hours (equal to B × C); in column E, the size of lamps, in watts; in column F, the current-consumption per lamp, in amperes; in column G, the number of amperes required for each location (equal to B × F); in column H, the number of amperes consumed per hour (equal to D × F); in column I, the power required, in watts (equal to B × E). The installation includes the wiring of the barn, and while the number and size of lights are modest, the estimate is probably not far from average conditions.

TABLE X. DATA USED IN COMPUTING THE SIZE OF A LIGHTING PLANT

A	B	C	D	E	F	G	H	I
LOCATION OF LIGHTS	NUM-BER OF LIGHTS	HOURS IN USE	LAMP-HOURS (B × C)	SIZE OF LAMPS, IN WATTS	AM-PERES PER LAMP	AM-PERES PER LO-CATION (B × F)	AMPERE-HOURS (D × F)	WATTS (B × E)
Kitchen	1	5	5	20	0.625	0.625	3.12	20
Dining-room	2	2	4	20	0.625	1.250	2.50	40
Living-room	2	4	8	25	0.781	1.562	6.25	50
Bedrooms	4	1	4	15	0.469	1.876	1.87	60
Halls	2	2	4	10	0.313	0.625	1.25	20
Bathroom	1	2	2	20	0.625	0.625	1.25	20
Basement	1	1	1	15	0.469	0.469	0.47	15
Porches	2	1	2	10	0.313	0.626	0.62	20
Barn	6	2	12	10	0.313	1.878	3.75	60
Total	21					9.536	21.08	305

It will be seen that 9.54 amperes will be required to operate all of the lights at one time and 21 ampere-hours will be required for the day's service. Now, while it is not probable that all of the lights will be turned on at the same time, there is a great deal of satisfaction in knowing that the plant will easily take care of all the lights if they are needed. Further, the storage battery, as has previously been noted, is rated in ampere-hours and will not only deliver the full-current capacity for the normal discharging-time of eight hours, but will deliver it at a correspondingly higher rate in a less number of hours. For example, referring to Table VIII, the first type of cell, size $6'' \times 6''$, with five plates to the cell, will furnish 10 amperes for three hours, or a total of 30 ampere-hours. (It will be noticed that this table does not rate the battery at the same ampere-hour capacity when discharging at a rate above the normal.) But 30 ampere-hours would run the assumed plant only one and one-half days at full capacity, since 21 amperes are required for each day's service.

FIG. 94. A larger view of the engine, switchboard, and generator shown in Fig. 93

An air-cooled engine is used

Under ordinary regulation this battery would probably run the circuit for two days or more. The 7-plate cell in the $6'' \times 6''$ size will deliver $10\frac{1}{2}$ amperes for five hours, or 52 ampere-hours, which is sufficient for a two-and-one-half days' run. This size is the regular 60-ampere-hour battery, and when discharging at the rate of $7\frac{1}{2}$ amperes, which would be a fair rate for the plant in question, would need charging only every third day. In summer one charging should last for many days.

There is always danger that too small a capacity will be chosen. It is invariably true that more lights will be used than are counted upon at first, and it is always better to have a reserve supply of current than to be overloading the battery.

The *capacity of the generator* is determined by the size of the storage battery, as well as by other purposes to which it may be put, as, for example, the operation of motors or heating-appliances. The size for lighting purposes only will first be considered. The storage battery has a voltage of 32 ordinarily; and when charged to full capacity, a voltage of about 40. The generator should have a voltage higher than this; hence a 40-volt or 45-volt generator will be required. The latter is the size usually furnished with low-voltage plants. At the normal rate of charge the generator must furnish 8 amperes; for excessive charging it should be able to furnish cur-

FIG. 95. A typical installation of a low-voltage plant

rent at the rate of 10 amperes. Generators are rated in kilowatts. A 10-ampere, 45-volt generator would furnish 450 volts, or a little less than $\frac{1}{2}$ kilowatt. A $\frac{1}{2}$-kilowatt size, then, should be chosen.

The plant, then, should be equipped with a 40-volt or 45-volt, $\frac{1}{2}$-kilowatt generator, and a 16-cell, 60-ampere-hour storage battery. The same kind of switchboard is suited to all ordinary farm plants.

Operation of motors and heating-appliances. It is possible to operate small motors from the storage battery, though it is not desirable to attempt too much in this direction. Table XI shows the size of motor commonly used for the machines specified, the current-consumption of each, and the number of twenty-watt lamps that could be operated on the same current.

An examination of this table shows that even the smallest motors require a large amount of current. Motors up to and

including one-eighth horse power may be used if they are oper
ated only a short time each day or week, as is the case for use
with a vacuum cleaner or a cream-separator.

TABLE XI. HORSE POWER AND CURRENT-CONSUMPTION OF THIRTY-
TWO-VOLT MOTORS FOR DIFFERENT MACHINES

Machine	Size, in Horse Power, of Motor required	Current-consumption, in Amperes, 50 Per cent Motor Efficiency	Number of 20-watt Lamps operated by Same Current
Sewing-machine	$\frac{1}{30}$	1.44	2.3
Vacuum cleaner	$\frac{1}{8}$	5.80	9.2
Washing-machine . . .	$\frac{1}{8}-\frac{1}{2}$	5.80–23.24	9.2–36.8
Cream-separator	$\frac{1}{8}$	5.80	9.2
Churn	$\frac{1}{4}$	11.62	18.4
Grindstone	$\frac{1}{4}$	11.62	18.4
Emery wheel	$\frac{1}{4}$	11.62	18.4
Meat-grinder	$\frac{1}{4}$	11.62	18.4

Table XII shows the amount of current required to operate
various heating-appliances, expressed in watts and amperes.

TABLE XII. CURRENT CONSUMED BY HEATING-DEVICES

Article	Power required, in Watts	Current-consumption, in Amperes, at 32 Volts, 100 Per cent Efficiency
3-pound flatiron	200	6.3
4-pound flatiron	280	8.8
6-pound flatiron	550	17.2
5-cup percolator	380	11.8
Toaster	500	15.6
Heating-pad	55	1.7
Curling-iron	15	0.46

The current-consumption of all of the above articles is so great
as to preclude their use with a storage battery.

Use of generator and storage battery combined. As previously
noted, a style of switchboard was selected by means of which it
would be possible to take current from the battery alone, from
the generator alone, or from the two combined. If it is found
to be very desirable to run relatively large motors or operate

heating-devices requiring a heavy current-consumption, it may be done by running the generator while the motor or heating-device is in use. For example, a 4-pound flatiron may be satisfactorily operated from the 10-ampere generator alone. At a small additional cost a 15-ampere or 20-ampere generator could be secured for heating or for motor work.

Cost of installation. The following estimated cost of installation (Table XIII) for an average low-voltage plant was furnished by a responsible company and represents reasonably accurate figures :

TABLE XIII. COST OF INSTALLATION OF AN AVERAGE FARM
ELECTRIC-LIGHTING PLANT

1 sixty-six ampere-hour battery, with 16 cells	$120.00
1 two-horse-power gasoline engine	90.00
1 one-half-kilowatt-hour, forty-volt generator	60.00
1 switchboard, all completely wired, ready to connect with generator and battery	78.00
1 piece leather belting	3.00
15 sixteen-candle-power, twenty-watt tungsten lamps . .	6.00
1000 ft. No. 10 rubber-covered wire	30.00
150 ft. No. 8 rubber-covered wire	6.00
3 switch-cabinets	10.00
Porcelain cleats and tubes	1.50
15 snap switches	4.50
1 three-light pendant, for living-room; 1 two-light pendant, for dining-room; 2 one-light pendants, for front hall and kitchen; 7 two-light bracket fixtures for bedrooms and for cellar; 5 drop-cords with ceiling rosettes and sockets	30.00
Incidentals	10.50
Labor (1 expert man, three days at $6)	18.00
Labor (1 helper, three days at $1.50)	4.50
Total	$472.00

Cost of operation. It is very difficult to make an intelligent estimate of the cost of operating an electric-lighting plant. The actual cash cost is made up chiefly of gasoline and oil for the engine, but there is a certain rate of interest on the investment and a certain amount of depreciation of the plant that must enter into the annual cost. The storage batteries depreciate more rapidly than any other part of the plant. The positive plates will need to be replaced in about five years, the negative plates in ten years. These elements will cost between $5 and $6 per

cell, the total annual cost for this one item of depreciation amounting to from $10 to $12. The depreciation on the generator, the switchboard, and the wiring, under ordinary care, is small; and since the engine is used in most cases

FIG. 96. A complete installation of a plant using nickel-iron storage cells

for other purposes, it is not fair to charge its depreciation entirely to the lighting plant. A fair rate of depreciation for the entire plant would be 5 per cent. A reasonable estimate would be as follows:

Interest, $475 @ 5 per cent	$23.75
Depreciation, $475 @ 5 per cent on whole plant	23.75
Taxes and repairs	5.00
Gasoline and oil	10.00
Total	$62.50

This makes a monthly charge of a little over $5. Hildebrand[1] estimates the annual cost on a four-hundred-dollar plant at $7.15 per month and adds that no farm electric-lighting plant of average size can be operated for less than $5 per month.

High-voltage plants. The preceding discussion has been concerned with low-voltage plants only. High-voltage plants (the term usually being taken to mean 110 volts) are not infrequently used for farm lighting purposes. With a high-voltage plant

[1] Economics of Rural Distribution of Electric Power, *Bulletin No. 1*, Vol. IV, Engineering Experiment Station, Columbia, Mo.

a 110-volt generator is most commonly used. All of the equipment, including switchboard, storage batteries, wiring, and lights, must, of course, be designed for similar voltage. Except for the storage battery the cost of the equipment is essentially the same as for the low-voltage plant. If a storage battery is used, however, — and, since without it the generator would have to be run whenever lights were needed, it is necessary, — at least 56 cells would be required, instead of 16 as in the low-voltage plant. This makes a heavy, cumbersome outfit, and the cost of the battery is considerably increased. The use of the high-voltage current, however, makes it possible to operate larger motors, and heating-appliances can be used more freely. Further, the cost of wiring a house is not so much, since a smaller wire is used. It is also possible to transmit a high-voltage current a longer distance without an appreciable drop in voltage, which is frequently an advantage, as in lighting distant tenant houses.

TABLE XIV. COPPER-WIRE DATA

Number (B. & S. gauge)	Area in circular mils	Weight, in pounds, per 1000 ft., of weatherproof wire	Ohms per 1000 ft.	Carrying-capacity, in amperes, of weatherproof wire
0	105,534	363	0.09829	185
1	83,694	313	0.12398	156
2	66,373	250	0.15633	131
3	52,634	200	0.19714	110
4	41,742	144	0.24858	92
5	33,102	125	0.31346	77
6	26,250	105	0.39258	65
7	20,816	87	0.49845	55
8	16,509	69	0.62840	46
9	13,094	56	0.79242	40
10	10,381	50	0.99948	32
12	6,530	31	1.58900	23
14	4,106	22	2.52660	16
16	2,583	14	4.01760	8
18	1,624	11	6.38800	5

A low-voltage current cannot be profitably carried for more than 500 ft., because of the excessive cost of the large wire which it is necessary to use. The size of the wire to be used depends upon the amount of current which must be transmitted and also upon the distance. The size may easily be figured from the following simple formula :

$$\frac{\text{Length in feet} \times \text{amperes carried} \times 11}{\text{Loss in volts}} = \text{area in circular mils.}$$

In a low-voltage plant the loss in volts should not be greater than 1 or 2. A high-voltage plant will stand a much greater loss. The resistance of 1 ft. of copper wire 1 circular mil (1 one-thousandth of an inch) in area is 11 ohms. The length in feet is the total length of wire used, which is twice the distance to the point to which the current is to be carried. For example, in the assumed plant approximately 2 amperes are required to operate the lights at the barn. If the barn is 300 ft. from the house, what size of wire will be required to carry the current with a loss of 1 volt?

$$\text{Length in feet} = 300 \times 2 = 600,$$
$$\text{Amperes carried} = 2,$$
$$\text{Loss in volts} = 1 ;$$
$$\frac{600 \times 2 \times 11}{1} = 13,200, \text{area in circular mils.}$$

By referring to Table XIV it is found that a No. 9 wire will be required. If a 2-volt loss were allowed, a wire having an area of 6600 circular mils would be required, which, according to the table, is a No. 12, the size commonly used in low-voltage transmission.

If, now, a 110-volt plant were in use, a drop of 3 volts would not be so serious as a drop of 2 volts in a low-voltage plant, and for such a loss a wire with an area of 4400 circular mils, or a No. 14, would be ample, and the cost would be materially reduced. Though the high-voltage plant has many advantages, the low-voltage plant is the one which is being most rapidly developed for farm use.

Location of the plant. It is most convenient to have the entire plant, including engine, generator, switchboard, and storage battery, close together. This makes regulation and control very easy. The basement is a good place for the plant, or it may be located in an outbuilding. The storage batteries will not freeze if kept charged, and consequently there is no danger from low temperatures unless the engine is water-cooled. In this case, however, proper precaution should be taken to prevent injury to it. The room must be well ventilated, as the fumes arising from the batteries when they are being charged are objectionable. If it is necessary, the engine and the generator may be located at a considerable distance from the batteries.

Driving the generator. The gasoline engine is without doubt more commonly used than any other source of power for driving the generator. This is naturally so, since the gasoline engine can be purchased in any size to suit the plant, and since it is easily operated and lends itself to almost any location. Water power and wind power are used to some extent for driving generators.

Water power is, of course, available only in a few localities. Where a stream of considerable size flows near a farmstead it is frequently possible to install a water-wheel which may be made to generate a current at an extremely low cost after the plant is once installed. A relatively heavy flow is required to develop even a small amount of power. For example, in the lighting plant assumed, a $\frac{1}{2}$-kilowatt generator was used. At least 1 H.P. will be required to operate it. If a stream were delivering 120 cu. ft., or 900 gal., per minute, over a dam 6 ft. high, and if it were possible to utilize the whole flow under the full head, there would be developed 1.36 theoretical horse power as verified in the following computation :

$$\frac{120 \times 62.4 \times 6}{33000} = 1.36.$$

Since water-wheels are only about 80 per cent efficient, approximately 1 H.P. would be delivered at the generator. There are, however, numerous streams the country over where thousands of horse power are going to waste that could be utilized for just such purposes as the lighting of farm homes.

The *windmill* has been used to only a limited extent for driving electric generators for power and light. *Bulletin No. 105* of the North Dakota Agricultural College describes a successful lighting and power plant driven by a 16-foot windmill. In this plant a 150-volt generator was used, and a 62-cell storage battery was installed in the attic of the house. The switchboard was placed in the kitchen.

The chief difficulty met with at this plant was the irregular speed of the wheel. A governing-device was designed in connection with the belt pulley, and there was an automatic cut-out to prevent the current from flowing back from the battery to the generator when the speed dropped below normal. All the difficulties seem to have been overcome in this case, but the inherent difficulties in the use of wind power are such as to make its wide use for farm lighting plants improbable.

CHAPTER X

SOURCES OF FARM WATER SUPPLY

The first question that should claim one's attention in a discussion of a farm water-supply system has to do with the source of the water. While it may be true that in the majority of cases the wells or cisterns are already in, a general consideration of the subject may be profitable for all concerned. There are two possible sources of supply: (1) surface waters and (2) underground waters.

Surface waters. Surface waters are not widely used for human consumption, though under certain conditions they may be used with impunity, and they are often, indeed, the most satisfactory source of supply. However, their use is largely confined to that for stock and laundry purposes. Surface waters may be roughly divided into two classes: (1) flowing streams and (2) ponds.

The water of *flowing streams* has its origin, as does all other water available for farm use, in rainfall. But rainfall may reach the stream in several ways. For example, it may reach it as surface run-off or drainage water, that is, as the water of under-drainage.

If a stream is supplied entirely, or even largely, by surface wash, possible sources of contamination are so many as to preclude the use of its water for domestic purposes. Water flowing over the surface of the soil comes in contact with and carries in solution, to a greater or less degree, certain soluble elements found in the upper layer of soil. Barnyard manure and commercial fertilizers applied to the land yield their share of soluble minerals and of certain organic substances which, while not positively dangerous, render the water distasteful. Further, surface waters come in contact with both human and animal wastes, thus adding an element of positive danger if used for human consumption. Decayed and rotting vegetation, particularly at certain times of the year, render surface run-off distasteful and dangerous. Moreover, the purity of the surface run-off may be influenced by the nature of the stream bed and the banks of the stream. Water that is quite unfit for human use may be rendered safe if allowed to flow for some distance in a stream having a rocky or gravelly bottom and sides. The action of the sun and the air has a purifying effect that is remarkable. The water of a stream that is fed largely by underdrains may be fairly pure and not objectionable to the taste. The water in reaching the tile has been filtered through two or three feet or more of earth, the extent of the filtering action depending, of course, on the type of soil. Since tile drains are usually found in clayey soils, organic substances as well as some of the mineral salts are removed by the soil. Streams thus fed represent only a temporary source of supply except in large drainage districts, where water flows from the tiles the greater part of the year.

In many regions *ponds* are relied on to furnish water for live stock during the summer months. Indeed they are often the only source of water for house use. Such ponds may be formed by a natural depression, by damming a draw of some size, or by scooping out over a considerable area a hole from three to four feet deep. They are usually made in regions where the soil is a stiff clay and holds what surface water finds its way into them until it is consumed by stock or evaporated. As long as rains are frequent and the weather cool, these ponds form a fairly satisfactory source of supply for stock; but in the dry summer months the water becomes filled with low forms of plant life and is quite unfit for any kind of stock.

Underground waters. Springs, as a general rule, form a most satisfactory source of water for the farm. The term "spring" is usually applied to a decided stream of water emerging from the ground at a more or less constant rate. There are certain forms of so-called "springs" which are really only seepage veins, the water escaping from a water-bearing stratum over a considerable area and oftentimes only in the rainy season, in which case they are sometimes called wet-weather springs.

Gravity, or seepage, *springs* are probably the most common kind encountered. The condition which usually gives rise to such a spring is shown in Fig. 97. The water-bearing stratum, which may be clay, gravel, sand, or a mixture of all of these materials, is found in more or less well-defined layers. Surface water from large areas percolates downward through this material until it encounters a harder, more impervious stratum; the water

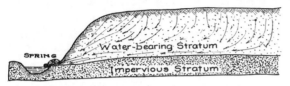

then finds its way along this layer, finally emerging, usually at some point along the

FIG. 97. The conditions which give rise to seepage springs

bank of a valley or stream, through a well-defined channel. If the vein from the hillside is not well defined, but emerges into a flat area as seepage water, it gives rise to swampy conditions. It is also frequently noticed that at times the flow is well defined, the water issuing forth in a fair-sized stream, while at other times this flow will cease or perhaps break out at some other place or come forth as seepage water.

The quality of the water from such springs varies widely; it is usually hard and contains minerals the nature of which varies with the kind of soil through which the water filters. Iron is nearly always found, and frequently an oily scum forms on the surface because of the decaying vegetation so often found about this type of spring.

An *artesian spring* is one whose waters bubble up out of the earth, and, if they are confined

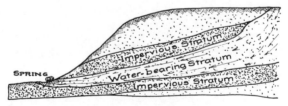

FIG. 98. Conditions which may give rise to an artesian spring

in a pipe, may rise for some distance above the surface. A possible condition under which such a spring may exist is shown in Fig. 98. The water finds its way into the water-bearing stratum and passes downward to an opening, as shown, from which it emerges with a force dependent upon the distance of the highest point of water-bearing stratum above the opening. These springs often have a deep-seated origin, as is attested by the temperature of the water, the opening through which they emerge being a joint in the overlying impervious strata.

The *water from springs* is, as a general rule, free from all impurities. If the water is contaminated in any way, it is usually from surface wash. Polluting elements may, however, enter the water-bearing stratum at a point some distance from the spring, where it may happen that the stratum approaches the surface very closely. If the spring is subject to contamination from either of these sources, it will usually become disturbed and show turbidity after heavy rains. If the disturbance comes from surface wash directly, some means should be provided to protect the spring. If there is adequate protection here, and the water roils after heavy rains, precaution should be taken that no privy vaults are open to the surface within a reasonable distance from the spring. This distance depends altogether upon the position of the upper strata. Frequently, by observing the general trend of stratification on eroded banks along streams, one may form an idea of their direction and of the distance from the spring at which the water-bearing stratum is likely to approach the surface.

Fig. 99. A satisfactory method of collecting and protecting spring water

The *proper protection* of a spring consists chiefly in preventing surface wash, leaves, and other foreign material from getting into the pool or basin in which the water is caught. Where the water flows in a decided stream and can be collected in a spout or pipe, the only precaution necessary is to keep live stock, dogs, etc., away. But often there is no distinct stream, and a basin of some kind must be provided. It is advisable never to do more digging about a spring than is absolutely necessary, as the flow may be very easily interfered with. A square plank frame, a hollow log, or a half-barrel sunk into the basin, with the earth cleaned out, forms a fairly satisfactory and inexpensive basin. Timber, under such conditions, will last a long time. A very satisfactory basin can be made by sinking one or more joints of sewer pipe. This affords a permanent installation which is easily cleaned and which is satisfactory in every way. Brick or concrete is an excellent material for this purpose, especially where a roof must be built over the basin to keep out leaves and trash. Fig. 99 gives an idea of how the basin and cover may be installed.

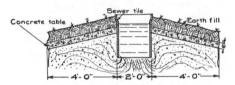

FIG. 100. A method of forcing spring water to collect in a central basin

Frequently the question arises as to the best method of forcing the water up into a tile or basin when it tends to rise to the surface over a considerable area. This is usually a difficult task. In Fig. 100 is shown an installation which has worked satisfactorily in many cases.

Wells. With but relatively few exceptions our farm water supply is taken from wells. As a rule they furnish pure water. It is well to consider possible sources of contamination, however, and to understand how different types of wells vary in adaptability, in cost, and in liability to pollution. The common types are dug wells, drilled wells, and driven wells.

The **dug well** is by far the most common type, particularly in the older parts of the country. It is only natural that this should be so, for this class of well was the most easily and quickly put down; the farmer could do the work with his own force, for neither skilled labor nor extensive equipment were required. This well, however, is limited to those sections where an adequate supply of water is encountered witnin fifty feet of the surface. Fifty feet is a reasonable maximum depth for a dug well, though depths considerably in excess of this are often reached.

The *size* of the hole dug varies from 4 ft. to 8 ft. in diameter. The size depends upon the material used in laying the wall, the nature of the strata into which the well is sunk, and the depth to which the well is likely to go. It is advisable to secure a free diameter for the well of not less than $2\frac{1}{2}$ ft. (better, of 3 ft.), in order to make as light as possible the labor of digging, laying the wall, and cleaning. Then, if two courses of brick are to be used in laying the wall, a total of 1 ft. 4 in. (8 in. on either side) would be taken up by the wall, an amount making necessary a hole at least 4 ft. 6 in. in diameter to maintain a free diameter of 3 ft. If building-stones — either limestone, sandstone, or cobblestones — are used, a wall 1 ft. thick is usually laid, and this thickness of course requires a correspondingly larger excavation.

The material in which the well is sunk is a factor in determining the size of the well, since this type of well is relatively shallow and does not frequently strike strong-flowing veins of water. It is desirable, therefore, to have a good-sized well, for the purpose of storing a considerable amount of water, so that the supply may not easily be exhausted in pumping. Further, in some formations into which such wells are dug no distinct veins are encountered and the total supply comes into the well as seepage water. Here it is especially desirable to have a large capacity for storage.

The *depth* to which the well is likely to go influences the size only as it is related to the amount of work involved. Naturally, if the well is to exceed a depth of, say, about forty feet, it would be wise to make it as small as possible in order to reduce the work of excavation. However, in an effort to save the volume of excavation, the mistake of making the hole too small is usually made, the result being that the workmen are hindered to such an extent that the digging is more costly than if the hole were larger.

In beginning the excavation a circle of the desired diameter is marked out and the hole sunk until it becomes difficult to throw the earth out by hand (a workman can throw the earth out of a hole from eight to ten feet deep without difficulty if the diameter is of good size). A windlass is then constructed over the hole and a bucket or tub lowered by means of a rope. The earth is best loosened by means of a crowbar or spud, a pick being advisable

in the larger holes. A plumb bob should be dropped from the surface frequently, or a mason's level used, to keep the walls plumb.
A try stick too should be at hand to test the diameter frequently.

Some difficulty is encountered at times from the caving in of
the walls. If caving is very troublesome, about the only way to
overcome it is to have a cylinder of wood
or sheet iron that may be slipped down as
the digging proceeds. However, in regions where dug wells are common the
earth is not subject to caving. The well
is sunk until a reasonably strong vein of
water is struck. At times such a vein is
suddenly encountered after the digging
has gone through an impervious stratum,
and in some cases the water rises very
rapidly, sometimes quite to the top of
the well. Often, to avoid difficulty in
laying the wall after the water is struck,
an experienced well-digger lays several
feet of the wall just before he enters the
water vein. Frequently a slow vein,
through which the water merely seeps
into the well, is struck, and it may be
necessary to carry the hole into and
through several such veins before enough
water will collect to make the well of
value. The material for laying the wall
should be close at hand, for use in case
a very strong vein is struck.

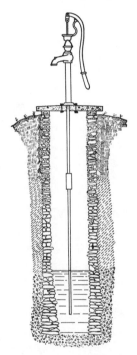

FIG. 101. A method of laying the wall of a dug well

The upper portion is laid with
cement mortar

The material generally used in laying
the wall is uncut stone, but bricks or
sewer tile may be used. These materials, which are laid without
mortar, make a wall ten or twelve inches thick. There is no
necessity for taking great pains to secure a smooth and even wall,
as it adds little to the value of the well. It is essential, however,
that all stones should be securely placed in the wall, so that none
may be dislodged to cause accident when the well is cleaned.
In Fig. 101 is shown a proper method of laying the wall.

The *wall* may be finished in many ways, but in each case the well should be so protected that nothing can fall into it. If the wall is carelessly laid at the top with loose stones only, and a poor curb provided, fishworms, toads, snakes, rats, or mice frequently fall into the well. Even a small fishworm may cause a considerable disturbance in the water, and a toad will render it unfit for drinking for many days. If the plan shown in Fig. 101 is followed (and this is not hard to do), little trouble will be encountered. In this case six to ten feet of the upper part of the wall are laid with cement mortar. This prevents worms or rats from getting into the well, even though they burrow some distance beneath the surface. Further, this water-tight wall tends to keep out surface wash with its impurities.

FIG. 102. A method of building and reënforcing a concrete well curb

While the *curb* may be made of a large flagstone or of wood plank, there is nothing so desirable as a concrete slab. This may be made in place by building up forms beneath and then knocking them out after the slab has set, or it may be molded to one side and later placed over the well. The concrete should be a 1–2–4 mixture and reënforced with fence wire or other rods as shown in Fig. 102.

It will be noticed that the top of the wall shown in Fig. 101 is also of concrete, thus giving a smooth surface on which to place the curb. Just before the slab is placed over the well, the top of the wall may be covered with cement mortar, so as to form a virtually water-tight joint. The center hole in the curb need only be large enough to take the pump cylinder. The holes for the bolts should be formed by inserting either the bolts themselves, or other rods slightly larger, while the concrete is being placed. If the bolts are placed they should be well greased and should be removed before the cement is thoroughly set. This is done in order to make it possible to put in new bolts when the threads on the old ones become worn or twisted off. The top of the curb should slope outward from the center.

In Fig. 103 is shown another method for protecting the water in a dug well. It has many things to recommend it, though one rather hesitates to cover up the water supply so completely as this method requires. One could rest secure, however, that nothing from the surface would find entrance into such a well.

The dug well should, for obvious reasons, be located at a point higher than the surrounding surface, so that all surface wash may flow away from the well. It is advisable to spend a little extra time digging, in order to secure such a location, rather than to place the well at a lower point. The distance from barnyards, cesspools, privies, etc., will vary with the nature of the soil. In heavy clay or heavy sandy or loam soil, where seepage is necessarily slow, a distance of from 50 ft. to 100 ft. may be considered safe. This is especially true if the well is rather deep and the water comes from a distinct vein instead of from seepage. If the well is shallow, however, and the soil is of an open nature, no cesspools or privies should be nearer than from 200 ft. to 300 ft.

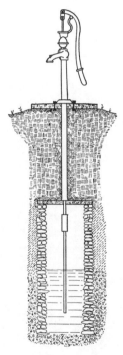

FIG. 103. Another method of protecting the water in a dug well

The *water of dug wells*, of course, always comes from clays, sands, gravels, glacial drift, etc. — the loose, earthy formations. The water from these formations varies decidedly, but because it dissolves a great many mineral constituents from the formations through which it seeps, it is usually of a mineral nature. Iron in greater or less quantities is nearly always present, and calcium and magnesium are found in varying amounts. Such minerals as are found are seldom objectionable.

The *cost* of the dug well varies with the size of the hole and the nature of the digging, but, as a rule, it will be from two to four dollars per foot for the ordinary depth, including the wall.

By way of a summary it may be said that the dug well is adapted to localities where water is found near the surface in unconsolidated strata. It is cheaply and easily constructed by the farm help; the outfit required for digging is not expensive; and the wall may be laid of cheap stone. It affords a large capacity for the storage from slow-seepage veins, and it responds quickly to rainfall. On the other hand, trouble may be had from caving while the well is being dug. Such a well is subject to pollution from the top and from underground seepage, and it cannot be dug in rock nor sunk to depths much in excess of fifty feet.

The **drilled well** is, next to the dug well, by far the most common type, and in newer parts of the country it is often the only type of well found. It is adapted to nearly all parts of the country, and it may be sunk in rocks of all kinds and to depths of thousands of feet, though for ordinary purposes the depth is usually less than three hundred feet.

A common type of well-drilling outfit is shown in Fig. 104. It consists of an engine, of several easily controlled drums on

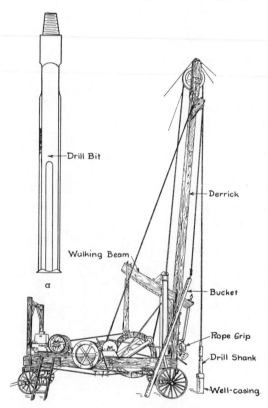

Drill Bit

Derrick

Walking Beam

a

Bucket

Rope Grip

Drill Shank

Well-casing

FIG. 104. A common type of well-drilling machine
At *a* is shown an enlarged view of the drill

which ropes are wound and given out at the will of the operator, and of a derrick with which the drills, the hammer, and the bucket are lifted and lowered. In the illustration the greater part of the drill is in the well-casing in the drilling position. Standing by the derrick is the bucket which is used to dip the material from the bottom of the well. The drill bit is shown enlarged in Fig. 104, *a*. The drill complete weighs from one to two tons.

An iron casing, usually from five to eight inches in diameter, is driven into the ground by suddenly dropping upon it a heavy hammer which is raised by means of the derrick and rope. After the casing has been driven down a short distance, the drill is lowered into the pipe, a little water is added, and the earth churned up to a thin paste. A long tubular bucket with a foot valve is then lowered into the pipe until the valve stem strikes the bottom; this opens the valve, and the bucket fills and is drawn out. After the pipe is cleaned it is driven down a few feet further and the operations repeated. Extra joints are screwed on the top of the casing from time to time as they are needed.

When rock is struck the drilling continues in the same manner except that the iron casing is not driven a great distance below the surface of the rock. It should, however, be carried into the rock several feet, to prevent any possible pollution from entering near the surface of the rock. When the casing is sunk into the rock, the drill is used to bore the hole and then the casing is driven. When a vein of water is struck, a pump is usually put in and the well tested by constant pumping for several days, to determine the strength of the vein and the quality of the water.

A *dry well* must be installed if the water is to be piped to a point at a distance from the well, as to watering-troughs, pressure tanks, etc., in order that pipes may be laid underground. Fig. 105 shows a drilled well with a dry well built of bricks. A six-inch casing is driven down until it extends a few feet into the limestone formation. The remainder of the drilled hole, which ends in a fissure in the limestone, does not require casing. The dry well is sunk to a depth of five feet and walled up with bricks or concrete, with a clear diameter of four feet remaining. This size is necessary in order to have plenty of room to work with wrenches and pipe tools. In the process of laying the walls of the well the pipes necessary to connect with the system to be used must be inserted. Since it is possible to obtain pumps that have a base-cap that will just fit well-casings of different diameters, complete protection to the well at the top is easily secured.

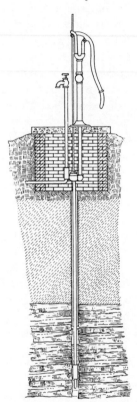

If it is possible to put in a tile drain to take care of any water that may collect in the dry well, this should be done. Otherwise it will be necessary to leave the bottom open so that such water may soak into the soil. If the water is drained off, a concrete bottom adds to the convenience of the workman when installing or altering pipe connections. There is some advantage in placing the dry well so that the well-casing will be to one side instead of exactly in the middle, as the side arrangement gives more room for the workman.

The question of *surface pollution* is not a matter of great concern in the location of a drilled well, since the depth of the well is usually such as to preclude any reasonable possibility of seepage waters entering the supplying vein, and since the iron casing keeps out all the immediate surface materials, provided the top of the casing is properly covered. The chief consideration is one of convenience.

FIG. 105. A drilled well with a dry well for underground pipe installation

The well should be as close to the point of delivery as possible, to avoid the use of needless pipes, and if the pump is to be operated by hand, it should of course be close to the house or barn.

The water of drilled wells may come from any of the sources mentioned in the discussion of dug wells and, in addition, from any of the rock formations in which water is usually found.

Aside from sands and gravels, which represent the most abundant sources of supply of unconsolidated materials, sandstone and limestone furnish the most of our water, the former being the best water-bearer of all the rock formations.

The *water from sandstone* is usually as pure as any unless it be that found in sand and gravels. Sandstones show considerable variation in structure, some being very coarse-grained, with open pores, others being fine-grained, with little pore space; but all are usually saturated and as a general thing give up their water readily. The water is not highly mineralized.

The *water from limestone* is usually found in open fissures, sometimes of small size, sometimes of vast dimensions. Of the latter, Mammoth Cave, in Kentucky, is an example. The water tends to dissolve the limestone and increase the size of the cavity in which it flows. As a consequence water from this formation should be carefully watched. Often underground cavities connect with smaller cavities which reach to the surface. Surface wash of all kinds may therefore be carried directly to the supply of a well which is thought to be sufficiently deep to preclude all possibility of pollution. In the great limestone regions some of these cavities are frequently used as cesspools, a practice which should be severely condemned if wells are near. The water from limestone is always hard, but it is usually not otherwise strongly mineralized.

Shales are usually poor formations to yield water. They are simply clays stratified and consolidated and are therefore so fine-grained as to yield water slowly.

The *cost* of the drilled well is usually from $1.50 to $2 per foot, including the casing. This estimate is for ordinary drilling. In hard limestones or in granites the cost may go as high as $5 per foot, or even higher. Good wrought-iron casing 4 in. in diameter weighs $10\frac{1}{2}$ lb. per foot and costs about 35 cents per foot. Casing 6 in. in diameter weighs about 27 lb. per foot and costs about $1.25 per foot.

By way of summary it may be said that a drilled well has no equal for general desirability. It is adapted to almost all regions. It may be put down to a depth of from ten feet to several hundred feet. It can readily be deepened if for any reason the vein goes dry. It can be located at any convenient place, and the deeper types are not affected by drought. On the other hand, it is rather high in first cost, as it requires an expensive outfit and skilled operators. The pipes rust and corrode. Water constantly standing in the pipes absorbs an iron taste, and there is little storage capacity if the vein is weak.

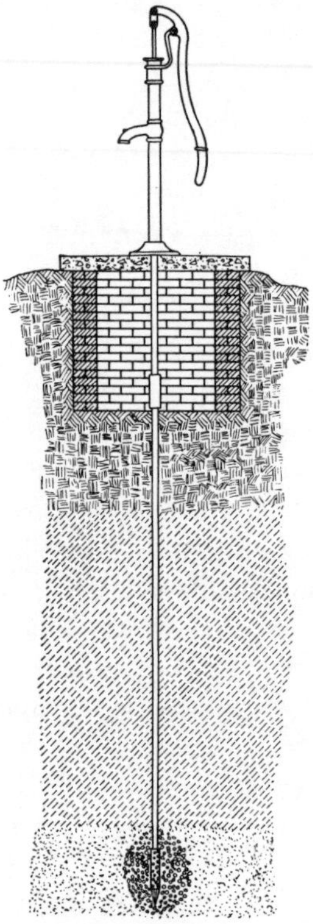

Driven wells are common in sections of the country where water may be found in sands or gravels within a distance of from 50 to 75 ft. and where stones or other obstacles to driving are not found. Driven wells are found most commonly where water occurs at a depth of not over 30 ft.

In the construction of this type of well an ordinary pipe, usually one and one-half inches in diameter, is fitted with a special *drive point*. This is then driven by means of a maul or sledge, extra joints being screwed on as the driving proceeds. From time to time a pump is attached to the pipe in order to ascertain whether water has been struck. As soon as the point punctures a vein of sand or gravel carrying water, the pump is operated rapidly for some time, until the screen of the drive point is cleared of sand and a more or less decided basin is formed at the bottom of the pipe.

In Fig. 106 is shown a common form of this type of well with the dry well installed for underground delivery to other points. Such an installation is frequently necessary in order to place the cylinder within at least twenty-five feet of the water. Often the vein is so close to the surface that a common pitcher pump may be placed on the pipe. In other cases it is necessary to dig the dry well to a depth of several feet in order to get the cylinder down far enough.

FIG. 106. A common form of driven well

Note the drive point at the base of the pipe

Where the water is more than 30 ft. below the surface, a 3-inch pipe is driven and the pump cylinder lowered into this pipe to the desired depth. Wells of this type, which require some form of power drive, may be sunk several hundred feet if necessary, but the average depth does not exceed 75 ft.

The *water of driven wells*, since it is usually found in sands or gravel, is pure and not subjected to polluting influences. There is no chance for surface wash to enter the well, and the seepage from privies, cesspools, etc. is not likely to find its way to the water vein, because sand is a good filter.

Under conditions that are at all favorable this is one of the least expensive types of wells. If a one-and-one-half-inch pipe is used, it will cost about 11 cents per foot. The driving is often the work of only a few hours if no disturbing circumstances, such as striking stones that stop or deflect the pipe, arise. There are in existence many wells of this type that were put down in three hours, some of them furnishing, the year round, all the water used on farms of considerable size.

The driven well is cheaply, quickly, and easily put down. It is virtually sealed from all sources of pollution and yields the pure water usually associated with sands and gravels. It is adapted only to limited areas and offers some little difficulty in operation, by way of clogged holes in the well point, especially if there is much iron in the water. In the larger pipes there are screens on the inside of the point which may be raised or lowered, a device which frees the point from any collecting scale.

The **artesian well**, since it is made possible only by certain geological formations, is found in a limited area. In certain regions there are large areas over which artesian wells are common, but these regions are few. The best flows usually come from sands and sandstones, although glacial materials afford many flowing wells. Artesian wells, except in certain regions, are not located in limestone formations.

Fig. 107 is a diagrammatic representation of conditions that give rise to flowing wells. If the water-bearing stratum is punctured at any point below the crest, or surface elevation, there will be sufficient head to force the water to the surface. In many cases this head is sufficient to throw the water several feet above the surface.

The nature of the water varies with the material from which it comes, and what was said of the waters of glacial drift, sandstone, and limestone in the foregoing discussion of different types of wells applies also to artesian wells. Frequently the source of the artesian well is at a great depth, and the water is usually pure and cold.

The water witch. The use of the mythical divining-rod in locating underground water-pipes, water veins, etc. has been discussed pro and con for years, and in the minds of many it represents a more or less infallible method of locating wells. It is a well-known fact that the course of underground water veins

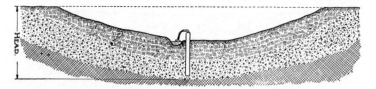

FIG. 107. Conditions which give rise to artesian wells

is far from regular, and there is no reasonable assurance that a well sunk even 30 ft. or less from a good existing well will not be a failure. If there is any reliable means that might be used in locating strong veins of water, thousands of dollars that are now consumed yearly in drilling holes could be saved. That there is any influence whatever, the power of which reaches from a distance of 25 ft., 50 ft., or 100 ft. below the earth's crust to the surface, and causes a twig from a peach or other tree to turn in one's hand when a supposed vein of water is approached, seems highly improbable; yet there are those whose experience makes them strong believers in the divining-rod.

One professed believer proceeds as follows :

Holding the branches of the fork, with thumbs down, the fork resting on the chest like the letter A, I walk back and forth. On crossing a vein of water, drain tile, sewer pipe, or water main, the fork will cave forward to the ground. When the depth is sought I grasp the branches in one hand, steadying the stick with the other, and while in a stooping posture I extend the fork forward over the vein. The A of the fork will begin to vibrate downward and with a stroke that indicates the strength of the vein, the number of full downward strokes will indicate the number of feet to the vein. I have had as good luck with the bitter elm or swamp willow as with the peach twig.[1]

Another believer says, "Any twig will turn whose fruit has a seed of any size."

Those of us who are inclined to search for a reason founded in fact will look with some suspicion on him who claims the power to locate our wells by such methods, and will hesitate to invest in his reputed ability. It would seem that the use of the water witch is a pseudoscientific process rather than a scientific one.

[1] *National Stockman and Farmer*, April 5, 1913.

CHAPTER XI

THE PUMPING AND PIPING OF WATER

In discussing the subject of farmstead installations it will be necessary to refer frequently to the friction of flowing water in pipes as related to the proper size of pipe to use. Further, the question of water pressure will be mentioned, as will the power required to operate a pump. So, in order to obtain an understanding of these and other terms, it will be well to discuss the general question of the flow of water in pipes and some of the general properties of this liquid as related to pumps and pumping.

Properties of water. Water at ordinary temperature is a liquid. Its density, and hence its weight per cubic foot, changes slightly as its temperature varies. It reaches its greatest density at 39.3° F., when its weight is 62.424 lb. per cubic foot. At 100° F. a cubic foot of water weighs 62 lb. In determining the weight of water, as, for example, in tanks, the number 62.4 is always used. A cubic foot of water contains $7\frac{1}{2}$ gal. One gallon weighs $8\frac{1}{3}$ lb.

The *pressure* in pounds per square inch at the base of a column of water, as in a standpipe, an elevated tank, or a pipe leading to the cylinder of a pump in a deep well, depends entirely upon the *height* of the column. The shape and size of the column do not affect the pressure in the least. Illustrations of this fact shown in Fig. 108 are typical. At *a* is shown a steel standpipe 2 ft. in diameter and 40 ft. above the faucet at the base. At *b* is shown an elevated tank, the top of which is 40 ft. from the faucet at the base of the tower. The pressure in pounds per square inch at the faucet is exactly the same in both cases as long as the level of the water stands at the same height in each. Consequently the pressure per square inch at the base of each is equal to the height of a column of water 1 sq. in. in cross section and 40 ft. high, provided both are full, as shown. How much is this pressure?

If a box 1 ft. in the clear on each side be filled with water, its contents would weigh 62.424 lb. Each face is 12 in. square and contains 144 sq. in. If the top face were divided into 144 equal squares, there would be a column of water 1 ft. high and 1 sq. in. in cross section for each square. Each column would weigh 62.424 divided by 144, or 0.434 lb., approximately. In the above cases, then, the pressure exerted at the faucets is 0.434 × 40, or 17.36 lb., per square inch. If the pipe is 1 in. in diameter, the total pressure is equal to $1^2 \times 0.7854 \times 17.36$, or 13.6 lb.

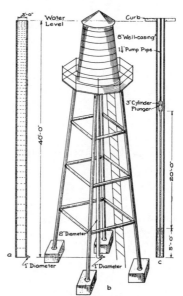

What is the total pressure on the base of the standpipe when it is full? The pressure on each square inch of the base is 0.434 × 40, or 17.36 lb. The area of the base is $24^2 \times 0.7854$, or 452.39 sq. in. The total pressure is, then, 452.39 × 17.36, or 7853.49 lb.

The same condition is shown in a somewhat different form in Fig. 108, c. The pump, pipe, and cylinder are installed in a well 40 ft. deep, with the water standing 5 ft. deep. In the actual operation of the pump, assuming that the water is delivered at the level of the curb, what is the downward pressure on the plunger of the pump cylinder?

FIG. 108. Pressure of water in a tank or a pipe

Pressure depends upon the height of the water column and not upon the shape of the vessel

Although the pressure of the atmosphere upon the surface of the water in the well will force the water up to the cylinder, the work done in creating the vacuum below the cylinder is equivalent to lifting a column of water 20 ft. high, since in this case the cylinder is 20 ft. from the water. The plunger, then, in being drawn upward is working against a column of water 35 ft. high. The pressure of this column is 35 × 0.434, or 15.19 lb., per square inch. The plunger is 3 in. in diameter; its area, then, is $3^2 \times 0.7854$, or 7 sq. in. The total pressure, then, on the plunger is 15.19×7, or 106.33 lb. Note that the problem was not concerned with the weight of a column of water 35 ft. high and $1\frac{1}{4}$ in. in area, which is, in reality, lifted by the plunger, but rather with the force of a column of water 35 ft. high exerted over the entire area of the plunger.

Flow of water in pipes. Water flowing through pipes follows the same general law as bodies falling through space. There are, however, certain factors which oppose the free passage of water in pipes, all of which represent some form of friction. For example, the friction in a rough pipe is greater than that in a smooth one. There is more friction in a long pipe than in a short one. A small pipe offers more resistance in proportion to the amount of water carried than a large one. Certain *laws of friction* may be stated, as follows: (1) friction is proportional to the length of the pipe, other factors remaining the same; (2) friction increases approximately as the square of the velocity; (3) friction varies inversely as the diameter of the pipe; (4) friction increases with the roughness of the pipe and with the number of bends. All of these laws have a practical bearing on the installation of farm water-supply systems. Often attention to the principles herein stated would save a great deal of power in pumping — notably through the use of a slightly larger pipe. Where water is piped for some distance the effective head can be very quickly consumed in friction if a small pipe is used. Table XV shows the loss in head because of friction in the sizes of pipes commonly used in farm water-supply systems. These figures are adapted from G. S. Williams's "Hydraulic Tables," and are for ordinary pipe.

The practical application of this table may be shown by citing an example or two. Some years ago the writer's attention was called to an installation by which water was piped to a barn from a spring 700 ft. distant. The total fall was 11 ft., and a $\frac{3}{4}$-inch pipe was used. The total flow of the spring did not exceed 2 gal. per minute. The water scarcely dripped from the pipe at the barn. By referring to Table XV it is seen that if a $\frac{3}{4}$-inch pipe is carrying water at the rate of 2 gal. per minute, the friction loss in each 100 ft. of pipe is 1.9 ft., or almost 2 ft.; that is to say, it requires 2 ft. of head to overcome the frictional resistance in each 100 ft. of pipe, or 14 ft. in the whole line. But in the above instance a head of only 11 ft. was available, a fact which explains why the water merely dripped at the barn.

TABLE XV. LOSS OF HEAD IN FEET AND IN POUNDS PRESSURE PER SQUARE INCH DUE TO FRICTION, IN ORDINARY IRON PIPE

Diameter of pipe in inches	Discharge per minute, in gallons	Velocity per second, in feet	Loss of head for each 100 ft. of pipe, in feet	Loss of head, in pounds of pressure, for each 100 ft. of pipe
$\frac{1}{4}$	0.5	1.54	7.80	3.38
$\frac{1}{4}$	1.0	3.08	28.00	12.15
$\frac{1}{4}$	1.5	4.62	60.00	26.04
$\frac{1}{2}$	1.0	1.05	2.10	0.90
$\frac{1}{2}$	2.0	2.10	7.40	3.21
$\frac{1}{2}$	3.0	3.16	15.80	6.85
$\frac{3}{4}$	2.0	1.20	1.90	0.82
$\frac{3}{4}$	3.0	1.80	4.10	1.77
$\frac{3}{4}$	4.0	2.41	7.00	3.03
$\frac{3}{4}$	5.0	3.01	10.50	4.55
1	3.0	1.12	1.26	0.54
1	4.0	1.49	2.14	0.93
1	5.0	1.86	3.25	1.41
1	6.0	2.23	4.55	1.97
1	8.0	2.98	7.80	3.38
$1\frac{1}{4}$	4.0	0.86	0.57	0.25
$1\frac{1}{4}$	5.0	1.07	0.84	0.36
$1\frac{1}{4}$	6.0	1.29	1.20	0.52
$1\frac{1}{4}$	7.0	1.50	1.59	0.69
$1\frac{1}{4}$	8.0	1.72	2.03	0.88
$1\frac{1}{4}$	10.0	2.14	3.05	1.30
$1\frac{1}{2}$	4.0	0.63	0.262	0.11
$1\frac{1}{2}$	5.0	0.79	0.398	0.17
$1\frac{1}{2}$	6.0	0.94	0.560	0.24
$1\frac{1}{2}$	7.0	1.10	0.740	0.32
$1\frac{1}{2}$	8.0	1.26	0.95	0.41
$1\frac{1}{2}$	10.0	1.57	1.43	0.62
$1\frac{1}{2}$	12.0	1.89	2.01	0.87
2	6.0	0.61	0.20	0.08
2	8.0	0.82	0.33	0.14
2	10.0	1.02	0.50	0.22
2	12.0	1.23	0.70	0.30
2	14.0	1.43	0.84	0.91

Now suppose a 1-inch pipe had been used. The table shows nothing smaller than a flow of 3 gal. per minute. At this rate the friction loss is $1\frac{1}{4}$ ft. for each 100 ft. of pipe, or a total loss of head of only 8.75 ft., leaving a free head of 2.25 ft. If the water were flowing at the rate of 2 gal. per minute, the loss in head for the total length would not be over 5 ft., which would leave a free working head of 6 ft. To go still further, if a $1\frac{1}{2}$-inch pipe were used, the total friction loss with a flow of 4 gal. per minute would be only 0.26 ft. per 100 ft. of pipe, or only 1.8 ft. for the total length.

This emphasizes the necessity, where the pipe is long, of using a sufficiently large pipe so that a great portion of the total head may not be consumed in overcoming friction. The principle that friction decreases with an increase in the size of the pipe is strikingly brought out in the table; as is also the fact that friction increases very rapidly as velocity, or quantity discharged, increases.

The last column in the table, giving the friction loss in pounds pressure per square inch, is obtained by multiplying the preceding column by the factor 0.434. This is useful in estimating the power necessary to force water into a pneumatic tank by means of a ram or common pump when a certain pressure must be attained in addition to that required to force the water through the pump pipe. For example, suppose that it is necessary to force water 500 ft. through a 1-inch pipe at the rate of 6 gal. per minute and discharge it into a pneumatic tank. It is desired to maintain a pressure of 40 lb. in the tank. What pressure will the pump have to work against? From the table the friction loss in pounds per square inch for each 100 ft. of pipe carrying water at the above rate is 1.97. The total pressure, then, necessary to overcome friction is 9.85 lb. The pump, therefore, must work against a pressure of 49.85 lb. This is equivalent to a vertical lift of 114.65 ft.

The *quantity* of water which a pipe of any given size will discharge depends upon (1) the head, or total fall, (2) the length of the pipe and the number of bends, and (3) the condition of the interior surface of the pipe. The *head* represents the difference in level between the surface of the water in the free chamber from which it enters the pipe and the center of the pipe at the point of free discharge.

A formula used in figuring the quantity of discharge is based on Darcy's formula for the flow of water in clean cast-iron pipes discharging water under pressure and is

$$Q = ac\sqrt{r} \times \sqrt{s},$$

where Q = quantity discharged in cubic feet per second.

Tables XVI and XVII give the values of the factors in the above formula for some of the common sizes of pipes and for various conditions in regard to fall, or head. It is not necessary, therefore, that the student know the meaning or the derivation of the remaining symbols in Darcy's formula.

TABLE XVI. VALUES OF THE FACTOR $ac\sqrt{r}$ FOR DIFFERENT SIZES OF PIPE

Diameter of pipe	Value of $ac\sqrt{r}$	Diameter of pipe	Value of $ac\sqrt{r}$
½ in.	0.00914	4 in.	2.5630
¾ in.	0.02855	5 in.	4.5610
1 in.	0.06334	6 in.	7.3068
1¼ in.	0.11659	7 in.	10.8520
1¼ in.	0.19115	8 in.	15.2700
1¾ in.	0.28936	9 in.	20.6520
2 in.	0.41357	10 in.	26.9520
2½ in.	0.74786	11 in.	34.4280
3 in.	1.2089	12 in.	42.9180

TABLE XVII. VALUES OF THE FACTOR $\sqrt{s}$ FOR DIFFERENT HEADS

Fall of 1 ft. in	Value of $\sqrt{s}$	Fall of 1 ft. in	Value of $\sqrt{s}$	Fall of 1 ft. in	Value of $\sqrt{s}$
372.1 ft. . . .	0.0515	150 ft.	0.0816	44 ft. . . .	0.1507
352.0 ft. . . .	0.0533	132 ft.	0.0780	40 ft. . . .	0.1581
330.0 ft. . . .	0.0550	120 ft.	0.0913	33 ft. . . .	0.1741
310.6 ft. . . .	0.0567	110 ft.	0.0953	24 ft. . . .	0.2041
293.3 ft. . . .	0.0583	100 ft.	0.1000	20 ft. . . .	0.2236
277.9 ft. . . .	0.0600	88 ft.	0.1066	16 ft. . . .	0.2500
264.0 ft. . . .	0.0615	80 ft.	0.1118	12 ft. . . .	0.2887
240.0 ft. . . .	0.0645	75 ft.	0.1155	10 ft. . . .	0.3162
220.0 ft. . . .	0.0674	66 ft.	0.1231	8 ft. . . .	0.3535
203.1 ft. . . .	0.0702	60 ft.	0.1291	6 ft. . . .	0.4082
188.6 ft. . . .	0.0728	55 ft.	0.1348	5 ft. . . .	0.4472
176.0 ft. . . .	0.0754	50 ft.	0.1414	4 ft. . . .	0.5000

An example will serve to illustrate the use of this formula. It is desired to pipe water from a spring to a house 1000 ft. distant. The total fall is 10 ft. How much water will a 1-inch pipe deliver?

From Table XVI the value of $ac\sqrt{r}$ for a 1-inch pipe is 0.06334. The fall is 10 ft. in 1000 ft., or 1 ft. in 100 ft. From Table XVII the value of $\sqrt{s}$ for this fall is 0.1. Substituting,

$$Q = 0.06334 \times 0.1$$
$$= .006334 \text{ cu. ft. per second}$$
$$= .38 \text{ cu. ft. per minute}$$
$$= 2.85 \text{ gal. per minute.}$$

If there are several elbows in the pipe line, 10 ft. should, in general, be added to the total length of pipe, for each elbow.

The operation of a pump. It is frequently necessary to determine the amount of water a given pump will deliver, as well as the power required to operate it under certain definite conditions.

The *size* of cylinder refers to its diameter and length. Common sizes are 2-inch, $2\frac{1}{2}$-inch, 3-inch, and $3\frac{1}{2}$-inch diameters and 10-inch, 12-inch, 14-inch, and 18-inch lengths. Which size to use depends upon the depth of the well. This matter is frequently overlooked and so large a cylinder installed that the pump is very hard to operate. An illustration will serve to show how the size affects the pumping.

Suppose a pump with a 3-inch cylinder is installed in a well 120 ft. deep. What force will be required on the end of the handle to operate the pump, the handle having arms 4 in. and 28 in. long? As previously shown, the pressure exerted on the plunger of the pump in pounds per square inch is determined by the height of the column of water which it supports. Assuming that it is 120 ft. from the pump spout to the surface of the water in the well, the pressure on the plunger would be as follows:

$$120 \times 0.434 = 52 \text{ lb. per square inch,}$$
$$3 \times 3 \times 0.7854 = 7 \text{ sq. in., area of plunger,}$$
$$52 \times 7 = 364 \text{ lb., total pressure,}$$
$$28 \div 4 = 7, \text{ leverage of pump handle,}$$
$$364 \div 7 = 52 \text{ lb. on end of handle.}$$

A person operating a pump cannot, with comfort, supply in continuous pumping a force in excess of from 15 to 20 lb. Therefore a 3-inch cylinder is out of the question.

What force would be necessary on the end of the handle if a 2-inch cylinder were used?

$$120 \times 0.434 = 52 \text{ lb. per square inch,}$$
$$2 \times 2 \times 0.7854 = 3.14 \text{ sq. in., area of plunger,}$$
$$52 \times 3.14 = 163.28 \text{ lb., total pressure,}$$
$$163.28 \div 7 = 23.32 \text{ lb. on end of handle.}$$

A 2-inch cylinder, then, requires a force of 23.32 lb. on the end of the handle. This is within the range of possibility, but still very difficult work, as would be expected in a well of this depth. Friction in the pump was disregarded in each case, as was the weight of the plunger rod, both of which would add something to the above results.

The *quantity* of water which a pump will deliver, depends upon the size of the cylinder, the length of the stroke, and the number of strokes per minute. Pumps should not be operated faster than 40 strokes per minute, or there will be undue wear on the leathers. How much water will a pump having a cylinder 3 in. in diameter and a 6-inch stroke deliver when operated at the rate of 40 strokes per minute?

$$3 \times 3 \times 0.7854 = 7 \text{ in., area of base of cylinder,}$$
$$7 \times 6 = 42 \text{ cu. in., volume of each stroke,}$$
$$42 \times 40 = 1680 \text{ cu. in., volume of 40 strokes,}$$
$$1680 \div 231 = 7.27 \text{ gal. per minute,}$$
$$7.27 \times 70\% = 5.08 \text{ gal. per minute, actually delivered.}$$

The last step allows an efficiency of 70 per cent for the pump; that is, the pump will deliver only 70 per cent of the total volume at each stroke, 30 per cent being a reasonable allowance for poor leathers, leakage, etc.

Power for pumping. All power is measured in terms of horse power. One horse power represents the amount of work done in lifting 33,000 lb. to a height of 1 ft. in one minute, or, briefly stated, it represents 33,000 ft.-lb. per minute. The same work would be done if 33 lb. were lifted to a height of 1000 ft. in one minute; any other transformation, also, would still be the equivalent, provided the proper relation of factors is maintained.

It follows, therefore, that in order to determine the *power required* for pumping water, it is only necessary to determine the amount per minute that is to be delivered, the height to which it is to be lifted, and the length of pipe through which it must be forced. An illustration will explain. How much power will be required to operate a pump which is lifting water from the bottom of a well 120 ft. deep and forcing it into a tank 40 ft. high at the rate of 10 gal. per minute? The tank is located 300 ft. from the well. All pipe used is $1\frac{1}{4}$ in. in diameter.

$$120 + 40 + 300 = 460, \text{ total length of pipe,}$$
$$3 \text{ ft.} = \text{friction loss per 100 ft. (Table XV),}$$
$$4.6 \times 3 = 13.8, \text{ friction loss in 460 ft.,}$$
$$120 + 40 + 13.8 = 173.8 \text{ ft., total lift,}$$
$$10 \times 8\frac{1}{3} = 83.3 \text{ lb. lifted per minute,}$$
$$83.3 \times 173.8 = 14,477.5 \text{ ft.-lb. per minute,}$$
$$14,477.5 \div 33,000 = 0.44 \text{ H. P. (theoretical).}$$

In order to allow for losses in the engine, pump, etc., the theoretical horse power should be doubled. This would give 0.88 in the above problem, a number requiring a 1-horse-power engine.

Table XVIII gives the capacity, at the rate of forty strokes per minute, of the sizes of cylinders mentioned, and the theoretical horse power required to lift the given quantity to the stated height.

This table, as stated, gives the theoretical horse power. The figures should be doubled to give the actual horse power required. In fact some writers recommend that the theoretical power be multiplied by three for pumps of small capacity under high lifts.

The windmill and the gasoline engine are two very common sources of power for pumping. However, the details of construction or of operation of neither will be discussed in this chapter, since each will be considered in detail in other chapters. But the question as to which is the more satisfactory for pumping water frequently arises and for that reason is briefly discussed here.

There is no doubt that the windmill affords the cheaper source of power. It requires almost no attention except oiling once a week; it will last for fifteen years if it is properly cared for, its bolts kept tightened, etc. Moreover, the wind costs nothing. On the other hand, it is essential that a sufficient amount of storage be provided to tide over possible days of calm. If much live stock is dependent on the mill for water, there are almost sure to be days when the water will give out. Intelligent care in keeping the tanks full will not allow this to happen often. Storage in winter means cold and frozen water; in summer, warm water. The windmill, too, is likely to be wrecked by storm.

TABLE XVIII. CAPACITY, AT FORTY STROKES PER MINUTE, OF PUMPS OF VARIOUS SIZES, AND POWER REQUIRED TO OPERATE THEM

DIAMETER OF CYLINDER IN INCHES	LENGTH OF CYLINDER IN INCHES	LENGTH OF STROKE IN INCHES	GALLONS PER MINUTE (forty strokes)	HORSE POWER REQUIRED TO LIFT WATER TO ELEVATION OF					
				50 ft.	75 ft.	100 ft.	150 ft.	200 ft.	300 ft.
2	10	6	3.26	0.04	0.06	0.08	0.12	0.16	0.24
2	12	8	4.35	0.06	0.09	0.11	0.16	0.22	0.33
2	14	10	5.43	0.07	0.10	0.14	0.21	0.28	0.42
2	16	12	6.52	0.08	0.12	0.16	0.24	0.32	0.48
2½	10	6	5.10	0.07	0.11	0.13	0.19	0.26	0.39
2½	12	8	6.80	0.09	0.14	0.17	0.25	0.34	0.51
2½	14	10	8.50	0.11	0.16	0.21	0.31	0.42	0.63
2½	16	12	10.20	0.13	0.19	0.26	0.39	0.52	0.78
3	10	6	7.34	0.09	0.14	0.18	0.27	0.36	0.54
3	12	8	9.80	0.12	0.18	0.24	0.36	0.48	0.78
3	14	10	12.25	0.15	0.22	0.30	0.45	0.60	0.90
3	16	12	14.68	0.18	0.27	0.36	0.54	0.72	0.08
3½	10	6	10.00	0.13	0.20	0.25	0.37	0.40	0.75
3½	12	8	13.33	0.16	0.24	0.32	0.48	0.64	0.96
3½	14	10	16.66	0.20	0.30	0.40	0.60	0.80	1.20
3½	16	12	20.00	0.25	0.37	0.50	0.75	1.00	1.50
4	10	6	13.00	0.16	0.24	0.32	0.48	0.64	0.96
4	12	8	17.33	0.22	0.33	0.43	0.64	0.86	1.20
4	14	10	21.66	0.27	0.40	0.54	0.21	1.08	1.62
4	16	12	26.00	0.32	0.48	0.64	0.96	1.28	1.92

The engine is being widely used for pumping water. Its first cost is less by one half than that of a windmill. The water can be pumped when needed, which means fresh water both summer and winter. It will not blow over, but it requires constant care, and the fuel cost for a year's pumping is considerable. All things considered, the windmill seems to be the better device unless from thirty to forty head of live stock are to be supplied, in which case the storage would become so expensive an item as to make an engine the more economical.

CHAPTER XII

PUMPS AND THEIR OPERATION

Before taking up a detailed study of the different types of pumps in common use it will be necessary to give some attention to the theory of pump operation, in preparation for a clear understanding of the reasons underlying the various constructions discussed.

Air in its relation to pumping. Nearly all our modern pumps depend upon and make use of certain properties of air, the chief of which are its weight and its elasticity, or compressibility. We are living at the bottom of a great sea of air which is many miles in depth. Just as a column of water supported in a vertical pipe exerts a pressure at the bottom of the pipe, so does this sea of air, which may be considered as made up of many columns, exert a pressure on all objects or surfaces at its bottom.

Several everyday phenomena illustrate this fact. If one is sucking cider through a long straw, the pressure of the air on the outer surface of the straw frequently causes it to collapse. If water is pumped through a rubber hose used as a suction pipe — for example, in a spraying-outfit — and if the entrance to the hose becomes clogged, it will collapse, because the pressure on the outside is greater than that on the inside. If a sirup can is filled to a depth of one inch or so with water and then placed on a stove until the water boils vigorously, a part of the air within the can is driven out. Now if the cap is screwed on tightly and the can set in cold water or even allowed to cool in the open room, the sides will soon begin to collapse. Here again the pressure on the outside is greater than that on the inside ; or, in other words, it is the weight of the air pressing on the surface of the straw, rubber hose, or can that produces the collapse. An open vessel does not collapse, because the air pressure is the same on all sides.

If a tube forty inches in length is filled with mercury and inverted and the open end placed in a vessel of mercury, at sea level it will be found that the surface of the mercury in the tube will be approximately thirty inches above the level of that in the vessel. The absence of air in the tube removes the pressure on the inside of the tube, and the weight of the air pressing on the surface of the liquid in the vessel, in order to preserve a balance of pressure, holds the mercury at this height.

If the tube were 1 sq. in. in cross section, there would be 30 cu. in. of mercury supported in the tube, and since 1 cu. in. of mercury weighs 0.49 lb., the total weight of this column of mercury would be $0.49 \times 30 = 14.7$ lb. In other words, there is a pressure upwards on the bottom of this tube equal to 14.7 lb. per square inch of the surface of the mercury in the vessel. If this is true of the mercury in the vessel, it is true of all surfaces at the sea level; and they are in reality found to be subjected to this same pressure of 14.7 lb. per square inch.

Mercury is 13.6 times as heavy as water; so that if water were substituted in the tube, it would rise 13.6 times as high, or $13.6 \times 30 = 408$ in., or 34 ft., which is recognized as the approximate height to which air pressure will lift a column of water under ideal conditions. When the piston, or plunger, of a pump is drawn upward it exhausts the air from the cylinder, and the pressure of thé atmosphere upon the water in the well forces the water up through the pipe and fills the cylinder. Theoretically, then, pump cylinders could be placed 34 ft. above the level of low water, but owing to valve leakage, worn leathers, etc., the maximum working distance is 25 ft., and 20 ft. is a safer working distance.

Atmospheric pressure is, as stated, 14.7 lb. per square inch at sea level. This pressure decreases as elevation increases, at an approximate rate of $\frac{1}{2}$ lb. for each 1000 ft., until at an elevation of 45 miles the air is so rare as to have no appreciable weight.

The *elasticity*, or compressibility, of air is made use of in pumping water in pneumatic systems of water supply. If a tightly fitting piston is forced into an air-tight cylinder until the volume of air originally contained is reduced one half, or until the same volume of air is forced into one half the space it originally occupied, it is found that the pressure contained is twice as great as it was before compression. If the same air is compressed into a space one third, one tenth, etc., as large as the original, the pressure of that air becomes three, four, ten, etc. times as great. On the other hand, if this compressed air is allowed to expand to a volume three, four, ten, etc., times as great as that which it originally occupied, the pressure will be reduced exactly one third, one fourth, one tenth, etc.

In pneumatic systems water is used in place of the piston, and the pneumatic tank in place of the cylinder. The action is exactly the same, with a few exceptions, and depends upon the principle that since water is virtually incompressible, it acts as a solid piston. It dissolves, or absorbs, air to some extent, however, and if air is not supplied at intervals, the volume of air originally contained in the tank becomes smaller and smaller until in time it may become completely absorbed by the water. More will be said of this when pneumatic systems are discussed.

Types of Pumps

There are upon the market many different types of pumps, each adapted to some specific purpose. The following sections will briefly describe the more common types and tell how they operate and what conditions they are intended to meet.

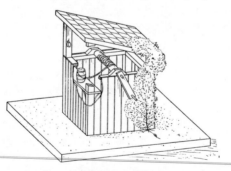

FIG. 109. A well-constructed, neat, and sanitary windlass and cover

The sweep. The sweep was one of the first mechanical devices put into use for lifting water from wells. It was an improvement over the bucket and rope, but is now only occasionally found.

The windlass. The windlass represents the next step in water-lifting devices, and associated with it for all time is "The Old Oaken Bucket." The windlass is still frequently used, and from the standpoint of sanitation it is fairly satisfactory if the well is properly protected. The effort required to lift the water is out of all proportion to the fancied advantages of the windlass, however, and too often it is the case that the housewife has the bulk of the water to lift. Fig. 109 shows a type of windlass and cover in common use.

The chain pump. There are two types of chain pumps, differing in the method used to raise the water. The first and older type has small *tin* buckets, holding about one pint each, mounted on an endless chain. As the chain is revolved each bucket dips into the water in the well, carries its portion to the top, and empties the contents into the delivery spout as it passes over the reel. Each bucket has a small hole near the bottom, to drain out all water in case of freezing weather.

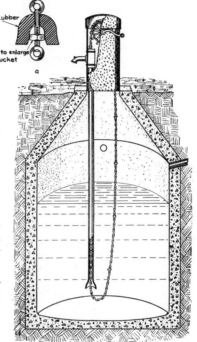

FIG. 110. A modern chain pump with rubber buckets and steel tube

At *a* is shown a section of an adjustable rubber bucket

The more modern type of chain pump is shown in Fig. 110. *Rubber* buckets are attached to the chain at intervals of several feet. These buckets, one of which is shown in Fig. 110, *a*, are drawn through tubing, and as each bucket is drawn upward it tends to leave a vacuum beneath it, the air pressure forcing the water up into the tube. As soon as another bucket enters the tube it lifts directly the water which is above it, and carries it to the top of the tube.

Formerly the *tubing* was made of wood, which was satisfactory material, lasting for many years. In a well of any depth, however, it was so heavy that it was a difficult task to lift it out of the well. The metal tubing is so much lighter and more satisfactory in every way that it is now rather generally used. The buckets are of different kinds, some being adjustable. The one shown is capable of being enlarged as the rubber becomes worn, if the nut on the threaded stem is turned up. This is a valuable feature, and buckets of this type should always be purchased.

The chain pump is best adapted to cisterns and shallow wells. There is no other type of hand pump that can be made to throw a larger stream, and hence in the shallow reservoir it is most satisfactory. In wells as deep as thirty feet, however, the weight of the chain is so great as to make the pump hard to operate. It is best adapted, therefore, to wells less than twenty-five feet in depth. The pump gives but little trouble. The buckets must be renewed every year or so, and the chain will, in five or six years, become worn at the wearing surfaces so as to give trouble from breaking. The deeper the well, the greater the wear. A good chain pump for a cistern or a shallow well costs about $12.

FIG. 111. A single-action lift pump

The plunger pump. The plunger pump represents a type of which there are several forms. All have the same general construction in that the pumping-parts consist essentially of a cylinder and of a plunger, or piston. Plunger pumps may be classified as (1) lift pumps and (2) force pumps. They may be further classified as (1) single-action pumps and (2) double-action pumps. A single-action pump may be a lift pump or a force pump; a double-action pump is always a force pump.

A *single-action lift pump* is shown in Fig. 111. It is called a lift pump because the top of the standard through which the plunger rod works is open so that water cannot be forced higher than the spout. It is called single-action because, as will be shown later, the greater part of the water is delivered on the up stroke of the plunger. The action of the pump is as follows : In Fig. 112, *a*, the plunger is being lifted by the down stroke of the handle. As it passes upward there is a tendency to create a vacuum below the plunger, but since the atmosphere is pressing down on the surface of the water in the well at the rate of 14.7 pounds per square inch at sea level, this force, in order to maintain equal pressure within the cylinder, will drive water up against the flap valve and into the cylinder. Thus, when the plunger reaches the limit of its upper stroke, the cylinder is almost full of water, although it is never completely full, since there is never a perfect vacuum created.

On the down stroke of the plunger (Fig. 112, *b*) the flap valve closes, the poppet valve is lifted off its seat, and the plunger finishes its stroke with all the water above it. In the next up stroke of the plunger, the water above it is lifted up to the spout, while at the same time a new charge is forced into the cylinder from below. It is seen that water is lifted to the delivery spout only on the up stroke of the plunger, which corresponds to the down stroke of the handle; hence the term " single-action pump." If one pumps fast enough it is possible to secure a more or less steady stream, although as a rule the flow is intermittent.

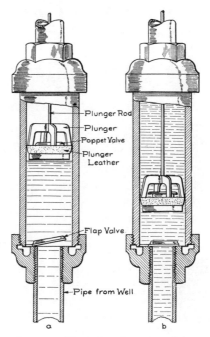

FIG. 112. Illustrating the action of the single-action pump

This pump is primarily intended for shallow wells. The pipe extending from the standard to the cylinder is called a set-length pipe, a term meaning that the cylinder is seldom placed nearer the water than the set length permits. This would limit the use of the pump to wells not over thirty-five feet deep. As a matter of fact the cylinder may be lowered any reasonable distance with satisfaction.

The *cylinder* may be made of cast iron, of galvanized iron, of iron lined with brass or with porcelain, or it may be made of solid

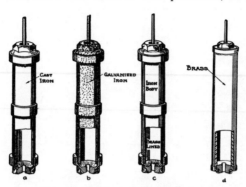

brass. An all-brass or brass-lined cylinder has the great advantage of unusual smoothness, an advantage which is conducive to long life of the leathers. An all-brass cylinder, however, is rather soft and cannot be readily clasped with pipe-wrenches without being dented. The

FIG. 113. Various types of cylinders

porcelain-lined cylinder is very smooth, but is likely to scale. It is used in pumping salt water or other material that would corrode iron. A first-class iron cylinder turned to a true diameter, ground, and polished, is cheaper than any of the others and is very satisfactory. It can be readily handled with wrenches and will not bend out of shape. Fig. 113, *a*, *b*, *c*, *d*, shows various types of cylinders. The inside-cap cylinder (Fig. 113, *d*) is for use in wells of small bore.

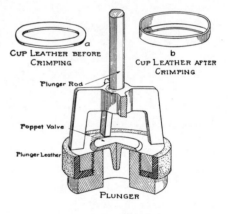

FIG. 114. Details of a pump plunger

The *plunger*, details of which are shown in Fig. 114, is one of the vital parts of the pump. The plunger leather, or cup valve, is a crimped leather and should always be made of oak-tanned leather of the best quality. It wears rapidly, and the efficiency of the pump depends in large measure on the quality and durability of this leather. The bottom of the plunger is screwed off, the leather inserted, and the bottom replaced.

The *poppet* valve is usually made of iron. Some manufacturers are providing a brass seat for this valve. Brass would not corrode and roughen as would iron, and it is readily seen that a perfectly smooth seat is essential. A ball valve is used by some manufacturers. This type possesses the advantage of wearing evenly all around, and sand is not so likely to interfere with its proper seating.

The *flap* valve, or suction leather, should be made of the best leather possible. The seat is usually of iron, though it may be of brass or glass. When quicksand is present, it is sometimes advisable to place a disk of leather beneath the valve, in which case the fine sand particles do not hold the valve off its seat so easily. A ball valve is frequently used, and where there is sand in the water this type is especially desirable.

The cost of the single-action lift pump with the 5-foot set-

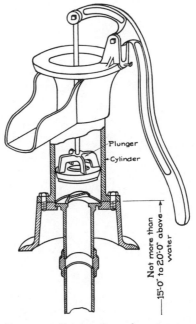

FIG. 115. Construction of a common pitcher pump, used chiefly in cisterns

length pipe is about as follows : 3-inch cylinder and $1\frac{1}{4}$-inch pipe, complete with iron cylinder, $5.75 ; with porcelain-lined cylinder, $6.75; with brass-lined cylinder, $7.25; brass-body cylinder, $8.25.

The *pitcher* pump, shown in Fig. 115, is a type of lift pump primarily adapted to cisterns. Its construction and operation are essentially the same as the lift pump just described, except that the cylinder is a part of the pump standard. This pump must never be set more than 20 ft. above the level of the water, and 15 ft. is a more common distance. It will of course lift water 30 ft. or more, but the handle is usually so short that pumping to this height is very difficult. The cylinder may be of the same materials as those mentioned for the lift pump. The porcelain-lined cylinder is commonly used for pumping salt water, milk, etc.

The *single-action force pump*, one style of which is shown in Fig. 116, differs from the lift pump in that the standard is enlarged into an air-chamber, and the plunger rod works through a stuffing-box in the top of this chamber. The action of this pump is quite different from that of the lift pump. As the water is forced upward by the up stroke of the plunger, a part of it goes out through the delivery spout, while a part acts to compress air in the air-chamber. Then, on the down stroke of the plunger, this air expands and drives the water out through the spout. With reasonably fast pumping, a steady stream is maintained; and since the top of the standard is closed, the water may be delivered against considerable pressure, a characteristic of the pump which gives rise to the term " force pump."

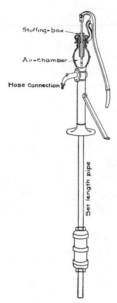

Fig. 116. A simple type of single-action force pump

At times, when all of the leathers are new and the stuffing-box is air-tight and water-tight, the air-chamber loses its effectiveness because of the fact that the water dissolves, or absorbs, the air, and so the chamber becomes filled with water. There is usually a plug in the chamber which may be screwed out to permit the chamber to fill with air. The packing around the plunger rod will need to be renewed occasionally, and the box must be screwed down at intervals as the packing wears. The air-chamber on this pump may be entirely separate from the pump standard and attached to the delivery spout by a short length of pipe. This arrangement is often seen in cistern pumps where the water is forced to an attic tank. One advantage in this type of pump lies in the fact that if a large air-chamber is needed, as when pumping the water to a considerable height or when pumping against high pressure of any kind, the chamber best adapted to the work to be done may be attached. This type of pump will cost about two dollars more than a common lift pump similarly equipped.

A *double-action force pump* is shown in Fig. 117. It will be noticed that this pump has two cylinders, a sectional view of which is shown in Fig. 118. In addition to the two cylinders there are the delivery pipe and the pipe forming part of the pump standard, which is used as an air-chamber. The action of the pump may be seen by referring to Fig. 118. On the up stroke of the plunger, water is drawn into the main cylinder by the action heretofore described. On the down stroke this water is transferred to the upper part of the lower cylinder. On the following up stroke (Fig. 118, *a*), while the lower part of the main cylinder is filling with water from below, the water above the lower plunger is being forced partly into the delivery pipe, partly into the secondary cylinder, and partly into the air-chamber. On the next down stroke (Fig. 118, *b*) the plunger

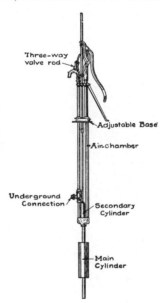

FIG. 117. A double-action force pump

in the secondary cylinder is forcing its contents out through the delivery pipe. At the instant between strokes the air in the air-chamber is permitted to expand and force still more water out of the delivery pipe. Thus it is seen that water is forced out through the delivery pipe on both the up stroke and the down stroke of the plunger; hence the name "double-action pump." It should be noted, however, that water is drawn from the well only on the up stroke of the plunger, the same as in a common lift pump. The term "double-action" is used here as opposed to the term "double-acting," which will be used later in connection with a type of pump that draws water from the source of supply at each stroke of the handle.

The secondary cylinder is usually one half the volume of the main cylinder, so that on the up stroke approximately one half the water enters the upper cylinder, and the greater part of the rest goes out through the delivery pipe. The presence of this upper cylinder makes this type a positive force pump, whereas the type just described as a single-action force pump is not positive, but relies entirely on the alternate compression and expansion of the air in the air-chamber to secure a steady flow.

As shown in Fig. 117, the secondary cylinder in this particular type is placed at a set length below the platform, usually five feet. The lower cylinder may be any distance below the upper cylinder, it being necessary only to lengthen the pipe and the plunger rod. This pump is adapted, then, to wells of any depth. In many cases the lower cylinder is placed beneath the water; in such a position the valve leathers never dry out and priming is never necessary.

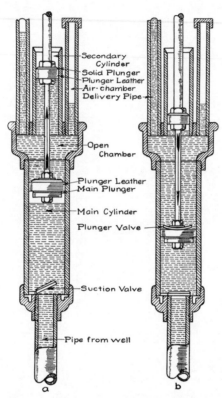

Secondary Cylinder
Solid Plunger
Plunger Leather
Air-chamber
Delivery Pipe

Open Chamber

Plunger Leather
Main Plunger

Main Cylinder

Plunger Valve

Suction Valve

Pipe from well

a   b

FIG. 118. Illustrating the operation of a double-action force pump

All of the piping, including the air-chamber which forms the standard of the pump, may be of either galvanized iron or black wrought iron. The galvanized-iron piping is slightly the more expensive, adding about 50 cents to the cost of the pump with set-length pipes, but it is considered to be worth the extra cost. The size of the pipe varies with the depth of the well and with the size of the cylinder. For less than 30 ft. in depth a $3\frac{1}{2}$-inch cylinder and a $1\frac{1}{2}$-inch pipe is used ; from 30 ft. to 40 ft. in depth, a 3-inch cylinder and a $1\frac{1}{4}$-inch pipe ; from 40 ft. to 50 ft. in depth, a $2\frac{1}{2}$-inch cylinder and a 1-inch pipe. Some manufacturers use a 1-inch pipe for nearly all conditions. A $2\frac{1}{2}$-inch lower cylinder is usually fitted with a $1\frac{1}{2}$-inch upper cylinder, and a $3\frac{1}{2}$-inch lower cylinder with a 2-inch upper cylinder.

The pump shown in Fig. 117 is fitted with an adjustable base. This is a decided advantage when the position of the set length is fixed, since no exact cutting of pipe is necessary in order to make a fixed base meet the platform properly. The eccentric lever on the pump spout controls a three-way valve at the point where the underground-pipe connection is made, so that water may be forced underground or delivered at the spout. Many of these force pumps are so made that it

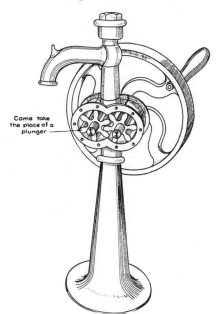

FIG. 119. Showing the construction of a simple hand-operated rotary pump

is possible, by unscrewing a cap at the base of the upper cylinder, to remove the plungers of both cylinders without disconnecting any of the pipes, provided the pump is in a shallow well and the lower cylinder attached directly to the set-length pipes.

The rotary pump. The rotary pump, one type of which is shown in Fig. 119, operates on the same principle as the plunger pump, with each tooth of the gears, or cams, acting as a piston. The parts are made of iron or bronze. The cams are usually well fitted and work with little friction. This pump is particularly adapted to lifting dirty water for irrigation purposes, since sand or other foreign matter does not readily interfere with its operation. It is not commonly used as a well pump, yet on lifts not exceeding 25 ft. it is very efficient, requires little power, and will work against a pressure of from 10 lb. to 50 lb., which is equivalent to a head of from 23 ft. to 115 ft. The capacity of such a type as shown in Fig. 119 varies from 5 gal. to 12 gal. per minute when the pump is operated at the rate of about 50 revolutions per minute. The cost of a pump of hand size made of iron is about $12 ; if it is made of bronze the cost is about $20.

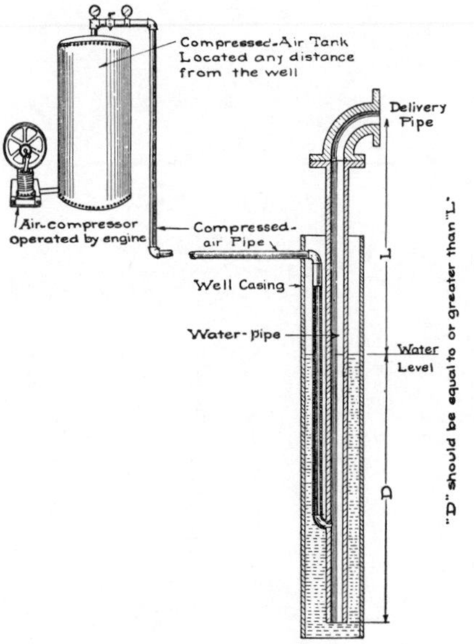

FIG. 120. Illustrating the principle of the air-lift pump

The air-lift pump. The air-lift pump is adapted to use in wells where the total height to which the water is to be lifted above the surface of the water in the well is not more — preferably less — than the depth of the water in the well. The principle upon which this pump acts is illustrated in Fig. 120. Here is shown an ordinary drilled well with a 4-inch casing. Within this casing is lowered a $1\frac{1}{2}$-inch casing, and just outside of the $1\frac{1}{2}$-inch casing is lowered another pipe $\frac{3}{4}$ in. in diameter which enters the $1\frac{1}{2}$-inch casing near the bottom. When compressed air is turned into the $\frac{3}{4}$-inch pipe, it flows into the water-pipe ; and since the pressure at the base of this pipe is exactly the same outside as inside, the compressed air, which enters the pipe a short distance above the bottom, tends to rise and forces up a column of water above it. The passage of the air upward creates a suction, another column of water flows in to fill the space, and a column of air falls in behind it, forcing it to the top of the pipe. Thus, there are alternate layers of water and air rising in the pipe as long as the air continues to enter at the desired pressure, giving rise frequently to an intermittent flow at the point of delivery. It is seen that there are no moving parts, nothing but ordinary pipes in the well. Sand, gravel, etc. will not interfere with its action. It is usually not desirable to attempt a lift of more than 200 ft. nor to carry the water more than 800 ft. horizontally, although some manufacturers say that there is almost no limit to the horizontal distance.

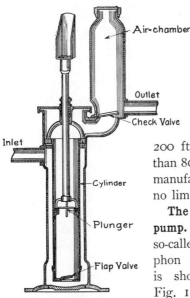

FIG. 121. Illustrating the principle of the so-called "siphon pump"

The siphon pump. The so-called " siphon pump " is shown in Fig. 121. It is used particularly where the pump cannot be set directly over the well. It works on the same principle as the single-action force pump, with the exceptions that the cylinder and the plunger in the siphon pump are below the inlet pipe, the air-chamber is set off to one side, and the water enters through a flap valve. The chamber around the cylinder is always filled with water ; hence the valve leathers are always kept moist. The term " siphon " arises from the fact that the water enters the chamber around the cylinder above the suction valve and hence the water flows upward into the cylinder.

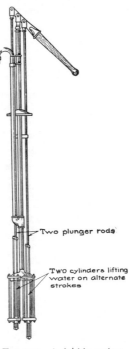

FIG. 122. A double-acting well pump

Double-acting pump. In Fig. 122 is shown a true double-acting pump. This pump has two cylinders. One lifts water from the well on the up stroke of the handle, the other on the down stroke. It is not much used in ordinary pumping except when the pump is operated by a windmill or by a gasoline engine. A modification of this pump is used on spraying-outfits where a high pressure must be maintained.

Windmill pumps. Almost any of the pumps shown in this chapter may be connected to a windmill. However, in Fig. 123 is shown a pump that is especially adapted for use with a windmill, as it is designed to throw the windmill into gear and out of gear automatically.

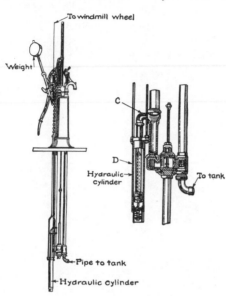

FIG. 123. A windmill pump with a hydraulic cylinder

As the tank into which the water is flowing fills, a float is made to close a valve in the pipe leading to the tank, upon which the water is forced into the hydraulic cylinder *D* through pipe *C*, Fig. 123. This forces the outer casing of this cylinder down and draws the wire leading to the wheel down, throwing the mill out of gear. At

FIG. 124. A dug well with a windlass and a concrete curb

Simple and old-fashioned, but the water is pure and cold

the same time the weight is raised. As the water in the tank is lowered, the valve in the water-pipe will gradually open and allow the water to flow into the tank, the hydraulic cylinder will resume its original position, and the weight will pull the mill back into gear. This feature is especially desirable if the well is at a considerable distance from the house. There is no reason why it should not operate in a satisfactory manner for several years if the float is kept in order and so protected that the stock cannot interfere with its action. A safety plug is provided in the bottom of the hydraulic cylinder which, in case any part of the device should fail to work, will be blown out and thus will prevent any material damage to the pump.

CHAPTER XIII

WINDMILLS

The windmill is now used almost exclusively in the operation of pumps, though its usefulness is not confined entirely to this work. Since it makes use of the wind as a motive power, it is unquestionably one of the most economical machines available within its more or less limited field. The small gasoline engine

FIG. 125. Showing the gears of a back-geared windmill

The strain comes between 2 bearings

is its only competitor, and elsewhere in this text the two are compared as to their value in pumping water. Though already in use in very large numbers, the windmill should be more common, because it is a real labor-saver and within the reach of nearly all farmers.

The tower. The modern tower upon which the wheel is erected is a 3-post or 4-post tower made of galvanized angle steel. The 4-post structure is to be preferred as offering a better support for the wheel, though it is slightly more expensive than the 3-post tower. Wood towers, though once common, are seldom used now. The height of the tower varies from 10 ft. to 100 ft. It should be high enough to raise the wheel above the level of all objects such as buildings, windbreaks, and hills, within 500 ft. of the mill. A clear and unobstructed sweep of the wind is essential to the mill's proper operation.

The *foundation* of the tower posts should be of concrete. Footings for the posts are furnished, and they should be set at least five feet in the ground, with the holes into which they are placed filled with concrete. If the footings are not provided with broad steel bases, the posts should be anchored to rods placed across the holes and covered with concrete.

FIG. 126. Showing gears at the end of the shaft

The strain comes on the end of the shaft which has only one bearing

The wheel. The wheel consists of a steel framework upon which are mounted the sails, which may be of either wood or steel, the latter being most generally used. The sails are set at an angle to the plane of the wheel. This angle varies from twenty to thirty degrees and is known as the *angle of weather.* There is a wide variation in the width of sail, though the wider sail, measuring some twelve inches, seems to be more generally used.

A *rudder*, or vane, is nearly always provided, its purpose being to keep the plane of the wheel perpendicular to the direction of the wind, thus realizing the greatest force possible from the wind's velocity. If the wheel has no rudder, the sails are so constructed as to present automatically a greater or less surface to the wind, this surface varying with the wind's velocity.

Gears. The shaft of the wheel must be supported upon long, well-constructed bear-

FIG. 127. Windmill having a bent crank and a rocker arm instead of gears

Note the brake around the end wheel

ings, to take the strain and weight of the wheel properly. Motion is transmitted from the shaft to the pump rod either directly, through a pitman-wheel connection, when it is known as a *direct-connected* mill, or indirectly, through spur gears, when it is known

as a *back-geared* mill. As the latter term signifies, the speed of the wheel is reduced, the ratio varying from 1 : 1 to 1 : 5. The purpose in back-gearing a mill is to permit the wheel to revolve more rapidly and still not operate the pump at more than thirty or forty strokes per minute. In the direct-connected mill the wheel must be so governed as to be

FIG. 128. Showing the construction and the operation of the governor on a windmill

thrown out of gear when only a moderate speed is reached, else the pump will be ruined by too rapid working. The back-geared wheel, because of its possible higher speed, is capable of

developing more power than the direct-connected type, though the latter will pump faster in light breezes.

Fig. 125 shows a back-geared mill with liberal bearings on either side of the gears, with the pump rod between. This represents good construction and is superior in this respect to most direct-connected mills, where the strain all comes on the end of the shaft (Fig. 126).

FIG. 129. Enlarged view of the brake wheel and the brake-wheel band shown in Fig. 128

Note the adjustment for the brake band, also the large oil cups

Governing the wheel. Since a pump should not be operated at a faster rate than forty strokes per minute, it is very necessary to have some device on the wheel that will keep the speed within a proper limit. Such a device is called a governor and operates in such a way as to turn the wheel toward or away from the plane perpendicular to the wind's

FIG. 130. An automatic windmill-regulator operated by a float

velocity, thus exposing more or less surface to the driving force of the wind.

During a high wind, when the wheel tends to turn into a plane parallel to the wind's direction and thus to be thrown out of gear, the governor, usually a long coiled spring, operates to hold the wheel toward the wind at a proper angle to secure the desired speed. The tension of this spring can usually be controlled so as to regulate the speed to the work which the mill has to do. In Fig. 128 the lower cut shows the rudder in a position to hold the wheel in a plane at right angles to the wind's direction. As the velocity of the wind increases the wheel tends to turn toward the rudder, thus placing the coiled spring under tension as shown in the upper figure. As the velocity of the wind decreases the coiled spring draws the wheel back into the wind.

A *brake*, usually in the form of a steel band surrounding the rim of one of the gears (Fig. 129), locks the wheel when it is out of gear so there will be no movement of wheel or pump. Automatic *regulators* may be attached to any mill by means of which, through a float connection with a near-by tank, it may be automatically thrown out of gear when the tank is filled and thrown in gear

FIG. 131. The head of a power windmill, showing driving gears

when the water in the tank is lowered. The regulator of Fig. 130 operates as follows: The arm of the ratchet wheel is attached to

the pump rod shown on the left, the vertical wire passes around the ratchet reel and up to the rudder. The horizontal wire (at the top) is connected to the float in the tank. When the tank is empty the float is down, the weighted lever is up, and the dogs are held out of engagement with the ratchet wheel. As the float rises in the tank the weighted lever drops and the dogs are permitted to engage the ratchet wheel. This wheel, then, operated by the pump rod throws the mill out of gear. As soon as the float is lowered the mill is permitted to be drawn into gear.

FIG. 132. The pump connections and line-shaft connections of a power mill

Power from windmills. The power to be derived from a windmill depends directly upon the force of the wind impinging upon the sails of the wheel. Since the force of the wind varies as the square of the velocity and since the amount striking the wheel varies directly as the velocity, theoretically the power of the wheel should vary as the cube of the wind's velocity, the size of the wheel remaining the same. For wheels of different diameters, then, the power developed should vary as the cube of

FIG. 133. A vaneless wheel

The wind blows from the side of the vane arm, and the force of a high wind on the ends of the sails closes the wheel. The weight opens the wheel as the velocity of the wind decreases

the wind's velocity and as the square of the diameter of the wheel, since surfaces vary as the square of like dimensions.

Smeaton's experiments seemed to show this to be the case, but later tests indicate that in practice the power varies as the square of the velocity of the wind and as one and one-fourth times the diameter of the wheel. The latter ratio is, quite naturally, cut down in the larger wheels because of the heavier construction necessary to withstand the added strain.

FIG. 134. Raising a windmill by means of a tackle

The mill was assembled on the ground and raised by hand to the height shown

The following table is given as a basis of judgment as to the power a windmill may be expected to develop. The accuracy of the figures is not vouched for, but they represent the claims of a reliable company, and a comparison with dependable tests seems to show that they are not far from the truth — near enough, at any rate, for all practical purposes.

TABLE XIX. POWER OF WINDMILLS FOR WHEELS OF DIFFERENT
SIZES AND FOR DIFFERENT WIND VELOCITIES

Wind Velocity per Hour, in Miles	Size of Windmill							
	4¾ ft.	6 ft.	8 ft.	9 ft.	10 ft.	12 ft.	14 ft.	16 ft.
6	0.010	0.020	0.047	0.067	0.092	0.16	0.25	0.38
8	0.018	0.035	0.084	0.120	0.164	0.28	0.45	0.67
10	0.027	0.055	0.132	0.187	0.257	0.44	0.70	1.05
12	0.040	0.069	0.189	0.270	0.370	0.64	1.02	1.52
15	0.060	0.125	0.296	0.420	0.580	1.00	1.58	2.37
20	0.110	0.220	0.530	0.750	1.030	1.78	2.82	4.21
25	0.160	0.350	0.820	1.170	1.610	2.78	4.41	6.58

For pumping purposes the 6-foot and 8-foot wheels are the most common. On the basis of pumping at the rate of 5 gal. per minute, which is a reasonable rate, through a vertical lift of 100 ft., a theoretical horse power of 0.12 would be required. Doubling this to get the working horse power required, gives 0.25, which, according to the above table, would require an 8-foot wheel and a 15-mile wind. These figures accord with common practice.

Use of the windmill. As before mentioned, the use of the windmill is confined almost exclusively to the pumping of water.

For this purpose it is fairly reliable if sufficient storage is provided when live stock is kept. Sufficient water should be stored to last at least three days.

The windmill is used in a limited way for grinding feed and for running machines,

FIG. 135. Method of arranging ropes

This view is just to the right of that shown in Fig. 134

such as grindstones, lathes, shellers, etc., if one is prepared to do the work when the wind is blowing. It has been used in a few instances for running a dynamo to generate an electric current, but difficulty in maintaining a uniform speed will probably prevent its wide use in this way. For small power purposes it never will successfully compete with the gasoline engine.

Care of the windmill. While the windmill needs but little care and attention, it needs that little very much. Lubrication is the one thing that should not be neglected. The automatic oilers provided with the better mills should be regularly filled. A few mills

FIG. 136. The mill erected

are now so made that the gears run in an oil bath. All nuts in the framework and the wheel should be kept tight.

CHAPTER XIV

THE HYDRAULIC RAM

In all sections of the country where a rolling topography prevails, many springs are to be found near farmsteads, but situated at a level considerably below that of the buildings. Frequently the only source of water for the house is just such a spring, and too often the duty of carrying the daily supply falls on the women of the household. Or it may be that at some distance from the barn there is a stream of relatively pure water flowing in abundance and that the water of this stream could be profitably used in barns or yards if the water could be easily and economically got to them. The hydraulic ram, which is serviceable in just such situations as these, may be described as a type of pump or engine which utilizes the power derived from a large part of the water of a flowing stream to lift a small part of this water and deliver it at some point above the level of the stream itself and at some distance from it if desired.

The essential parts. The essential parts of a hydraulic ram are shown in Fig. 137, which is a diagrammatic cross section of a ram. The base G of the ram affords the framework on which the other parts are built and receives the water from the supply pipe A, which connects with the spring or other source of supply. The air-chamber C is mounted on the base,

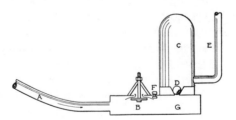

FIG. 137. Diagrammatic section of a hydraulic ram

with the check valve D connecting the two. Leading from the air-chamber is the delivery pipe E, connecting with the point of discharge. The waste valve B leads from the base and, in its natural position, is open, as shown. At F is a small snifting valve, which opens inward from outside pressure at a certain phase of each stroke. There are only three moving parts about a ram — the waste valve, the snifting valve, and the check valve. There are several types of valves, some of which will be shown later. Many rams do not have the snifting valve.

The operation. The operation of the ram is as follows: The water from the spring or other source of supply flows down the pipe A, which is laid with considerable fall, and entering the chamber G flows out through the waste valve B, which is open. This flowing water soon attains a considerable momentum, and, pushing up on the waste valve, closes it. The escape here being suddenly shut off, the water lifts the check valve D and enters the chamber C. As the flow into C continues, the air in the chamber is compressed. Soon the pressure overbalances the force of the incoming water and the flow ceases. Just at this point there is a rebound, or backward surge, in the base of the ram and in the supply pipe, as there is when one object strikes another. At this instant the pressure below the waste valve is sufficiently decreased to permit it to open and allow the supply water to escape. Flow past the waste valve will continue until there is sufficient force to close the valve; then the above action is repeated. The operation is entirely automatic, and gives an intermittent flow at the point of delivery, the intermittency corresponding to the cycles, or beats, of the waste valve.

The general installation. The general conditions required for the successful installation of the ram are set forth in Fig. 138. The ram itself is placed some distance down the stream from the source of supply and usually in a pit A, as shown. The supply water comes from the pool shown at B, through the supply pipe C. The length of this pipe, which must be laid with considerable fall, must bear a definite relation to the height to which the water is to be lifted, and its size must be proportionate to the amount of water available and to the size of the ram used. The delivery pipe E, which leads to the point of delivery, be it an elevated tank at the barn, a watering-trough, or a tank in the kitchen sink, bears a definite relation in size to the supply pipe. The vertical and horizontal length of the delivery pipe is limited by the total fall of the supply pipe, the amount of water available, and the amount desired at the point of delivery.

The source of supply. As before noted, the water to operate the ram must come from a flowing stream, a spring, or an artesian well. Whatever the source of supply, there must be a basin constructed in which a constant supply of water may be maintained. If a spring furnishes the supply it is usually a simple matter to build a containing-basin of brick or concrete. A barrel or a twenty-four-inch sewer-pipe tile, sunk below the surface, will furnish an adequate chamber; or an earth bank may be thrown up and made

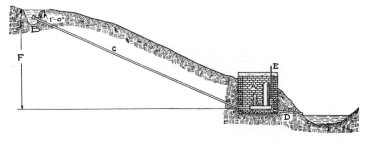

FIG. 138. Showing the requirements for the installation of a ram

to hold a sufficient supply, but the earth bank is not so permanent and does not afford adequate protection to the water.

If a stream furnishes the supply, care must be taken to protect from overflows the basin from which the supply is taken, as sediment and trash are likely to be washed in. In this case it is well to build a containing-basin to one side of the stream and to connect the two by a short line of tile or pipe. The basin can then be covered, and high water does not interfere with the operation of the ram. In the case of flowing wells it is possible to connect the supply pipe directly to the casing of the well by suitable connections, forcing the entire flow through the ram. If the water is delivered from the well under considerable force, this force is equivalent to a head equal to the distance the water would rise in a standpipe, and the ram may be placed near the well and on a level with it. The essential feature in all cases is to maintain a constant supply which will not become sufficiently roiled to permit silt or sand to enter the pipe.

The supply pipe. The supply pipe should be laid on an even grade from the basin to the ram, without bends or elbows except where it enters the ram base. Here the pipe should be bent on a smooth curve, no connections being used. The mouth of the pipe should be placed at least one foot below low-water level in the basin. This is necessary to prevent air from entering the pipe and stopping the ram. The end of the pipe should be further protected by a strainer, or screen, to keep out sand and sediment. The length of the supply pipe should be just about equal to the vertical height to which the water is to be lifted; that is, if the water is lifted to a tank 40 ft. above the ram, the length of the supply pipe running from the basin to the ram should be

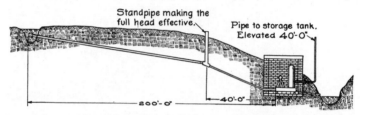

Standpipe making the full head effective.

Pipe to storage tank. Elevated 40'-0"

200'-0" 40'-0"

FIG. 139. Showing how the total head may be realized when the ram is at a considerable distance from the spring

40 ft. In cases of short lifts, however, the length of the supply pipe should not be less than from eight to ten times the total fall, where the fall is 5 ft. or less. For example, if the water is to be delivered to a height of 15 ft., by the rule stated above, a drive pipe 15 ft. long would be required. However, this is not sufficient for a fall of 5 ft. or less. If the fall were 5 ft., the drive pipe should be 8 × 5, or 40 ft. long.

In many installations it will be found necessary to go downstream quite a distance from the supply basin in order to secure the proper fall. Suppose, for example, it becomes necessary to go a distance of 200 ft. downstream in order to secure a fall of 4 ft. The total lift is to be, say, 40 ft. Proper regulations would call for a drive pipe 40 ft. long. Now if the flow from the spring is small, too much of the force due to the total head would be used up in friction arising from the passage through the 200 ft. of pipe, so that the effective head at the ram would be very much less than 4 ft. — so much less, in fact, that the ram would not operate. This difficulty is overcome by a device such as that shown in Fig. 139. In the instance above referred to, the standpipe would be connected to the supply pipe at the proper distance, 40 ft., from the ram. The water rises in this pipe to the same level as the water in the spring, thus giving the full force of the total head to the operation of the ram. This stand-pipe may be a short pipe a little larger than the supply pipe and connected to it by a T-connection, or it may be a barrel sunk in the ground with the supply pipe from it to the ram con-nected in the ordinary way. The pipe from the spring to the standpipe should be somewhat larger than the drive pipe proper.

The size of the supply pipe is governed by the flow of the spring and by the quantity of water it is desired to deliver. The smallest size that it is desirable to use is $\frac{3}{4}$-inch pipe; it is found on No. 2 rams, which require from 2 to 3 gal. per minute to operate them. For ordinary farm purposes the largest size is usually 2 in.; it is found on No. 6 rams, which require from 5 to 12 gal. per minute to operate them. A gate valve should be placed in this line next to the ram so that the water may be turned off in case the ram needs repairs.

The fall. The fall, or head, is the difference between the level of the feed water and the point at which it enters the ram, and is designated by F in Fig. 138. As a general rule this should be 1 ft. for each 7 ft. of vertical rise in the discharge pipe, with a minimum fall of from 2 to 3 ft. no matter how small the vertical lift. This fall too should not greatly exceed the maximum required by the lift, as an undue strain will be put upon the ram.

The delivery pipe. The delivery, or discharge, pipe shown at E in Fig. 138 is usually one half the diameter of the supply pipe. This pipe is laid according to the rules for laying all water-pipes, that is, with as few elbows and turns as possible, because each elbow increases the friction in the pipe and cuts down the total efficiency of the ram. It may be laid on a gradual incline, as is usually the case; it may extend horizontally the desired distance and then rise vertically; or, it may first rise vertically and then extend horizontally to the desired place. In case of extremely high lifts or long horizontal distances this pipe should be made larger than one half the diameter of the supply pipe in order to reduce friction. A gate valve should be placed in this line next to the air-chamber.

The pit. The ram is usually placed in a pit built of bricks or concrete. This is done chiefly as a protection in freezing weather. The pit may be covered with a concrete or plank covering, and if the weather becomes very severe, additional protection, such as corn fodder, horse manure, etc., may be provided. In this way the operation of the ram is not interfered with in the least by cold weather.

Frequently, if the fall is slight, an increase may be secured by placing the ram in a pit and then providing a drain, Fig. 138, D, for taking care of the waste water. If the pit were not provided, it would be necessary to go so far downstream that the increased friction in the pipe would more than equal the head gained. The drain for the waste water is, of course, necessary, whatever the purpose for which the ram is placed in a pit.

The valves. As before stated, the waste valve and the check valve represent the only moving parts about the ram. The snifting valve is, of course, a moving part, but so little wear is occasioned by its action that it may be disregarded so far as wear is concerned.

The *waste valve* is frequently made of iron throughout and rests on an iron seat as well. This sort of valve is efficient and wears well, but is rather noisy, and for that reason is not desirable if the ram is located where noise might be an objection. Other valves are leather-covered or rubber-covered. This decreases the noise materially and, though the wear is more rapid, the parts are cheaply replaced. Fig. 140, b, shows the construction of a rubber-covered valve. In Fig. 140 the waste valve is seen to hang from an arm pivoted near the middle, at P, and working on an adjustable bolt at O, where the length of the vertical lift of the valve may be controlled. The full vertical travel is about one inch. Tests have been made which show that the highest efficiency is reached when the working stroke is about 60 per cent of the full vertical lift of the valve. The weight W on the arm supporting the valve is adjustable; it may be so moved as to increase or decrease the force required to close the valve and hence increase or decrease the frequency of the cycle. The proper adjustment of this weight, as well as the length of the stroke, depends upon the quantity of water passing through the ram and upon the quantity of water desired at the point of delivery. An adjustment should be made that will permit a smooth, steady stroke. The more frequent the strokes, the less the amount of water delivered; and conversely, the slower the beat, the more water delivered.

The *check valve* leading to the air-chamber may, like the waste valve, be of iron throughout, or it may be covered with leather or rubber. There is not so much wear on this valve as on the waste valve, but it should be easily accessible in case it needs replacing.

The *snifting valve* (Fig. 137, *F*) is for the purpose of keeping the air-chamber supplied with the proper amount of air. When water is forced into the air-chamber against considerable pressure a certain amount of air is absorbed. If additional air is not supplied in some way, the water soon fills the chamber completely, and the chamber fails to serve the purpose for which it was intended — that of equalizing the flow at the point of delivery. The snifting valve is placed close to the check valve and in the base of the ram, opening to the outside. At each backward surge of the water, as previously explained, a partial vacuum is created; the result is that a small amount of air is drawn through this valve and at the next impulse is carried into the air-chamber. Thus the air supply is automatically controlled.

Starting the ram. After the ram is installed and before any pipes are covered, all pipes in the system should be filled with water and tests made for leaks. After the system has been tested and the pipes covered, the supply pipe should be opened; water will at once begin to flow through the waste valve. This valve should then be operated by hand, with regular beats at the rate of about fifty per minute, until the ram and all the pipes are filled; then the valve should begin to operate automatically. When the ram is new this valve is likely to stick occasionally and may need close attention for a few days.

Ram troubles. If the ram ceases to operate, several things may be at fault. If the water in the supply basin has fallen below the mouth of the supply pipe, permitting air to enter the ram, action will cease, and the ram must be started by hand. If silt or sand gets into the ram the valves may not seat properly, and the ram either will cease to work or will work imperfectly. The ram should be thoroughly flushed and both valves and valve seats cleaned. The valves may become so worn as to fail to hold properly. In this case the ram will begin to work imperfectly and finally will stop altogether. New valves should be put in. If the snifting valve is not working properly or if there is none, as is sometimes the case, the air-chamber will fill with water, and the ram will then cease to operate. In such a case the air-chamber should be drained by a plug usually provided for that purpose, and allowed to fill with air, after which the ram should be started by hand. If no plug is provided, it will be necessary to remove the air-chamber and allow it to fill with air. The supply pipe will sometimes become so filled with foreign substances, such as an incrustation on the walls, that the flow is decreased and the ram stops. This, however, does not often happen.

The size of the ram. The size of the ram is governed by the flow of the spring or other source of supply and by the amount of water desired at the point of delivery. Table XX, which is furnished by a reliable pump company, gives the sizes adapted to ordinary farm use, together with the proper size for supply and delivery pipes and the quantity of water required for operation. While the number given to each size may be taken as a standard, yet a ram of the same size may be differently numbered by different companies. The quantity of water required to operate the ram should be the guide to size.

TABLE XX. THE SIZE OF RAMS, THE QUANTITY OF WATER REQUIRED, AND THE SIZE OF SUPPLY AND OF DELIVERY PIPES

Size of Ram	Water to operate, in Gallons per Minute	Size of Pipe		Weight in Pounds	Approximate Price
		Supply pipe	Delivery pipe		
No. 2	2–3	$\frac{3}{4}$ in.	$\frac{1}{2}$ in.	27	$6.00
No. 3	2–4	1 in.	$\frac{1}{2}$ in.	35	8.00
No. 4	3–7	$1\frac{1}{4}$ in.	$\frac{3}{4}$ in.	53	11.00
No. 5	6–12	2 in.	1 in.	94	18.00

Efficiency of the ram. As was said in the beginning of this chapter, the hydraulic ram uses the power derived from a large part of the water of a flowing stream to lift a small part of the water to some point above. The quantity of water lifted varies directly with the fall. That is, with a fall of 4 ft., approximately twice as much water will be delivered to a given height as with a fall of 2 ft. Further, the quantity delivered varies inversely as the height to which it is to be raised. That is, other things being equal, if 6 gal. per minute are delivered to a height of 10 ft., 3 gal. would be delivered to a height of 20 ft. and 2 gal. would be delivered to a height of 30 ft.

The last two statements are made on the theoretical basis that if the fall is doubled, twice as much power will be available ; and that hence twice as much water will be delivered provided the height of lift remains the same. On the other hand, if the fall remains the same, the same power is available, so that if the lift is doubled, trebled, etc., the quantity lifted will be decreased by one half, one third, etc. Practical results will not vary greatly from these rules, but there are limitations, of course, beyond which a ram will not work.

As a working rule, a ram can be counted upon to lift to a reasonable height only from one tenth to one seventh of the total quantity delivered to the ram. Table XXI gives the relation that should exist between the length of supply and discharge pipes and the minimum quantity of water required to operate the specified sizes under the fall indicated, together with the quantity that will be delivered, the specifications being those at which the ram will reach its highest efficiency.

TABLE XXI. SPECIFICATIONS FOR THE INSTALLATION OF RAMS OF DIFFERENT SIZES

Size of ram	Height of delivery, in feet	Fall in feet	Length of supply pipe, in feet	Supply, in gallons, per minute	Amount delivered, in gallons per hour
No. 2	20	3	30	2–3	10–15
No. 3	30	4	30	2–4	10–20
No. 4	40	5	40	3–7	15–35
No. 5	50	7	50	6–12	30–60
No. 6	60	8	60	11–20	55–100
No. 8	100	14	100	30–60	150–300

By the aid of Tables XX and XXI it is possible to select the proper size of ram for any condition, as well as the proper size of supply and delivery pipes. If, for example, a spring flows 4 gal. per minute and it is desired to lift the water vertically 40 ft. under a 5 ft. fall, by turning to Table XX one can see that either ram No. 3 or No. 4 will operate on this amount. From Table XXI it is seen that ram No. 3 works most efficiently at a lift of 30 ft. and that ram No. 4 gives the highest efficiency at a 40-foot lift. It is clear, therefore, that, although the No. 3 ram will work, a No. 4 should be chosen. Table XX shows that the No. 4 ram calls for a $1\frac{1}{4}$-inch drive pipe and a $\frac{3}{4}$-inch delivery pipe, and from Table XXI it will be seen that a ram of this size will deliver about 20 gal. per hour.

The second column in Table XXI, giving the height of delivery for each size, does not represent the maximum height to which these sizes will lift the water. It is never advisable, however, to use the very small sizes for high lifts.

While it may seem, at first thought, that a spring flowing, say, 3 gal. per minute will not supply an adequate amount for house and barn use if only one tenth of it can be delivered, yet the fact that the flow is constant, day in and day out, through the year should not be forgotten. For instance, the above-mentioned flow means 21.6 bbl. of 50 gal. each, or more than 1000 gal., per day.

Life and utility of the ram. There is practically no limit to the life of a ram. The moving parts are easily and cheaply replaceable. In many cases rams have given continuous service for over twenty years. The ram may be installed to lift water into an elevated tank at the house or barn or into a pneumatic tank if the lift is not too great. In this case it should be remembered that in pumping against the pressure of a pneumatic tank 2.3 ft. should be added to the vertical lift for each pound of pressure registered by the tank gauge. For example, if it is desired to force water into the tank until the gauge shows 25 lb., it would be necessary to make allowance for a lift equivalent to 2.3 times 25, or 57.5 ft., in addition to the lift from the ram to the tank. Near Dayton, Ohio, there is an installation where a ram pumps water into a pneumatic tank maintaining a pressure of 70 lb. When this pressure is reached, a safety valve is

released and the water flows away through a waste pipe. The
spring supplying this ram is of course a very strong one.

The ram may also be used to lift water into a small tank on
the kitchen sink, from which it may flow to the milk-house, to
troughs at the barn, etc. Though it is possible to stop the ram at
any time by holding the waste valve shut for a short time, it is
better to let it run continuously if the water is available. If, however, it is necessary to stop the ram, a wire for such purpose may
be attached to the waste
valve and the valve ma-
nipulated from the house.

The double-acting ram.
It frequently happens that
a spring flowing such a
small amount of water
that it would not operate
a ram under the usual
conditions is located close
beside a stream the water
from which is not fit for
human consumption. The
double-acting ram is de-
signed to make use of the
water in such a stream to
lift practically all of the
water from the spring to
the desired height. A section of such a ram is
shown in Fig. 140 and a

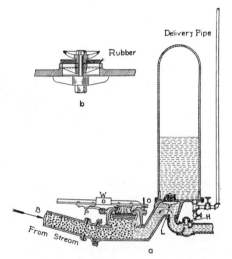

Fig. 140. A sectional view of a double-
acting ram

The check valve is shown enlarged at *b*. The stream
water fills the space covered by the heavy dots; the
remaining space is filled with spring water

complete installation in Fig. 141. The water from the basin,
which is supplied by the stream, flows down the supply pipe *B*
and operates the ram exactly as heretofore described, considering
the valve at *H*, Fig. 140, closed. The pipe *D*, Fig. 141, should be
laid to a fall of not more than two feet; if the fall is more than
this or if the spring is at some distance from the ram, a standpipe
E should be erected next to the ram. If this is made the proper
height, any excess fall is eliminated, and any undue friction is
overcome. Water must rise in the standpipe at least two feet.

Now after the ram has begun to operate on the stream water it will be seen that at the time of the backward surge which occurs during each beat of the ram, just following the time when the check valve (L, Fig. 140) closes, a small amount of spring water enters this partial vacuum, forced in, in part, by the two-foot head. On the next beat of the ram this spring water, being next to the main check valve leading into the air-chamber, and

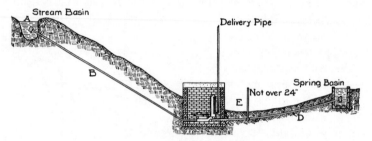

FIG. 141. Details of installation of a double-acting ram

being held by the check valve H in the spring-water supply pipe, is forced up into the air-chamber. On the closing of the main check valve this action is repeated. Undoubtedly some of the spring water escapes through the waste valve, as shown in the figure; but the amount thus escaping is very slight and nearly all of the spring water is lifted to the point of delivery.

Only a few companies manufacture double-acting rams. One of the largest hydraulic-ram companies, however, claims that 25 per cent of its business is with this kind of ram. They are slightly more expensive than the single-acting type.

CHAPTER XV

POWER FROM STREAMS

In the rolling sections of the United States there are many streams, some large, some small, which are flowing under conditions that would make it possible for them to develop a considerable amount of power if properly harnessed. It is the purpose of this chapter to discuss conditions which must exist before power installations are possible and to refer to the various water-wheels commonly used in farm installations.

Source of power of a stream. A stream is capable of developing power because of the fact that its head, or fall, causes its water to flow at a certain velocity. In the usual installations a dam is built across the stream, and the water is confined and made to flow over the dam or through a side channel or mill race in which the flow may be controlled. The head is the distance from the level of the water above the dam to the level of the water below the dam.

How to determine flow and head. In order to determine whether or not it is possible to obtain a sufficient amount of power to make an installation worth while, it is necessary to make a fairly accurate determination of the volume of flow and the possible head. The volume of flow may be determined by the float method or by the weir method.

Fig. 142. Method of finding the average depth of a stream

The average depth here equals $8 + 18 + 20 + 12$ divided by $4 + 1 = 11.6$ in.

The *float* method, which is as follows, will give only an approximate result. A representative section is selected, and the depth is measured at several points at equal distances apart on the same line across the stream. The sum of these figures divided by the number of measurements plus

207

one is the average depth of the stream at this point. The method is illustrated in Fig. 142. The velocity is secured by measuring off a given distance, say, two hundred feet, throwing a cork or chip into the middle of the stream, and observing the time it takes to cover the measured distance. Two or three trials should be made and the average taken. Inasmuch as there is a great deal of friction along the sides and bottom of the stream, the mean velocity has been found to be only about 0.8 of the surface velocity. It is necessary, therefore, to multiply the velocity as determined above, by this factor, to obtain the mean velocity of the stream. The cross-sectional area in square feet multiplied by the velocity in feet per minute will give the flow of the stream in cubic feet per minute.

$$Q = av,$$
where $\quad Q =$ discharge in cubic feet per minute,
$\quad\quad a =$ cross-sectional area in square feet,
$\quad\quad v =$ velocity in feet per minute.

The *weir* method should be used to determine the volume of flow if accuracy is desired. Fig. 143 shows the method of constructing a weir. The notch is cut beveled, as shown, so as to afford as little resistance as possible to the passage of water. The width of the notch should be about two thirds the height of the weir dam.

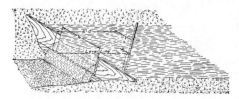

FIG. 143. The weir method as used to determine the volume of flow of streams

The ends of the plank must of course be embedded in the banks and bottom of the stream so that all the water will flow through the notch.

It is necessary now only to measure the head that is forcing the water through the notch. It will be noticed that the surface of the water as it flows through the weir slopes toward the notch and that the depth of the water is not so great at the weir as it is a few feet upstream. To measure the real head, then, some six feet back from the weir a stake should be driven, the top of which should be exactly level with the bottom of the notch. The depth of water flowing through the weir may then be measured by holding a rule on the top of the stake as the water is flowing normally. The depth of the water and the width of the weir being known, the volume of flow is

$$Q = 3.33 \times W \times h\sqrt{h},$$

where
$Q =$ discharge in cubic feet per second,
$W =$ width of notch, in feet,
$h =$ depth, in feet, flowing over weir.

The *head*, or fall, is determined by the height of the dam. The height to which it will be possible to dam the stream depends upon the nature and height of the banks and upon the slope of the stream bed. The latter may easily be determined by means of a drainage level; or, if this is not at hand, an ordinary carpenter's level may be used. If such a level is fastened to the top of a stake some three or four feet long and successive measurements taken, the total fall available for the conditions presented may be found. With the flow and head of the stream thus accurately determined, the theoretical horse power may be figured by the following formula:

$$\text{Theoretical horse power} = \frac{Q \times 62.4 \times h}{33000},$$

where
$Q =$ flow in cubic feet per minute,
$62.4 =$ weight of one cubic foot,
$h =$ total head, in feet.

As an illustration let the following conditions be assumed: In measuring a stream by the weir method the notch in the weir was found to be 6 ft. wide and the depth of flow 1 ft. If it is possible to erect a dam 10 ft. high, what theoretical horse power will the stream develop?

$$Q = 3.33 \times 6 \times 1\sqrt{1}$$
$$= 19.98.$$

$$\text{Theoretical horse power} = \frac{19.98 \times 62.4 \times 60 \times 10}{33000}$$
$$= 22.66.$$

Inasmuch as water-wheels will develop about 80 per cent of the theoretical horse power, such a stream has a sufficient flow and fall to make a power plant worth while.

There is a very common misconception as to the quantity of water required to develop even a small amount of power at a reasonable head. For example, a flow of three hundred and sixty gallons per minute, which, at first thought, would be considered a heavy flow, would have to fall through a head of eleven feet to develop one theoretical horse power. Hence the necessity of carefully measuring streams when the installation of a power plant is contemplated.

WATER-WHEELS

Water-wheels are resorted to as a means of harnessing a stream so that the water may be made to do useful work. Though there are a large number of different kinds of water-wheels available, there are only three which are used to any extent in small farm installations; namely, the overshot wheel, the turbine wheel, and the impulse wheel.

FIG. 144. A steel overshot water-wheel as installed in a small farm plant

The large pipe carries the water from the dam to the wheel, which operates an electric generator in the small building

The overshot wheel. The overshot water-wheel is one of the older types of wheels that has been largely used, but which, for reasons to be noted, has been rather generally replaced by other forms of wheels. It has, however, much to recommend it, and one company in particular is manufacturing this wheel on a large scale. The wheel is giving satisfaction in small farm plants. Fig. 144 shows the general construction and the principle of operation.

The water from the dam is delivered by appropriate means on top of the wheel just back of the center. Coming in at such a point, the flowing water strikes the buckets with some force, tending to impart motion to the wheel by reason of the velocity of the flow. The greatest force exerted, however, is due to the weight of the water in the buckets, which, in the best forms of wheels, is carried from the highest to the lowest point of the wheel before it is discharged.

The power to be derived from a wheel depends upon its diameter and its width. The former must be just about equal to the height of the dam; the latter must be controlled by the flow of the stream. Wheels ranging from 1 ft. to 75 ft. in diameter, and from 6 in. to 20 ft. in width, are made. As a rule, the bottom of the wheel should hang clear of the discharge water, owing to the increased friction caused by the wheel's running in backwater. The modern steel wheel, however, will stand a considerable amount of backwater without a very great decrease in efficiency.

It will be seen that this wheel is large, heavy, somewhat cumbersome, and slow in speed. There is, further, some danger from clogging and freezing. On the other hand, the construction and installation are not complex, and

FIG. 145. A skeleton view of a turbine wheel

the efficiency is high. Tests made on a steel wheel, at the University of Wisconsin, showed an efficiency as high as 92 per cent. In actual use such wheels should have an efficiency of 80 per cent to 85 per cent. The overshot wheel is best adapted to medium or large flows and to medium heads. For small farm installations, where the head is from 6 ft. to, say, 12 ft., this wheel may well be given consideration.

The turbine wheel. There are many different turbines on the market, the types differing chiefly in the manner in which the water is received and discharged. Fig. 145 illustrates the general principle upon which the turbine operates. The water enters from

the sides and imparts motion to the shaft by reason of the velocity with which it strikes the vanes. Furthermore, the vanes are so shaped that the falling water tends to impart motion to them and hence to the shaft. These two features give rise to the names " impulse turbine " and " reaction turbine."

Fig. 146 shows the general method of installing a turbine where the available head is small. The turbine is contained within the box, or penstock, the water from the dam flowing directly into this box. Passing into and through the turbine, the water is

FIG. 146. Showing the usual method of installing a turbine wheel under a small head

The water flows in at the side of the submerged wheel and drops through into the tailrace

discharged into the tailrace. The draft-tube, or lower portion of the turbine, projects into the tailrace water several inches, to assist in maintaining or creating suction for the discharge water. The total head is the distance from the water in the penstock to the water in the tailrace. The wheel is provided with gates by which the amount of water delivered to it may be readily controlled. In Fig. 147 is shown

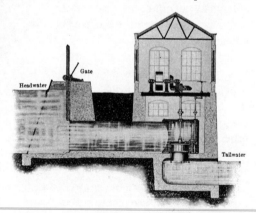

FIG. 147. A turbine installation showing the arrangement of gears and line shaft

Note the method of controlling the flow to the wheel

a complete installation, including the method of controlling the flow and the disposition of gears and line shafting.

In comparison with the overshot wheel, the turbine is small and light in weight and runs at a high rate of speed. It is adapted to medium and large flows and to any head up to several thousand feet. One of the smallest wheels made by a leading company requires a head of 7 ft. and a flow of 384 cu. ft. per minute, and under these conditions it is claimed that it will develop 4.1 horse power. The efficiency of the turbine varies a great deal with the conditions under which it operates, but ordinarily an efficiency of from 70 per cent to 80 per cent may be expected.

The impulse wheel. The impulse wheel, a notable example of which is the Pelton, is adapted only to high heads and small flow. While frequently installed with a twenty-foot head, this type of wheel is usually found with a head of one hundred or more feet. The wheel is operated by water flowing from a nozzle under high pressure and impinging against the vanes of the wheel. It is small and light in weight and runs at a high speed. It has only an occasional application in rural plants.

Use of water powers. The power developed by a water-wheel may be put to a number of uses. The wheel may be attached to a grinding-mill if the proper location can be secured, and, through a system of pulleys and shafting, may be used for other power purposes. Perhaps there is no more desirable or convenient use to which small water powers may be put than that of generating electric current for light or power. Even though the stream may be at a considerable distance from the house, the generator may be located at the wheel and both controlled from the house. If the power developed is great enough, electric motors may be installed about the house or barn; and they are a most convenient source of power.

CHAPTER XVI

WATER–SUPPLY SYSTEMS

Every farm and farm home has some system of water supply, even if it is nothing more than a well with a common hand pump. This well is expected to furnish water for use at both house and barn. There is generally a cistern also, which is located at the house. In this chapter will be considered some of the possibilities open to every farmer whereby he may provide his home with an adequate and convenient water-supply system. While especial attention is given to the question of conveying water into the house, the barn is not neglected.

The simpler systems will receive first consideration; then the more extensive as well as the more expensive systems will be discussed, in the hope that some of the ideas presented may find application in many of our farm homes. While a complete hot-and-cold-water system is greatly to be desired, it is often neither practical nor wise to attempt its installation; available means should always determine the extent of the system to be chosen. It is too frequently the case, however, that while the barn equipment has been improved and added to, the housewife has been forced to worry along under most unsatisfactory conditions, not the least of which is the lack of a convenient water supply.

The amount of water actually consumed per day about the barn can be quite accurately determined. It is estimated that a horse will consume 12 gal. a day; a cow, 10 gal.; a hog, 2 gal.; and a sheep, 1 gal. Where a house is equipped with a bathroom and attendant conveniences, there will be consumed an average of 20 gal. per day for each occupant of the house. This of course includes the allowance for laundry purposes. If the house is not equipped with a water-supply system of any kind, the water-consumption would probably amount to from 5 gal. to 8 gal. per day for each person.

The Cistern

Size. With very few exceptions every farm home has its cistern. In too many cases the cistern is much too small. There are two things which should determine the size of the cistern: (1) the roof area from which it will be filled, and (2) the amount of water that will be consumed. The average house presents a roof area of about 1000 sq. ft. The average monthly rainfall for Ohio is about $3\frac{1}{4}$ in. Allowing the $\frac{1}{4}$ in. as waste, one month's rainfall will yield 1875 gal. from the average roof. A rainfall of 6 in. per month is not at all uncommon, in which case 3750 gal. would be caught if a cistern of adequate size were provided. A family of 6 persons using 20 gal. each per day will consume 3600 gal. per month, or just about the equivalent of 6 in. of rainfall. A cistern should by all means hold one full month's supply to tide over periods of drought. It is during times of drought that the most water is used, and some allowance should be made for this. It should be remembered too that the cistern is never full at the beginning of the dry months. A cistern

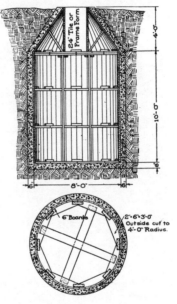

FIG. 148. Section of a concrete cistern
Note the construction and bracing of forms

8 ft. in diameter and 8 ft. deep to the arch will hold 3000 gal. A cistern 8 ft. in diameter and 10 ft. deep to the arch will hold 3760 gal., which is equivalent to 119.3 bbl. of 31.5 gal. each. A cistern of this size will be easily filled from the average roof and will furnish none too much water. The cistern ought to be no smaller than this — especially if the installation of a hot-and-cold-water system is contemplated, in which case the amount used will be materially increased.

Materials. Cisterns are undoubtedly most easily built from brick. Concrete makes a cistern that is in many ways superior to one built of brick, but the building of forms often involves an additional expense for lumber and labor. If, however, old lumber is at hand for the forms and if sand and gravel can be obtained for the hauling, the concrete cistern may prove less expensive than any other kind.

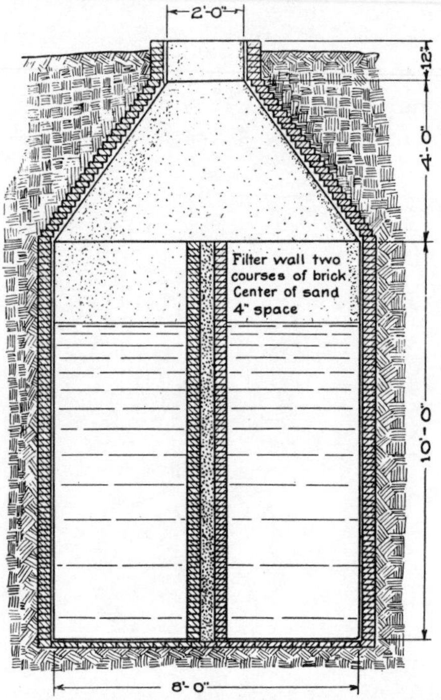

Fig. 148 shows a *concrete* cistern in section, a sufficient amount of detail being shown to enable one to construct the forms. The circular supports for the inner form would need to be cut out on a band saw. They may be hewed to shape, but sawing would be much easier. The inner form, as high as the arch, should be completely set up and securely fastened across the top, so that the bottom and sides can be placed in one operation. The form for the arch should be all ready to place as soon as the walls are finished.

FIG. 149. Section of a one-course brick cistern with a two-course brick filter

Nothing but good Portland cement and clean sand and gravel or crushed rock should be used. If bank or creek gravel is used, it should be run over a $\frac{1}{4}$-inch screen — the part passing through being used as sand; and the part running over, as coarse aggregate. The materials should then be mixed in the proportion of 1 part cement, 2 parts sand, and 4 parts gravel (see the chapter on concrete for details in mixing and placing). It is wise to reënforce the arch with No. 9 fence wires spaced 6 in. apart.

The forms should be left in place for from four to six days. When they are removed the surface should be painted with a thin cement wash to fill all air-holes and to secure smoothness.

To build such a cistern as that shown in Fig. 148 there will be required

12.75 bbl. cement @ $1.60	$20.40
3.5 cu. yd. sand @ $1.00	3.50
7 cu. yd. screened gravel @ $1.00	7.00
500 ft. lumber @ $25.00	12.50
Total cost of materials	$43.40

Fig. 149 shows a one-course *brick* cistern coated with cement plaster. This construction has the advantage over the concrete type in that no forms are required. It can be made perfectly water-tight and, all things considered, is perhaps more easily and readily constructed than the concrete cistern.

The cost of materials for such a brick cistern would be approximately as follows:

2800 bricks @ $8.00 per M (if filter is desired, add 1200 bricks)	$22.40
6.5 bbl. cement @ $1.60	10.40
2.4 bbl. lime @ $0.75	1.80
3 cu. yd. sand @ $1.00	3.00
Total cost of materials	$37.60

Thus, the total for materials is less than in the case of the concrete cistern. The labor cost would be less, also, although the service of a skilled mason would be required.

Cistern filters. If the cistern water is to be used for drinking purposes, a filter of some kind is very much to be desired. Even for laundry purposes the water is much cleaner if filtered. Of course if a house is provided with a good slate or sheet-iron roof and if care is taken always to prevent the first washings from the roof from entering the cistern, the use of a filter is not so essential; but even then a filter will prove a great aid in keeping rain water clean. In Fig. 149 is shown a filter that is very commonly used — at least in a modified form. As shown in the figure, two single courses of bricks are laid across the middle of the cistern, leaving a four-inch space between the courses. This space may be filled with sand. If the water entering the cistern is very dirty, the pores of the filter, both bricks and sand, tend to become clogged; so that the filter loses its effectiveness. The brick sur-

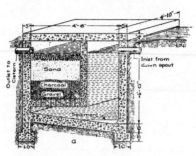

FIG. 150. An effective cistern filter

The filter bed may be easily replaced

face should be cleaned with a wire brush if the coating becomes too heavy, and the sand should in a few years be replaced with a fresh supply. The two courses of bricks may be laid close together and the sand omitted; even a single course of bricks will prove very effective.

A simple form of brick filter often used consists of a square crib, or box, of single-course bricks, with sides about two feet long, built up in the center of the cistern. The pump pipe is placed inside this crib.

Another form of filter that is extremely effective is shown in Fig. 150. It is a little more complex and expensive than the brick filter described above, but it has great filtering power. The bottom of the filter bed may be made of a slab of concrete with numerous small holes made by inserting greased pins one-fourth inch in diameter into the slab while the concrete is green. A piece of perforated slate will serve the same purpose. The charcoal layer may be eliminated, but it adds greatly to the effectiveness of the filter. In Fig. 151 is shown still another form of filter that is easily and inexpensively arranged.

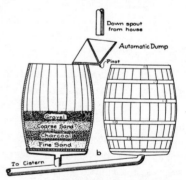

FIG. 151. An inexpensive but fairly effective cistern filter

The 2 barrels are used to take care of heavy rainfalls

Two barrels are buried by the house, at the down spout, and filled with layers of gravel and sand as shown. A bucket that automatically dumps the water from the down spout first into one barrel and then into the other is placed between the tops of the barrels as shown. The barrels may be placed on top of the ground if they are protected during freezing weather.

If the water in a cistern has a disagreeable odor, the best thing to do is to pump it out and give the cistern a thorough cleaning. If the loss of the water would be serious, the water can be purified to some extent by aëration; that is, by forcing air through it, as by forcing an upturned bucket deep down into the water and then releasing the air by turning the bucket. Vigorous agitation will help to aërate the contents. A teaspoonful of permanganate of potash sprinkled on top of the water just before it is agitated will eliminate some of the impurities.

THE ELEVATED TANK

The elevated tank is perhaps most frequently used as storage for well water. It may be placed out of doors, as on the windmill tower (Fig. 152), on a tower built especially for the purpose, or on the silo. In any case it is subject to freezing in the winter, the water becomes warm in the summer, and the tank is exposed to the weather. Any or all of these objections may be overcome to some extent. If a double-walled wooden tank is provided and the space between the walls is packed with sawdust or with specially prepared material, the danger from freezing is virtually eliminated. If a concrete tank is built, weathering has no effect on it. The concrete elevated tank is expensive because of the heavy supporting columns necessary; but it is nearly indestructible

FIG. 152. A substantial installation of an elevated tank

and may prove the less expensive in the long run. Cement blocks are available for the construction of tanks aboveground — the same kind of blocks that is used in silo construction. The use of the blocks eliminates expensive forms, and cisterns built from such blocks have proved very satisfactory.

Table XXII gives the common sizes and the approximate prices of tanks of different materials used for storing water. The prices of course will vary in different places.

TABLE XXII. SIZE, CAPACITY, AND APPROXIMATE PRICE OF WATER-TANKS

MATERIAL	SIZE		CAPACITY IN GALLONS	COST
	Diameter in feet	Height in feet		
Steel	6	5	1050	$42.00
Steel	7	7	2000	65.40
Galvanized iron	6	5	1050	30.00
Galvanized iron	6	8	1690	49.00
Galvanized iron	8	6	2250	56.00
Cypress	6	5.5	1160	35.00
Cypress	6.5	6.5	1600	45.00
Cypress	7.5	6.5	2150	55.00

Steel towers are now generally used for the support of the elevated tanks. The heights of the more common towers, with the quantity which they are designed to support, and their prices, are as follows:

15 ft. high, supporting from 1000 to 1500 gal. $60
20 ft. high, supporting from 1000 to 1500 gal. 85
27 ft. high, supporting from 1000 to 1500 gal. 92
39 ft. high, supporting from 1000 to 1500 gal. 125
20 ft. high, supporting from 2000 to 3000 gal. 115
27 ft. high, supporting from 2000 to 3000 gal. 122
39 ft. high, supporting from 2000 to 3000 gal. 165

A tank built in the attic of the house is hardly to be recommended, though such tanks are common. Heavy construction is usually necessary to prevent sagging, for water in large quantities is very heavy. For example, a tank holding five hundred gallons weighs over two tons when filled with water. The danger from leakage, too, is always a menace, though a sheet-iron tray provided with an outlet is usually placed beneath the tank for the purpose of catching the leakage. The tank in the attic possesses the one great advantage of being protected from the weather; and with a little additional protection it will not freeze. The tank is frequently placed on a level with or below the eaves, so that it may be filled directly from the eaves spout.

Fig. 153 shows a scheme in which the force of gravity is utilized. There is no pumping — no effort except the turning of faucets. This system is especially adapted to locations where the house is on a lower level than the barn, although it has been installed in many places where both house and barn were on the same level. It is essential in such an installation to have the

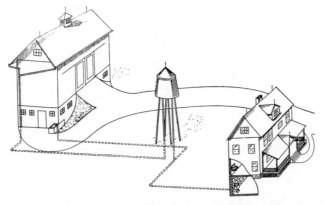

FIG. 153. An installation which makes use of the force of gravity

It is best adapted to locations where the house is lower than the barn

down spout well constructed and provided with a valve at the bottom so that it may be drained in freezing weather. There are many modifications of this idea. A cistern may be built in the approach to a bank barn or in a sidehill near the barn. Instead of taking the water to the tank beneath the ground, the tank may be located closer to the barn, and the water carried across to the top of the tank.

A SIMPLE KITCHEN INSTALLATION

Fig. 154 shows an inexpensive and simple yet convenient installation for a kitchen. Many kitchens are provided with a sink on which is mounted a cistern pump. With very little additional expense a twenty-five-gallon tank may be placed on the end of the sink and filled with well water supplied from a pump outside, or from a flowing spring, or from a hydraulic ram. If the supply is furnished from a windmill or a flowing stream, all of the water for barn use may be passed through the tank and the overflow taken to the barn. This keeps a constant supply of fresh water

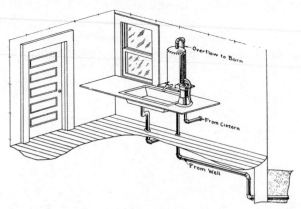

FIG. 154. A simple kitchen installation

Note that the sink is located near a window where there is good light. The tank is for well water, the overflow from which may lead to the barn

in the kitchen. If the tank is filled by hand, the men of the house can see to its filling once or twice a day. Following is a statement of the probable cost of such an installation :

1 enameled kitchen sink (18″ × 30″)	$5.00
1 galvanized iron tank (16″ × 3′, 30 gal. capacity)	8.00
1 cistern pump (3-inch cylinder)	5.00
25 ft. 1¼-inch galvanized-iron pipe @ 10¢	2.50
50 ft. 1-inch galvanized-iron pipe @ 7¢	3.50
Labor	5.00
Total	$29.00

THE TANK-IN-ATTIC SYSTEM

Fig. 155 shows an installation making use of the attic tank. As was said in the discussion of elevated tanks, this system has some serious objections, but it will give fair satisfaction if the tank is properly supported and possible leakage provided for.

Hot-water tank. The system shown in Fig. 155 includes a hot-water tank which is located by the side of the kitchen range. The water is heated by means of a water front placed in the fire-box of the range. This may consist of a simple rectangular metal box, or it may be composed of a series of coils made of a one-inch pipe. The latter offers more heating-surface, but the small pipes frequently become completely filled with deposits from the water. This difficulty is worse with some waters than with others, those having a large amount of lime being the worst. The rectangular box, although it does not heat the water so quickly, does not, on the other hand, become clogged so readily. There seems to be no cheap and effective way of preventing this incrustation, and the only practical remedy is to

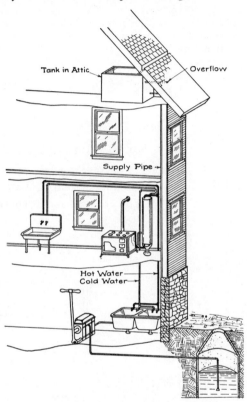

Fig. 155. A pressure system, using an attic tank

The tank may be filled directly from the roof or by means of a pump, which may be located in the basement

supply a new water front when the old one gives out. If the water carries a high percentage of lime, this may be necessary every three or four months.

The cold-water pipe, which is taken into the tank at the top, is extended nearly to the bottom. The hot-water pipe is taken directly from the top of the tank. The tank is usually 1 ft. in diameter and 4 or 5 ft. high, and holds 25 or 30 gal. The cost of installing this system would be approximately as follows:

1 pump (double-acting)	$15.00
1 cypress attic tank (3½ ft. diameter; 3 ft. deep; 216 gal. capacity)	15.00
1 hot-water tank (30 gal. capacity)	7.50
1 water front and connections	3.50
1 enameled sink (18″ × 30″)	5.00
1 enameled tub (2 compartments)	17.00
25 ft. 1¼-inch pipe @ 10 ¢	2.50
60 ft. ¾-inch pipe @ 5 ¢	3.00
Labor (estimated)	25.00
Total	$93.50

THE HYDROPNEUMATIC SYSTEM

Fig. 156 shows a possible scheme for the installation of a so-called "hydropneumatic" system of water supply. This system consists of an air-tight tank, usually located in the basement of the house, a pump to force the water into the tank, a hot-water boiler for heating a portion of the supply, and a piping system leading to various parts of the house.

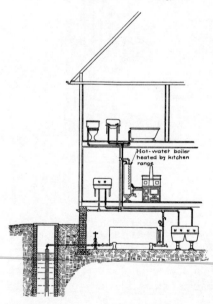

FIG. 156. An installation of a hydropneumatic system

The dark-colored pipes carry hot water. A hand pump is located in the basement

The tank. The tank is the most expensive single item of the system. It must be made of good material in order to stand the pressure to which it is subjected. The best tanks are made of heavy galvanized iron, though the tank known as the black-steel tank is very good and is less expensive than the galvanized-iron tank. The mistake is frequently made of getting a tank that is too small. It should be remembered that the tank is never completely filled with water. As the water is pumped in, the air is compressed more and more, until at 5 lb. pressure the tank is one-fourth full of water, at 15 lb. pressure the tank is one-half full of water, at 45 lb. pressure the tank is three-fourths full of water, and at 60 lb. pressure the tank is four-fifths full of water.

Since the working pressure seldom exceeds 40 lb., the tank is never more than three-fourths full. Furthermore, a tank will not deliver all the water that it contains to a point above the level of the tank itself unless the air within the tank is first charged to a pressure determined by the height to which the water is to be raised. For example, the bathroom fixtures are usually about 20 ft. above the tank. It will require a pressure of 20 × .434, or 8.68 lb., to lift the water in these pipes. Hence, if all the water from the tank is to be delivered into the bathroom, there must be a pressure of 8.68 lb. left in the tank. In other words, if the tank is charged to about 10 lb. by forcing in air before pumping begins, all of the water will be delivered to the second story. This is usually not done, so that when the water ceases to run on the second floor, the tank will still be about one-third full of water. One must not overlook this fact when purchasing a tank.

TABLE XXIII. SIZES AND CAPACITIES OF PNEUMATIC TANKS

Size of Tank		Total Capacity in Gallons	Working Capacity in Gallons	Approximate Cost
Diameter in inches	Length in feet			
30	6	220	145	$32.00
36	6	315	210	41.00
36	8	420	280	51.00
36	10	525	350	58.00
42	8	575	385	75.00
48	10	940	625	118.00

Table XXIII gives the sizes of tanks most frequently used, together with the total capacity, the working capacity, and the cost of each.

It was said that the tank is usually located in the basement. It may, however, be buried in the ground just outside the basement, with one end projecting through the basement wall. This keeps the water cool in summer and prevents freezing in winter. The fact that the end projects into the basement makes possible the convenient connection of pipes, gauges, etc.

The pump. The pump used to fill the tank may be a hand pump placed in the basement, as shown in Fig. 156, provided the water is not more than twenty feet below the level of the pump. An ordinary force pump may be placed directly over the well or cistern and operated by hand, by windmill, or by a gasoline engine.

Since the water absorbs a certain amount of air, it is necessary to supply air to the tank at more or less regular intervals. Pumps for this purpose are so designed that air may be forced in with the water. Sometimes a separate air pump is supplied, but this is not necessary.

Cistern or well water. Unless two tanks are put in, only one kind of water can be furnished. This should be soft water, by all means, since the chief household needs call for soft water. If hard water is desired, another and smaller tank may be put in and both systems operated by the same pump provided the well is not too deep.

Cost of the system. The following estimate is intended to cover an average farm installation, with fixtures of reasonably good quality. This estimate is based upon the experience of a large company dealing in systems of this kind.

1 pump (double-acting, hand-operated)	$20.00
1 pneumatic tank (galvanized-iron, 350 gal.)	50.00
1 hot-water tank (galvanized-iron, 50 gal.)	7.50
1 bathroom outfit (including tub, lavatory, and closet), good quality enameled iron	50.00
1 enameled kitchen sink (18″ × 30″, with drain board) . .	10.00
40 ft. 4-inch soil-pipe @ 25 ¢	10.00
10 ft. 2-inch soil-pipe @ 15 ¢	1.50
100 ft. ½-inch galvanized-iron pipe @ 4½ ¢	4.50
20 ft. ¾-inch galvanized-iron pipe @ 5 ¢	1.00
Pipe-fittings	25.00
Labor	60.00
Total, hand-operated plant	$239.50
1 two-horse-power gasoline engine	40.00
Total, engine-operated plant	$279.50

The Pneumatic System

The objection has been raised to the hydropneumatic system just discussed that the water must be stored. This is true, and if it is used for drinking purposes, this may be a real objection. In order to overcome this possible objection the pneumatic system, or so-called "fresh-water" system, has been devised.

General installation. Fig. 157 shows the necessary features of such an installation. An air-tank is placed in the basement or other convenient place and charged with air by means of an air-compressor. This compressor must be operated by a gasoline engine. An air-pipe conducts the air from the tank to a pump in the well. Leading from this pump is another pipe which carries the water to the various

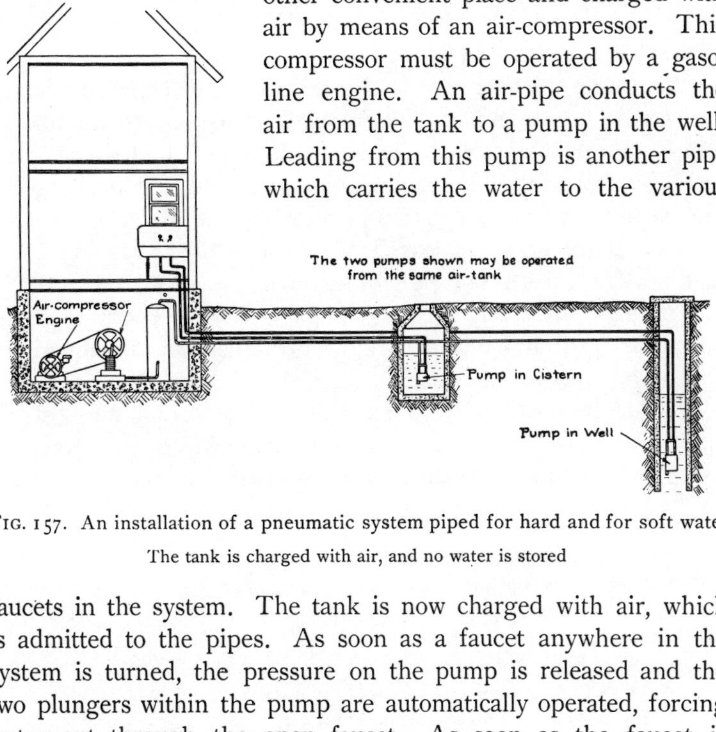

The two pumps shown may be operated from the same air-tank

Air-compressor Engine

Pump in Cistern

Pump in Well

FIG. 157. An installation of a pneumatic system piped for hard and for soft water

The tank is charged with air, and no water is stored

faucets in the system. The tank is now charged with air, which is admitted to the pipes. As soon as a faucet anywhere in the system is turned, the pressure on the pump is released and the two plungers within the pump are automatically operated, forcing water out through the open faucet. As soon as the faucet is closed the action of the pump ceases.

The tank. The tank is essentially of the same construction as that described under the hydropneumatic system, though it must be built to withstand a higher working pressure. The degree of pressure which it is necessary to maintain depends upon the depth of the well and upon the distance from the well to the point to which the water is to be carried. For example, if the well is 75 ft. deep, it will require a pressure of 75 × .434, or 32.5 lb., to lift the water to the surface. If it is to be conducted through an additional length of, say, 200 ft., making a total of 275 ft. of 1-inch pipe, at the rate of 5 gal. per minute, the friction loss would be approximately 9 ft. of head, making the total lift 84 ft.; consequently there will be required a minimum pressure of 84 × .434, or 36.5 lb., to deliver the water to the faucet at the above rate. In order to maintain this pressure the initial pressure must be considerably higher than this. The tank is usually charged to a pressure of 100 lb.

The pump. The pump is the complex and expensive feature in this system. It is a long tubular device, made in different sizes, but small enough to fit into a four-inch well-casing. It is made up of two cylinders with plungers and a complex set of valves to admit of automatic operation by the air. The material is brass throughout, and excellent workmanship is required. The pump alone costs about eighty-five dollars.

The air-compressor. An air-compressor is necessary to charge the tank. An engine is required to operate it, and though simple in its construction, it is rather expensive.

Cost of the system. For an average installation the cost, not including house fixtures or plumbing for house fixtures, would be as follows (figures furnished by a responsible dealer) :

1 No. 5 pneumatic pump	$75.00
1 air-compressor ($3\frac{1}{2}'' \times 4''$)	50.00
1 two-horse-power gasoline engine	50.00
1 galvanized-iron air-tank ($30'' \times 5'$)	50.00
2 pressure gauges ($3\frac{1}{2}$-inch)	5.00
1 leather belt ($3'' \times 16'$)	5.00
500 ft. $\frac{3}{4}$-inch galvanized-iron pipe, for water	25.00
200 ft. $\frac{1}{2}$-inch galvanized-iron pipe, for air	9.00
5 hydrants @ $2.50	12.50
Labor	25.00
Total	$306.50

The great advantage of this system lies in the fact that no water is stored. Yet, if the well is some distance from the house, the pipes must be drained before cool, fresh water is to be had. By the use of one air-tank it is possible to operate two or more pumps in different wells or cisterns. The objectionable feature is the expensive and complex pump. If there happens to be sand in the water, the working of the valves is likely to be interfered with. Many installations are giving satisfaction, while others have given considerable trouble. The system is much more expensive than the hydropneumatic system and can scarcely be considered so reliable.

THE AUTOMATIC SYSTEM

Where an electric current is available the hydropneumatic system may be equipped with an electrically operated pump. The motor is supplied with an automatic switch connected to the pressure tank in such a way that it is thrown out when the pressure reaches the desired maximum point, and thrown in (thus starting the pump) when the pressure drops to the lowest point permissible. But little current is required to operate the motor, and the system seems to be giving the best of satisfaction.

CHAPTER XVII

SEWAGE–DISPOSAL FOR FARM HOMES

Since good health is regarded as a natural heritage of life in the country and since it is common to hear the country spoken of as the home of rosy-cheeked children and aged men and women, the question, Why is there need to discuss farm sanitation? might well be asked. As a matter of fact, such statistics as are available seem to show that there is very little difference between rural and urban districts in respect to the death rate, and that, so far as certain diseases are concerned, — for example, tuberculosis, typhoid fever, and, in general, diseases traceable to poor water, — the country has distinct advantages. Influenza seems to be one disease which is more prevalent in the country than in the city, the country death rate from this disease being twice as high as the city. But the question of disease and death does not offer the only excuse for this chapter. Virile manhood possessed of an active brain is not assured even though sickness is not common. Healthy bodies are frequently found in houses that are slovenly kept; but self-respect, dignity and poise, culture and refinement, are not found there.

Farm sanitation in its broadest sense is concerned with all factors relating to the health of those who live on the farm. These factors include the proper location of the house in regard to drainage, the construction and ventilation of house and stable, and the nature of the water supply, as well as the general tidiness and care of the place. The subject is here taken as referring to the proper disposition of night soil, or sewage from the house.

The common privy. Almost every farm has its outdoor privy, which represents the common method of disposing of night soil. It must be said, to our shame, that too often the privy is little short of loathsome, a place to which one goes with much reluctance even when he is forced to do so. It is often placed several rods from the house, and at times it is necessary to travel through mud and storm to reach it. Rather than endure these discomforts those who are compelled to use it are likely to postpone their visits as long as possible, a circumstance which results in a deranged system.

A better construction should be secured, not only for the comfort and convenience of those who must use the privy but also to guard against the spread of disease. Too frequently the privy vault is entirely open, and flies find easy access. Flies revel in filth, and it may be quite possible that they fly from just such places as a privy vault direct to the dinner-table or to the baby's rattle, depositing the germs of some deadly disease. Further, the seepage from a privy vault may find its way to the well, the spring, or other source of water supply, carrying the germs of typhoid fever or other diseases.

A good privy must be fly-proof, so constructed that there is no possibility of its polluting the water supply, and reasonably comfortable in cold weather. A common method of construction is to dig a vault, over which the house is built. Sometimes the sides of the vault are walled up with brick, plank, or concrete; in other cases there is simply a hole in the ground — usually with no bottom provided, so that the liquid may better seep away. This is a dangerous mode of construction and should be avoided unless the privy is located from one hundred and fifty to three hundred feet from the well.

If a vault is used, it should by all means have the walls and bottom made of concrete. If such a vault is protected from flies it is reasonably safe, but it is a most disagreeable task to clean it out. A large vault does not have to be cleaned often, of course, but the accumulation of many months renders the use of the privy disagreeable.

The dry-earth closet. What is perhaps one of the best constructions for the common privy is what is known as the dry-earth closet. It is a common observation that when dead organic matter comes in contact with the surface soil it is very soon decomposed and made a part of the soil. Rotting weeds, manure, fecal matter, dead bodies, etc., on top of or slightly covered by the soil, are readily and almost greedily attacked by the millions of bacteria in the soil, which, acting as scavengers, soon render the decomposing mass unobjectionable.

If, now, a convenient receptacle for receiving the night soil in the closet is provided and a liberal amount of dry earth sprinkled over the soil each time the closet is used, the result will be surprising. The fecal matter will be practically consumed if this method is followed; and if the dry earth is persistently used, the task of cleaning will not be objectionable provided it is frequently done. Lime, road dust, or screened cinders may be used, but they do not possess the purifying power that live earth does.

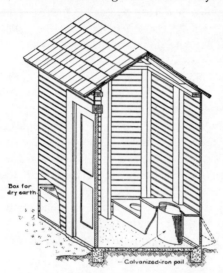

Box for dry earth

Galvanized-iron pail

FIG. 158. A method of constructing an inexpensive but satisfactory dry-earth closet

There are several designs which may be used for the receptacle. In some cases a concrete box is built and is cleaned from the rear by means of a shovel; in other cases a concrete floor is put in and a long wooden box slipped under the seat. The size of the box is such that it may easily be removed at the rear and lifted into a wagon. Fig. 158 shows a plan that has proved very satisfactory. A concrete floor is laid, and a concrete seat-front, also, is advisable, for the front of the seat soon becomes foul and ill smelling if made of wood. Buckets are provided under the seats as containers; galvanized garbage cans, which are easily handled and cleaned, serve the purpose very well.

If this method is to prove satisfactory, constant care is necessary. Children, for example, may neglect to use the dry earth and thus foul the cans. Persistently and regularly used, however, the earth will virtually eliminate the solid matter. Slop jars should never be emptied into the can, because the earth will not absorb a large amount of water.

The cans should be emptied at least once a week, although twice a week would be better. The contents may be buried or may be hauled some distance from the house and scattered over the field. It must be remembered, however, that, since the dry-earth process does not kill any disease germs that may have been voided in the excrement, great care must be exercised in disposing of the waste. It should be seen to, also, that such waste is not scattered near the buildings, where flies are likely to find it.

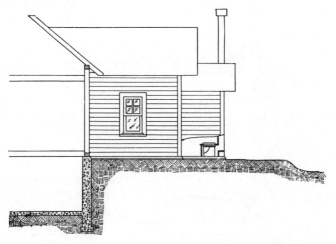

FIG. 159. A pail closet in close connection with the house
Such a closet is convenient and, if properly cared for, sanitary

If this type of privy is carefully managed, it need not be far from the house and, if possible, should be connected with it by means of a covered walk.

The pail closet. Fig. 159 shows what is designated as the pail closet, a simple application of the dry-earth-closet principle. It may be located in the woodshed or in any building adjoining the house. The receiving pail is placed in a tight box provided with a closely fitting hinged cover. A vent flue leads from this box directly to the outside or into a chimney flue and so conveys away objectionable odors. If the can is emptied every few days and dry earth liberally used, the scheme is very satisfactory and exceedingly desirable, especially for children and aged people.

The chemical closet. The chemical closet is a patented device which has recently been placed upon the market and which is finding a wide use in homes not supplied with running water. The system is used to good advantage in extremely cold climates and is sometimes found even in small hotels where much trouble results from frozen water-pipes.

Fig. 160 shows the usual installation. The closet is best located on the first floor of the house. Second-floor installations are possible, but not at all desirable. The closet may be placed in a bathroom or in a woodshed adjoining the kitchen. A vent removes disagreeable odors, so there is no objection to locating the closet in or adjacent to the house.

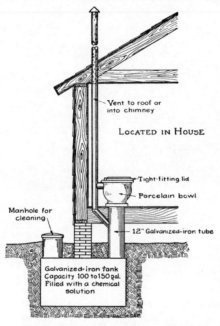

The tank, which is usually of heavy steel and holds from 100 to 150 gal., is buried in the ground beneath the closet. One end projects beyond the foundation of the house so that cleaning is readily accomplished. The inner end of the tank may project into the basement. The closet seat is a white porcelain bowl with a tightly fitting hinged lid. Leading from the bowl to the tank is a 12-inch galvanized-iron tube. A vent tube, frequently made of 4-inch heavy sheet iron, white-enameled, leads from the bowl up through the roof; or it may discharge into a chimney flue. In all cases it is necessary that a proper vent be provided.

FIG. 160. A common installation of a chemical closet

The caustic material is furnished in cans, each can being sufficient for one charge. A certain quantity of water is added and the tank is ready for use. While the solution is strong enough to render practically harmless the solid matter with which it comes in contact, it will not completely sterilize the solid matter unless the latter is broken up in some way. Agitators are frequently provided for this purpose, and if they are not provided, the material should at frequent intervals be stirred in some other way.

To clean the tank it is only necessary to place a small pitcher pump over the outside opening in the tank, pump out the liquid, and remove any sludge that may collect in the bottom. This is not a disagreeable task. Some companies claim that the tank will not need cleaning oftener than twice a year. This may be true under certain conditions, but the chances are that, if satisfactory results are secured, a cleaning every month or so will be found necessary where the family is large.

It will readily be seen that this system has its drawbacks. There is some expense connected with each charging. It takes considerable time to clean the tank, and the total first cost of the installation would amount to from twenty-five to fifty dollars. Moreover the tube leading to the tank frequently becomes soiled and so requires attention. On the other hand, this system affords a comfortable closet where water is not piped into the house, and with reasonable care it will prove less objectionable than the common privy.

The cesspool. None of the methods for the disposal of sewage thus far discussed involve the use of running water. As soon as a home is supplied with a complete water-supply system, other and better methods for disposing of sewage are available.

The cesspool is not to be classed as one of the better methods, but questions concerning it are so frequently asked that some discussion is here necessary. As ordinarily constructed, the cesspool is nothing more than a hole in the ground some 12 ft. deep and 6 or 8 ft. in diameter, loosely walled up with stones. The bottom is not covered. The sewage from the house is drained into the hole, and the liquid gradually seeps into the surrounding soil. The solid matter sinks to the bottom, and although much of it is decomposed by bacterial action, a considerable amount of sludge collects.

The liquid contents of the cesspool must all be absorbed by the soil immediately surrounding the pool itself. This means that the soil soon becomes clogged by the material from the tank and loses its purifying power. If the cesspool is located near a well, the water vein is likely to become polluted through the seeping of sewage into it. If once the contents of the pool find their way into a water vein, they may travel long distances. Should a person carrying typhoid germs use a closet emptying into the cesspool, the entire family, and possibly other families, may become infected through the water supply. It is no argument for this method to say that certain cesspools have been in operation for years without serious results. One death from such a source is all too much to pay for the needless risk, and on the whole the use of the cesspool must be severely condemned.

The septic tank. Without any question the septic tank is the best means yet devised for disposing of the sewage from the farmhouse. It is not expensive, it is easily installed, and, above all, it is safe. The form of tank most generally adopted is composed of two chambers. The chamber receiving the sewage from the house is known as the *settling*-chamber, and the second compartment is known as the *dosing*-chamber.

Operation of the septic tank. Two distinct steps are recognized in the disposal and purification of sewage by means of the septic tank. The material from the bathroom, the kitchen sink, etc., is conducted into the first chamber of a water-tight tank, where it is allowed to settle and where it remains without undue agitation or disturbance until a certain kind of bacteria, called anaërobic, or rotting, bacteria, has transformed a large portion of the solid matter into a liquid or gaseous state. The bacteria which bring about this stage in the process of purification do their work only in the absence of light and air. Fortunately they possess in large measure the power of creating their own favorable conditions. They will bring about the formation of a scum over the surface of the liquid in which they work, thus effectually excluding both light and air.

From the settling-chamber the liquid content seeps into the second chamber of the tank; a small amount of solid matter is carried over with the liquid, and the action which took place in the first chamber is here continued until nearly all the solid matter is consumed.

From the second chamber the liquid is discharged into a disposal system, where it is exposed to conditions favorable to the action of another kind of bacteria known as aërobic bacteria, which work only in the presence of air. It must never be forgotten that the liquid coming from the tank is foul and likely to be laden with disease germs. A tile drainage system is perhaps the best means by which to provide the necessary conditions for the further purification of the sewage. This takes advantage, as does the dry-earth closet, of the purifying action of the upper layer of soil, which soon renders the sewage virtually harmless if it is properly distributed.

The discharge from the tank into the disposal system may be by gradual seepage, as through the upper outlet shown in Fig. 161, or it may be by intermittent discharge. In the latter method the second chamber is allowed to fill to a certain height, and then the contents are flushed into the disposal system either by the removal of a plug such as that shown in Fig. 161 or by the action of an automatic siphon, as shown in Fig. 162. While discharge by gradual seepage seems to be giving satisfaction, intermittent discharge serves to flush the entire disposal system and tends to secure better distribution of the liquid over the disposal area.

Location of the septic tank. Since there is almost no odor coming from the tank, it may be located by the side of the house. It is perhaps best placed from twenty to fifty feet from the house. It should not be much further away, as in that case the pipe leading to the tank would be more likely to become clogged. The tank may be covered completely, so that there need be no objection to having it in the yard.

Construction of the septic tank. Fig. 161 shows the simplest possible construction for a septic tank. This is a double-chamber tank built of concrete. It may be built of bricks thoroughly plastered with good cement plaster as in cistern construction. The hole is excavated to the desired size and the inner form lowered into place and supported from the top. The concrete is then mixed in the proportion of 1–2–4 and the bottom first placed. The bottom may be laid before the inner form is put in. Care should be taken not to have the mixture too wet, as it tends to flow out from the bottom of the inner form when the sides are being placed. After the sides are completed the bottom should be smoothed over with the trowel and given the desired slope. The forms should be left in for at least three or four days. As a matter of precaution it is advisable to reënforce the walls (especially, near the top) with No. 9 fencing-wire placed at intervals of eight or ten inches.

The cover is made up of concrete slabs, which may be molded in separate forms and then laid over the tank. A wood cover would answer for a time, but the concrete is much more satisfactory. A manhole is sometimes built into the cover as a convenience in cleaning, but it is not difficult to remove one or two slabs for this purpose, even if the tank is completely buried.

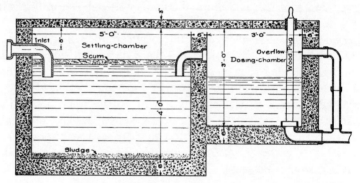

FIG. 161. A double-chamber septic tank

For the average farm family it should be 2½ ft. wide (inside measurement)

The inlet pipe leading from the house to the tank is a 4-inch vitrified sewer pipe laid to a fall of from ⅛ in. to ¼ in. per foot. The pipes are laid with the bell end toward the house, and the joints are thoroughly cemented in order to prevent the seeping of sewage into the soil near the house. Cementing also holds the joints in line. Care should be taken to have the inside perfectly smooth. A swab should be made of old rags on a stick, and each time a joint is laid and cemented it should be wiped out so that there will be no projections to clog the pipe. The depth should be at least 2 ft. and if the slope will permit, a greater depth is desirable. The warm water from the kitchen will prevent freezing under ordinary conditions, however, and it is not advisable to place the tank too far beneath the surface. It is a good idea to lay a Y-joint, with the Y turned up, in the inlet pipe, about midway between the house and the tank. The hole in the Y is then plugged, and in case the inlet ever clogs it will be convenient in cleaning the pipe. It is necessary that the inlet pipe should have a branch inside the tank, extending down into the liquid, to prevent unnecessary agitation of the contents of the tank and avoid breaking the surface scum.

Fig. 162 shows a double-chamber tank equipped with an automatic siphon. As the dosing-chamber fills, the weight of the water column forces the air in the siphon bell down into the long leg of the siphon, driving the water down farther and farther

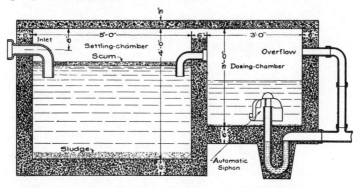

FIG. 162. A double-chamber tank equipped with an automatic siphon

into the U-tube ; finally the air seal is broken, and the entire contents of the dosing-chamber enter the disposal system. A siphon of this sort costs about fifteen dollars. It seems to work with fair satisfaction. The only difficulty encountered comes from the collection of foreign matter on the parts of the siphon, which at times interferes with its action. However, should it become clogged it is not difficult to clean.

The regulations of the Ohio State Board of Health require that the joint extending into the tank be a T-joint, with one end extending down into the liquid and the other end reaching well above the liquid, thus allowing a free movement of air from the upper part of the tank back into the plumbing system of the house. They also require that there be a vent of some kind in the cover of the tank to aid further in the free circulation of air in the tank. A great deal of gas collects above the liquid in the tank, and this must have a means of escape. The tank shown provides escape into the outlet pipe, a method which has given satisfaction in many installations, though the requirement referred to provides more complete circulation.

The disposal system. When the liquid is discharged from the tank, it is still far from pure; in fact the sewage has been

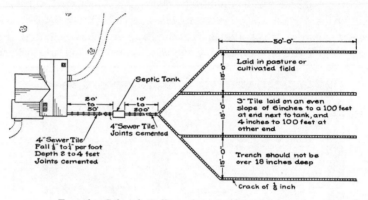

FIG. 163. Subsurface disposal system for a septic tank

purified but little during the action which has taken place within the tank. It is important, therefore, that the effluent be properly disposed of.

A tile drainage system, such as that shown in Fig. 163, represents one of the best methods available for disposing of the effluent from a septic tank. The drain leading from the tank to such a system should be laid with sewer tile, with the joints cemented, in order that none of the sewage may seep out near the well or cistern, and that it may be carried to the several drains, where it will be distributed over a large area of soil. The grade should be at least from 4 to 6 in. per 100 ft. Its length should not be greater than is absolutely necessary — from 50 to 100 ft. usually being sufficient.

The tile drains should not be over eighteen inches deep, as this depth allows a more or less free circulation of air over the liquid and into the soil. Furthermore the sewage is thus permitted to seep out into the upper layer of soil, where the bacteria which are relied upon to purify it further are most abundant. A considerable space is left between the joints of the tile, especially in stiff clay soils where seepage is likely to be slow. In unusually retentive soils it is wise to cover the drains with a few inches of cinders or gravel.

The disposal system may be located anywhere conveniently near the tank, a pasture or a meadow being perhaps the best place. There is no objection, indeed, to locating it in the garden. There should be from 20 to 50 ft. of tile for each occupant of the house. An average of, say, 40 ft. would probably suffice for the ordinary soil, but the length required increases with the stiffness of the soil.

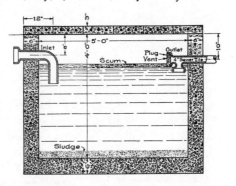

The effluent from the tank is frequently taken into a tile drain laid for ordinary drainage purposes. This is permissible and safe if the tile drain does not empty into a stream the water of which is used for human consumption.

FIG. 164. A single-chamber septic tank

Owing to the absence of adequate light and air little purification will take place, however, if the tile are laid to a depth of three feet, as tile drains should ordinarily be laid.

The effluent may also be taken directly into an open stream if the water is flowing the year round and if it is not used for house purposes. In such a case, however, there is always danger that someone may use the water and that the method may thus lead to the spread of disease.

The single-chamber tank. Fig. 164 shows the construction of a single-chamber tank. This kind of tank is essentially the same as the double-chamber tank except that the second chamber is omitted. Such a tank does not provide for the intermittent discharge of the contents into the disposal system, which in the opinion of many is not necessary. General practice, however, seems to favor a second chamber in the belief that more complete action is thus secured. Fig. 165 shows the method of con-

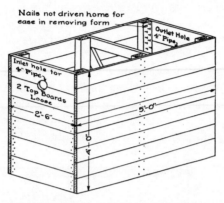

FIG. 165. Form-construction for a single-chamber concrete tank

structing the inner form for a single-chamber tank built of concrete. The form for a double-chamber tank may be similarly constructed.

Fig. 166 illustrates the construction of a single-chamber tank in which a sludge-drain is provided. In all the tanks shown above it is necessary to pump out the liquid and remove the sludge with a shovel when the tank is cleaned. With the sludge-drain provided, it is necessary merely to agitate the contents, remove the drain plug, and allow the material to flow out. In rolling country where a convenient outlet

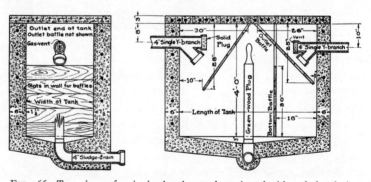

FIG. 166. Two views of a single-chamber tank equipped with a sludge-drain

Note the form of outlet tile and inlet tile and the position of the baffle boards

for such a drain is easily provided, this system is perhaps advisable. In level sections, however, there is too much work involved in providing an outlet for the drain. The tank shown in Fig. 166 is also provided with three baffle boards which serve to break the fall of incoming sewage, to prevent undue agitation, and to prevent so far as possible the escape of solid matter into the outlet tile.

Size of tank. The size of the tank depends upon the number of persons served. The tank shown in Fig. 161 is, when made two and one-half feet wide (inside measurement), designed to meet the needs of a family of six persons. Table XXIV [1] specifies the proper dimensions for single-chamber tanks the designs for which are taken from the bulletin mentioned in the footnote. The size of the first chamber of double-chamber tanks is essentially the same as for single-chamber tanks. The dosing-chamber should be of such a size as to hold approximately one third as much as the settling-chamber. If an automatic siphon is used, a minimum depth must be secured and the specifications for the size of siphon used must be carefully followed.

TABLE XXIV. DIMENSIONS FOR SINGLE-CHAMBER TANK

NUMBER OF PERSONS	DIMENSIONS OF TANK		
	Inside length, in feet	Inside width, in feet	Inside depth, in feet
6 or fewer	5	$2\frac{1}{2}$	4
8	6	3	4
10	7	3	4
12	8	3	4
14	8	$3\frac{1}{2}$	4

Care of tank. The tank, properly installed, needs but little attention. Under ordinary conditions it will need cleaning but once in from three to five years, so completely is the solid matter in the tank consumed by the bacterial action. What solid matter there is collects in the bottom of the tank as sludge, a fine loamy material which is not very disagreeable to handle. To clean the tank it is necessary to pump the water out and remove the sludge with a shovel if a sludge-drain is not provided.

Grease interferes with bacterial action, and consequently a little care should be exercised in this regard. However, the small amount of grease which ordinarily finds its way to the tank from the kitchen sink and the laundry will not be harmful.

[1] H. W. Riley, *Bulletin No. 59*, Cornell Reading Course, Cornell University, Ithaca, New York.

Scheme of installation. The general scheme of installation is shown in Fig. 167. The tank shown is completely covered with earth. No flushing system is provided, the liquid being permitted to seep out into the disposal system. The inlet and outlet joints, as well as the joint connecting the two chambers, are T's rather than elbows. A free circulation of air is thus provided between the two chambers of the tank and between the disposal system and the house plumbing.

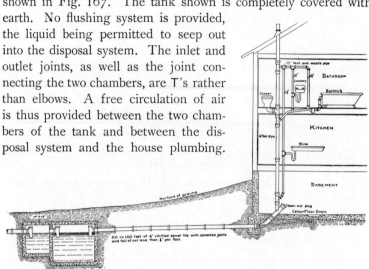

FIG. 167. General scheme of installation of a septic tank, together with the plumbing system required

Drain for kitchen sink. Fig. 168 shows a good way to provide a drain for a kitchen sink. Too frequently the drain from the sink empties its contents on the surface of the ground in the back yard, where they are likely to produce unsanitary and unsightly conditions. The scheme shown keeps the discharge beneath the ground and eliminates trouble from freezing. There is also a certain amount of septic action in the barrel.

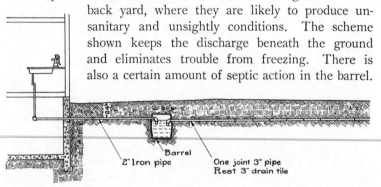

FIG. 168. A barrel drain for a kitchen sink

CHAPTER XVIII

THE PLOW

The plow is the basic tillage tool, the fundamental farm implement. It is not merely a tool for inverting the furrow slice, but it is the most efficient pulverizer of the soil in use. As the moldboard turns the furrow, each particle of soil is forced to slip against the particle adjoining, a process which results in a tilth that no other single operation approaches. The general impression prevails that the plow is a simple tool, requiring but little adjustment and less care. This is far from the truth, however. Without question it is the most complex tool on the farm, in that it requires the greatest skill for adjustments, the grain-binder and the gasoline engine not excepted. More effort has been expended in the slow process of development of this seemingly simple tool than in that of any other implement on the farm. Careful study of its construction, adjustment, and use will be amply rewarded.

The Walking Plow

Mechanics of the plow. The mechanical principle underlying the construction of the plow embraces the application of three simple machines: the wedge, the inclined plane, and the screw. The wedge is formed by the ground line and the slope of the share face; while in the slope and twist of the moldboard are found the inclined plane and the screw.

Materials used. The moldboard, the share, and the landside may be made from either chilled iron or soft-center steel.

Chilled-iron parts are manufactured by pouring the molten metal into a mold having its face lined with metal. At times this metal lining is hollow and water is made to circulate through it. This hastens the cooling of the molten mass and changes the minute construction of the resulting piece, rendering it extremely hard and brittle. A section of a chilled-iron moldboard is shown in Fig. 169.

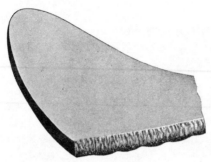

FIG. 169. Section of a chilled-iron moldboard

Note the uniform texture of the metal

A chilled plow bottom, then, possesses the following characteristics : (1) it is extremely hard ; (2) it takes a good polish ; (3) it has a long life, wearing especially well in gravelly soil ; (4) it does not rust deeply and it repolishes easily ; (5) it is heavy and somewhat cumbersome ; (6) it breaks easily if struck a sharp blow.

Soft-center steel is manufactured by taking two layers of very hard steel, placing between them a layer of softer steel, and then rolling the three together at welding heat. The effect is to produce a sheet of steel, thin and light in weight, yet extremely tough. The soft center serves as a cushion to all blows and sudden strains. In Fig. 170 is shown a diagrammatic section of a soft-center steel share.

A steel bottom has the following characteristics : (1) it is tough and not easily broken ; (2) it takes a good polish and scours well in sticky soil ; (3) it does not wear so well as a chilled plow in gravelly soil ; (4) it is light and easily handled — a boy's plow ; (5) it often rusts and pits badly if left exposed to the weather.

Cast-Steel Patch ⅛"thick) Making ⅜"of
Finest Cast Steel   ) Hard-Temp-
Soft Steel   ered Steel
Finest Cast Steel

FIG. 170. Section of a soft-center steel share

A patch of extra-hard steel is welded on top of the point for the purpose of resisting wear

The modern tendency seems to be toward the exclusive use of the steel plow. In sections where the soil is largely gravelly loam or of a coarse, sandy nature, however, the chilled plow will outwear one made of steel. The pitting of the steel plow when it rusts is due primarily to the process by which the steel is manufactured. The phenomenon, which is not dissimilar to the rusting of modern fencing-wire, constitutes a defect which seems difficult to overcome.

The frog. The frog is the heart of the plow, around which all other parts are built. It is that part of the plow bottom to which are attached the moldboard, the share, and the landside. The beam may also be attached to it. There are three materials out of which frogs may be made : cast iron, malleable iron, and steel.

The *cast-iron* frog is confined almost entirely to wooden-beam plows. The reason for this is that the wood beam requires a standard of considerable size because the entire force required to draw the plow is applied at this point ; and since the standard and the frog are of one piece, both must be large. Cast iron is sufficiently strong, and at the same time is less expensive than either steel or malleable iron. A cast-iron frog is absolutely rigid and forms a satisfactory base to which to attach the moldboard, share, and landside.

The *malleable-iron* frog is frequently used in plows where the frog is of medium size. If cast iron were used, the thinner parts would break, and yet the frog is too large to permit of the economical use of steel.

The *steel* frog is now almost universally used on steel-beam plows. It has the advantage over other materials in being strong, light in weight, and easily shaped. With all its lightness in weight, however, it seems to provide a sufficiently substantial base for other parts. There are two kinds of steel frogs, the cast-steel frog and the forged-steel frog. The cast-steel frog is made by pouring the molten steel into a mold which is the exact shape of the frog. The forged-steel frog is made by placing a red-hot sheet of steel over a form of the desired shape and size and striking it a heavy blow with a drop hammer. A forged-steel frog is smaller than a cast-steel frog, and a plow equipped with the former must be rigidly braced if good construction is to be secured.

248

A convenient method of determining whether a certain piece is made of cast iron or of malleable iron is by the use of a hammer

Fig. 171. A sod moldboard

This type of moldboard is long, gently sloping, and has considerable twist

and chisel. If made of cast iron, the piece subjected to this test will chip; if of malleable iron, it will dent. Of course, soft steel also, will dent, but it is easy to tell whether or not a frog is made of steel. If the number of the part is stamped into the metal by a die, we may usually conclude that the part is steel; if the number is raised, the part is cast or malleable.

The moldboard. The moldboard has three distinct functions; namely, to lift, to turn, and to pulverize the furrow slice. To perform these functions in different types of soil and under different conditions of moisture, tilth, etc., mold-boards of different shapes are required. The *sod* mold-board must raise the furrow

FIG. 172. A stubble moldboard

It is short, steep, and bends abruptly

slice gently and at the same time give it sufficient twist to keep it from falling back into the furrow. Then, too, it must not

FIG. 173. A general-purpose moldboard

This type stands halfway between the sod and stubble moldboards

bend the furrow slice so much as to cause buckling. This type of moldboard, therefore, is long, gently sloping, and characterized by considerable twist. The *stubble* moldboard is used in stubble ground or ground free from a stiff sod. Here it is not so necessary to turn the furrow slice completely over, and since there is no tendency to buckle, more thorough pulverization will be secured if the moldboard is steep and short, with much bend. The *general-purpose* moldboard stands halfway between the sod and stubble types. It is the one most generally used in the older sections of the country, where all farms have some sod to break, but where there is little virgin soil.

The *breaker* is a type of moldboard used in stiff prairie soil. It has an extremely long and gently sloping form. In extreme types it has a length of several feet. The *rod breaker* is the type of plow used in very sticky soil,

FIG. 174. A breaker moldboard

This type of moldboard is used in stiff prairie sod

where it is impossible to get a moldboard plow to scour. The moldboard of this plow is made up of rods or of flat pieces of steel.

Figs. 171 to 175 illustrate different types of moldboards.

The landside. The landside is necessary in the walking plow to take the pressure exerted by the furrow slice on the moldboard and to aid in giving the plow a steady motion. There is a wide variation in the height, length, and shape of landsides. They are classified as high, medium, or low, according as they measure about 8 in., 6 in., and 4 in. respectively. The height should approach very closely to the depth of the furrow, else there is likely to be undue friction between the furrow bank and the unprotected part of the plow. The friction between the landside and the furrow slice is independent of the area of contact. A long landside aids in the proper

FIG. 175. A rod moldboard

This type is used in extremely sticky soils

handling of the plow, rendering it less susceptible to variation in the line of draft because of an unsteady land horse.

Fig. 176 shows several types of landsides as regards the shape and angle of the face. The frequent tendency of a plow to rear up behind is overcome by the projecting sole on the landside, and thus more even running is secured. It is claimed for the sloping face that the furrows, when turned, fit more closely the one on the other, leaving less space between and thus interfering less with the rise of capillary moisture. It is doubtful, however, whether such a result is secured. On the contrary the slanting landside rather increases the tendency of the plow to rear up behind; moreover the slanting landside does not cut so clean a furrow slice, leave so smooth a furrow bank, nor afford so much room for the furrow horse as does the straight landside. In fact its effect is just opposite to that of the landside with a projecting sole.

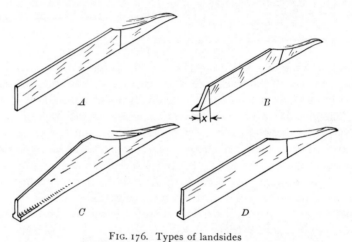

FIG. 176. Types of landsides

A, rectangular plain-faced type; *B*, slanting type; *C*, projecting-sole type; *D*, widened-sole type

The greatest wear comes upon the sole of the landside, and the heel takes the most of this. Several methods are in use for reënforcing the sole. In Fig. 180 is shown a detachable heel which is easily replaced when worn. A detachable sole is frequently provided, and it is easily replaced when it becomes worn. The practice of widening the sole (Fig. 176, *D*) is frequently resorted to in order to prolong the life of the landside. In many steel plows the landside proper is not reënforced in any way, but the landside back, to which it is attached, takes all the wear. It is doubtful whether this is the best construction, as a worn landside is more easily replaced than a landside back.

The share. The share may be made of chilled iron or of steel. The *steel* share has several decided advantages. It may be sharpened at the forge and thus made to last several years. It should be said, however, that this is a difficult task, requiring much skill and practice for its successful operation. Both the bearing at the wing and the suction must be altered during the process, and the smith should have the plow at hand for a trial fit before he can be assured that the share is properly set. The steel share, although it costs two or three times as much as the chilled share, is probably more economical in the end. It can be made to carry a sharper edge than the cast share, and it is to be preferred in land where there are tough roots, as in alfalfa, shrubbery, bushes, etc. A poorly sharpened steel share, however, is worse than a dull chilled-iron share.

The *chilled-iron* share, commonly called a *cast* share, is recommended by the fact that it is cheap and, on becoming dull, may easily be replaced by a new one. It is possible to grind this share

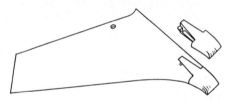

Fig. 177. A detachable point for a cast share

Such a point may be turned over when it becomes dull, and hence is called self-sharpening

on an emery wheel, but the suction, which is decreased with wear, cannot be increased, so that the share seldom works well after being sharpened. A sharp edge must not be provided, since it will be easily nicked and broken. It is possible to improve a dull cast share slightly by turning the plow upside down and chipping the point by sharp blows with a hammer, at the same time supporting it from beneath, as with an iron wedge.

Fig. 177 shows a detachable point for the cast share. This usually costs about 10 cents, and although it is easily put on and is reversible (a feature which gives it the name of self-sharpening point), it has never been popular.

The beam. The beam may be made of either wood or steel. Since good material is becoming rather scarce, the number of *wooden* beams in use is rapidly decreasing. The wooden beam (Fig. 178), however, has some advantages over the steel beam.

FIG. 178. A wooden-beam plow equipped with jointer and beam wheel

Note the heavy cast-iron frog and standard, the two being in one piece. Note also the ribs on the back of the chilled-iron moldboard; they serve as braces to prevent breaking. The landside has a widened sole

FIG. 179. A steel-beam plow equipped with jointer and beam wheel

The point of the jointer is slightly to the rear of the point of the share

It is lighter in weight, and the adjustment for width of furrow and for two or three horses is made at the rear end of the beam instead of at the clevis. Thus, the set of the plow is interfered with less than when the adjustment is made at the end of the beam. On the other hand, the wooden beam is frequently broken, and has less clearance, which is a disadvantage when one is plowing under trash or coarse manure.

The *steel* beam, shown in Fig. 179, is now quite generally used. Being made of high-carbon steel, it is not easily bent and has plenty of clearance. Moreover in a few makes there is a special device for landing the beam at the rear, so that it possesses the one great advantage of the wood beam. This device, shown in Fig. 180, consists of two wedges which, after the bolts at the base of the beam have been loosened, may be slipped in between the beam and the frog or landside. This device will swing the end of the beam through a range of several inches. The chief faults of the steel beam are that it is rather heavy and that it can hardly be brought back to its original position if it is once bent out of shape. In fact it is quite impossible to do this unless it be returned to the factory and reshaped in the original mold.

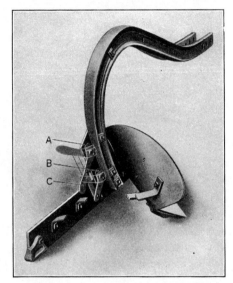

FIG. 180. A wedge attachment for adjusting a steel beam at its rear end

When the nuts at the base of the beam are loosened, the wedges *A* and *B* may be forced in by raising the lever *C*. Note the wedge at the wing of share for altering bearing

The set of the plow. When the walking plow rests on a level surface (Fig. 181) but three points of the bottom touch this surface; namely, the point, the heel of the landside, and the wing of the share. The proper relation of these points to the level surface, together with the adjustment of the beam or the hitch at the end of the beam, constitutes the set of the plow.

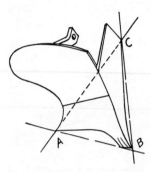

FIG. 181. The bottom of a properly adjusted walking plow rests on the three points *A, B, C*

Suction, the force which draws the plow into the ground, is secured by dipping the point of the share downward below the bottom line of the landside. It is measured as shown in Fig. 182. It should be from $\frac{1}{8}$ in. to $\frac{3}{8}$ in. for 12-inch to 14-inch plows, and about $\frac{7}{32}$ in. for 16-inch plows. As a share dulls, suction is destroyed, as shown in Fig. 183, and all penetrating power is lost. If the share is of steel the point may be bent downward, thus increasing the suction. This cannot be done with a cast share, but it is possible, by loosening the bolts in the share, to insert shims of tin or leather behind the bolts, thus throwing the point downward. If there is too much suction, it may be decreased in a similar manner. Raising the hitch does not change the suction. It may help to secure penetration when the share is dull, but it always interferes with the proper running of the plow.

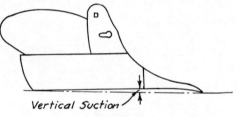

Vertical Suction

FIG. 182. Plowshare having good vertical suction

Vertical suction is secured by dipping the point of the share below the bottom line of the landside

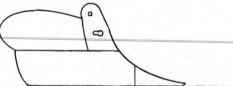

FIG. 183. Plowshare without vertical suction

A dull share destroys the suction. It is impossible to adjust the hitch so as to overcome this defect

The term "landing the point of the share" refers to the projection of the point toward the land, sometimes called horizontal suction (Fig. 184). It measures $\frac{1}{8}$ in. to $\frac{1}{4}$ in.

The *bearing* at the wing of the share is measured as shown in Fig. 184. It varies from ¾ in. for 10-inch plows up to 1¼ in. for 16-inch plows. Next to the hitch, proper bearing at the wing is most responsible for the level running of the plow. Too little

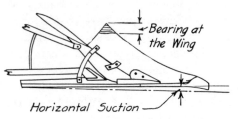

bearing will cause the plow to " wing over " away from the land, and too much bearing will have the opposite effect. On steel shares the bearing may be altered by forging the wing up or down. On some plows a special

FIG. 184. Illustrating bearing at the wing of the share and horizontal suction

device in the form of a movable wedge is attached to the underside of the share in such a way that by moving it outward or inward the bearing is increased or decreased. Frequently a plow which will run properly in a dry soil will wing over from the land if used in wet soil, and vice versa, so that some adjustment is desirable. Fig. 180 shows such an adjusting-device.

The winging over of a plow is often due to an improper hitch or to poor adjustment of the beam. This is not the only cause, however. If the land horse is considerably larger than the furrow horse and a rigid clevis is used in the bridle, the slant of the doubletree may cause the plow to wing over from the land.

By the " landing of the beam " is meant the adjustment of the beam (Fig. 185), or of the hitch at the end of the beam, in a horizon-

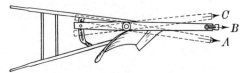

FIG. 185. Adjustment of beam

A, set for 2 horses ; *B*, set for 3 horses ; *C*, set for 4 horses. If the beam is rigid a corresponding change must be made in the clevis at the end of the beam

tal plane. The purpose of this is to cut varying widths of furrow and to change the hitch from 2 to 3 horses, or vice versa. If a narrower furrow is desired, the beam or the hitch should be moved toward the land ; for a wider furrow it should be moved in the opposite direction. If it is desired to change the hitch

256

from 2 to 3 horses, the beam or hitch should be moved toward the land. This is due to the fact that when the third horse is added the line of load is moved toward the line of draft so that the two may fall as nearly as possible in the same straight line.

Fig. 185 shows the proper landing of the beam for 2, for 3, and for 4 horses. For 3 horses the beam is virtually on a straight line with the landside, while for 2 horses the landside of the beam is almost directly above the middle of the point of the share. This is not an absolute setting and will need to be varied to suit the size of the team, the length of the doubletree, etc.; but the setting shown is standard, and steel beams that are rigidly set conform closely to it. It should be noted that many steel-beam plows are now provided with an adjusting-device for landing the beam at its rear end. Such an adjusting-device is shown in Fig. 180.

Line of draft. Fig. 186 shows the correct line of draft for a walking plow. This line starts from a theoretical point about

two inches toward the moldboard side of the shin and just above the junction of the share and the moldboard. The

FIG. 186. The line of draft in a walking plow

hitch at the beam is supposed to occupy a position which will direct this line to the horses' hames in such a way that the plow may be drawn with the least friction on the furrow bottom. Any variation from this straight line will influence the operation of the plow. Raising the hip straps, for example, will break this line vertically, and poor adjustment at the clevis may destroy the line horizontally. Every effort should be made to keep this line perfectly straight.

Plow attachments. Since a bare plow will seldom do satisfactory work, all plow-users should give careful study to the specific purpose of each attachment. The most important attachments are the jointer, the various forms of coulters, or cutters, and the beam wheel.

The *jointer* is the most important single attachment found on plows, whether walking plows, sulky plows, or gang plows. Its form is shown in Figs. 179 and 187. It finds its most effective use in the plowing of sod. The jointer turns the edge of the furrow over in such a way that grass cannot grow up between the edge of the furrow slices if the plowed field stands for several weeks before being worked. Moreover it aids in covering manure and trash of any sort. It is impossible to do first-class plowing in sod without this attachment. The use of the jointer also reduces the work of preparing the seed-bed. In many cases it saves one harrowing, because of the way in which the furrow slice is turned. A mistaken impression is held by some that

FIG. 187. A wooden-beam plow with jointer and beam wheel

The jointer is set above the point of the share. It should run at a depth of 1½ in. and should be set about ½ in. to the land side of the shin

the rolling coulter takes the place of the jointer. The functions of the two are quite different. The jointer should be so set that (1) its point is above or just back of the point of the share, (2) it runs $1\frac{1}{2}$ in. to 2 in. deep, (3) it runs $\frac{1}{4}$ in. to $\frac{1}{2}$ in. to the land side of the shin of the plow.

The *coulter*, or cutter, takes many forms, of which Figs. 188 and 189 show several. The purpose of the coulter is to cut the furrow slice from the land, thus leaving a clean-cut furrow bank. If no coulter is provided, the shin of the moldboard must do the work of a coulter; but since in the absence of a coulter the face of the share begins to lift the furrow slice before the shin has had an opportunity to cut it off, a ragged job is sure to result.

The *rolling* coulter is not well adapted to the walking plow, though it is sometimes used. The fin or the hanging coulter when used on walking plows improve the quality of the work and

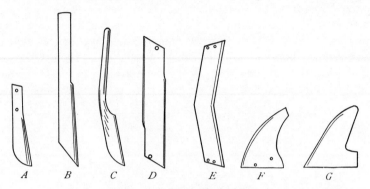

FIG. 188. Various types of coulters

A, B, C, hanging coulters; *D,* reversible knife coulter; *E,* reversible coulter; *F, G,* fin coulters

materially decrease the draft. The rolling coulter should be set back of the point of the share, at a depth equal to about one half the depth of the furrow, and from one fourth to one half an inch outside the line of the shin. All other forms of coulters should, when it is possible, be set in this same relative position.

The effect of a *beam wheel* is to cause the plow to run more steadily and thus to make the work easier for both man and team. The hitch should be so adjusted as to cause the wheel to press firmly but not too heavily on the ground. It should be set near the end of the beam and on a line with the landside. The use of a beam wheel always results in a more uniform furrow

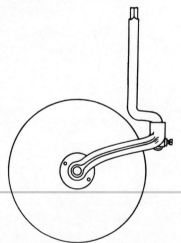

FIG. 189. A castered rolling coulter

This type of coulter is in no sense a substitute for the jointer and, in most cases, in a material reduction in draft. Two-wheeled trucks are used to a limited extent, with favorable results, but their weight is against their common use.

The Sulky Plow

The sulky plow is the result of an effort to reduce friction as well as to provide a means for the operator to ride. The size of the plow is usually either 14 or 16 in., and it is essentially a 3-horse plow. The plow bottom, together with the frame, is mounted on 3 wheels, a feature which changes into rolling friction the sliding friction of the walking plow. Hence it is possible to add the weight of the frame and the driver and still not materially change the draft.

The high-lift sulky plow. The high-lift sulky plow, a type of which is shown in Fig. 190, was the first to come into prominent use. In this type

FIG. 190. A double-bailed high-lift sulky plow

A, *B*, bails; *C*, point where rear furrow wheel is given lead; *D*, point where suction is altered; *E*, point where bottom is set to float

the framework is supported by and carried upon the three wheels, two running in the furrow and known respectively as the front and rear furrow wheels, and the other running upon the land. The frame may be raised or lowered upon the wheel-supports by means of two levers, one controlling the land side of the frame through the land wheel, the other controlling the furrow side by raising or lowering the frame upon the shank of the furrow wheel.

The plow bottom is attached to the frame by bails, the plow being designated as a single-bailed or a double-bailed plow, according to the number of bails. A foot lever is provided which, by means of the bails, lifts the bottom sufficiently high for turning purposes, so that it is not necessary to use the hand levers after the plow is properly leveled.

The furrow wheels are on casters and inclined to the vertical, so that they may run in the furrow without undue friction and

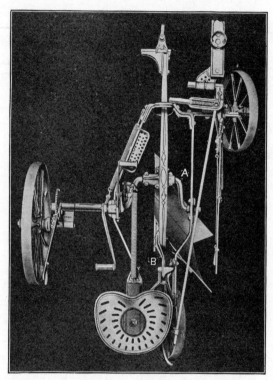

may better take the pressure of the furrow slice on the moldboard. The front furrow wheel, which is connected to the rear furrow wheel by a flexible rod, is guided by the tongue, which is connected directly to the front wheel.

The frameless sulky plow. The frameless sulky plow, shown in Fig. 192, consists of little more than a walking plow minus the handles, with a truck under the end of the beam, a seat attached, and a wheel substituted for the landside.

FIG. 191. Top view of a single-bailed high-lift sulky plow

The single bail is shown at *A*. At *B* is shown a leveling device; suction is also altered at this point

There are two levers to control the bottom — one to raise the end of the beam on the front furrow wheel, the other to level the plow by controlling the land wheel. By means of these levers the point of the share may be lifted free from the ground, but there is no way to lift the rear end. The front and rear furrow wheels are inclined from the land in order the better to take the pressure of the furrow slice on the moldboard. The front furrow wheel is always castered; the rear one is usually castered, but in some types is rigidly fastened, and so becomes in reality a rolling landside.

This plow is usually operated without a tongue, although in some plows the tongue may or may not be used. In case a tongue is not used, the front wheel may be controlled by a hand lever for

FIG. 192. A frameless sulky plow

The front furrow wheel is controlled by the hand lever shown. The rear furrow wheel is rigid — in reality a rolling landside

convenience in turning, or by a connection from the hitch at the end of the beam. If the rear wheel is castered it is connected to the front wheel, so that both are controlled by the same lever or by the same hitch connection. Because this plow is short-coupled — the rear wheel, especially in the rigid form, running close to the bottom — and because of the short and rigid connection between the bottom and the wheels, it is possible to turn either a right-hand or a left-hand corner with equal ease. Moreover it is not necessary to lift the plow from the ground in turning in either direction. This type usually sells for about fifteen dollars less than the high-lift type. For this reason, and because of its general desirability, it is likely to grow rapidly in favor.

The set of the sulky plow. The set of the sulky plow differs in many ways from that of the walking plow. The point of the share is the only part of the bottom that touches the floor when the plow is properly leveled. The wing of the share just swings free of the floor, while the heel of what little landside there is does not touch at all. The *suction*, then, is not measured by the amount the point dips, but rather by the amount the heel of the landside is raised from the floor. Since the length of the landsides differs greatly, the suction cannot be stated in terms of distance of the heel from the floor unless the distance back to the point of the share is given. In general, at a distance of 18 in. from the point, the landside should be $\frac{1}{2}$ in. from the floor. Except in a few instances there is a

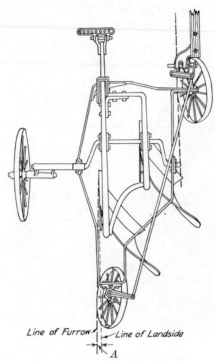

Line of Furrow — Line of Landside

A

FIG. 193. A plan view of a frameless gang plow

The furrow wheels may be given lead either toward or away from the land. The rear wheel is also set outside the line of the landside, as shown at *A*

means provided for regulating the suction, by which it can be varied from zero to about 1 in. This device, which is usually found in connection with the shank of the rear furrow wheel, provides a means for raising or lowering the rear end of the frame. In some frameless sulkies with a rigid rear wheel it is impossible to alter the suction in this way.

The furrow wheels are given *lead* either toward or away from the land, as illustrated in Fig. 193. The front wheel is frequently given lead toward the land in an effort to throw the line of load as far to the land as possible. This is particularly true of gang plows. The rear furrow wheel is given lead from the land. There is considerable pressure on this wheel, a pressure which tends to crowd it into the furrow bank, and it leads away in order that it may have no tendency to climb over the bank. Different devices are provided for giving these wheels lead.

The rear furrow wheel is also set *outside the line* of the landside, as shown in Fig. 193, *A*. This is for the purpose of taking all friction off the landside. The amount the rear furrow wheel is set over varies from ¾ in. to 2 in., but is usually about 1 in.

The front furrow wheel must be properly adjusted to the width of the furrow; that is, this wheel should always be kept running in the bottom of the furrow and against the furrow bank. If the hitch is changed to cut a wider or a narrower furrow, a corresponding change must be made in the wheel.

It is possible, too, to set the high-lift plow to *float*. Ordinarily when the bottom is lowered by the foot lever, it is locked in position and cannot be raised unless the frame is lifted with it. In nearly all cases a set-screw (Fig. 190, *E*) is found in connection with this foot lever, which may be so adjusted as to prevent its locking, so that if the bottom strikes a stone or root, it alone will be thrown out of the ground, swinging upward on its bails. This device is useful in the plowing of stony or stumpy ground.

Attachments. Almost any of the various types of *coulters* may be used on sulky plows. A *jointer* attachment should be secured also. The ideal combination uses both the jointer and the rolling colter, the latter being set forward. A *weed-hook* is usually supplied, and it is attached to the beam, being carried just ahead of the moldboard. It is of great assistance in turning under weeds or tall grass. A cable chain is frequently used instead of a weed-hook; one end is fastened to the doubletree, behind the furrow horse, the other end to the beam, there being a long loop that is permitted to drag in the furrow just ahead of the moldboard. Sometimes this loop is weighted to hold it to the bottom of the furrow. This device is even more effective than a weed-hook.

Harrow attachments are now provided for both sulky plows and gang plows. They may be of either the spike-tooth or the disk type. They are fastened to the plow by a more or less rigid connection and can be raised from the ground by convenient levers. They are undoubtedly useful, particularly in the fall, when the upturned soil is rather lumpy and dries quickly. They insure immediate harrowing, a thing very much to be desired and too frequently neglected.

Bearings. The bearings, particularly of the front and rear furrow wheels, are constantly covered with dirt, and must be dirt-proof as far as possible. Removable boxings should be provided in order that wear may be taken up without the purchase of a new wheel or axle. In addition, means should be provided for oiling, so that this essential in the proper use of the plow will not be neglected.

THE GANG PLOW

Gang plows are now quite generally used in states west of Ohio, and are growing in popularity in the East. Farmers in the latter section have been

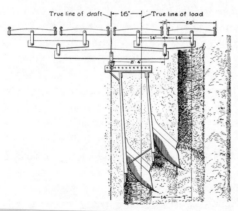

FIG. 194. A four-horse-abreast hitch

There is side draft when such a hitch is used, because, as shown, the line of draft falls outside the line of load

slow to adopt them, the chief reason being that farms are small and the horse power necessary is frequently not available. There has also been a feeling that the draft is great when compared to the work done, and that the quality of the work does not conform to the standard of many Eastern farmers. There is some merit in these objections, to be sure, but the observed difference in the draft is more apparent than real, the apparently greater draft being due to the hitch. It is possible to do first-class work with the gang plow.

Types of gang plows. Gang plows are made in both *frameless* and *high-lift* types, the latter being far the more common. It may be predicted, however, that the frameless type will come into wider use as plowmen become familiar with it.

Adjustments. The adjustments discussed under sulky plows apply to gang plows, also with the difference that the lead in the furrow wheels is usually greater in gang plows than in sulky plows.

Hitches. The greatest objection to be urged against gang plows is that of side draft. Fig. 194 shows clearly just why there is side draft when 4 horses are hitched abreast to a 2-bottom gang plow. Here the line of draft is shown to fall 16 in. outside the line of load. The line of load is found by locating the theoretical points of resistance on the two bottoms as shown and described under "Line of draft" (p. 256) and then dividing

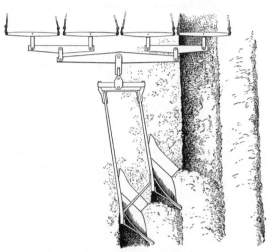

FIG. 195. A four-horse-abreast hitch

The beams are set well toward the land in an effort to bring the line of draft and the line of load together

this line at the middle. If 12-inch right-hand plows are used, this line would be 8 in. to the right of the shin of the land plow. Anything that brings the horses closer together will alleviate side draft but will not eliminate it. Fig. 195 shows how the beams of the gang plows of a certain company are set, in an effort to bring the line of draft and the line of load together. It should be noted, however, that the change in the beams does not alter the line of load. The only way to eliminate side draft is to hitch tandem. In Fig. 196 a tandem hitch is shown in which longer doubletrees are used than shown in Fig. 194. That side draft is virtually eliminated is shown by the fact that the line of draft falls inside the line of load. Fig. 197 shows two methods of hitching thus. The pulley and cable is satisfactory for 2-horse teams, but the lever must be used for other combinations. While the tandem hitch makes the handling of the teams more awkward, especially in turning, its merits in other ways make one wonder why it is not more commonly used on gang plows.

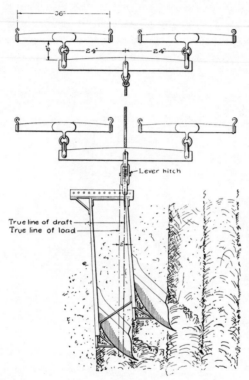

FIG. 196. A tandem hitch

The line of draft falls just inside the line of load, thus virtually eliminating side draft

Disk plows. Disk plows, in which a rolling disk is substituted for the moldboard, share, and landside, are the result of an effort to reduce draft by transforming sliding into rolling friction. Fig. 201 shows a disk plow. There seems to be a reduction in the draft, but it is secured at the expense of efficiency in general plowing. The disk plow does not cover trash nor pulverize soil so well as does the moldboard plow. It finds its greatest use in the extremely sticky soils of the West and the Southwest. In the East it is used to some extent for plowing extremely hard ground.

Deep-tilling plows. With the demand for deeper plowing have come several plows of both moldboard and disk construction designed especially for this purpose. The double-disk plow, shown in Fig. 202, represents one type of deep-tilling plow and differs radically from the disk plows above described. It has 2 disks, each 24 in. in diameter, and turns but 1 furrow. The front disk runs at a

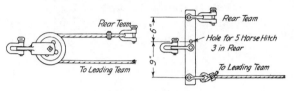

depth of from 6 to 10 in.; the rear disk in the bottom of the same furrow turns from 5 to 12 in., making a

FIG. 197. Tandem-hitch devices

A tandem hitch may be secured by means of the pulley or the lever

total of from 11 to 20 in. or even to 24 in. It covers trash well and pulverizes the soil to an astonishing degree. It is rather

difficult to use the plow in stiff sod, but ordinary sod is satisfactorily handled. The tandem pulley hitch (Fig. 197) is used on this plow, 4 horses being required. Several moldboard plows designed for deep plowing are giving satisfaction.

The draft of plows. Plowing is one of the farm operations that calls for the expenditure of a large amount of energy. The question of draft, therefore, is an important one, and if anything can be done to decrease the draft of a plow ever so little, the total saving during a

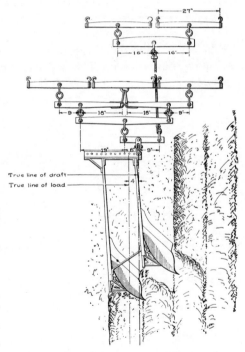

FIG. 198. A five-horse tandem hitch

season's work may be immense. Quite an extensive series of tests has been carried on at the Ohio State University under the supervision of the Department of Agricultural Engineering, in an effort to determine the relative draft of different types of plows, as well as the effect of different attachments.

The draft was taken by means of a recording-dynamometer. This is nothing more than a spring balance, which, by means

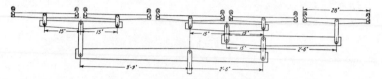

FIG. 199. A five-horse-abreast hitch

of a moving finger playing over a revolving drum on which is fastened a slip of paper, records the number of pounds of force necessary to draw the plow.

Table XXV gives the results of tests made in the spring of 1916 on a heavy timothy sod. The soil was a stiff clay loam and the moisture content was almost perfect for good plowing. A frame-less sulky plow equipped with a 14-inch steel bottom and a

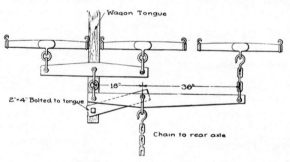

FIG. 200. A simple and satisfactory method of hitching three horses to a wagon or other tongued implement

An ordinary 3-horse evener is used, and the hitch is made directly to the rear axle

general-purpose moldboard was used. The object of this series of tests was to determine the effect of the jointer, of the rolling coulter, and of a combination coulter-and-jointer attachment upon the draft of the plow. The coulter was set to run one half the depth of the furrow, and the jointer to run about $1\frac{1}{2}$ in. deep. The same team

FIG. 201. A disk gang plow

The disk plow is used in very sticky or in very dry **soils**

FIG. 202. A double-disk deep-tilling plow

The relative depths of the 2 cuts may readily be seen

FIG. 203. Turning a square corner with a frameless sulky plow

It is possible to turn a square corner either to the right or to the left with a frameless plow. The driver has just shifted the front furrow wheel

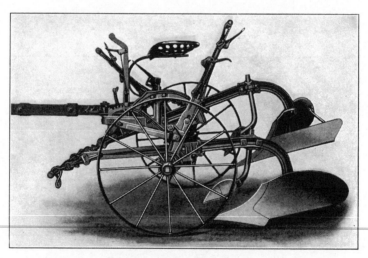

FIG. 204. A reversible sulky plow

Such a plow is used on hillsides or in places where a dead furrow is objectionable

and driver were used throughout the tests, and unusually uniform results were secured. The tests were carried on in series; that is, five furrows were run on a narrow land with the bare plow, then five with the jointer, five with the rolling coulter, and five with the combination, after which the second series was started. This was done in order that the soil conditions under which the different attachments were tested might be as uniform as possible. The ground was uniform, and the tests were made within a period of six weeks. The general average represents the average of forty tests and is therefore fairly reliable. The figures give the draft

FIG. 205. First-class plowing

The furrows are clean cut, well proportioned, and properly turned. A jointer would improve the quality of the work

in pounds per square inch of furrow slice. That is, the total pull in pounds was divided by the cross-sectional area of the furrow slice in order to reduce the results to a common basis of comparison. The total draft of the furrows varied widely owing to the unavoidable variations in both the width and the depth of furrow. When the total draft, however, is reduced to terms of pounds per square inch of furrow slice, the variation in size of furrow is not material. The furrows averaged $7\frac{1}{2}$ in. in depth and 14 in. in width.

TABLE XXV. EFFECT OF ATTACHMENTS ON THE DRAFT OF A
SULKY PLOW

SERIES	PLOW ATTACHMENTS			
	Bare	Jointer	Rolling coulter	Combination coulter and jointer
No. 1	5.610	5.848	6.328	6.877
No. 2	5.786	5.265	6.157	6.487
No. 3	5.503	5.396	5.919	7.190
No. 4	5.801	5.319	6.095	6.484
Average . .	5.675	5.457	6.124	6.759

The Iowa State College of Agriculture reports the following
tests comparing the draft of walking, sulky, and gang plows:

TABLE XXVI. RELATIVE DRAFT OF WALKING, SULKY, AND
GANG PLOWS

PLOW	SIZE OF FURROW IN INCHES	TOTAL DRAFT IN POUNDS	DRAFT PER SQUARE INCH OF FURROW SLICE, IN POUNDS
Walking	14 × 6.5	440	4.83
Sulky	16 × 6	474	4.93
Gang (two bottoms) . . .	14 × 5	700	5.00

Several tests have been made at the Ohio State University
comparing the draft of a double-disk deep-tilling plow with
moldboard plows. Table XXVII gives the relative draft of the
double-disk plow and a twelve-inch walking plow in a stiff timothy
sod. The figures are the averages of three tests. The results
show that the double-disk plow pulled 10 per cent more easily
than the moldboard plow, when the furrow turned is considered.

TABLE XXVII. A COMPARISON OF THE DOUBLE-DISK PLOW AND A
MOLDBOARD PLOW

PLOW	SIZE OF FURROW IN INCHES	TOTAL DRAFT IN POUNDS	DRAFT PER SQUARE INCH OF FURROW SLICE, IN POUNDS
Moldboard	12.7 × 6.93	526.7	6.98
Double-disk	10.4 × 12 (depth)	785.4	6.29

CHAPTER XIX

TILLAGE TOOLS

In its broadest sense the term "tillage tools" includes all tools used in the preparation of the soil for the seed. This would include the plow, but since plowing is a process so complete in itself and so different in its method, it seems logical to exclude the plow from the class of tillage tools, remembering, however, the statements made in the opening paragraph of Chapter XVIII. For the purpose of this discussion, then, tillage tools will include harrows, weeders, rollers, drags, and cultivators — chiefly those tools which are used in preparing plowed ground for the seed and in caring for the crops during their period of growth.

HARROWS

The spike-tooth harrow. Next to the plow, the spike-tooth harrow seems to be the tool most common to Eastern and Western farms. It is virtually indispensable. Its chief use is as a leveler, since it will not penetrate hard ground to any depth, though it stirs the surface soil and crushes clods to some extent.

The *steel-bar* harrow has been the most popular harrow in recent years. The bar is made in a number of different forms. Fig. 206 shows several forms and several methods in common use for attaching the teeth to the bars. This is one of the points which should not be overlooked in purchasing a harrow. Some forms of clamps have a tendency to work loose, and if the teeth which they hold are not enlarged at the top, teeth will frequently be lost. In the best types of harrows the ends of the bars are protected by guard rails, as shown in Fig. 207, a feature which prevents them from catching on posts, stones, and other obstructions. The teeth are usually triangular, round, or square. In any case they should be so fastened that they may be turned around and thus be, in a sense, self-sharpening. The teeth must

273

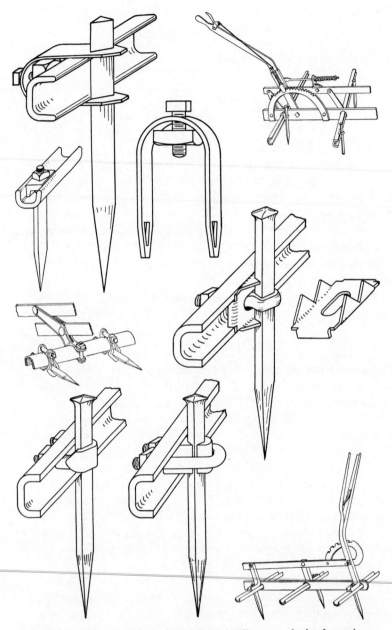

FIG. 206. Several types of harrow bars and different methods of securing
the teeth

not be too large, else they will make too much of a furrow, especially when they gather trash. The levers should permit of a wide range in the adjustment of the angle of the teeth, this angle vary-

FIG. 207. One section of a steel-bar harrow

The guard rails protect the ends of the bars and help to brace the harrow

ing from about 15° back of a vertical position to a horizontal position. Runners or some other device should be provided for transporting the harrow. These runners, which are usually attached to the bars, are let down as the teeth

are slanted backward. The first part of a harrow to wear out is usually the link attachment between the evener bar and the sections

of the harrow. This connection, therefore, should be quite heavy.

Of late the *wood-bar* harrow (Fig. 208) seems to be coming back into favor. The wooden bars afford a rigidity of construction which is usually lacking in the steel-bar harrow. The teeth are usually driven through

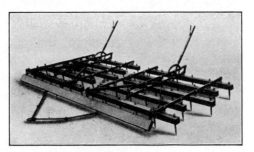

FIG. 208. A substantial wood-bar harrow

The wooden bars are stiff and afford simple means for bracing. The bars should be riveted at each tooth

the wooden bar, and should be riveted on either side of the tooth.

Following is a list of the common sizes of spike-tooth harrows :

Two-horse harrow, 2 sections, 60 teeth, cuts 10 ft.
Two-horse or three-horse harrow, 3 sections, 72 teeth, cuts 12 ft.
Three-horse harrow, 3 sections, 90 teeth, cuts 15 ft.
Four-horse harrow, 4 sections, 96 teeth, cuts 18 ft.
Four-horse harrow, 4 sections, 120 teeth, cuts 20 ft.

The spring-tooth harrow. Fig. 209 illustrates a common type of spring-tooth harrow. This harrow is furnished either with or without wheels. Wheels or runners should generally be included, since they enable the operator to control better the depth to which the teeth will penetrate and since they are a great aid in transport-

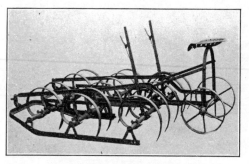

FIG. 209. A spring-tooth harrow with riding truck and runners

The runners are for gauging the depth and for transportation. The cart does not carry the weight of the harrow

ing the harrow from field to field. The teeth may be furnished with removable points. This is an advantage, since teeth of varying shapes and sizes may then be used with the same harrow for different kinds of work. For example, this harrow is very generally used now in preference to the disk harrow for cultivating alfalfa, since the more or less flexible teeth do not cut off so many of the root crowns as does the disk. But for this particular purpose the points of the teeth should be long and narrow (Fig. 210), and if removable points are provided they can be changed to suit the kind of work being done. Fig. 211 shows a spring-tooth harrow in which the framework is carried on high wheels. This makes an excellent harrow. The weight of the frame holds the teeth in a fixed position and elimi-nates the tendency found in the com-

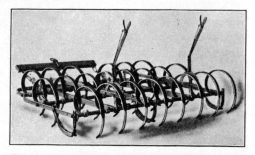

FIG. 210. A type of spring-tooth harrow especially intended for harrowing alfalfa

mon type to jump and jerk about, especially in rough ground.

The spring-tooth harrow is superior to the disk harrow in stony and in shaly ground, and is especially desirable for orchard work in such soils. It has excellent penetration and can be used

FIG. 211. A spring-tooth harrow on a high-wheeled truck

Even in exceptionally hard ground the operator can control the depth to which the teeth penetrate. The teeth run more steadily than in the common type

FIG. 212. The harrow cart is a valuable attachment

The illustration teaches a lesson in the economy of man labor

effectively in stirring very hard ground. It does not, however, adapt itself to as many different conditions as does the disk. The following sizes of spring-tooth harrows are in common use:

Two-horse harrow, 15-tooth, cuts 4½ ft.
Two-horse or three-horse harrow, 17-tooth, cuts 5½ ft.
Three-horse harrow, 23-tooth, cuts 7½ ft.
Four-horse harrow, 25-tooth, cuts 8½ ft.

The disk harrow. The disk harrow, like the spring-tooth harrow, is used to stir the ground to a considerable depth. It is an all-around harrow, being adapted to a variety of conditions. It is

very generally used in preparing plowed land for corn or other crops, in preparing corn-stubble land for oats in the spring or for wheat in the fall, in cultivating alfalfa, and, in recent years, in harrowing sod previous to . breaking. Fig. 213 shows a good type of the single disk harrow.

FIG. 213. A well-constructed disk harrow

A truck is an indispensable attachment to most disk harrows; it lightens the burden of the team

There has been a distinct evolution in the size of the disk used in this harrow. A few years ago the disks were as small as 10 in. and 12 in. in diameter; now the prevailing sizes are 16 in. and 18 in. Other things being equal, the smaller disk will penetrate better than the larger one, but in working over trashy ground the small disk is not so effective, and it probably makes for heavier draft. The disks may be of the *solid* or of the *cutaway* type, as shown in Fig. 214. The cutaway disk will penetrate hard ground, but it does not stir all of the soil to the same depth, or cut trash so completely as the solid type. The points are likely to bend, the bottom of the scallops become dull, and the disk as a whole is difficult to sharpen.

The *double*, or *tandem*, disk is the more modern type of disk harrow. Fig. 214 illustrates a common construction. In the single disk harrow each gang throws the soil out, and consequently the ground is left uneven; to level the surface it is necessary to lap half on each succeeding round. With the double disk harrow the front gangs throw out and the rear gangs throw in, thus leaving the ground perfectly level. In addition, the disks of the rear gangs are so set that each runs between the furrows cut by the

FIG. 214. A tandem disk harrow with fore truck

The rear gangs are of the cutaway type. Each of the 4 gangs is separately controlled.
The rear gangs may be taken off

two disks immediately ahead, thus stirring nearly every inch of the soil. The ground is covered twice as fast with a tandem disk as with a single disk of the same width, and at the same time the work is done more efficiently. The power required is, of course, increased, but it is not doubled.

There are two general types of construction used in the tandem disk harrow. As shown in Fig. 214, one type is nothing more than a single disk harrow with another set of gangs attached behind by some coupling-device. This construction offers one advantage in that the rear gangs may be taken off and the

280

harrow then used as a single disk harrow. This type is always provided with a tongue truck. It will be seen that the weight of the frame rests entirely on the front gangs, and that the rear gangs cannot be very rigidly connected to those in front. In very hard ground the rear gangs therefore have a tendency to slip to one side, so that their disks follow in the tracks of the disks on the front gangs.

The other type of construction is shown in Fig. 215. There is no tongue truck, the frame being supported equally on the front

FIG. 215. A cutaway tandem disk harrow

The frame is supported equally on the front and rear gangs. There is no fore truck with this type. A tongue may or may not be used

and rear gangs; thus the gangs are rigidly connected. Because of the rigid connection of the gangs, this type of harrow is rather difficult to turn; it is, in fact, quite impossible to turn it squarely around. There is, however, no tendency for the rear disks to run in furrows made by the front disks. It is provided with a stiff tongue, but works as well or better without it.

The factors which influence the *depth* to which a disk harrow will penetrate are (1) the angle of the disks, (2) the weight of the harrow, (3) the sharpness of the disks, (4) the size of the disks, (5) the dish of the disks, and (6) the angle of the hitch. Of these factors the first three are the most important, and all are within the control of the operator.

The levers for varying the angle of the gangs should be conveniently located and easily operated. In the tandem disk there are usually 4 levers, 1 for each gang. In a few harrows there are but 2 levers, 1 for the front gangs and 1 for the rear gangs. The latter construction is not so desirable as the former.

The disks should be sharpened every two or three years. Very few farmers attend to this important matter. It is an easy task to remove the disks and have them ground on an emery wheel at the blacksmith shop. Sharp disks relieve the harrow of much strain; if they are dull, the angle of the gangs must be increased if the disks are made to run deeply enough. This increases the pressure on the bearings.

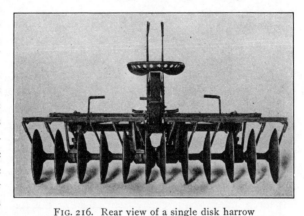

FIG. 216. Rear view of a single disk harrow

The bearings are oiled by grease-cups on short tubes. The bumpers between the gangs relieve the bearings of considerable side thrust

Whatever the type of harrow, there are certain things that should be looked after in purchasing. The bearings may be either of *chilled iron* or of *maple* soaked in oil; roller bearings are only occasionally used. The bearings should be amply long, well protected from the dirt, easily removable, and easily oiled. The last feature is extremely important. One of the best methods of oiling is shown in Fig. 216. A large cup on a short tube, which keeps it up out of the dirt, may be filled with cup grease or with oil. In oiling some harrows it is necessary to use a wrench in removing a setscrew, and if the wrench is not at hand the bearing is likely to go unoiled. Sometimes long tubes reaching up above the disks and closed at the top by a cotter-pin plug are provided. This is very satisfactory, though long tubes for conducting oil are always objectionable. Hard-maple bearings are found to be satisfactory; they reduce friction to a minimum, they wear well and are easily and cheaply replaced when worn out.

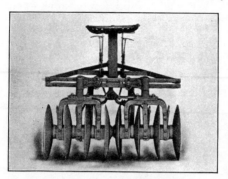

FIG. 217. An extension disk harrow

The long bolts holding together the disks of each gang are called *arbor* bolts. They should be provided with heavy heads and nuts, and in harrows where the heads of the arbor bolts take the end thrust of the gangs (Fig. 216) there should be large and substantial bumpers. The bearings and the spools between the disks are sure to become worn because of this end thrust, and it should always be possible to take up the wear through the arbor bolts.

In both single and double disk harrows there is a tendency for the inner ends of all the gangs to be forced out of the ground. Adjustable *snubbing-blocks* or bars should be provided to force these ends down and secure an even penetration at all points.

A tongue truck should always be furnished with the single-disk harrow. It takes all unnecessary weight off the horses' necks and allows them to turn the harrow with their traces rather than with their necks.

The size of a disk

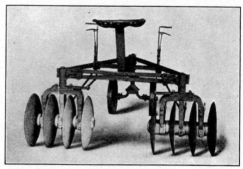

FIG. 218. The extension disk harrow of Fig. 217 with disks extended

This harrow is adapted to orchard use. The gangs are shown extended so as to reach under trees. They may also be reversed so that the soil can be thrown in or out

harrow is specified by stating the number of disks, which are placed 6 in. apart. The common sizes in the single disk type have 8, 10, and 12 disks, covering 4, 5, and 6 ft. respectively.

In the double-disk type the common sizes have 16, 20, 24, 29, and 33 disks and cover 4½, 5½, 6½, 7½, and 8½ ft. in width respectively. The extra half foot comes from the fact that each end disk of the rear gangs is set 3 in. outside of the corresponding disk in front. The last two sizes have an extra disk in the middle to stir the soil between the two rear gangs, hence the odd number of disks.

The Acme harrow. The Acme harrow is an excellent tool for preparing sod ground for corn. The crooked knives have a slicing effect; they mash clods well and are very effective in leveling the

FIG. 219. An alfalfa harrow

The sharp teeth penetrate to a considerable depth but do not injure the root crowns

ground. This type of harrow cannot be put to as many uses as the disk or the spring-tooth, and hence has never been widely used.

WEEDERS

Although the spike-tooth harrow is used a great deal in stirring the soil after spring crops — chiefly corn and potatoes — are planted, the weeder is in many cases more effective. Its numerous fine teeth stir almost every inch of the soil and tear out weeds, but yet do not seriously injure corn or potato plants which may just be coming up. By many the weeder is used with good results when corn or potatoes are several inches high. It should not be used in early morning, when the young plants are brittle and easily broken.

The best modern weeders are now supplied with wheels, such a weeder being shown in Fig. 220. This makes it possible to control the depth better and to turn the weeder more easily when in the field. The teeth should be long, small and sharp at the ends, with plenty of spring.

ROLLERS

The roller is a tool that must be used with care and judgment. Properly used, it is efficient in the preparation of the seed-bed, but improperly used it does far more harm than good. It packs and firms the soil in dry weather, mashes lumps, and levels the land. In sod ground newly plowed it may be used with profit, since it presses the furrow slices against the subsoil and thus

FIG. 220. A weeder with a truck attachment

The truck enables the operator to control the depth to which the teeth penetrate

establishes capillary action. For meadowland, wheat land, or pasture land that has heaved badly the roller is the only effective tool. On plowed lands the roller should always be followed with a harrow to prevent the formation of a crust and to provide the necessary surface mulch.

Homemade rollers are very satisfactory. A round log with lag screws in the end for supporting the frame is the simplest type, but a 1-piece roller is difficult to turn. A *log* roller may easily be made in 2 pieces and will last for many years. Old mower wheels may be made to serve as a foundation for a *plank* roller.

FIG. 221. A cast-iron drum roller in three sections

FIG. 222. A tube roller
This type of roller crushes clods well and leaves the surface ridged

FIG. 223. A combination roller-crusher

Four wheels are required to make a roller, 2 for each half. Holes $\frac{3}{8}$ in. in diameter and 4 in. apart are drilled in the rims of the wheels, and $2'' \times 4''$ planks, slightly beveled to fit closely together, and of proper length, are bolted to the wheels. A suitable axle and framework may be easily contrived by the average farmer. The whole makes an inexpensive and satisfactory drum roller.

Cast-iron and *steel* rollers made in two or more sections (Fig. 221) are now widely used. One type has a narrow middle drum which may be removed for the purpose of rolling ground after the corn is up. A roller should be of large diameter, and of course it must be heavy. The following table gives standard sizes and weights:

Length	Diameter	Weight
6 ft.	24 in.	485 lb.
7 ft.	24 in.	540 lb.
8 ft.	24 in.	585 lb.
7 ft.	26 in.	620 lb.
8 ft.	26 in.	670 lb.
8 ft.	30 in.	680 lb.
9 ft.	30 in.	715 lb.

The *tube* roller shown in Fig. 222 possesses some advantage over the ordinary

FIG. 224. A demonstration outfit which shows the action of the roller-crusher

Fig. 225. The work of roller-crusher

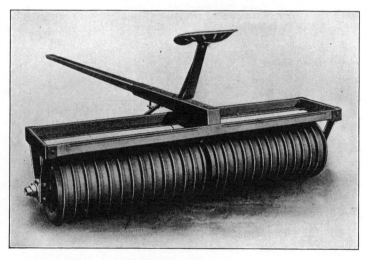

Fig. 226. A single-gang roller-crusher of large size

kind. It is a well-known fact that if the surface of the soil is ridged there will be less evaporation and less tendency to form a crust. In spite of this advantage, however, this type of roller has

never come into common use. One reason for this probably lies in the fact that it is not generally satisfactory for rolling wheat land or meadowland in the spring.

FIG. 227. The subsurface packer

Used chiefly in arid and semiarid regions

A still newer type of *roller-crusher*, shown in Fig. 223, is now on the market. This roller, which weighs 700 lb. for a length of 6 ft. and a diameter of 12 in., does unusually effective work in crushing clods. It pulverizes and packs the soil, but at the same time leaves a ridged surface on which a crust will seldom form. This culti-packer, as one company calls it, is believed by many to be the best tool

of its kind on the market, and it will undoubtedly become popular. Fig. 225 shows this tool in action on the Ohio State University farm. It will probably find its greatest use in the preparation of the seed-bed for spring and fall crops. It has been used with success on fields after the

FIG. 228. The crow-foot roller

A good clod-crusher, but not in general use

corn has been planted, a use which is especially beneficial in a dry season. The *subsurface packer*, shown in Fig. 227, is used very generally in semiarid regions, and by some in humid regions, with excellent results.

DRAGS

There are numerous forms of drags, all of homemade type. The drag is perhaps more valuable to the average farmer than the roller, since it is even more efficient than the roller in crush-

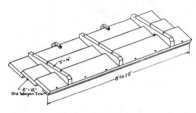

FIG. 229. A common but effective drag

The iron shoe takes the wear and assists materially in crushing clods

ing clods, and is, besides, a good leveler. Figs. 229 and 230 show two common types of drags. The common plank drag is perhaps the best for all purposes. The drag made of 4 × 4 oak timbers is excellent in crushing hard clods, but clogs easily in damp soil.

A drag made of four 2 × 4 scantlings placed one foot apart is used chiefly as a leveler. It may be made quite long, thus making short work of a field where the soil is already in fairly good condition. Eight feet is the standard length of a drag; if it is longer than this, it does not touch throughout its length at all times. Some attempts have been made to overcome the slight tendency there is for the soil to crust after its use, by driving a

FIG. 230. A drag made of 4″ × 4″ timbers

This type is very effective as a crusher

row of heavy spikes or harrow teeth through the back of the rear plank — a good practice if the teeth can be kept from bending and if there is no trash to be dragged.

CULTIVATORS

The garden cultivator. This tool, shown in Fig. 231, ought to be more generally owned and used in the farm garden. Work can be much more rapidly done with it than with the hoe, and just as efficiently. There are so many different attachments adapting it to various uses that when it is once used it is always used.

FIG. 231. A garden cultivator
This tool should be more generally used in farm gardens

The one-horse cultivator. No farm can do without its 1-horse cultivator. For cultivating the garden, small truck patches, and corn after it is too large for the 2-horse cultivator, nothing will take its place. There are many forms of shovels for this tool. There should be at least 5 shovels, and the width of the cultivator should be easily adjustable through a wide range. The shovels should be adjustable as to depth, and it is often an advantage to be able to turn the two outer shovels to throw toward or away from the row, though where the shovels are small this is of minor im-

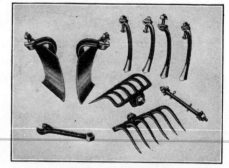

FIG. 232. Attachments for the garden cultivator shown in Fig. 231

portance. A gauge-wheel is important in properly controlling the depth. The harrow-tooth cultivator is good for breaking a crust, but it is almost useless among large weeds. Moreover it is rather difficult to keep it running smoothly when open to its full width.

The two-horse cultivator. The walking cultivator (Fig. 233) is still in quite general use in the East. On farms cultivating large

areas it is more rare, but even on such farms there are those who wish their corn cultivated the first time with the operator walking. This of course accords with the fairly well-established fact that it is not usual for an operator to do as good work in small corn when riding as when walking.

FIG. 233. A walking cultivator with an attachment for distributing fertilizer

The 2-shovel gangs are not to be recommended

The chief difference in sulky cultivators lies in the style and control of the gangs. In the various illustrations shown there is found a wide variation in the form and type of gangs in common use. Nothing less than a 3-shovel gang should be considered. The use of the old-fashioned 2-shovel type with each shovel from

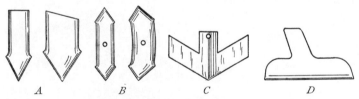

A   B   C   D

FIG. 234. Different types of shovels used on cultivators

A, common single-pointed shovels; B, reversible shovels; C, thistle sweep; D, gopher, or surface, blade

4 to 6 in. wide can no longer be justified. There are gangs with 4, 5, or 6 shovels, though 3 or 4 shovels are most common. Not a great deal of importance need be attached to the distribution of the shovels on the gang. The illustrations show several forms, any one of which is satisfactory. The spring-tooth gang is

more widely used on walking than on sulky cultivators. It does
excellent work except in very hard ground, when the shovels are

likely to bend back-
ward too much.

It will be noticed
(Fig. 234) that there
is a difference in the
shape of the shovels.
Some are reversible;
that is, they are
pointed on both ends.
This type of shovel is
curved and gives con-
siderable difficulty by
failing to scour in
loose soil, the soil

FIG. 235. A combination walking or riding cultivator with spring-break shovels

sticking to the upper end of the shovel. The double-point
feature is scarcely valuable enough to overcome this objection.

In regard to control of
gangs, sulky cultivators may
be divided into four classes:
(1) the pivot axle, (2) the pivot
gang, (3) the pivot frame, and
(4) the direct foot control.

A *pivot-axle* cultivator is
shown in Fig. 236. The gangs
are guided by controlling the
wheels by means of suitable
levers. These levers, shown
at the right and left of *A*,
Fig. 236, are worked by the
feet, and the whole cultivator
is shifted from side to side,
the gangs being absolutely
stationary in this regard.
Since the operator simply

FIG. 236. A pivot-axle cultivator

The foot levers are the horizontal bars to the
right and left of *A*

changes the direction of the wheels, the team must pull the cultivator forward before it will be drawn to one side, and this makes

it slow in action. It is necessary, too, that the feet be held firmly against the levers at all times, else if a stone or clod is struck the cultivator will swerve to one side. In rough ground this puts a constant strain on the operator. Shifting from side to side, as in crooked corn, makes the work hard for the team, as it imparts a constant seesawing motion to the tongue. Further, the distance between gangs cannot be varied quickly; so that if a scattered hill is encountered a part of it is likely to be plowed out. On the other hand, for sidehill work this type is excellent; one is able to keep the cultivator uphill and make it straddle the row. In cultivating around trees and stumps there is also a considerable advantage with this cultivator. Likewise, in turning, it is possible to steer the wheels around hills of corn. The depth is controlled by the lifting-levers, and it is possible to force the gangs to a considerable depth even in very hard ground. The gangs may be raised separately, or the levers may be locked so that one

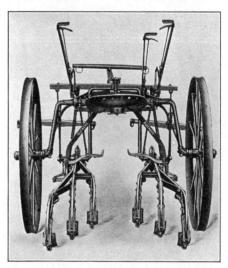

FIG. 237. A treadle-guide cultivator

The gangs are controlled by the foot levers. The arched bars may be used to connect the two gangs; otherwise they work independently of each other

lever will raise both gangs. A separate lever is provided to adjust the width between the gangs. There is always a tendency with this type of cultivator to set the gangs rather too far apart, especially if the corn is crooked.

A *pivot-gang*, or treadle-guide, cultivator is shown in Fig. 237. The gangs are pivoted and controlled by a system of foot levers so placed that the feet are moved straight to the front to throw the gangs out. There is usually a spring to bring them back toward the row. Usually each gang is controlled independently

FIG. 238. A pivot-frame cultivator

The frame is pivoted about the tongue. Notice the pulley and track at the rear end of the tongue

of the other, though an arch may be attached to the gangs so that they may be moved together. In cultivating crooked rows it is better to work them independently. Since the gangs are controlled directly, they may be moved more quickly than in the pivot-axle type. Moreover there is less strain on the operator, and the work is not so hard on the horses. It is possible, too, to swing the gangs in between hills if necessary, a thing which cannot be done with the pivot-axle type. There is less tendency to rack the cultivator, since nothing but the gangs are moved. On the other hand, each gang must usually be raised separately, there is no means of forcing the gangs into the ground, and on sidehills the control is not so complete as with the pivot-axle type.

A *pivot-frame* cultivator is shown in Fig. 238. This type is guided by shifting the whole frame from side to side. The frame is pivoted at

FIG. 239. A direct-foot-control cultivator

The gangs are raised by means of the upright levers

the rear end of the tongue, and by swinging the seat to one side the direction of the frame and wheels is changed, so that when the cultivator is pulled forward it travels to one side just as in the pivot-axle type.

The *direct foot control*, as the name implies, is a type in which the gangs are controlled by the feet, which are placed in stirrups on the gangs. Figs. 239 and 240 illustrate this type. The lifting-levers with handholds are not effective in guiding the gangs. The

Fig. 240. In a direct-foot-control cultivator with gangs which are raised by the hands

This type is sometimes called a hammock-seat cultivator, since the seat is swung from the bars at either side of the operator

great advantage of this type is that the feet control the gangs directly; the work is harder than in the former types, however, since no leverage is taken advantage of in the movement of the gangs. This type is often called the hammock-seat cultivator, a feature greatly prized by some, since it not only gives greater freedom to the feet but affords a better view of the row than does the straddle-seat type.

The *parallel-beam* feature is now found on many one-row and two-row cultivators. Fig. 242 illustrates this feature with the attendant advantage. It is seen that when the gangs are kept

parallel while being shifted, the shovels always travel straight to
the front and thus are effective to their full width at all times,

FIG. 241. Side view of a pivot-axle cultivator

Notice the penetrating curve on which the shovels are set

stirring all of the soil ;
but if the gangs are
not kept parallel, the
wide angle of shift
makes it necessary to
draw the shovels at an
angle, and this destroys
their effectiveness and
leaves narrow strips
of soil untouched.

In many sulky cul-
tivators, the tongue is
thrown up as soon as
the gangs are raised,

since the rider is so placed as exactly to balance the tongue with
the gangs down. The *balance-frame* feature which is now found
on some cultivators is so arranged as
to shift the wheels when the gangs
are raised or lowered, thus maintaining a balance at all times. In many
cases this is automatically done. It
should be possible in all types to adjust the balance for operators of different weights.

Since the width of rows which must
be cultivated varies, there should be
some easy means for widening and
narrowing the cultivator. This should
apply not only to the width of tread
but to the distance between gangs
and, if possible, between the shovels.

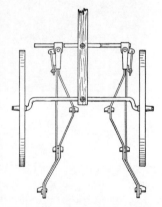

FIG. 242. The principle of the
parallel-beam feature

The gangs instead of swinging on a
pivot at the front end are by appropriate levers pushed from side to
side on the bar shown in front

It should be possible to raise and
lower each shovel on its shank so that
the depth next the corn row may be
varied at will. Besides, each shovel should turn on its shank so
as to throw the dirt toward or away from the row. It is often

FIG. 243. A pivot-axle cultivator in a vineyard

The shovels can be adjusted to different heights as well as to different distances apart;
they may also be turned to throw soil toward or away from the row

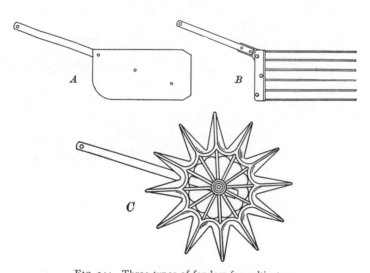

FIG. 244. Three types of fenders for cultivators

A, a solid fender, is perhaps the most common; *B* is light and allows fine soil to pass
through, which helps to cover weeds; *C*, a star fender is not often used

298

an advantage, too, to be able to vary the width of the gangs. For example, in potato culture the practice is followed of cultivating immediately after planting. If the cultivator gangs can be spread

sufficiently to cover the space between the rows, it is sufficient to straddle alternate rows. Fig. 243 shows a cultivator with this possibility. The bar supporting the shovels is pivoted in front and may be swung out at will.

FIG. 245. A sulky cultivator with a weeder attachment

The weeder is supported between the gangs and is raised and lowered with them

Fig. 245 shows a *weeder* attachment suitable for any cultivator. It is merely a section of a weeder having from six to eight teeth; it is attached to the gangs and is raised and lowered with them. The depth to which it runs can be adjusted. This attachment is especially valued by potato-growers and may be used until the potatoes are from 6 to 8 in. high. It may be used on corn if the soil is not too lumpy.

The wheels of the cultivator should have removable boxings so that the boxings may be replaced when worn. There is a great amount of wear here, especially in the pivot-axle type of cultivator, and loose bearings make the handling of the cultivator more difficult. The bearings should be lubricated every day when in use, and twice a day is sometimes necessary to prevent their becoming dry — this is always true if oil is used instead of grease.

FIG. 246. A surface cultivator

An excellent tool to break the crust and create a mulch in relatively soft ground

The *disk* cultivator having, usually, three disks on a gang does not meet with general favor. It is excellent for pea vines, heavy weeds, or trash, but is difficult to use in small corn because it covers the corn badly. Then, too, there are bearings to wear out, and the gangs are heavier.

FIG. 247. A surface cultivator at work

The rake attachments are just to the rear of the surface blades and serve to level and fine the soil

There are several other special types of shovels, such as those used on the surface cultivator, which are useful only under certain limited conditions. This particular type is shown in Fig. 246. It is excellent for breaking a surface, but is not effective in stirring hard ground.

The two-row cultivator. The two-row cultivator is coming into more general use each year, because of an increasing desire among farmers to place more power at the command of a single driver. One man with a single-row cultivator and 2 horses cannot

FIG. 248. A two-row cultivator

This type of cultivator cultivates 2 rows

FIG. 249. A two-row cultivator

This type cultivates 2 spaces

properly care for more than 25 acres of corn. With 3 horses and a two-row cultivator, however, he should be able to handle at least 40 acres. With level land and with the rows straight it is possible to do fairly satisfactory work with this implement.

There are two general types of two-row cultivators, as shown in Figs. 248 and 249. The one straddles and cultivates 2 rows; the other straddles 1 row and cultivates 2 spaces. With the first type

FIG. 250. A convertible cultivator

The outside half of each gang can be removed, thus converting it into a 1-row cultivator

it is possible, when cultivating in the direction in which the field is planted, to straddle two rows planted at one passage of the planter. Such rows are exactly the same distance apart. This type requires 3 horses, and its wide type of construction makes it somewhat hard to handle.

The second type, which requires but 2 horses, is compact and easily handled. But since it cultivates 2 spaces, and since there are no two adjacent spaces in a field at a uniform distance apart, it is not possible to cultivate as close to the corn with it as with the former type. In several makes it is possible to use it either as a 1-horse or a 2-horse cultivator, the outer gang on either side being removable.

CHAPTER XX

SEEDING-MACHINERY

The importance of the proper selection, care, and adjustment of seeding-machinery cannot be overemphasized. No matter how well the ground is fertilized nor how well it is prepared, if the machines for distributing the seed are not what they ought to be, good crops are impossible; and if the seeding is poorly done, the loss is irreparable. No one can afford to take chances with an old corn-planter or grain-drill. Often indeed the investment in a new one yields a high return.

CORN-PLANTERS

The corn-planter has undergone many changes within the past ten or fifteen years. The old hand planter, or jobber, is now used only for replanting, or in sections where a small acreage is grown.

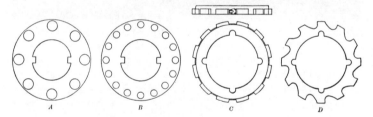

FIG. 251. Types of corn-planter plates

A, full-hill-drop; *B*, cumulative-drop round-hole; *C*, cumulative-drop edge-selection; *D*, cumulative-drop flat-selection

The older styles of horse planter, which made it necessary for the field to be marked out one way and for one man to drive the planter while another rode and dropped the two rows by tripping just as the planter shank crossed the mark, are now obsolete. That type of check-row planter too in which the wire turned the

301

plate is seldom found. In place of these types the modern cumulative-drop check-row planter is now almost universally used.

Plates. The cumulative-drop check-row planter is fitted with a variety of plates suited to every purpose. Fig. 251 shows the types in common use. The *full-hill* plate is seldom used. The other types are all classed as *cumulative-drop* plates, the idea being that but 1 kernel is selected at a time, the cells being large enough for but a single grain. In the full-hill plate it is quite possible to find 4 kernels small enough to fit into a 3-kernel cell, or 2 kernels

FIG. 252. An edge-selection plate (on the left) and a flat-selection plate as they operate in the bottom of the seed-box

large enough to fill the same cell. On the other hand, it is quite impossible to find 2 kernels so small as to slip into a cell intended for but 1. It seems that there is less variation in the thickness of the kernel than in any other dimension, a circumstance which is the fundamental reason for the design of the cumulative plates. Each planter is supplied with an assortment of plates adapted to small, to medium, and to large kernels.

The drop. The drop is spoken of as being *full-hill* or as being *cumulative*. In the first type a full hill is deposited as each cell is passed over the shank of the planter. In the cumulative drop, since each cell of the plate holds but a single kernel, it is necessary to accumulate the kernels one at a time until the full hill is collected. This is accomplished by turning the plate through a portion of its circumference until the desired number of cells has passed over the upper valve. For this purpose a clutch is provided which is tripped by the knot on the check wire and which turns the plate the desired distance. When this distance is reached, the plate is thrown out of engagement until tripped again. This clutch is one of the extremely important parts of the modern planter and is usually the first part to cause trouble. It is essential, whatever the construction, that the parts engage quickly and positively, and that there be no chance of the plate's slipping out of engagement until it is thrown out at the end of the travel.

It will be noticed from Fig. 253 that the *clutch* is on the drop shaft, which, in turn, revolves the plates. In the older check-row corn-planters, each time the clutch was tripped the drop shaft was turned through one complete revolution. The gear on the drop shaft which turned the seed-plate was

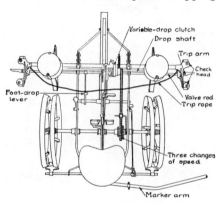

FIG. 253. Plan view showing the main features of a check-row corn-planter

so timed as to revolve the plate through one fourth of its circumference. Hence, if there were 4 cells in each quarter of the plate, 4 grains would be deposited. If a 3-kernel hill were desired, it became necessary to put in a plate with 3 cells in each quarter. These planters were regularly supplied with 8-cell, 12-cell, and 16-cell plates. If required, 10-cell plates were provided, so arranged as to drop 2 kernels in one hill and 3 kernels in the next, thus suiting the fancy of those who felt that 3 kernels made the corn too thick and 2 kernels made it too thin. If each type of plate were furnished for small, for medium, and for large corn, at least 18 plates would be required for each planter.

Nearly all of the planters now on the market, unlike the older planters, are equipped with a *variable-drop* device. This device is found in connection with the drop shaft, either on the clutch or at the plate. Fig. 254 shows a type in which the shifting

lever controls the distance the drop shaft travels. Each time the clutch is tripped, if the lever is in notch No. 4 (the top notch), as shown in the lower figure, the drop shaft makes one complete turn, which causes 4 cells to pass over the upper valve. If the lever is in notch No. 3, as it is shown in the upper figure, the clutch does not engage the drop shaft through a complete revolution, but by means of the cam A the dog B is thrown out of engagement so that the drop shaft is made to skip one quarter of a turn, thus causing but 3 cells to pass over the valve. The plates in nearly all cases have 16 cells.

FIG. 254. A variable-drop clutch

In the lower figure the lever is set for 4 kernels, in the upper figure for 3 kernels; C is the drop shaft

Fig. 255 shows how the same thing is accomplished in another way. The clutch turns the drop shaft through one complete revolution each time it is tripped. The drive plate beneath the seed-plate has three rows of teeth, and as the variable-drop lever is shifted, the gear on the drop shaft engages with different-sized gears on the

FIG. 255. Another type of variable-drop clutch

The distance the plate travels is regulated by the rows of teeth on the drive plate

plate, and turns the plate through varying distances, according to whether 2, 3, or 4 kernels per hill are desired. In many ways this

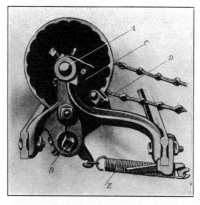

type is better than that shown in Fig. 254, since the clutch is not interfered with at all.

Figs. 256 and 257 illustrate another type of planter clutch. In Fig. 256 the dog is locked in such a position that it does not engage with the notched wheel, which revolves continuously around the drop shaft. When a knot on the check wire passes through the trip arm in the check head the dog *C* is released by the trip *D* and permitted to engage with the notched wheel, as shown in Fig. 257. It remains in engagement through one revolution, when it is thrown out by the trip *D*.

FIG. 256. Still another type of clutch

A, drop shaft; *B*, valve rod; *C*, dog; *D*, trip; *E*, trip spring. The clutch is thrown out and the parts are not engaging

The variable-drop device is an advantage where it is desired to plant the corn thinner on the poorer parts of the field, because

it makes it possible for the operator to vary the number of kernels per hill in a single round without stopping the team. Further, not so many plates are required, since the assortment need vary only for the variation in size of kernel; that is, there need be but three plates — small, medium, and large — for each box.

The *accuracy* of drop is influenced by several things. Perhaps the most important is

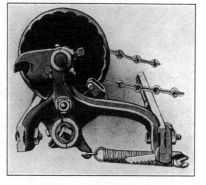

FIG. 257. The clutch shown in Fig. 256 with the parts in engagement

the condition of the corn in regard to uniformity of kernel. Then, too, the kind of box bottom, the style of plate, the speed with which the plate is driven, the accuracy of the valves, the roughness of the ground, the fullness of the corn-boxes, and, no doubt, many other matters help affect the accuracy of the drop.

It is possible for the operator to control the most variable factor — the uniformity of kernel — and reduce the inaccuracy to a minimum. In a series of tests on ungraded, hand-graded, and machine-graded corn, performed by students in the course in Farm Machinery at Ohio State University, the results are uniformly in favor of the machine-graded corn.

The three grades were obtained as follows: the ear was butted and tipped and the remainder shelled. This remainder comprised the hand-graded corn. After this grade was tested the butts and tips were mixed with the hand-graded corn, the whole forming the ungraded corn. This grade having been tested, the corn was run through a simple hand grader to obtain the machine-graded corn. The general average of several classes, the experiment extending over several years and embracing tests on at least seven different makes of planters, is herewith given:

TABLE XXVIII. THE RESULT OF GRADING CORN

	NUMBER OF HILLS OUT OF A POSSIBLE 100					
	0 kernels	1 kernel	2 kernels	3 kernels	4 kernels	5 kernels
Ungraded	0	3	8	77	10	2
Hand-graded	0	3	7	84	5	1
Machine-graded	0	1	6	86	6	1

The figures at the head of the columns represent the number of kernels per hill. The figures in the various columns give the percentage of hills having 1, 2, 3, 4, and 5 kernels per hill. Thus, with a 3-kernel hill as the ideal, ungraded corn gave 77 per cent perfect; the hand-graded, 84 per cent; and the machine-graded, 86 per cent. These tests are not given as final by any means, but such a general average uniformly in favor of the machine-graded corn is worthy of careful attention.

The construction of the bottom of the planter box has much to do in determining the accuracy of the drop. The plate should be so arranged as to aid the kernels in every possible way to find their places in the cells of the plate. To this end the bottom should be cone-shaped, so that it turns the kernels up on edge in the edge-selection type, and thus puts them into a position

FIG. 258. A corn-planter check head
A, valve rod; *B*, trip rope; *C*, check wire; *D*, trip arm. The wire is stationary

to slip naturally into the cells. The cut-off spring should work smoothly and not too stiffly, else it will tend to knock kernels out of the cells unless they fill the cells perfectly.

The edge-selection planter has been criticized because it cracks a good many kernels. This, it seems, is particularly true when the kernels are not of fairly uniform size, in which case it is possible for two kernels to slip endways into a single cell. When this cell reaches the cut-off spring both kernels may be knocked out of the cell, one only may be knocked out, or one or both may be broken off. This difficulty is not so likely to occur in well-graded corn.

It is always advisable to test the planter after the seed corn is prepared, to determine the proper plate to use. The planter should be placed on a box or other support so that the wheels may be freely turned by hand, the valve rod tripped, and a hundred hills or so run out, a record being kept of the number of kernels in each hill. If there are too many twos, a larger

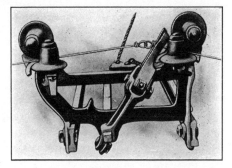

FIG. 259. Corn-planter check head when tripped by check wire

The knot has drawn the trip arm backward, thus tripping the clutch and opening the valves

plate should be put in, while if there are too many fours, a smaller plate should be tried (it is assumed· that three kernels are ideal). This test obviates guessing and takes but little time.

The valves. It has been said that the hill is accumulated on the upper valve of the planter shank. One other valve is

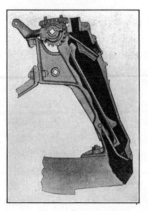

FIG. 260. Section of planter shank, showing the valves

The upper and lower valves are closed, with a hill on each

absolutely essential, and this is the one found in the bottom of the shank. These two valves are operated by the knot on the check wire, through the valve rod, as shown in Figs. 258 and 259. They open and close in unison, the corn being dropped from the top valve as it opens, and caught on the lower valve, which opens and closes while the hill is dropping from the upper to the lower valve.

It is possible, by holding these two valves open or by opening them very slowly, to allow both the lower and the upper hill to drop in the same place. This might happen if the team were to stop while the knot on the wire

was in process of tripping the valves (Fig. 259). To safeguard against this possibility most planters have a third valve in the shank, placed about midway between the upper and lower valves. This intermediate valve is timed so as to open when the others close and close when the others open. Thus, in case the upper and lower valves are held open, the hill from the upper valve will be caught on the intermediate valve and held there until the others close, when it drops to the lower one. In ordinary field operation this valve does not function at all, since it closes and opens again before the corn from the upper valve reaches it. Figs. 260, 261, and 262 show the location and operation of valves in the planter shank.

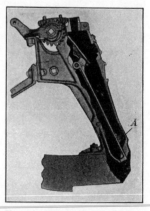

FIG. 261. Planter shank, showing function of intermediate valve

The upper and lower valves are open; the intermediate valve, *A*, is closed and will catch the hill above if the upper and lower valves are not closed before the corn reaches it

The action of the lower valve and the way in which it deposits the corn are important. It should give the hill a slight backward

direction, but should not deposit it with force, else if the speed of the team is rather fast it will throw the hill out of line and scatter it as well.

Drilling. Experiments seem to indicate that, if the field is properly cared for, more bushels per acre can be grown from drilled than from checked corn. Ordinarily, however, the increased yield does not pay for the extra labor required to keep a drilled field free from weeds.

To set a planter for drilling, it is necessary to open the valves and keep them open, and at the same time to permit the clutch to remain in engagement. This is done by drawing back the trip arm and fastening it in this position. If there is an intermediate valve, it must be opened and locked open (usually by a separate device), since otherwise opening the upper and lower valves will automatically close this one.

FIG. 262. Planter shank with valves set for drilling

All three valves must be locked open when corn is being drilled

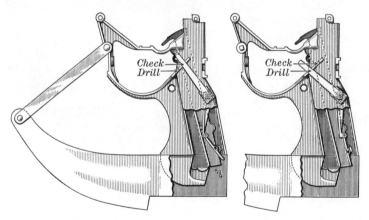

FIG. 263. Another arrangement for planter valves

At the left the valves are set for checking, and the intermediate is seen holding a hill. At the right the valves are all open

The *distance* between kernels in drilling is determined by the number of cells which pass over the planter shank for each revolution of the main wheels.

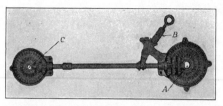

FIG. 264. A gear drive for a planter

A, main shaft; *B*, variable-drop lever; *C*, drop shaft. The main shaft is driven by gears rather than by sprockets and chains. The different rows of teeth are for the purpose of controlling the size of hill

In Fig. 253 it is seen that there are a number of sprockets on the main shaft by means of which the drop shaft may be driven at different rates. The actual drilling-distance for a particular setting is determined as follows: if the sprocket on the main axle has 18 teeth and that on the drop shaft 6 teeth, then for each revolution of the main wheels the drop shaft will turn three times around. The variable-drop lever is usually set in notch No. 4, so that for each revolution of the drop shaft 4 cells pass over the planter shank. Thus, 12 kernels would be dropped for each revolution of the ground wheels, or in a distance of 94.24 in. for a wheel 30 in. in diameter. This would place the kernels 7.85 in. apart. By working the drive chain on different-sized sprockets, or by changing the variable-drop device where its method of operation will permit its use when set in other positions than the one for a 4-kernel hill, or by changing the seed plates, a wide variation in the drilling-distance is possible.

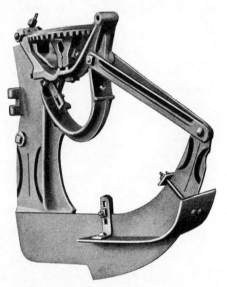

FIG. 265. A shoe furrow-opener with a gauge shoe attached

The gauge shoe maintains a uniform depth in loose ground

Furrow-openers. Figs. 265, 266, and 267 show several styles of furrow-openers. The *curved* runner is satisfactory and is the runner in most common use. The *stub* runner is usually adapted to land where there are sticks, stones, and pieces of sod to contend with, the stub nose getting under such obstructions and throwing them to one side. The *disk*, either single or double, penetrates well, but is hard to guide, has bearings to wear out, and in mellow ground is likely to plant the corn too deep.

Gauge shoes or depth-regulators, one type of which is shown in Fig. 265, are frequently used, and if the mellowness of the soil is variable they are of value. Many of the numerous makes may be attached to any planter. One manufacturer attempts to secure more even depth by bringing the wheel up closer to the planter shank, thus forcing the furrow-opener to follow the wheel over ridges and into depressions. The distance from the rear valve to the bottom of the wheel in this planter is about half the distance found in the average planter. The construction is therefore awkward, and the planter will never become popular.

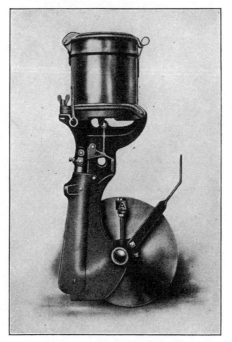

FIG. 266. A disk furrow-opener

The grease-cup, *A*, on a short tube, provides a convenient method of oiling

Covering-devices are sometimes to be advised and are found in various shapes. Fig. 268 shows one type and the method of attaching it.

Wheels. The *open* wheel is now almost universally used. It does not pack the ground immediately above the hill, and hence this ground will not bake, as is often the case when the solid wheel is used. In very loose ground, however, or in a dry season the use of the *solid* wheel is to be advised. The *double* wheel is said to cover better than the single wheel, since it has more gather, but it is awkward and does not meet with general favor, though some prefer it.

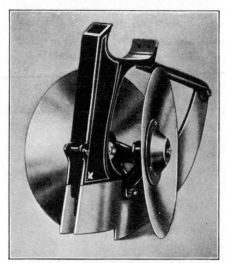

FIG. 267. A combination shoe and disk furrow-opener

The check wire. The check wire is carried on a reel which may be swung from the main frame under the seat and driven by a sprocket and chain from the main axle or which may be carried on the side of the frame and driven by friction from the main wheel. The advantage of this second method is said to lie in the fact that the last rows can be planted and the wire reeled up at the same time. The position, however, is awkward; the weight of the reel unbalances the planter, and very few operators would attempt reeling up the wire while planting if, indeed, it were practicable.

Wire may be furnished with knots 3 ft. 6 in. or 3 ft. 8 in. apart and it is usually furnished in 80-rod lengths. At intervals

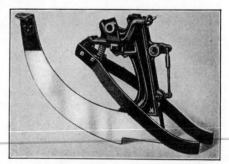

FIG. 268. A shoe furrow-opener with covering-device attached

of 5 or 6 rd. are spreading links, at which places the chain may be separated for convenience in passing trees or similar obstructions.

Conveniences. Some planters are provided with double markers, making it unnecessary to transfer the marker from one side to the other. These markers are raised by levers operated from the seat. Where there is only a single marker, it is well to have an arch on the planter to carry the end of the marker rope. In this case a ring is slipped from side to side on the arch, and there is no interference with the reins.

At the rear end of the tongue is a device making possible an adjustment which keeps the planter shanks at the same angle though the height of the team may vary. By lowering the front part of the frame or by raising the rear end of the tongue in a slotted bracket, the bottom of the planter shanks may be thrown backward or forward and the hill made to fall in the proper line.

There is an advantage in being able to see the corn at some point in its path from the box to the ground. A *sight-feed* arrangement, if present, is usually found at the top valve so that the hill may be seen as it is being accumulated.

FIG. 269. An auxiliary furrow-opener device

This device serves to press back the clods and to keep them from falling upon the hills

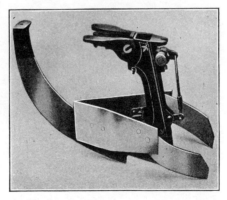

FIG. 270. An auxiliary furrow-opener with covering-device

314

FIG. 271. A corn-planter with fertilizer attachment

Fertilizer attachment. Many farmers desire to fertilize their corn in the hill. All planters may have an attachment such as that shown in Fig. 271 put on for sowing fertilizer. This is operated by a separate sprocket from the main shaft and deposits the fertilizer just behind the hill; it may also be set to sow in rows. It is not advisable to fertilize heavily in the hill. It is perhaps better to drill the fertilizer broadcast by means of a fertilizer-drill. However, a little fertilizer in the hill may have a beneficial effect.

FIG. 272. A one-horse corn-drill with fertilizer attachment

This drill is found largely in hilly regions

Operating the check-row planter. The planter should be started on the straight side of the field if there is one. The wire is unreeled next the fence, one end having been first fastened by a stake so set that it is in line with the last furrow and if possible in solid ground. After turning the team at the opposite end, the check wire, if it has not all been used, should be unjointed and the other stake set directly behind the planter tongue in solid ground. The chain should then be brought to a firm tension. After driving across the field the wire should be released from the drop head, the team turned, and the stake reset straight back of the tongue. Great care should be taken to bring the chain to the same tension as before while the stake is driven home. Some stakes are provided with graduated springs which make it easy to secure the same tension every time.

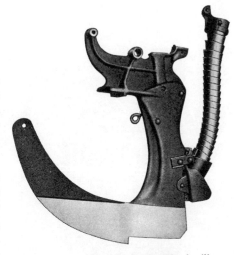

FIG. 273. A method of attaching the fertilizer tube to planter shank

The fertilizer may be checked with the hills or it may be drilled in the row

GRAIN-DRILLS

Grain-feeds. The device for feeding the grain or the fertilizer is the heart of the drill and should receive first attention. There are in common use two types of

FIG. 274. A fertilizer-tube set to drill the fertilizer just back of the hill

grain-feeds, which are designated as the fluted-wheel feed and the internal double-run feed, both being force feeds.

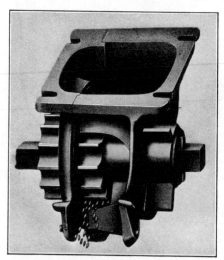

FIG. 275. The fluted-wheel force feed

The wheel is set so that only a portion of its surface is in contact with the grain

FIG. 276. The wheel is here set to sow the maximum quantity per acre

The fluted-wheel feed. This is the simpler of the two and is shown in Figs. 275 and 276. There is a fluted wheel for each furrow-opener, and all are mounted on a shaft running from one end to the other of the grain-box. The shaft is run directly from the main axle by sprockets and chain. To regulate the *quantity* per acre, a greater or less portion of the fluted wheels is exposed to the grain in the box. A lever attached to the rear side of the drill-box controls the shaft to which the wheels are fastened. A dial plate is usually found beneath this lever, on which is indicated the proper setting for different quantities of grain per acre.

The simplicity of this fluted-wheel feed is its best recommendation. Besides, it is quickly changed from one rate of seeding to another, there being no troublesome tables or other directions to follow. (In some drills directions for setting the rate of seeding

are printed on perishable paper, and if this becomes destroyed
or lost the owner is helpless. Drills with such a makeshift

device should not be pur-
chased.) A further advantage of the fluted-wheel
feed lies in the fact that
there is a wide variation
in the quantity which it
is possible to sow. The
chief difficulty with this
feed is that it cracks some
of the kernels. This is
especially true with the
larger seeds, such as beans,

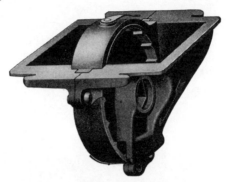

FIG. 277. An internal double-run force-feed cup
The 2 compartments have throats of different sizes
for drilling large and small grains

cowpeas, corn, etc. Some
companies, however, are
now making a fluted-wheel
feed with a much larger throat,
so that large seeds will pass
under the fluted wheel without
danger of cracking. Another
objection that has been brought
against the fluted-wheel feed
is that it tends to bunch oats
in seeding.

*The internal double-run
force feed.* Fig. 277 shows
the construction of this type
of feed. There is a double-
throated seed-cup for each
furrow-opener. One throat is
relatively small and is intended
for wheat, rye, and other small
grains. The other is larger,
and through this such grains
as oats, peas, beans, etc. are
sown. If the smaller-throated
side is in use the larger throat

FIG. 278. The disk-gear method of driving the internal double-run force-feed cups

The speed of the wheel, and hence the quantity
per acre, is regulated by shifting the movable
pinion on the disk gear. The graduated scale
for different grains is conveniently located

is covered by a metal lid ; if the larger-throated side is in use the smaller side is covered. The little ribbed wheel, seen in the right-hand compartment (Fig. 277) forces out the grain, as the wheel is revolved by the shaft to which it is fastened.

The *quantity* per acre is regulated by changing the speed of the ribbed wheel ; if the revolving wheel turns out a given quantity in one revolution, two revolutions will turn out twice as much. There is always the same wheel surface exposed to the grain.

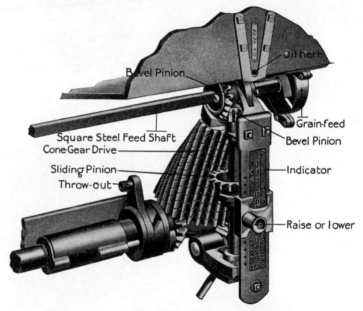

FIG. 279. The cone-gear method of driving the internal double-run feed cups
As the sliding pinion is moved upward on the cone the quantity sown is decreased

Many devices are used for varying the *speed* of the ribbed wheel. Figs. 278 and 279 illustrate two common methods. Perhaps the most common is the disk gear with the movable pinion. The feed shaft is operated by the movable-pinion shaft, and as the pinion is moved from the center outward on the disk gear the quantity per acre is increased. This permits as many rates of seeding as there are rows of teeth on the disk, usually from six to nine.

The chief advantage of this feed lies in the fact that it has a large throat on either side and will not crack the kernels of such grains as corn, cow-peas, etc. It probably is not so positive as the fluted-wheel feed, since the ribs on the internal wheel are rather small. The more or less complex device required to control the quantity per acre is objectionable, too. For example, the teeth on the disk gear above described become worn so that the driving-pinion may skip a tooth occasionally. Unless these driving-parts are rigidly supported, trouble is certain. The directions for setting the drill should be attached to the drill-box in such a way that they may not be lost or destroyed. In some drills a paper envelope containing the directions is inserted in a pocket on the box lid, but this method is not to be commended.

FIG. 280. The disk-gear method in a different form

The feed shaft is driven indirectly from the main axle, by sprockets and chain

FIG. 281. The general arrangement of the wizard feed

The feed is driven by the disk gear, which, in turn, drives the feed plates through the beveled gears

Fertilizer-feeds. There are three types of fertilizer-feeds in more or less common use: (1) the wizard, or finger, feed, (2) the Marks, or cone, feed, and (3) the revolving glass-plate feed.

FIG. 282. Arrangement of plates in the box

The size of the gate opening is controlled by the lever at the end of the box

The wizard, or finger, feed. Figs. 280, 281, 282, and 283 illustrate the principle of this feed. There is a finger plate in the bottom of the box for each furrow-opener. These are revolved by a common shaft. The fertilizer is carried by the fingers through gate openings in the back of the box and is knocked into the grain-tubes by small weights which play over the fingers as they revolve. The *quantity* per acre is controlled by varying the speed of the plate and by varying the gate opening. By means of the two the quantity per acre may be varied from nothing to one thousand pounds or more.

The *speed* of the plate is controlled as shown in the internal double-run grain-feed.

The Marks, or cone, feed. This feed is shown in Fig. 286. The inverted cone with its projecting lip is stationary, but the plate beneath it revolves.

FIG. 283. Details of the wizard feed

The gate has a long and a short end. The weighted lever on the left is hung back of the gate and forces the fertilizer from between the fingers of the plate

As the fertilizer is carried to this projecting lip, the lip gathers up a certain amount, carries it to the center of the cone, and drops it to the grain-tubes. The *quantity* is controlled by varying the speed of the plate beneath the cone and by changing the cone, the cones varying in the size of the lips. A certain manufacturer supplies what is known as standard, half-standard, double-standard, lime, and hen-manure cones, these different types giving a wide range in quantity. The speed of the plate is controlled as in the other types.

FIG. 284. Another method of varying the speed of the feed plates

The great objection to this feed is that damp fertilizers stick inside the cone and do not drop out. At times the cone becomes so clogged as to twist off the shaft pins which fasten it.

The revolving glass-plate feed. This type is not very commonly used. Figs. 287 and 288 show its construction. The glass plates are partly inside the box and partly outside. As they revolve, the fertilizer is carried to the gates and passes into the tubes leading to the furrow-openers. There is an agitator inside the box which keeps the fertilizer evenly distributed over the bottom. The quantity per

FIG. 285. A bottom view of Fig. 284

acre is controlled chiefly by varying the size of the gate opening, though the speed of the plate may be varied. This type of feed is very simple, and the glass plates do not corrode. It cannot, however, be regarded as a positive force feed. Its simplicity is its strongest recommendation.

FIG. 286. The Marks, or cone, fertilizer-feed

The cone is stationary; the plate beneath it revolves

Grass-seed feed. The feed in nearly all grass-seed attachments is of the fluted-wheel type and is controlled in the same way as the feeds in the grain-box. The seed-spouts are so arranged that

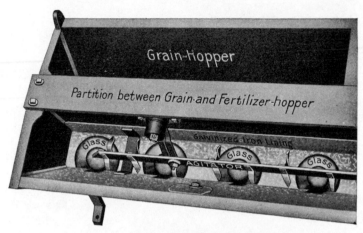

FIG. 287. The revolving-glass-plate feed

The view is taken looking down into the fertilizer-box

the seed may be taken into the grain-tubes (Fig. 289) or delivered either in front of or behind the furrow-openers. One method of driving the grass-seed attachment is shown in Fig. 290.

Furrow-openers. The *hoe* furrow-opener shown (Fig. 291) is the oldest type in common use. It forms a good furrow if the ground is not too hard, and it covers well, the earth falling in from either side. Each hoe is provided with a single or a double point. The double point has the

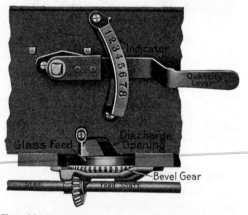

FIG. 288. Rear view of a portion of the box in Fig. 287

The plates are driven by beveled gears on the feed shaft. The lever is used to raise and lower the gates. The figures indicate hundredweights

advantage that it may be reversed when one end of the point becomes dull. It is essential that these points be kept sharp, a requirement which necessitates their being removed and sharpened every two years at least. The hoe clogs somewhat in trash, but if a zigzag setting is used, the trash must be very thick to cause much difficulty. There seems to be a tendency on the part of many farmers to return to this type of furrow-opener after having used the disk type for a number of years.

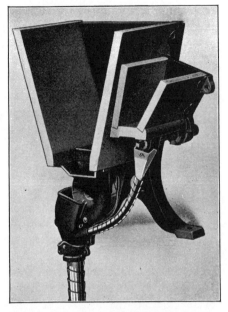

FIG. 289. The grass-seed-tube inserted in the grain-tube

The *single-disk* furrow-opener, shown in Fig. 292, has good penetration, cuts through trash well, and does not easily clog. On the other hand, the bearing becomes worn, the disk loosens, and, owing to the fact that one half of the disks on a drill will throw the soil down the grade, it does not cover well on sidehills. In fact it is not easy to cover well on the level in soil that is not thoroughly prepared. It covers chiefly from one side, and in this respect is

FIG. 290. The grass-seed attachment is driven from the grain-feed shaft

324

inferior to the hoe furrow-opener. Several kinds of boots are used in connection with the single disk to aid in opening up the furrow and in covering the seed. Some of these are very effective.

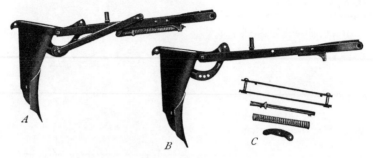

FIG. 291. The hoe furrow-opener

A, spring hoe ; *B*, pin-break hoe ; *C*, parts of spring device on *A*

They should all be rather well closed to prevent clogging and should deliver the seed at the deepest part of the furrow. This means that in the absence of a special boot, the seed should be deposited as nearly as possible below the center of the disk.

FIG. 292. A single-disk furrow-opener

The boot on the left of the disk assists in opening the furrow. A good method of oiling is shown. The cup is intended for machine oil

The *double-disk* furrow-opener is composed of two rather flat disks set at an angle one to the other (Figs. 294 and 295), and throws the soil both ways in opening the furrow, thus covering from both sides. In this particular it is superior to the single-disk. One of the disks is usually larger than the other, the smaller one running just a little back of the larger one. Since the two must fit snugly together at the front, neither can be given much dish. For this reason the double disk does not penetrate hard ground so well as the single disk, which is given more suction. The claim is made for the double-disk furrow-opener that the seed is sown in a double row, and that, because of this better distribution, larger yields are insured. As shown in Fig. 296, there is a tendency to sow a double row, but experiment stations have not yet proved the truth or falsity of the above claim.

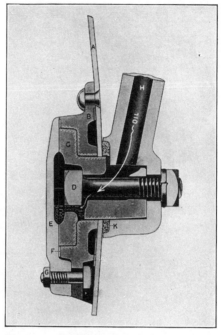

FIG. 293. Sectional view showing a single-disk bearing

A, disk; *B*, hub; *C*, bushing; *D*, bolt; *E*, cap; *F*, washer; *G*, cap bolt; *H*, oil-tube; *K*, felt oil-retaining ring

Both single-disk and double-disk furrow-openers are open to the objection that there are bearings to wear out, to be cared for, and to give trouble. A great deal of pressure is put upon the bearings in order to secure penetration; hence they should be well oiled, and a convenient means for oiling will add to the life of the bearing. In some cases hard-oil cups are used and are fairly satisfactory. The oil-tubes for machine oil should project well above the bearing and be capped to prevent the entrance of dirt.

Covering-devices. It is often found advisable to use a covering-device. The most common type is the drag chain. There are various types of press-wheels, too (one of which is shown in Fig. 298), which are use-ful in a dry season.

FIG. 294. A double-disk furrow-opener

Size of drill. The size of the drill is determined by the number of rows it will sow and by their distance apart. A drill sowing 12 rows with the rows 7 in. apart is known as a 12 × 7 drill. It is advisable, unless the land is too hilly, to buy a drill with at least 9 furrow-openers, and a drill having 10 or 12 can be drawn by 2 horses on level land without difficulty. A drill with 12 furrow-openers is usually supplied with either a 2-horse or a 3-horse hitch. Where the custom of seeding corn ground is generally practiced

FIG. 295. Double-disk furrow-opener of Fig. 294, with right disk removed
The seed is deposited directly below the center of the disks. Note the oil-tube

the width of the corn rows should determine, in part at least, the width of the drill. For example, a 12 × 7 drill will just cover 2 corn rows where the rows are 3 ft. 6 in. apart.

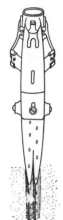

Not many years ago all drills were built with the furrow-openers 8 in. apart. Recently, however, narrower rows have been very much in demand among farmers, and there are now more 7-inch drills on the market than any other size. Some drills are made with 6-inch rows, and a few companies are making a drill with rows only 4 in. apart. Experiments have not proved conclusively that there is any advantage in this narrowing of rows.

Seed-tubes. Fig. 299 shows the *steel-ribbon* seed-tube. All things considered, it is the best type, since it is not easily drawn out of shape and returns to position if it is. The *steel-wire* seed-tube is very satisfactory, but if it becomes stretched it does not resume its original shape. The *rubber* seed-tube is satisfactory while it

FIG. 296. There is a tendency for the double disk to sow a double row of grain

lasts, but it breaks at the top of the furrow-openers and also gives trouble from clogging. The *steel telescope* seed-tube (Fig. 300) as used in some drills is very satisfactory and does not clog easily, although it is adapted only to certain types of furrow-openers.

Wheels. The wheels may be of wood or of steel, the trade being about evenly divided between the two. The *wooden* wheels wear out quickly, especially in the larger-sized

FIG. 297. A shoe furrow-opener

This type of furrow-opener is not in common use

combination drills, but they are very substantial and offer means for a good hub attachment. The *steel* wheels last better than the wooden. The chief objections to steel wheels are that they slip on hillsides and that they have a tendency to pick up dirt and drop it on the exposed gears.

The pawls in the hub. The pawls in the hub are important. In some drills it is possible to turn the wheel forward several inches before the pawls engage the ratchets and start the seeding; consequently there are frequently seen in drilled fields bare strips

FIG. 298. A single-disk drill with press-wheel attachment

several inches wide and as long as the width of the drill. These bare strips show that the drill was stopped at this point and that, in starting, the wheels moved forward quite a distance before the pawls engaged the ratchets in the hub; there should be at least three pawls in each hub, and no two should engage at the same time. Lost motion in the gears would bring about the same difficulty.

The frame. A heavy, substantial frame is essential. Not only must it carry the drill-box with its grain, fertilizer, and grass seed, but it must be substantial enough to hold all gears in perfect alignment.

Convenient attachments. Every grain-drill should be equipped with a *surveyor*. It is quite unlikely that a drill will sow all kinds of fertilizers with equal accuracy and according to specified setting, but if the operator watches the amount put in the box and observes the surveyor while sowing this known quantity, he can check the fertilizer-setting. The same is also true of the grain and the grass seed, especially of the latter. All parts should be well protected, so that fertilizer will not fall on the gears and cause them to rust and thus become difficult to set and to operate.

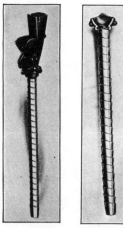

FIG. 299. Steel-ribbon seed-tubes

A *footboard* upon which the operator may stand is of service. The operator can watch the drill and the team better while riding, and his weight does not materially affect the draft.

A *power lift* is desirable for the larger sizes; that is, for drills having 16 or more furrow-openers. If there are as many as 12 furrow-openers, they should be arranged in 2 sections, with a lifting-lever for each.

All parts should be automatically thrown out of gear when the hoes or disks are raised and should likewise be thrown in gear when these are lowered. Further, it should be possible to throw the fertilizer and grass-seed attachments out of gear while the grain-compartment is in use.

FIG. 300. A steel telescope seed-tube

The lower section is fastened to the furrow-opener and telescopes as the furrow-openers are raised

Calibration of the drill. Every drill should be frequently tested to ascertain whether it is sowing the desired amount of grain per acre. It is not uncommon to find an error of 25 per cent in the setting of drills. This error will vary with the kind and purity of grain used. Seed grain should always be recleaned. There are always straw joints, if nothing else, left in by the thresher, and these will clog the drill and lead to inaccurate sowing.

To calibrate the drill it is necessary to raise one or both wheels off the ground. The number of revolutions to seed one acre should be determined by dividing the area of one acre by the width of the drill, and this by the circumference of the wheel. For example, if the drill has 12 disks 7 in. apart it will sow a strip 7 ft. wide; then, $43,560 \div 7 = 6222.8$; $6222.8 \div 12.56 = 495.4$, the number of revolutions required to seed 1 acre. The drill should then be set at a certain rate, the box filled with grain, and the wheel turned through a sufficient number of revolutions to seed $\frac{1}{4}$ acre or $\frac{1}{2}$ acre. The weight of the grain delivered is then determined. A comparison of this weight with the setting of the drill will demonstrate the error if there is one.

Care of the drill. Each season, after the drill is stored away, all parts should be thoroughly cleaned, especially if fertilizer has been used. The metal parts corrode rapidly if fertilizer is left in the box all winter or through the summer. The disks of a disk drill should be well cleaned and oiled or greased. The bearings become filled with dirt and will rust if not cleaned and oiled. One hour spent in such work at the proper time will save several hours' work later, and besides do much to keep the operator in even temper.

One-horse drills and hand drills. There are on the market several one-horse drills devised for sowing grain or grass seed in standing corn. There are also several types of hand seeders now in use for seeding lawns. They are very effective and give an even distribution of seed, covering it at the same time.

Alfalfa drills. The extensive growing of alfalfa has been largely responsible for the manufacture of a drill for sowing all kinds of grass seed. As now made, this is usually a disk drill having 20 disks 4 in. apart. It is really a grain-drill on a small scale, the disks being only from 8 to 10 in. in diameter. This seeder is also made with a fertilizer-compartment.

This type of seeder is coming to be widely used in sowing clover seed in wheat in the spring of the year. If this custom is followed it is necessary to wait until the ground is in tillable condition. It is claimed that the drill effects a saving in seed, since a much larger percentage of the seed will germinate if it is covered when put into the ground. It is further claimed that the cultivation which the wheat receives during the seeding of the clover is beneficial.

FIG. 301. A knapsack seeder

The distributing-wheel in this type of seeder revolves in a vertical plane

Broadcast seeders. Many types of broadcast seeders are on the market. They are used for sowing all kinds of grass seed and some larger grains, chiefly oats. Fig. 301 shows one type of *knapsack* seeder. The wheel in front of the sack is revolved by a crank. This wheel has several radial ribs which scatter the seed in all directions as it falls upon it through the graduated opening above. In some types of knapsack seeders, and usually in the more common type, the wheel revolves in a horizontal plane ; in other forms there are two wheels, one above the other, the upper receiving one half of the seed and revolving in one direction, the lower wheel receiving the other half and revolving in the opposite direction. The two wheels, it is thought, result in a more even distribution of the seed. In older seeders the wheel was revolved by a fiddle-bow action, the string of the bow being wrapped about

FIG. 302. An end-gate broadcast seeder

Used more particularly in seeding oats broadcast

the axle of the wheel in such a way as to revolve it first in one direction and then in the other. The objection to this type was that the wheel came to a full stop at both ends of the stroke.

The *wheelbarrow* seeder has never come into very wide use. There seems to be no question that the seed can be more evenly distributed with this type than with any of the knapsack seeders, since the box is carried close to the ground, and the seed does not have far to fall. An agitator which is kept constantly moving inside the box prevents the holes through which the seed passes from clogging. The fact that clover seed is very often sown early in the spring when the ground is frozen or rough has prevented the wide use of this seeder.

The *end-gate* seeder, shown in Fig. 302, is constructed on the knapsack principle and is used where large areas are to be sown. It finds a wide use in oat-growing sections where the seed is sown broadcast.

CHAPTER XXI

MANURE-SPREADERS

There is no longer any question as to the utility of the manure-spreader. Being a labor-saver, it is regarded as a necessity on every farm producing from seventy-five to one hundred loads of manure per year. In the application of manure with the spreader there is real economy, too, since it is the means of making a

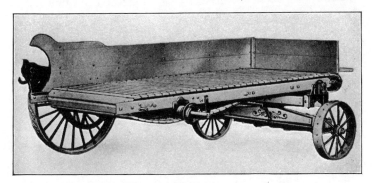

FIG. 303. An endless-apron manure-spreader

given amount of manure cover a greater acreage and cover it more effectively than when it is spread thickly, as is nearly always the case when the work is done by hand.

The apron. The apron and the means of driving it constitute one of the vital parts of the spreader. There are three types of aprons in common use: (1) the endless apron, (2) the return apron, and (3) the solid bed with carrier.

The *endless* apron is shown in Fig. 303. It consists of an endless web passing around the front and rear apron shafts. The web is held together by two, sometimes by three, endless chains, to the links of which the slats of the apron are fastened. In some spreaders the slats are riveted to the chain links, but it

333

334

is much better to have them bolted, in order that broken parts may be easily replaced.

Between the front and rear shafts the upper fold of the apron is supported on bed rails as shown in Figs. 304 and 305. If there are but two of these, the slats must be very strong to support the load properly without undue sagging. A third rail through the middle of the apron slats makes possible more substantial construction. Fastened to these rails, as shown in Fig. 304, are small pulleys which carry the entire weight of the load, thus reducing friction to a minimum. The rollers should be firmly fastened to the bed rails by a heavy bolt or a lag screw.

FIG. 304. A substantial apron support

The middle bed rail keeps the slats from sagging in the middle. The rollers which carry the apron are mounted between the bed-rail parts

In some spreaders the bed rail is grooved and the pulleys are supported in this groove. This construction occurs more often when steel rails are used, but whether steel rails are used or not, excellent support is provided for the pulleys.

As compared with the return apron the endless type is simple in construction, since no reversing gears are necessary. The apron is always ready to load;

FIG. 305. Another good apron support

The rollers are bolted to the sides of the outer bed rails

that is, it does not have to be run back after the load is off, as is the case with the return apron. No front end-gate is required either, a circumstance which eliminates a possible source of trouble.

Further, with this type of apron it is possible on long hauls to pile the manure above the highest loading-line, and so after the apron has been run back a short distance the top of the load may be thrown forward. On the other hand, this apron is very heavy, since both upper and lower folds are slatted. Manure that filters through the cracks in the upper fold lodges, in part at least, on the lower fold, and in freezing weather may be the source of some trouble; one company overcomes this difficulty by hinging the slats on one edge (Fig. 306), so that they turn down as they pass along the under fold, and thus allow any trash to fall to the ground. There is some difficulty in spreading the very last of the load evenly with the endless type, for when all but three or four

FIG. 306. An endless apron with hinged slats

bushels of the load has been spread, the remainder is rolled backward by the beater, and it is quite impossible to spread this last bit at the same rate as the rest of the load. This fault may be partially overcome by speeding up the apron at the finish.

The *return* apron, as shown in Fig. 307, is very similar in construction to the endless apron except that but one fold, the upper, is slatted. The load is run off and the apron then returned to its original position before loading is started again. A front end-gate is provided which moves back with the apron, and consequently the load is spread evenly to the finish. The end-gate is circular in form, to fit the shape of the beater, so that all of the manure is picked up and thrown out by the beater. Since but one fold of this apron is slatted, it is much lighter in weight than the endless type, and all danger of fouling is eliminated. In loading this type of apron from the rear, as from a stable door, it is possible to return it only part of the way, and after the front end is loaded the apron may be completely returned by hand and the rear end loaded. It is also possible to stop this apron at any point while unloading, without stopping the beater, by simply pressing

FIG. 307. A manure-spreader with a return apron

There are no slats on the lower fold

the return-gear lever. This is an advantage in crossing swales or similar places where no manure is needed. On the other hand, this type of apron requires a reversing gear to return it after each load is run out. Formerly this gear gave much trouble, but in modern spreaders little difficulty is had with it. It consists of a

FIG. 308. A spreader having a solid bottom with carrier apron

positive clutch on the rear axle, which is thrown in gear by a foot lever near the seat. The clutch is held in gear only during the time the foot lever is held down. When the apron is completely returned, the lever on which the foot rests is thrown upward and the clutch disengaged. The front end-gate is a point of weakness in this apron; it is usually not very well supported, and there is danger of its running into the beater if the device for throwing the beater out of gear is not properly adjusted. This arrangement is automatically controlled.

The *solid bottom* with carrier, which is used on several makes of spreaders, is shown in Fig. 308. The load is pushed back over the solid bed by the endless carrier. This type affords unusually

FIG. 309. The ratchet apron drive

The power to operate the ratchet-wheel is taken from the beater shaft

substantial construction for bed and frame, but it would seem that there is a noticeable disadvantage in sliding the load as against carrying it on rollers. In hauling very dry manure the carrier is likely to slip under the load, though this seldom happens.

The apron drive. The mechanism for driving the apron constitutes one of the weakest points in any spreader. There are two common methods in use : (1) the ratchet drive, and (2) the worm-gear drive.

In the *ratchet* drive, shown in Fig. 309, the ratchet-wheel is mounted on the rear apron shaft. This wheel is actuated by one pawl — sometimes by two — the pawls in turn being driven by an upright arm pivoted at the bottom and receiving a reciprocating motion from the pitman driven by the beater shaft. The quantity per acre is regulated by raising or lowering the horizontal arm connected directly to the pawls on the upright arm driven by the pitman.

As compared with the worm-gear drive, next to be discussed, this method of driving the apron has several advantages. In the first place the rachet-wheel is usually large — much larger as a rule than the spur gear actuating the shaft in the worm-gear drive — and therefore greater leverage is possible. There are not

FIG. 310. A rachet drive in which the power is taken directly from the rear axle

The quantity per acre is controlled by regulating the backward travel of the pawls

that constant strain and steady grind so noticeable in the worm-gear drive. Moreover there is a wide range in the number of loads that it is possible to apply per acre, this range in some cases extending from nothing to sixty-five loads per acre. It is possible, too, to change the rate of spreading while the team is in motion, without danger of breaking any of the parts.

On the other hand, this drive imparts an intermittent motion to the apron. While the effect of this cannot be noticed in the spreading, the load must be started from a dead stop following each backward travel of the pawls, thus forcing an excessive strain on the teeth of the ratchet-wheel. In frosty weather the teeth are likely to be stripped from the gear, though if good material is used in its construction this seldom happens. In the cheaper spreaders this wheel is frequently made of cast iron and the teeth are easily stripped. The power for driving the ratchet-wheel is in nearly all cases taken from the beater shaft. This is objectionable because the beater is subjected to a great strain in doing its own work, and if it must drive the apron in addition it is the more likely to be strained or broken. One company resorted to a very ingenious device to overcome this objection, as shown

in Fig. 310. The ratchet-wheel in this device is driven directly from the rear axle by a set of cams. In still another spreader, where the beater is on the axle, the ratchet drive is used for the apron, the power being taken from the axle through an eccentric (Fig. 311). In most cases where the ratchet drive is used there is nothing to prevent the apron from racing; that is, running backward faster than it is being driven, as in going up a hill. Then, too, the apron in such cases has a tendency to work back in driving to

FIG. 311. A ratchet drive in which the power is taken directly from the rear axle by an eccentric

The beater of this spreader is on the rear axle

the field, especially if the road is rough or upgrade. If there is no rear end-gate, this jars the load into the beater. To overcome this objection some companies put a brake on the front apron shaft to be operated by the driver if the apron has a tendency to race.

The *worm* gear is shown in Fig. 312. The large disk gear shown may be fastened directly to the rear axle, or it may

FIG. 312. A worm-gear apron drive

The disk gear is on the rear axle. The quantity per acre is controlled by shifting the movable pinion into different rows of teeth on the disk

be mounted on a separate stud just to the rear of the axle but driven by it. There are usually four rows of teeth on this gear.

Extending from it back to the spur gear on the rear apron shaft is a short countershaft on the front end of which is a movable pinion which may be set to mesh with any one of the four rows of teeth on the disk gear. On the rear end of this short shaft is the worm gear, which meshes with the spur gear on the apron shaft. The quantity per acre is regulated by shifting the movable pinion on the disk gear.

By comparing the worm-gear drive with the ratchet drive it will be seen that this drive takes its power directly from the rear axle, thus relieving the beater of extra strain. It gives a uni-

FIG. 313. A worm-gear apron drive in which the disk gear shown in Fig. 312 is replaced by a train of spur gears

formly steady motion to the apron, and the apron will not race, since it cannot move backward faster than it is driven by the gears. On the other hand, there is a great strain on the worm and spur gears as well as on the disk gear and pinion. If all parts are not held in proper alignment and kept thoroughly greased, they will wear out rapidly.

Many companies are now inclosing the worm and spur gears in a tight casing so that the parts may be run in a bath of oil. If the oil bath is not present, axle-grease, and not oil, should be freely used several times a day when the spreader is in use. There are usually but four changes possible in the rate of spreading, but this range in most cases covers the rates in common use. It is not safe to attempt to change the rate of spreading while the team is in motion for fear of stripping the disk gear or pinion. All things considered, the ratchet drive will probably give the average operator less trouble than the worm-gear drive and will give longer service.

A *combination* ratchet and worm-gear drive is shown in Fig. 314. The crank on the small pinion driven by the spur gear on the rear axle actuates the pawl arm. With such a drive the apron is locked so that it does not race and cannot be jostled backward while going to the field with the load.

The beater. The beater must spread all kinds of manure in various states of physical condition. It must therefore be very strong and well supported on its bearings. These bearings could well be self-aligning, since the bed in time is likely to become racked, in which case stiff bearings will cause undue friction.

The bars of the beater may be made of either steel or wood. Whatever the material, the teeth must be firmly fastened to them. In several makes using wooden bars the teeth are simply driven into the bar. This, however, is poor construction; the teeth should pass through the bar and be fastened by a nut. Some are riveted, but in case a tooth is broken it is rather difficult to replace it.

FIG. 314. A combination ratchet and worm-gear apron drive

This circular type of beater is placed above the apron

There is considerable variation as regards the position of the beater in relation to the apron. Sometimes the beater is placed well forward and above the upper fold of the apron (Figs. 313 and 314), the ends of the teeth in their lowest position just clearing the slats. In this position the teeth are forced to work against the manure as it presents itself, thus adding to the total draft. In other spreaders the beater is quite to the rear end of the apron (Fig. 320), the teeth extending below the line of the apron's upper fold. In this position the teeth receive the manure and lift it upward with the least possible draft. In the first position the beater would be more efficient as a pulverizer, but the beater working against the manure must literally dig its way through, thus probably slightly increasing the draft.

It is frequently found to be difficult to spread manure evenly the full width of the spreader bed, there being a tendency to spread most thickly at the middle. To overcome this trouble each

beater bar is sometimes made in two parts and these parts set at an angle to the beater shaft; that is, each bar makes a wide V with the point of the V at the middle of the beater. This tends to throw the manure outward from the center. In another form the beater is composed of two sections (Fig. 315). One company places a circular beater on its spreader (Fig. 316). This type of beater will spread much

FIG. 315. A V-shaped beater made in two sections

wider than the bed. It is claimed that the circular beater makes better traction possible, in that it is not necessary to run one wheel on manure previously spread, as is the case with the average spreader.

In this connection it should be said that there are several *wide-spreading* devices on the market. All of these consist of an additional attachment put on just to the rear of the regular beater. In one type large pans are provided which are

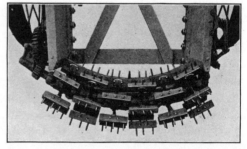

FIG. 316. A circular beater made in six sections
The beater is driven by beveled gears

placed in a horizontal position. These pans receive the manure from the beater and, being revolved at a rapid rate, spread the manure in a strip two or three times as wide as the spreader bed. Another company has a similar device except that the pans revolve in a vertical plane. It does not seem, however, that it is at all necessary to equip a spreader with this extra mechanism. It adds a great deal to the cost and increases the draft of the spreader. Moreover it is possible without such an attachment to spread the manure as thinly as it should ordinarily be spread.

The *proper loading* of the spreader has a great deal to do with the way in which the contents will be spread. In loading a wagon it seems easier to throw the manure into the bed, piling it up in the middle and letting it roll off on either side. As a result the load is packed much more in the middle than on the side. If the same plan is followed in loading a spreader, the beater cannot possibly

FIG. 317. A spreader with two beaters

The upper beater takes the place of a rake, and being in 2 sections and set as shown, secures a more even distribution

spread the load evenly the full width of the bed. The manure as loaded should be spread evenly over the bottom of the bed, and if rather dry material is being handled it should be well tramped when the box is nearly filled. In case rather heavy, coarse material is being handled it will be spread much more easily if, in loading, the load is started at the front end and continued to the rear. In hauling flaky sheep manure the beater will tear up the flakes better if the reverse order is followed in loading.

The beater drive. There are two methods in general use for driving the beater and for reversing its motion; that is, for driving it in a direction opposite to that of the travel of the rear wheels. The first of these is shown in Fig. 318. The large sprocket passes around the main axle. It is not fastened directly to the axle, but by means of a lever conveniently operated by the driver

344

it may be made to revolve with it. Fig. 319 shows a section of the rear axle with the sprocket wheel and clutch used to throw

the beater into and out of gear. A chain is run from this sprocket to another sprocket carried on a separate stud, which is fastened to the spreader bed. Fastened to this sprocket is a large spur gear which in turn meshes with a smaller gear on the beater shaft. The motion is reversed and at the same time multiplied at this point. The beater usually makes about fifteen revo-

FIG. 318. One method of driving the beater

This method uses sprockets, chains, and gears

lutions to one revolution of the main wheels. On some spreaders it is possible to use either one of two speeds, the higher speed being used when applying the manure in large quantities per acre.

This method transmits the motion and reverses it at the beater. Another similar method reverses the motion at the main axle and then transmits it to the beater. The latter method probably provides a more substantial support for the reversing gears, but because of minor difficulties in throwing the beater into and out of gear it is seldom used.

The second method used for driving the beater is shown in Figs. 320 and 321. This method uses sprockets and chains alone. The idle pulley to the front of the main sprocket is lowered or raised to throw the beater in or out of gear. This chain drives a sprocket on

FIG. 319. The large sprocket shown in Fig. 318

The right half of the clutch is fastened to the main axle. To throw the beater into gear the sprocket wheel is shifted and caused to engage the right half of the clutch

a separate stud, as shown. In order to multiply the motion this stud carries a second, larger sprocket which drives the sprocket on the beater shaft.

This method possesses the great advantage of all chain drives, namely, it has no gear teeth to break; for it is better to break

FIG. 320. A single beater driven by sprockets and chains

The additional step at the rear is taken to increase the speed of the beater. The 2 sprockets on the beater provide for 2 speeds

a link in a chain than a tooth in a gear. One disadvantage is evident; the chain working over the main sprocket engages only a few teeth. But even at that more teeth take the strain than in the case of the two spur gears in the first method.

One company places the beater on the rear axle, such a spreader being shown in Fig. 322. This position calls for a different method of driving. The mechanism used is shown in Fig. 323. The planetary gears are operated directly from the rear axle. The three idle gears reverse and transmit the

FIG. 321. Two beaters driven by sprockets and chains

To throw the beater out of gear the front roller, around which the chain passes, is raised

motion to the outer shell of the gear-case to which the beater is fastened. There is a great advantage in having all of the gears used in driving the beater inclosed in a tight case and running in oil. There seems to be no reason why this mechanism should not give satisfaction.

The rake. Several different types of rakes are shown in the different illustrations in this chapter. A rake of some kind is necessary on every spreader, for without it the manure will be thrown out in bunches, and lumps will not be effectively broken up. The rake should have long, flexible teeth so that the load

FIG. 322. A spreader in which the beater is mounted on the rear axle
This construction affords substantial support for the beater

will not be clogged easily. In some spreaders a second beater which is smaller than the main beater and placed just above and to the front of it takes the place of the rake, as shown in Fig. 327. It revolves in a direction opposite to that of the main beater and assists materially in breaking up lumps and in securing even spreading.

The rear end-gate. Without a rear end-gate the manure in loading or in driving to the field is packed against the beater; and as a result, when the spreader is thrown in gear, the beater throws out a bunch of manure. An end-gate of some kind prevents this difficulty and at the same time makes it easier to start the spreader. In some spreaders the rake and the end-gate are

combined. A lever is provided for raising and lowering the
device. When lowered, it serves as an end-gate; when raised, as
a rake. In at least one make the rake automatically drops when
the load is off, serving in the capacity of
an end-gate when down. When the unloading begins, the manure automatically
raises the end-gate to the proper position
for a rake.

In Fig. 329 may be seen a novel arrangement used to prevent the manure
from packing against the beater. This is
a sort of concave, the bars being circular
to fit the curve of the beater. While the
spreader is being loaded, these bars are
turned forward a few inches so that the
manure cannot touch the beater. When the spreader is thrown
in gear, the bars of the concave are thrown backward until they
almost touch the beater bars. In this position the teeth of the
beater project through the concave, and the manure is more

FIG. 323. Planetary-gear
drive for the beater shown
in Fig. 322

effectively torn to pieces
than would otherwise be
the case.

The wheels. Spreader
wheels are now rather
generally made of steel, a
material which enables
them to withstand wear
and to afford good trac-
tion. A weak point in
many steel wheels, how-
ever, is found in the construction of the rim. The
edges are usually turned
backward from the face of
the tire to prevent the

FIG. 324. A combination chain and planetary-
gear drive

The planetary gear is essentially the same as that
shown in Fig. 323

wheels from slipping sideways; but this forms a channel in which
mud and slush or dust collect. This material is carried upward as
the wheel revolves and is dropped over the gears of the spreader.

This trouble may be largely overcome, however, if several large holes are provided in the tire to let water and slush drain out.

FIG. 325. Method of driving the circular beater

The truck. The front truck of the spreader may be either wide or narrow. It is said to be wide when it is the same width as the rear truck. In soft and slippery ground the front wheels of the wide truck sink through to hard ground and so give better traction for the rear wheels.

With the narrow truck four separate tracks are made, and while the rear wheels may have a tendency to slip occasionally, it is seldom that any of the four tracks are deep enough to damage the turf. Where but two tracks are made, as with the wide truck, they are frequently so deep as to damage the sod. The narrow truck whips the tongue less than the wide truck, because of decreased leverage. The wide truck, as a general rule, offers better support for the bed.

Fig. 308 shows a common method of attaching the front truck to the bed. Because of the arched axle the pull of the team tends to draw the truck from under the load and produces a severe strain on its attachment to the bed. A wide truck (Fig. 330) is not open to the same criticism.

FIG. 326. A stationary rake located above the beater

The 2 springs above the rake permit the rake bar to spring back slightly

In a few spreaders a *single wheel* in front takes the place of the truck. This construction has never been very popular, though on level land there is no objection to the single wheel. Of course

Fig. 327. A spreader with two beaters and a pulverizer

The paddle attachment secures more even spreading and breaks up lumps

all whipping of the tongue is prevented, and there is no undue tipping of the bed as when one wheel of a two-wheeled truck drops into a hole. There is, however, a tendency for the single wheel to slide when the spreader is turning a sharp corner.

In Fig. 333 is to be seen a novel type of truck. The wheels here are of the automobile construction, there being no fifth wheel. This permits of an unusually strong support for the front end of the bed, and there is no whipping of the tongue. While it is not possible to

Fig. 328. Upper beater and ratchet drive driven from the lower beater

turn so short as with the other trucks, one is attracted by the very substantial appearance of the front end of this spreader.

350

Height of the spreader. In recent years nearly all manufacturers have turned to the low-down spreader. The top of the

FIG. 329. A concave that is really a slatted end-gate

In unloading, it is thrown back against the beater bars, the teeth of the beater projecting through it

bed has been lowered about one foot, the average height now being about forty inches. To accomplish this result the wheels in nearly all cases have been lowered. In many types, in order to avoid making the front wheels too low, they have been set out in front of the bed, as shown in Fig. 331. In either case the draft has been increased, since the draft becomes greater as the wheels are lowered, and the pull becomes harder as the

distance of the team from the load increases. But even with the increased draft, the low-down spreader has come to stay. It is much more easily loaded than the other, and at the same time, since it is easier to load the bed evenly, the efficiency of the spreader when unloading is increased.

Miscellaneous details. Only the best of materials should be used in the manure-spreader. Hard wood or steel, for example,

FIG. 330. A wide front truck placed beneath the spreader bed

This gives a short-coupled spreader and has the appearance of compactness

FIG. 331. A narrow front truck set in front of the spreader bed

is much to be preferred to pine, which is used for the bed rails in some cheap spreaders. All gears should be of malleable iron

or of steel and should be thoroughly protected from dust and mud. Oil and grease should be used freely and frequently. A little attention to this simple detail will well repay the time and money thus spent. The spreader should not be thrown into or out of gear while the team is in rapid motion. It is better to take the time to stop than to buy a new gear. All levers for making the necessary adjustments should be easily

FIG. 332. A front view of the spreader shown in Fig. 331

Note the narrow truck

reached and controlled from the seat. *Lime hoods* may be secured for nearly all spreaders at a slight additional cost. They are very satisfactory, but it is disagreeable to attempt to spread

FIG. 333. Automobile front-truck construction

No fifth wheel is required, and excellent support is provided for the bed

352

hydrated lime with a manure-spreader even if the spreader is equipped with a hood. *Drilling-attachments* are also furnished and are used chiefly by truck gardeners.

LIME-SPREADERS

Lime in its various forms is now so widely used in correcting soil acidity that some special machine to secure its proper application to the land is almost a necessity. In a small way the manure-spreader is used for this purpose, but with it the work

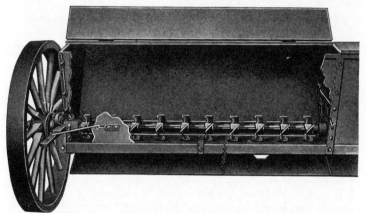

FIG. 334. A type of feed common in lime-spreaders

is slow and, especially with hydrated lime, rather unsatisfactory. Some have attempted to use the grain-drill for applying lime, but the range of quantity per acre is not great enough in drills to permit the application of lime in sufficient quantity without going over the land two or more times. The lime-spreader, then, becomes a necessity.

The lime-spreader distributes the lime broadcast and on top of the ground. It must be provided with an unusually strong feeding-mechanism, since the spreading of raw-ground limestone rock is not easily accomplished. One feeding-device is shown in Fig. 334. The winged wheels are located just above holes in the bottom of the hopper and are really nothing more than agitators. In supplying raw-ground rock there is a tendency for it to bridge over, especially if it is a little damp. In Fig. 335 is shown a type of feed which, in addition to the fact that it is more positive than the feed in Fig. 334, prevents the bridging over of the material being spread.

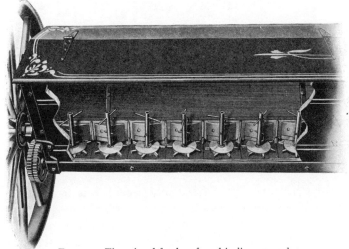

FIG. 335. The wizard feed as found in lime-spreaders

The upright bar and cross arm prevent the lime from bridging over

The quantity per acre is regulated by simply controlling the size of the openings in the bottom of the hopper. The range usually runs from three hundred pounds to as much as four tons of raw rock. The lime-spreader may be used for sowing fertilizer broadcast on the surface of the ground if the quantity which it is desired to sow is not too small and if the fertilizer is dry and fine.

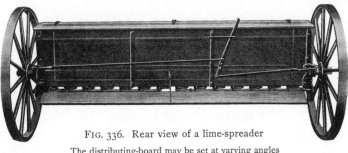

FIG. 336. Rear view of a lime-spreader

The distributing-board may be set at varying angles

CHAPTER XXII

HAYING MACHINERY

Few crops grown on the farm can be as completely handled by machinery as the hay crop. While the investment necessary to provide a more or less complete equipment may seem large, the investment pays for itself not only through a saving in labor but through value added to the crop by promptness in making and saving it.

Mowers

The mowing-machine is too frequently regarded as a simple tool requiring little care and less adjustment. As a consequence it is much abused, and often comparatively good machines are thrown away as worthless when a little adjustment and repair would prolong their usefulness for many years. Fig. 337 shows a plan view of a mower which illustrates several features to which attention will be called.

The frame. It will be noticed that the frame proper is of one piece of cast iron. Cores are inserted in the mold to provide bearings for the main axle and for the countershaft. It is a cast-iron casting and therefore much cheaper than if made of steel; at the same time it is sufficiently strong to withstand all ordinary strains.

The bearings. In the great majority of mowers the main axle is provided with roller bearings as shown (Fig. 337, *D*). The secondary shaft may or may not have roller bearings. The bearings of this shaft are important, since they are subjected to a great deal of wear and strain. The best construction has two bearings with the gears in between or with one gear between the bearings and one outside. This shaft is frequently provided with a device for taking up the wear between the beveled gears. One device is shown in Fig. 340, *A*. This is a very commendable feature and

354

should be found on a great many more machines. The counter-shaft leading to the pitman wheel is nearly always provided with solid bearings. The bearing next to the pitman wheel could not well be a roller bearing, since the reciprocating motion of the pitman would soon wear the rollers out of round. These solid bearings are removable in all cases and so may be replaced when worn. They are made of bronze or of Babbitt metal — more commonly of bronze. Unfortunately it is so difficult to remove these bearings when they become worn that, although they are said to

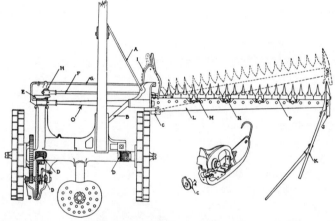

FIG. 337. Plan view of a mower

A, draw bar; *B*, push bar; *C*, aligning-device; *D*, roller bearings; *E*, pitman wheel; *F*, pitman rod; *G*, protector; *H*, pitman crank; *I*, inner shoe; *J*, outer shoe; *K*, grass-board; *L*, cutter bar; *M*, wearing-plate; *N*, knife clip; *O*, hinge bar; *P*, knife

be replaceable, new ones are seldom put in. There are a few exceptions to this rule, however, as some mowers provide easily removable bearings.

The *pitman* rod connects the countershaft to the knife. One end of the pitman is connected to the crank pin of the pitman wheel by a replaceable bearing, usually of bronze. It is very important that this bearing should be replaced when it becomes worn, for a little wear at this point causes undue strain upon other parts of the machine. The other end of the pitman rod is fastened to the knife head, usually by some form of ball-and-socket joint. It is needless to say that this joint must be kept tight.

356

In several mowers a ball bearing is provided just back of the beveled gear on the countershaft, as shown in Fig. 338, *B*. This is to take the end thrust, which would cause a great deal of unnecessary friction on a plain friction bearing.

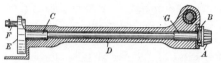

FIG. 338. Section through a countershaft

A, countershaft pinion; *B*, ball bearing; *C, G*, bronze bearing; *D*, portion of frame; *F*, crank; *E*, pitman wheel

Transmission of motion. Motion may be transferred from the main axle to the knife by gears alone or by chains and gears. The mower is just the reverse of the gasoline engine from the point of view of the transmission of the initial force to the point where the work is done. The engine converts the rectilinear motion of the piston into the curvilinear motion of the belt wheel. The mower converts the curvilinear motion of the ground wheels into the rectilinear motion of the knife. Either type of conversion calls for a more or less complex construction.

Transmission by gears alone is illustrated in Figs. 339, 340, and 341. Fig. 339 shows the most common method of arranging these gears. The large gear is keyed to the main axle, and meshes with the small spur gear on the secondary shaft. The large beveled gear on this shaft in turn meshes with the beveled pinion on the countershaft.

Fig. 340 shows another method of arranging these gears. The large gear attached to the main axle is called an *internal* gear, the teeth being on the inside of the rim. The chief

FIG. 339. External and beveled gears

Two steps are taken to increase the motion; both by external gears

advantages of this arrangement are that the strain is at all times distributed over more teeth, and the large gear by passing around the smaller one tends to draw it in. This tendency opposes the

FIG. 340. Internal and beveled gears

The larger gear is called an internal gear. More teeth are in contact than in the gear in Fig. 339. *A*, nut for taking up lost motion in the beveled gears

action of the beveled gears, which tend to force the secondary shaft outward.

Fig. 341 shows the gear device used by one manufacturer in which a circular gear-case, or *bell* gear, is substituted for the secondary shaft in the other types mentioned.

In the cases shown, two steps are taken to multiply the motion. These gears are usually of such size that the pitman wheel revolves about twenty-five times for each revolution of the ground wheels. Some mowers are provided with another pair of gears and thus take three steps to multiply the motion, and still others have a third pair of gears so arranged as to make it possible to give two different speeds to the knife. This is some advantage in cutting thin grass, wheat stubble, etc., as such mowing does not require the knife to be run fast.

FIG. 341. Beveled and bell gears

The bell gear takes the place of the secondary shaft

Transmission by chain and gears combined is shown in Fig. 342. This method offers the usual advantage of the chain drive — that it is better to break a link in a chain than a tooth in a gear. It is difficult, however, to keep the chain tight enough to prevent lost motion and still not give rise to undue friction.

The cutter bar and the knife. Fig. 337 shows the relation of the parts of the cutter bar and the knife. The guards are placed three inches apart, and the knife has a travel of three inches each

FIG. 342. Transmission by sprockets, chain, and gears

The small sprocket is on the short secondary shaft. Note the 4 pawls in the pawl hub

way. The sections of the knife when the pitman wheel is on the outer center are found exactly centered in certain guards. As the pitman moves to the opposite center, the sections move to the next adjoining guards, where they should again center.

The knife is said to *register* when each section is found to center in its guard. This is

essential, since in this position the motion of the knife is zero, and it should not be possible for it to cut anything. As the pitman-wheel crank moves up to a position 90° in advance of center, the motion is fastest, and the knife should be cutting the most grass. From this point motion decreases and is zero

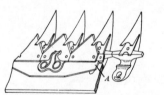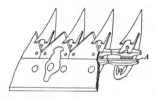

FIG. 343. Sections of cutter bars

Two types of wearing-plates, *A*, *A*, are shown

again at the other center. Knives may be thrown out of register by a strained bar, by loose joints between bar and frame, by misadjustment of the bar, etc.

It is not often that the knife fails to register properly except in very old machines. Nearly all mowers, however, provide some means for adjustment should it be found necessary. The bar (Fig. 337, *O*), sometimes called the hinge bar, just in front of or to the rear of the pitman rod, is usually threaded at its outer end and provided with a nut by means of which the inner shoe and the yoke in which the bar is hung may be drawn in or forced out as occasion requires.

The knife rests on *wearing-plates*, as shown in Fig. 343, *A*. It is essential that the rear part of the knife should be kept at the proper level with respect to the ledger plates. Should the rear part of the knife drop a little too low, the sections would not fit squarely on the ledger plates. The wearing-plates may be replaced when they become worn.

The *ledger plate* (Fig. 344) is that part of the guard against which the knife cuts the grass — the other blade of the shears, so to speak. The edges of the ledger plate are serrated that they may better grasp and hold the grass. It is essential that a close shearing action be maintained between the sections and the ledger plates. The *knife clips*, shown on top of the knife in Fig. 337, *N*, should at all times force the sections down snugly on these

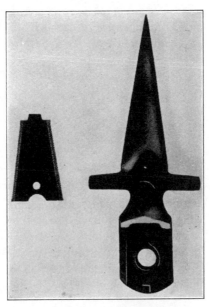

FIG. 344. A mower guard with its ledger plate removed

The edges of the ledger plate are serrated

plates. If the clips become worn, as soon happens, they may easily be bent downward by striking them a sharp blow, repeating the action, if necessary, until the proper fit is secured. The clips are for this reason made of malleable iron. They should not be pounded down so close as to cause the knife to bind, and the upper part of the guard should never be pounded down in an effort to force the sections close down on the plates.

The guards should be kept in a true line at all times. If they become slightly bent in any direction, they may be hammered back into place, since they are made of malleable iron. If they are out of alignment, the proper cutting action is interfered with and the knife is under a strain.

It will be noticed from Fig. 337 that the knife, the cutter bar, and the pitman are all in perfect alignment and must be kept so if free and easy motion of the knife is maintained. The cutter bar frequently becomes strained when stumps, posts, etc. are encountered and falls back of the true line. Long wear will often cause the outer end to lag behind and thus cause undue strain on all wearing-parts. It is necessary, therefore, that there should be

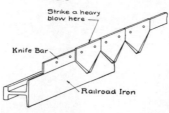

FIG. 345. Method of removing sections from a knife

some device for *aligning* the cutter bar. One method, found on a well-known mower, is shown in Fig. 337, *C*. An eccentric bushing surrounds the rear shoe pin. By applying a wrench to this bushing the outer end of the cutter bar may be moved through a distance of several inches. Other machines have different methods for accomplishing the same thing, but a few have no such provision.

The knife should be frequently ground, and when the ends of the sections become rounded by wear, new sections should be put on. This is a simple task which anyone can accomplish. Fig. 345 shows how to remove sections from a knife. Care should be taken not to bend the knife bar any more than necessary, as it is difficult to get it perfectly straight again. It is well, too, to keep a file in the mower box so as to touch up the sections if they become nicked or bent. Care in this regard will save the gears, the most expensive part of the machine.

The levers for raising the cutter bar should be easily manipulated. The foot lever (the kind on which the weight is thrown downward rather than forward seems best) should raise the bar high enough for turning. Some levers will bring the bar to a vertical position — a thing to be desired if one is cutting in new ground where stumps and trees are frequent. Otherwise it is of no great advantage. The tilting-lever for throwing the guards up and down at the inner and outer shoes will make it possible to cut high or low. Now that it has become a general custom in many parts of the country to clip wheat stubble in the fall of the year, it is desirable that the above adjustment should have enough range to allow the stubble to be cut at least four inches high.

FIG. 346. Pawl hub with three pawls

Lost motion in the mower. Lost motion in a mower is evident if the knife fails to start as soon as the main wheels begin to revolve. This permits the mower to be drawn into the grass before the knife starts, and choking down is the result. Lost motion may occur in several places : (1) *In the hub of the wheel.* Loss of motion here is due to the fact that the pawls do not engage the ratchets all the time. Fig. 346 shows a pawl hub with three pawls. It will be seen that only one pawl is in engagement at a time. This is as it should be ; but it is possible to turn the wheels a considerable distance at times before any one of the pawls will engage ; four pawls would therefore be better than three. (2) *In the device for throwing the machine into gear.* It is often the case that the wheels will turn one quarter of the way around before the gear clutch will engage. Of course the clutch should be thrown in before cutting is ready to begin. (3) *In the gears for transmitting motion.*

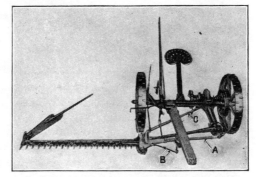

FIG. 347. A combination draw-bar and push-bar cut

A, hinge bar ; *B*, draw bar ; *C*, push bar

There is very little lost motion of this sort in a new machine ; but in time the teeth become worn, and unless there is some way of taking up this wear, unusual strain will be thrown upon all wearing-parts. As before mentioned, the secondary shaft may be provided with a device for taking up wear between the beveled gears. (4) *At the crank end of the pitman rod.* Wear at this point is usually taken up by providing a new bushing. (5) *At the knife-head end of the pitman rod.* These parts should be kept tight at all times.

Draw-bar and push-bar cut. Mowers were formerly nearly all of the push-bar type; that is, the cutter bar was pushed by the frame connections, and no force was applied directly to and in front of the cutter bar. The draw-bar cut was just the opposite — a rod connected the doubletree hitch and the inner shoe of the

FIG. 348. A draw-bar-cut mower

The draw-bar is shown at *A*

cutter bar, so that the bar was drawn rather than pushed. Nearly all mowing-machines are now combinations of the two types. Both draw bar and push bar are shown in Fig. 347.

Size of mower. This is determined chiefly by the width of the cut, although the size of the truck may vary for the same width of cut. Formerly the 5-foot cut was the standard, with the 4-foot cut common. Now there are many 6-foot and 7-foot cuts and a few 8-foot cuts. It is doubtful whether it is advisable for the cut to be wider than 7 ft., as the side draft and the general strain on the whole machine are very much increased. A wide truck should always accompany a wide cut.

Windrowing attachment. For the cutting of clover for seed there are attachments for the cutter bar which make it possible to throw the clover in a windrow or to drop it in bunches. One such attachment is shown in Fig. 349.

FIG. 349. A bunching-attachment

This is used in the cutting of clover for seed

RAKES

The modern steel *dump rake* is found on nearly every farm. Its superiority over the older wooden-frame, wooden-wheeled, hand-dump rake is evident. Nearly all such rakes are now dumped by power, through a clutch operated by the foot. A lever near the operator's foot serves to engage the tooth-bar with the wheels of the rake, thus causing the teeth to be lifted by the team. The advent of the loader, however, since it makes necessary a long windrow, created a demand for another type of rake — one that would make such a windrow possible. To meet this demand the side-delivery rake was produced. There are two types of side-delivery rakes upon the market, one known as the revolving-cylinder rake, the other known as the tedder rake.

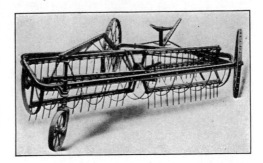

FIG. 350. A revolving-cylinder side-delivery rake

As the rake is drawn forward the hay is gathered into a windrow and thrown to the left

The *revolving-cylinder rake* is shown in Fig. 350. The construction of this rake is very simple. The revolving cylinder consists of three rake bars carried at an angle to the direction of travel of the team. The cylinder is long enough to cover two swaths, and the hay, which is rolled to one side as the rake is drawn forward, is thrown up into a loose windrow. The cylinder may be raised or lowered so that the teeth of the bars may run the proper distance from the ground. They should be set so as just to brush the ground and not dig into it. Two swaths usually make a sufficiently large windrow for a loader, but if the hay is thin, four or even six swaths may be thrown together. The way in which this rake handles the hay is a material help in curing it, and the use of the tedder is less necessary. The objection is frequently raised that this rake rolls the hay, making it difficult to handle in loading when a loader is used. In very long timothy hay this is noticeable, perhaps, but for average hay it is not a serious objection.

FIG. 351. A tedder side-delivery rake

This type of rake is very useful in clearing trash from ground which is to be seeded; for instance, in clearing potato vines and weeds from a potato field after the potatoes are dug. The windrows are tumbled over until they are sufficiently large, when they may be burned or hauled off.

The *tedder rake* is shown in Fig. 351. This type kicks rather than rolls the hay, and probably handles it more roughly than the cylinder rake. In some makes this rake can be reversed and used as a tedder.

In the opinion of many users the side-delivery rake is to be preferred to the dump rake whether or not a loader is used, the chief advantage being that it forms a continuous windrow of any desired size and that it rakes cleaner perhaps than the dump rake.

TEDDERS

The all-steel hay-tedder, in which the fork shaft is run by sprockets and chains or by gears, is now the most popular type. Fig. 352 shows a common style. In this type the fork shaft is driven from the middle and the shaft is in one piece. In some makes the shaft is in two pieces and driven from the ends. The latter type throws less strain on the driving mechanism. In

nearly all the modern tedders one fork is carried outside the wheels, so that the newly tedded hay will not be run over on the succeeding round.

It is essential that the tedder forks be provided with substantial springs that will permit of considerable freedom of movement

FIG. 352. A modern steel gear-driven tedder

should an obstruction be encountered; and yet they must be strong enough not to let the forks yield in handling a heavy bunch of hay. The coiled spring shown in the figure is perhaps one of the best types.

Fig. 353 shows an older type of tedder, but one that has given satisfaction. The fork shaft, which is in two pieces, is driven from the ends by gears alone. The fork bars are of wood.

The tedder is subjected to much vibration; it is therefore essential that all nuts be securely locked to prevent their working

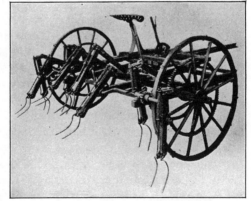

FIG. 353. A wooden-wheel wooden-bar tedder

The fork shaft is in 2 pieces, and each half is driven by gears at the end of the shaft

loose. Oil should be freely used on the tedder bearings, as the fork shaft revolves rapidly and the bearings are subjected to great strain. Oil is cheaper than new bearings or a new shaft.

LOADERS

The loader has come to be regarded as a necessity on farms where hay is one of the principal crops, not only because it is a labor-saver, but because the same work can be more easily accomplished with less labor and in less time than could possibly be the case if hand methods were followed. There are two general types of loaders commonly used, the fork (or rake-bar) loader, and the cylinder (or carrier) loader.

The fork loader. Fig. 354 shows a typical fork loader. The forks work close to the ground and are carried back and forth through a travel of several inches by the crank motion shown. Several different devices are used for giving the forks this vibrating motion, but they all accomplish the same purpose. The hay is forced up the elevator by a series of shoves, each upward movement of the bars pushing it up a few inches. The hay is thus handled rather roughly, and there is a tendency to shatter the leaves, particularly of clover, if very dry.

FIG. 354. A fork loader

The wheels on the side boards help to give a substantial support

This loader is wide enough to cover two swaths, and it takes hay from the swath well; in fact, it is sometimes called a swath loader. It will load from the windrow, however, if the hay is not too thick. If there is much trash on the ground, the forks have a tendency to pick it up with the hay. The elevator is usually narrowed at the top so that the hay is not dropped on the edges of the load.

The cylinder loader. Fig. 356 shows the simplest type of cylinder loader. The cylinder is made up of eight bars, each carrying several teeth, as shown in the figure. These bars, which are made to turn in their end supports, are guided in such a way that the teeth project downward when they are nearest the ground and while in this position pick up the hay. As the loader moves forward and the cylinder revolves, the teeth are turned upward, so that they grasp the hay firmly until the bars reach the top of the cylinder. Here they are permitted to turn backward, thus releasing the hay, which is deposited upon the carrier and elevated to the wagon. The slatted carrier, or web, as the figure shows, surrounds the cylinder. A separate view of a single cylinder is shown in Fig. 357, in which the position of the teeth on the various bars is more clearly shown. Although this type of loader will take hay up from the swath if the hay is not too thin on the ground, it is essentially a windrow loader. It is not wide enough to cover two swaths.

FIG. 355. Rear view of a fork loader

The elevator is narrowed at the top so that the hay will fall nearer the middle of the wagon

Figs. 358 and 359 show a *two-cylinder* loader. This is virtually the same as the single-cylinder type, with an additional cylinder carried behind which revolves in a direction opposite to that of the front one. This loader is made wide enough to cover two swaths and will take hay from the swath in a satisfactory manner. The rear cylinder adds a great deal to the complexity of the loader, since it requires additional support and since the drive chains or the gears must reverse its motion. It also adds materially to the draft. The gathering-boards on either side of the carrier guide the hay to the center of the wagon.

Fig. 360 shows a loader with a *jointed elevator*, the joints allowing the carrier to be straightened as the load becomes higher.

FIG. 356. A single-cylinder loader

The truck in front is a valuable attachment. Some loaders do not have it

This possesses two advantages. It is possible to deliver the hay farther to the front during the greater part of the loading process, and at the same time the hay does not have so far to fall. This is some advantage, particularly in windy weather.

The essential advantages and disadvantages of the loaders mentioned may be enumerated as follows: The fork loader seems to be the best for swath loading and is not so complex as the double-cylinder type. While it handles the hay roughly, it is easier to load after than the cylinder type, because if the hay piles up in front of the elevator, the fork loader continues to push it forward and does not drag it back off the load as the cylinder loader does. The fork loader may be used to take hay from either swath or windrow. The single-cylinder type is a windrow loader, but is without doubt the lightest-draft and the simplest of all the types mentioned.

FIG. 357. Details of a cylinder

The cylinder is in position to travel toward the left. Note the different positions of the teeth and the bars around the cylinder

It handles the hay without shattering the leaves and does not pick up trash so readily as does the fork loader. In a windrow loader there seems to be little need of the second cylinder.

FIG. 358. A two-cylinder loader

The rear cylinder revolves in a direction opposite to that of the front cylinder. The elevator is the same width at top and bottom, but the gathering-boards guide the hay to the middle at the top

The argument is offered that a swath loader is the most economical, since, if it is used, it is not necessary to rake the hay. This may be true from the standpoint of economy of time, but it would seem that a better quality of hay could be made if it were raked up and allowed to cure in part in the windrow rather than if it were left to lie in the swath until completely cured. In the latter case, of course, the top of the swaths is likely to be burned and the quality very much impaired.

The method of attaching the loader to the wagon is important and the work should be easily accomplished. Loaders with four wheels afford the best connection to the wagon and do not throw extra weight on the rack. It should be possible to disconnect the loader without getting off the load.

FIG. 359. Front view of a two-cylinder loader

The front truck adds greatly to the ease of handling

In working after the loader some operators prefer to keep the load level from the start. Others load the rear half up to a

FIG. 360. A two-cylinder loader with a jointed elevator

The hay is deposited further forward on the wagon than with a straight elevator and does not blow off the wagon when the load is being started

level with the loader and then load the front end. There is a new type of loader on the market which is provided with a carrier that rests in a horizontal position and that may be stretched out to the front end of the rack and then automatically drawn to the rear, the hay being distributed over the whole load. When it has been completely drawn back, it is shot forward again and the operation repeated. Still another handy loading-device provides a car extending half the length of the rack and rolling on top of it. It is first drawn to the rear end, and one half the load built upon it. By a windlass and rope attached to the front standard the car is then drawn to the front and the rear half of the load put on. It is doubtful whether such a device accomplishes much as a time-saver.

FIG. 361. A single-cylinder loader in operation

The windrow is picked up and elevated simply and easily. There are no scatterings left on the ground

BARN EQUIPMENT

The modern barn equipment for handling hay consists of a track and a carrier arranged for unloading at the end of the barn or from the inside of the barn. The track is suspended from the peak to the rafters and should be as close to the top as possible. There is a variety of tracks and cars. The former may be a wood track, but more commonly it is made of angle steel. The car should be of the swivel type so that it may be quickly changed from end to end of the barn without the necessity of unthreading. Figs. 362 and 363 show some of the common tracks and cars.

Fig. 364 shows the forks commonly used. The *double* harpoon fork is in highest favor and is especially good in short, dry hay. The *single* harpoon fork is more easily handled, however, and works very well if the hay is not too dry and too short. The *grapple* hook (Fig. 365) is especially useful in unloading straw or sheaf grain.

Slings are very much in favor in many parts of the country. Fig. 366 shows a good style — a sling that opens at the middle. The argument

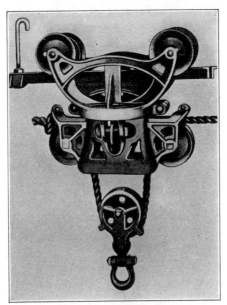

FIG. 362. A nonreversible carrier

To change the fork from one end of the barn to the other, the rope is drawn through the carrier

for the slings is that the load is taken up without any of the difficulties encountered in the use of the fork, such as the scattering of hay on both sides or the failure to clean up at the finish. In actual operation slings are used as follows : They are taken to the field, where one is put on the bottom of the wagon. When about one fourth of the load is put on, another sling is spread out, and this process is repeated until about four slings to the load are used. At the barn the ends of the slings are hooked into pulleys of a special car and drawn up. The sling is then tripped at the middle.

There is some inconvenience in getting the slings to the field. One way is to hang them on the front and rear standards. If a loader is used, the slings should all be hung on the front standard in such a manner that each may be easily and quickly spread over the load when needed ; this is probably the best manner in which to handle them. Another way is to carry the slings

on a cart or sled hitched to the wagon. Where hay is taken in from the end of the barn a somewhat larger door is required to admit a sling load than to admit a fork load ; further, it is quite difficult to finish a mow with slings, since they hang low and are very much in the way. It is customary, therefore, in some localities to take off the slings and use a fork in finishing a mow. A great many farmers use one sling on the bottom and take off the top of the load with a fork. This assures the cleaning up of the wagon on the last load and, except for the slight inconvenience of changing from fork to sling, is a very satisfactory arrangement.

FIG. 363. A reversible carrier

To change the fork to the opposite end of the barn the lower part of the carrier is turned on a swivel

In some localities instead of using slings two harpoon forks are attached to the rope and carrier. One of these forks is set at the front end of the load, the other at the rear end. In this way a complete layer of hay is taken up from the wagon, and the trouble arising from the hay's hanging together and falling back before the load has reached the mow (an incident of frequent occurrence where a single fork is used) is avoided.

Figs. 367 and 368 show some common methods used in equipping a barn with rope and carrier. Two different devices are shown for returning the car by means of weights. Fig. 368 shows a combination of two sizes of rope. In this device the large rope, usually three quarters of an inch or one inch in diameter, is used to draw the load up to the car. At this point the end of the smaller rope, a half inch in diameter, is hitched to the doubletree, and the car is drawn to the end of the track by it. In some cases the team is turned at the end of the smaller rope, which is passed around a pulley at the point shown, so that the car is drawn to the end of the track

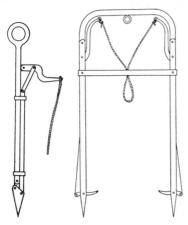

FIG. 364. A single and a double harpoon fork

on the return trip. This materially lessens the distance the team must travel, especially where the barn is long.

Various kinds of hay-hoists are used in connection with barn tools which, since they are operated by gasoline engines, effect a saving of time and horse power. Fig. 369 shows a cleverly arranged outfit. The man on the load has complete control of the hoist, and no time need be lost in taking the load off. Fig. 370 shows a similar device.

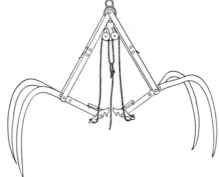

FIG. 365. A grapple hook

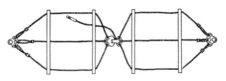

FIG. 366. A hay-sling that opens at the middle

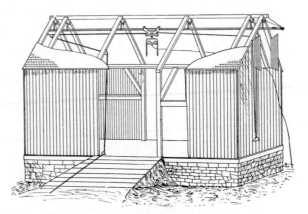

FIG. 367. The common method of installing carrier and rope

The hay is here taken in at the end of the barn. The weight is for the
purpose of returning the car

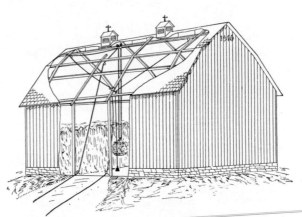

FIG. 368. Taking hay in at the middle of the barn

Two sizes of rope are used in this installation

374

Stacking-tools

One very common method used in stacking is to cock the hay and then to haul the cocks to the stack. Figs. 371 and 372 show the most common devices used for hauling the cocks. One advantage which the pole has over the rope is that cocks can be hauled as soon as put up, while with the ropes they must have settled. The rope must be tucked under the cock on both sides at the front, to prevent turning over, and must be left untucked

Fig. 369. A hay-hoist operated by a gasoline engine

The operator controls the hoist by the ropes running to the wagon. By shifting levers the load may be drawn up and the car returned to the end of the track

at the rear to prevent the rope from pulling under. After the rope has been tucked the foot should be placed on the rope at the rear of the cock in order to hold the rope close to the ground until the horse has started the cock. This prevents the rope from tipping the cock over and also causes the hay to be taken up better than if the rope were not so held. It is best to tie the rope in the hame ring. If a hook is put on the rope, it is invariably troublesome in unhitching from the cock at the stack. There should not be even a knot in the rope. This method of stacking is useful only where the stacks are built in or near the field. With two pitchers at the stack three horses with riders

FIG. 370. A hay-hoist and engine mounted on a home-made truck

At least a 4-horse-power engine is required to run such a hoist

and one boy to tuck ropes are generally required to keep the work going rapidly. Such a force can put from 15 to 18 tons of hay into stacks in a half day. When the stacks reach such a height as to make pitching from the ground difficult, a wagon may be run alongside the stack and the hay pitched first upon the wagon and then from there to the stack. The stacks should always be allowed to settle before they are finally topped out. Where the fields are close to the barn, the cocks may be hauled to the barn by means of ropes and taken up with the fork or with slings.

Several tools are available for drawing the hay up to and placing it upon the stack. Figs. 373 and 374 illustrate one such outfit. Figs. 375, 376, 377, and 378 show home-made devices used in stacking. Their construction is simple, though some companies have them for sale.

The equipment shown in Figs. 373 and 374 is especially desirable where

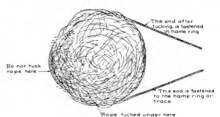

FIG. 371. Top view of a haycock showing method of hauling by rope

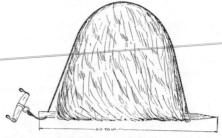

FIG. 372. Method of hauling haycocks by means of a pole and a rope

FIG. 373. A stacking outfit

A rake load of hay is being deposited on the derrick platform. It will then be elevated by the team on the right and dropped on the stack

FIG. 374. A rake for carrying hay to the derrick shown in Fig. 373

377

it is necessary to stack a large amount of hay each year. The hay is taken directly from the swath and placed on the stack with a minimum of man labor — a feature which commends the outfit to owners of large farms. Its cost, however, makes it prohibitive to the small landowner.

FIG. 375. A handy stacking-outfit

The simpler devices for stacking shown in Figs. 375, 376, 377, and 378 commend themselves to the small farmer who has, say, 30 or 40 tons of hay to stack each year. The outfits shown in Figs. 375 and 378 are in common use and seem to give entire satisfaction. In the former a special car carried on a wire cable is necessary, while in the latter the rope, pulleys, and fork required are the same as those used in the barn.

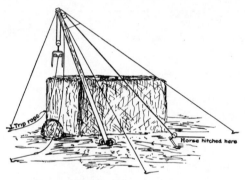

FIG. 376. A single-pole stacking-outfit

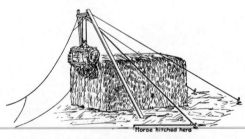

FIG. 377. A two-pole stacking-equipment

In stacking hay it is a much better plan to make a few large ricks than several small stacks. The essential thing to hold constantly in mind when building a rick is to keep the middle full and well tramped. The edges of a stack should be tramped but little if at all. The hay should be pitched from both sides if possible. If all the pitching is from one side, the stack is much more solid on that side, and in settling it will invariably lean toward the opposite side. The sides should be raked down with a hand rake to put them in better condition to shed water.

A good type of hayrack is shown in Fig. 379. The irons may be purchased from almost any hardware dealer, and it is a simple task to make the rack. Some prefer a rack with a flat top made of matched lumber; this type of rack may be provided with side boards and end boards for the purpose of hauling loose grain and ear corn, or it may be converted into a stack rack by equipping it with side boards and end boards of proper height.

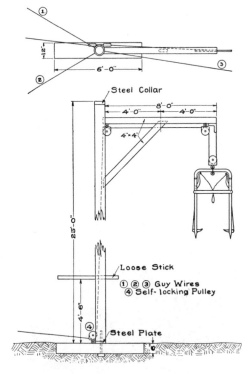

FIG. 378. Another type of single-pole outfit

The fork load is drawn up to the cross arm and locked. The pole is then turned on its base and the load dropped on the stack

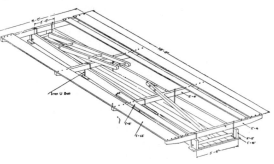

FIG. 379. A good type of hayrack

CHAPTER XXIII

GRAIN-BINDERS

The evolution of wheat-harvesting machinery which has taken place within the past sixty years forms one of the most interesting phases of modern industrial development. Within the memory of men still living, the cradle, and even the sickle, has been replaced by the modern four-horse eight-foot-cut grain-binder now used in almost every country in the world where wheat is grown. This short chapter, since it cannot take up in all its detail the construction and operation of the binder, will discuss what are deemed its more important features.

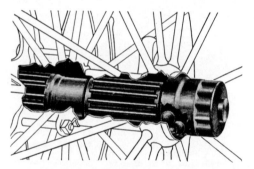

FIG. 380. Roller and ball bearings as found in the master wheel

The master wheel. Naturally the entire machine is built up around the main wheel. In addition to furnishing the traction to run all moving parts this wheel must carry the weight of the binder, which totals about fifteen hundred pounds. The necessity for strength is therefore evident. It must be wide and have strong heavy climbers to insure traction under all conditions. Its bearings, as shown in Fig. 380, are always of the roller type, with ball bearings at each end to take the end thrust. A convenient method should be provided for oiling these bearings. Too frequently it is made very difficult for the operator to attend to this important duty. The device provided for raising and lowering the machine on the main wheel should be amply strong and easily operated.

The secondary shaft. The secondary shaft, shown in Fig. 381, is just to the rear of the master wheel and operated by it through sprockets and chain. This shaft is carried on two long roller bearings, as shown. The coiled spring holds in place the clutch

used to throw the machine in and out of gear. At the left end of the shaft is shown a large nut by means of which wear between the beveled gears at the right end of the shaft may be taken up and a close mesh assured. An enlarged view of the end of the shaft is shown

FIG. 381. The secondary shaft and its relation to the countershaft

in Fig. 382. A similar device should be found on all binders.

The drive chain. The drive chain may be made of *malleable-iron* links or of *steel* links. The former are most in favor since they do not wear the sprockets so fast and are more easily put together. There are two styles of links, the *hook* link and the *pin* link. The hook link should be put on with hooks up, and to the front. This style of link is the one most commonly used for the main chain as well as for the elevator chain. In removing this kind of link from a chain, however, it is necessary to bend two of the links back on each other in order to slip them together. In putting on the main drive chain it fre-

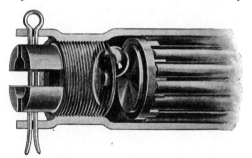

FIG. 382. End of secondary shaft showing method of taking up wear in the beveled gears

quently becomes impossible, therefore, to get the chain as tight as desired. The pin link, shown in Fig. 383, is not open to this objection. Some hook-link chains are provided with two pin links to overcome the above objection.

It will be seen from the figure that oil-holes are provided in the pin links. In sandy soil it is not advisable to use either oil or grease on the main chain, since the grit will cut out both chain and sprockets more quickly than friction from lack of oil. If sand is not troublesome, axle-grease may be used.

The countershaft. As shown in Fig. 381, the countershaft is driven by beveled gears from the secondary shaft. On the rear end of this shaft is a sprocket that runs the rear elevator chain, and on the front end is the pitman wheel and crank which runs the knife. Thus it is from the countershaft that motion for all parts of the binder is taken. The countershaft is usually provided with a roller bearing at the rear, as shown, but with a solid bearing in front.

FIG. 383. A main drive chain

The pin links are made of malleable iron

The cutting mechanism. The construction of the cutter bar, the knife, and the pitman is essentially the same as that of similar parts in the mower and differs only in some minor details. The travel of the knife is twice as great as in the mower and covers two guards at each movement. The guards are smaller, since they do not run close to the ground and hence do not encounter obstacles, as the mower guards do. The knife is made up of sickles rather than of plain sections, since dry grain is more easily cut by a serrated knife edge. The wearing-plates and the ledger plates are essentially the same. The cutting-mechanism is not put to so severe a strain as that of the mower; hence no device is found for aligning the cutter bar and none for bringing the knives to register. The knife will frequently last for several years, and the guards seldom need adjustment.

The reel. It is the function of the reel to deliver the grain in proper shape to the platform after the knife has cut it off. It begins its work before the grain is cut.

The reel may be driven by any one of the following devices: (1) by sprockets and chains, (2) by beveled gears and shafts, (3) by knuckle joints. The chain drive (Fig. 384) seems to permit the greatest amount of lost motion in the reel. The beveled gear and shaft seem to give the least opportunity for lost motion or play. In nearly all cases the power for driving the reel is taken from the upper roller of the lower elevator, which, in turn, is driven by the elevator chain. At least one binder provides a special shaft for driving the reel, taking its motion from the

FIG. 384. A reel driven by sprockets and chains

The power is taken from the elevator rollers

secondary shaft and running to the front of the machine near the base of the elevators.

The levers provided for the control of the reel should permit of a wide range in adjustment, both as to height and as to position forward, the latter adjustment being especially useful in lodged grain. It should be possible to bring the reel down to within about four inches of the guards but no lower. After a time the outer end of the reel is likely to sag and catch the guards if the reel is dropped to the lowest point of adjustment. There should be some means available for keeping the reel level at all times, as by the small diagonal rod running to the top of the reel bar shown in Fig. 385. In the wider cuts the outer end of the reel is provided with a special support, as shown in Fig. 389.

In grain that stands up straight the reel fans should strike the grain about six inches below the heads, just as the knife is cutting it off. If the reel is run too low, the grain will be thrown back too far on the platform, and a poor bundle will result. In grain that is leaning from the machine the reel should be well forward and low. A multitude of conditions must be met, and the making of poor bundles may frequently be traced to poor

FIG. 385. A reel driven by gears alone

The diagonal rod is for the purpose of keeping the reel level

reel-adjustment. The most common fault is that of working the reel too low and too far to the rear.

The platform. The platform with its canvas receives the grain and carries it to the elevators. It is securely bolted to the main frame at the inner end, while the outer end is carried on the grain-wheel. This wheel must be rigidly supported and must run true or it will knock down the standing grain. The underside of the platform is covered with sheet iron, which must be heavy enough not to bend or it will interfere with the operation of the platform canvas. The outer grain-divider is frequently made to fold up, for convenience in passing through narrow gates or in storing. The same is true of the inner grain-divider.

The platform canvas is driven by the inner roller, this roller receiving its motion from the elevator chain. There should always be some device for tightening the canvas. This device is usually found in connection with the outer roller, as shown in Fig. 386. It is difficult, by means of buckles alone, to draw the canvas tight enough to prevent slippage. If there is a tightener, it should be loosened and the canvas buckled; then the tightener may be adjusted to secure the proper tension. Moreover the dew and damp weather will shrink the canvas and sometimes break the straps if the tightener is not released.

There is often furnished with the machine a piece of strap iron which fastens to the outer grain-divider and lies loosely on the canvas, extending the full length of the platform, as shown in Fig. 385. It is placed on the platform where the heads of the grain fall, the purpose being, especially in short grain, to retard the heads, which being heavier than the straw cling more closely to the canvas, and so tend to make the grain go lengthwise into the elevator canvas.

FIG. 386. A device for tightening the platform canvas

By means of the tilting-lever the platform may be tilted forward and the guards made to run closer to the ground. This is for adjustment, to suit short grain or to take up lodged grain better. The platform should always be tilted slightly forward, since it seems to take the grain better in this position than when run perfectly level. The wind-shield on the rear platform is not essential, but is helpful if the wind is blowing in the direction of travel, in which case the proper handling of the grain is interfered with.

The elevator. The elevator is made up of the upper and the lower elevator canvases, with the necessary framework and rollers. Obviously its function is to elevate the grain and deliver it upon the deck. The lower canvas is driven from its upper roller, which, in turn, drives the upper roller of the upper canvas, the motion being transmitted and reversed by means of spur gears at the front end of the rollers. One company provides an extra-large lower roller for the upper elevator, the claim being made that it permits more spread between the upper and the lower canvases, so that clogging will not be so likely to occur.

FIG. 387. The upper and the lower elevator
A, diagonal rod for squaring the elevator; *B*, lever for tightening the canvas

Frequently the elevator canvases begin to creep; that is, one end runs ahead of the other and the slats do not run parallel with the rollers. The slats in such cases often become broken and then the proper delivery of the grain to the deck is interfered with. If this happens the elevator frames are not square. To ascertain whether the frames are square, the diagonals of each frame should be measured; they should of course be equal if the frames are square. In most cases there is a device for shifting the upper portion of the framework forward or backward far enough to make the diagonals equal. The diagonal-rod shown in Fig. 387, *A*, is for squaring the upper elevator. Canvas-tighteners should be provided, as on the platform canvas. A canvas-tightener for the platform canvas is shown in Fig. 386 and one for the upper elevator canvas in Fig. 387, *B*.

The seventh roller operates between the upper roller of the

FIG. 388. A steel-belt butt-adjuster

lower elevator and the deck. Its function is to carry the grain over to the deck and to assist in passing the grain on to the packers.

The deck. As the grain is delivered from the elevator it must pass down the deck to the packers. A steep deck is a decided advantage, since clogging will be less likely to occur. Decks that are flatter, though, are not so high and so reduce the amount of work necessary to elevate the grain; this, however, is insignificant when the actual power required is estimated.

The *butt-adjuster*, or butter, is provided to assist the grain down the deck and to feed it to the packers as evenly arranged as possible. There are two forms of butters, the vibrating butter, operated by a crank movement from the elevator rollers, and the

FIG. 389. A seven-foot-cut binder
In the wider cuts the outer end of the reel is provided with a special support

belt butter. The belt butter, shown in Fig. 388, consists of two rollers with a canvas or steel belt. A canvas belt is used by some manufacturers, but since it must be driven at a high speed, it wears out quickly. The vibrating butter, such as that shown on the machine in Fig. 385, seems to be the most satisfactory.

The butter should be run for the most part in a position straight down the deck at right angles to the grain. The common practice of drawing the butter back if it is desired to bind the bundles nearer the butts is wrong and will result in a bundle with uneven butts. The binder head should be moved forward rather than the butter backward. Only in very short grain is it necessary to draw the butter in.

388

The binder head. After the grain is delivered to the packers the binder head does the rest of the work of binding and dis-

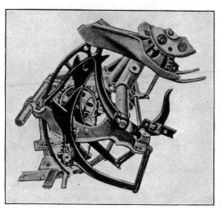

FIG. 390. Portion of a binder head

The needle, the packers, and the trip arm are shown in heavy black

charging the bundle. The essential parts of the binder head are shown in Figs. 390 and 391. These include the packers, the needle, the knotter, the discharge arms, the tier shaft — all parts, in fact, which have to do with the tying of the bundle. The binder head may be driven in either of two ways: (1) from the elevator chain, as shown in Fig. 392; or (2) by a separate chain, the power being taken from near the front end of the countershaft. The sprockets-and-chain connection may be seen in Fig. 390. The latter method is really the better, since it relieves the elevator chain of this extra strain.

Most binders are provided with two packers. Some, however, have three, the argument for the third being that by virtue of its position well to the front it assists the butter in bringing down the grain. The packers should reach

FIG. 391. View of a binder head

This view shows the tier shaft, the knotter, the trip arm, the packers, and the needle

up quite close to the seventh roller, — within four to six inches of it, in fact, — so as to reduce the tendency of the deck to clog. In at least one make the packers are stopped while the bundle is being bound, or, more particularly, while the needle is above the deck. This prevents the packing of grain against the needle while the needle is in the tying position. It will often be noticed that when a bundle is being discharged the machine chokes just as the needle is partially withdrawn. This is often due to the

FIG. 392. A method of driving the binder head

The elevator chain drives the packer shaft and through it the entire binder head

fact that the packers have forced the grain down against the needle, binding it tightly as it is disappearing beneath the deck.

The packers gather the grain from the deck and force it down against the *trip* arm and the *bundle-sizer*, or compressor, arm. These two devices may be in one piece, as shown in Fig. 391, *A*,

FIG. 393. Rear view of a binder

A, trip arm; *B*, bundle-sizer, or compressor, arm

or in two pieces, as shown in Fig. 393. It will be seen from Fig. 391 that the upright arm just beneath the knotter is bolted to a bracket which in turn is fastened to the small shaft extending to the front end of the binder head. By means of short

FIG. 394. Front end of a binder head

A, nut for adjusting length of needle pitman; *B*, trip spring; *C*, trip-arm shaft

arms this shaft is connected to the small coiled spring shown just beneath the tier-shaft wheel.

The packers drive the grain down against this upright arm, forcing it back against the tension of the *trip spring* (Fig. 394, *B*) until finally the dog in the clutch at the front of the binder head is tripped, this action throwing the head in motion with the rest of the machine. As soon as the tier shaft begins to revolve, the needle delivers the twine to the knotter; one end already being held by the twine disk, the knot is tied; the discharge arms kick the bundle off the deck; and, as the tier shaft resumes its original position, the dog drops back in place, and the binder head is thrown out of gear.

It will be seen that the tighter the tension of the trip spring referred to above, the tighter will the bundles be bound. Although many believe that tightening the twine tension will increase the tightness of the bundles, this is not so. The twine tension (types of which are shown in Figs. 395, 396, and

FIG. 395. A roller twine tension

This type of tension will pass uneven twine without difficulty

397) is merely to keep the twine from being fed to the needle too rapidly, and it should simply be tight enough to keep slack out

of the twine. To make the bundle *larger* or *smaller* the *compressor* arm should be moved out on the bracket as shown in Fig. 391, *A*,

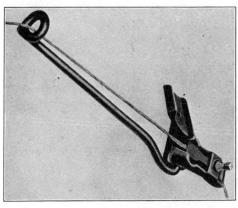

FIG. 396. A spring twine tension

A very satisfactory tension, though it is claimed that it tends to increase the kinking of the ball in the box

and ample provision is made for this adjustment.

If the trip arm and the compressor arm are not combined, the former is connected to the small shaft (Fig. 394, *C*) and through this to the trip spring, while the compressor arm is supported on its separate bracket. The compressor arm is so called because in most binders it is given a slight backward motion against the bundle just as the needle is delivering the twine to the knotter; thus the bundle is compressed from both sides at the moment of tying. This compressor arm, when separate from the trip arm, is provided with a compressor spring in order that the packers may not be obliged to force the grain against a rigid arm during the process of tying the bundle.

As the needle travels forward in the process of tying the bundle it is preceded by one of the packers and so is not used in compressing the grain. This

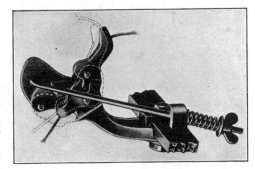

FIG. 397. Another type of spring twine tension

helps to prevent the needle from being bent out of its proper position. Should it for any reason become bent out of shape, it may be readily bent back again, as it is made of malleable iron.

392

The travel of the needle is controlled by the length of the *needle pitman*. This pitman, which is located at the front end of the binder head, is adjustable for length; so that if for any reason the needle should fail to travel far enough forward to deliver the twine to the cord-holder, the proper travel may be secured by adjusting the length.

FIG. 398. A portion of the tier shaft and the knotter head

The *knotter*, or knotter head, is undoubtedly the most delicate and most complicated part of the grain-binder. As shown in Fig. 398, it is made up of several parts, which must work together in closest harmony. An actual demonstration of the tying of a knot on a binder head is essential to a proper understanding of the function of the various parts of the knotter.

When the machine is properly threaded, one end of the twine is held by the *twine disk* (Fig. 399, *A*). As the grain collects above the breast-plate in the desired quantity, the binder head is set in motion; and the needle, which comes up from beneath the deck, carries the twine around the bundle, laying it across the bill hook and delivering it to the twine disk. The bill hook now makes a complete revolution, producing a loop in the twine, the ends of which are held by the twine disk. Just as the bill hook completes its revolution it grasps the

FIG. 399. The twine disk and its driving-gears

ends of the band, the knife cuts the twine between the bill hook and the disk, and the stripper slips the knot off the bill hook, the ends just cut off being drawn through the loop about the bill and finally completing the knot. The twine disk retains one end of the twine, and as the needle is withdrawn it lays the twine across the bill hook ready for the succeeding knot.

The knotter illustrated and used in modified forms on nearly all binders is known as the *Appleby* knotter, because it was invented and patented by John P. Appleby. The *Holmes* knotter, used on a leading make of binder, does not use the familiar bill hook. The Holmes knotter ties a bowknot. The criticism is sometimes made that it uses more twine than the other knotter, which ties a straight knot. This criticism is not true, however, for the knotter which ties a straight knot cuts off and throws away a short piece of twine for every bundle, while the Holmes knotter puts this short piece into the knot. Both knotters use the same amount of twine.

Knotter-head troubles. Troubles with the knotter head make up about 90 per cent of all binder troubles. In endeavoring to locate and remedy a trouble one should make only one adjustment at a time, for if two or three different remedies are tried at the same time, it is impossible to determine which is the real remedy. If after making one adjustment no benefit is derived, this adjustment should be brought back to its original position before another is attempted. By thus systematically going about the work one is almost sure to locate the trouble and so is able to apply the proper remedy.

Some of the more common troubles with the knotter head are the following:

1. *Loose twine disk.* The twine disk should hold the twine so tightly that a pull of about fifty pounds is required to draw it from the disk spring. If this spring becomes loosened, two conditions may be met with: (*a*) a band may be found clinging to the bill hook with a loose knot in the end, while the free end has the appearance of having been cut squarely off. The trouble here is that the twine-disk spring was so loose that it released one end of the twine but the other end was placed across the bill hook. Thus a knot was tied in one end and the twine remains on the bill. (*b*) A band may be found lying with a discharged bundle, there being a loose knot in one end of the string and the other end being cut squarely off. In this case the twine disk held the

twine until the knot was nearly completed, but one end of the twine slipped out of the disk just before being made a part of the knot, and the other end was tied in a loose knot around this freed end. Sometimes the knot will hold until the bundle is picked up, and then one end will slip out. The remedy is to tighten the twine-disk spring.

2. *Twine disk too tight.* (*a*) If a band with a knot in one end and with the other end presenting the appearance of having been chewed off is found with a discharged bundle, it is an indication that the disk is too tight. When the bill hook revolves, one end is pulled from the disk and does not enter into the completed knot, being similar in this respect to 1 (*a*). In this case, however, the ragged end shows that the disk was so tight as almost to hack the twine off. (*b*) If a band is found with both ends presenting the appearance of having been chewed off, it is an indication that the disk was so tight that it would not allow the twine to slip at all as the bill hook revolved. The result was that both ends were pulled out broken from the disk. The remedy is to loosen the twine-disk spring.

3. *Bill spring too loose.* If there is found with a discharged bundle a band having both ends cut squarely off and each end bent over as though a knot had been tied, it is an indication that the bill spring is too loose. As the bill hook revolved it made the loop in perfect order, but after the twine was cut and the stripper forced the loop off the bill, the ends, instead of being held tightly enough to be drawn through the loop, slipped out, and the knot was never completed. The remedy is to tighten the bill spring slightly.

4. *Bill spring too tight.* It is possible, though it does not frequently happen, that the bill spring may be so tight that the stripper will not slip the twine off the bill, and the discharge arms, in seeking to kick out the bundle, will break the twine, leaving the knot on the bill. A rough or rusted bill will cause the same trouble. Not infrequently the bill becomes worn in a groove where the twine crosses it, giving rise to a similar trouble.

5. *Twine tension too tight.* If the twine tension is too tight, the difficulties mentioned in 1 and 2 may be increased, so much force being required to draw the twine from the box that the

sudden passage of the needle upward pulls the twine from the disk instead. Broken twine is frequently the result of having the twine too tight. In this case the needle becomes unthreaded.

6. *Needle trouble.* If a bundle is discharged with the twine extending back to the needle eye, it is an indication that the needle failed to deliver its twine to the twine disk. As a result the loop and knot were made in the usual way, but only one end was cut off. The disk of course was not threaded for the following bundle. This trouble may come from the fact that the needle pitman does not permit the needle to travel sufficiently far forward, though this is seldom the case. What happens more frequently is that straws or trash interfere with the proper placing of the twine in the disk. On the discharge of the following bundle the disk may catch the twine and the third bundle will be properly bound.

7. *Several bands clinging to bill hook.* This is usually the result of several successive misses and may be caused by any of the preceding troubles where the knot is left on the bill hook.

More general troubles are the following:

1. *Loose drive chain.* If the main drive chain is too loose, it attempts to climb the teeth in the small sprocket on the secondary shaft and results in a jerky motion. The tension should be tightened or a link removed.

2. *Creeping canvases.* If the canvases are too loose or if the elevators are not square, the canvases creep; that is, the slats do not remain parallel to the rollers. The remedy is obvious.

3. *Ragged bundles.* Ragged bundles may be due to (*a*) improper manipulation of the reel, (*b*) improper setting of buttadjuster, (*c*) improper position of binder head, (*d*) creeping canvases. The explanation of ragged bundles as related to these difficulties is made upon the assumption that the grain is in good condition. There are times of course when the condition of the grain makes good bundles impossible.

4. *Choking on the deck.* This frequently happens in light, fluffy, overripe grain. The only remedy is to lower the deck cover if possible.

5. *Tier-shaft motion irregular.* If the tier shaft, or the whole binder head, in fact, starts tardily when tripped, or, after starting,

runs with a jerky motion or makes successive revolutions without stopping, the trouble is with the dog in the binder-head clutch. When the trip arm releases the dog stop, a spring behind the dog should force it to engage the clutch with the driving motion and start the binder head at once. It should remain in engagement throughout the complete revolution of the tier shaft. The dog stop may become so worn that it will not throw the dog out of engagement with the clutch, and the tier shaft continues to revolve. The face of the stop may be filed, or its length adjusted to remedy the trouble. The length of this stop should be such as to prevent play in the tier shaft.

6. *Discharging very small bundles.* This is due to imperfect contact between the dog and dog stop. The remedy is the same as that in 5.

7. *Choking machine in wet ground.* This trouble is often unavoidable. Only a part of a swath should be cut, and relief may be had by tying the bundles looser and making them smaller.

The bundle-carrier. There are two types of bundle-carriers in common use. In one (Fig. 385) the fingers of the carrier are held at right angles to the direction of travel, and in discharging bundles they fold backward and downward. This type is a little difficult to hold in position if high stubbles or other obstructions are in the way. It is also sometimes difficult, particularly in heavy grain, to return it quickly enough to catch the first bundle delivered after dumping; hence the piles are likely to be scattered. In the other type the fingers point backward and are carried parallel to the direction of travel. To discharge the load the carrier is simply dropped to the ground. This carrier tends to scatter bundles in going up hill, but it discharges the load quickly, as a rule, and makes neat and regular bunches. Either type should be so adjusted as to lock when receiving bundles, so that the operator will not be required to hold the carrier in place by sheer foot pressure.

The tongue truck. All binders having a seven-foot or eight-foot cut should be equipped with a tongue truck (Fig. 393). A truck takes all the weight off the horses' necks. The horses, too, turn the machine with their traces rather than with the neck yoke, and if there is any side draft the truck takes it off the team.

Better adjustment of the machine is possible with a truck than without one. The so-called "quick-turning" truck is best, as it does not tip over in turning a corner.

Size of binder. Not many years ago 5-foot cuts were common and the 6-foot cut was large. Now, however, all companies are selling more 7-foot cuts than anything else, and a large number of 8-foot cuts are sold. The 8-foot binder is a 4-horse machine, and, indeed, 4 horses ought to be used on the 7-foot binder. If one has as much as 30 acres of grain each year, an 8-foot machine will be found profitable.

Transport trucks. The transport trucks should be so made as to be quickly and easily removed. In most binders one man can now easily truck or un-truck a binder except for putting the tongue on. Formerly it took two or three men to perform the task.

Care of the binder. The binder should be carefully inspected at frequent intervals when it is being used, to make sure that all nuts are tight and all parts in proper working order. A lost nut is

FIG. 400. A self-rake

The chief use of this machine is that of cutting clover for seed

frequently the cause of hours of delay. All bearings should be oiled at least twice each day while the faster-running parts, such as the packers, should be oiled several times a day. At the end of each season the binder should be carefully cleaned and put away under cover. It should not be left out in the field for days or weeks to rust and rot. The knife, the end of the needle, and the knotter should be well oiled or they will rust badly, even though the machine is kept in a shed. While in use the binder should be gone over frequently to see that all nuts are tight. This will often prevent broken parts. The canvases should be removed at night or should be well covered to prevent their becoming wet from rain or dew; when the binder is stored for the winter they should be taken off and hung up in a dry place where mice cannot get at them.

The header. In the extreme western part of the country the header is used to some extent. This is an adaptation of the modern binder in which the cutting-parts, platform, and reel are similar to those of the common binder. The machine, which is pushed ahead of the team of from 4 to 6 horses, cuts a swath from 12 to 20 ft. wide. The heads of the grain are clipped off and elevated into wagons drawn along by the side of the machine. Some types are provided with a binding-attachment, in which case they are called header-binders. The combined header and thresher is in rather common use in some of the Western states. In one operation the grain is cut, threshed, and sacked. The sacks are dropped on the ground as the work proceeds and may lie there for weeks before being hauled away, as no rain occurs at this season of the year. These machines may be propelled by horses or by engine power, and they are capable of harvesting 100 acres per day.

CHAPTER XXIV

CORN-HARVESTERS

Cutting corn is undoubtedly one of the most difficult and disagreeable tasks that the farmer must perform. Though a great effort has been made to develop machinery to make this task less arduous, nothing has been perfected thus far that may be considered a complete success. It cannot be said that the machines are always at fault, for some of them work well under favorable conditions. But the corn crop is so easily blown down when near maturity that it is the exception rather than the rule to find a field where the corn stands straight and even. There are several types of simple cutters which are widely used the country over, and both the binder and the shocker are used with a considerable degree of success.

The sled cutter. The "sled cutter," so-called, is one of the simpler machines that works satisfactorily if the corn stands straight. This cutter is usually mounted on wheels, though it may be drawn on runners. It is drawn by one horse and cuts two rows at a time, requiring two men to operate it; the operators, one on either side, stand or sit just back of the stationary knife. As the cutter is drawn forward they grasp the corn just before the knives cut it off. When an armful is collected, the horse is stopped and the corn carried and set up. Obviously the operators cannot stoop to gather up stocks that are down.

Modifications of the sled type. Efforts have been made to devise some means for collecting the corn on the platform so that the operators need only carry it to the shock. One harvester employs a large screw about 10 in. in diameter and 6 ft. long, extending backward from a point at the extreme front end of the machine at an angle of 45° with the ground. The rotation of this screw carries the corn back, as the knives cut it off, into an arm which holds it in a vertical position. The

399

horse is stopped as usual and the corn carried to the shock. This type has met with only fair success and is used very little.

FIG. 401. Front view of a one-horse cutter

Another cutter, illustrated in Figs. 401 and 402, carries the corn back by chains and drops it on the platform in a horizontal position. The operators have simply to carry the corn to the shock. It is not necessary to stop the horse if the men can keep up with the machine. This machine is used to advantage in cutting corn for the ensilage-cutter, though of course it does not bind it. Owing to its low first cost and to its simplicity it is meeting with a great deal of favor and promises to become popular.

Still another modification provides a platform with a central tree around which the operators set the corn as it is cut, until a full shock is accumulated. It is then tied, and by means of a windlass the tree is raised and the shock set off to the rear. The tree is then withdrawn and placed in its original position. This cutter has not met with much favor, for the shocks are not large enough to be set up well and consequently soon fall down.

FIG. 402. Rear view of cutter shown in Fig. 401

The corn-binder. The corn-binder has not proved so popular as was anticipated when it was first put upon the market in a large way. There are several objections to its use, the more common ones being the following : (1) it does not do a neat job ; (2) it knocks off too many ears ; (3) it is difficult to get men to shock after it ; and (4) if the corn were being cut by hand, the teams could be used in preparing the ground for wheat where it is customary to follow corn with wheat. Not all of these objections are real, however ; some are purely local, and others do not obtain at all. Where men are not to be had for cutting by hand, it is conceded that corn is more

FIG. 403. Side view of a corn-binder

The bundles are bound while standing in a vertical position. There are no packers on this machine, though most of the other makes have them

quickly cut by means of the machine. For those who have silos to fill, the binder is in great favor.

Fig. 403 shows a side view of a typical corn-binder. The long projecting noses on the rails of the binder can be set close to the ground, so as to pick up lodged stalks surprisingly well. They will pick up nearly all the lodged stalks except those leaning directly away from the machine. Many stalks lying rather flat are broken off by the binder noses, however, because of the weight of the ear. The corn is conveyed to the reciprocating knife by elevator chains, there being at frequent intervals links, known as picker links, provided with fingers. These elevator chains force the corn back to the knife, which is usually provided with three sections and a short pitman.

After the corn is cut off by the knife, it is conveyed to the binder head. In some machines the corn is bound while in a vertical position. In this case the packers receive the corn as it leaves the elevator chains, and then force it against the trip arm, as in the grain-binder. The binder head is nearly the same as that found on the wheat-binder except that all parts of it are slightly heavier.

FIG. 404. Gasoline engine attached to a corn-binder

With the engine attached 2 horses can easily draw the binder

If the corn is bound in a horizontal position, it drops upon the deck after leaving the elevator chains, and there it comes within the reach of the packers. A butter is used on most machines to assist in passing the corn from the elevator chains to the deck.

One binder which binds the bundles while in a vertical position has no packers (Fig. 403). It is claimed, and the claim seems reasonable, that as a result fewer ears are knocked off than where packers are provided. It is also considered that where the corn drops upon a horizontal deck, additional ears are knocked off. A bundle-carrier similar to that of the grain-binder is provided with all machines.

A stubble-cutter, which is a great convenience in seeding, is frequently used if wheat is to follow the corn. It consists of a knife carried along close to the surface of the ground. The corn may be cut at different heights by raising or lowering the binder on the two wheels. Ample adjustment should be provided so that the elevator noses may be set to run very close to the ground if the corn is badly lodged.

In operating the binder it is the custom in many parts of the country first to "heart" the field; that is, stools are tied and 2 rows are cut on each side. This opens up the way for the binder, and since it provides a substantial support for the shocks, very few of them fall down. The other plan is to go around the field and cut all of the corn with the machine, using a horse, or tree, to start the shock. The corn-binder is essentially a 3-horse machine, but inasmuch as it is somewhat difficult to handle 3 horses in a cornfield, some prefer to use only 2 horses, changing teams in the middle of each half day.

The size of the shocks, whether cut by hand or by a machine, varies greatly in different sections of the country. Where the ground is seeded to wheat, the shocks are commonly made 4 by 24, 5 by 20, or 12 by 12; that is, the shocks are made to contain 96 or 100 or 144 hills respectively. In the first two sizes the shock rows are not seeded at all, but in the last, wheat is seeded around the shocks. If the ground is not to be seeded, the corn is usually cut 10 by 10, making 100 hills to the shock.

The corn-shocker. The corn-shocker stands less in favor than the binder, but many farmers are using the shocker and liking it. They find it a one-man machine, and by care seem to be able to do good work with it. Others have tried it and failed. The chief trouble seems to be that the shocks do not stand up well. It would seem that if the bottoms were made larger the shocks would stand better; from the way in which the shock is formed, it is next to impossible to make one that will stand up straight for any length of time. The shock is collected around a central tree, tied, and set off to the rear by means of a windlass. The tree is then pulled out and replaced ready for another shock.

The picker-husker. In sections where the fodder is not valued highly, the picker-husker is used to some extent. This machine has a pair of rolls which snap the ears off and carry them up to husking-rolls. After passing over these rolls, which remove the husks, the ears are elevated into a wagon which is drawn alongside the machine. There are other machines which simply pick the ears but do not husk them.

Cost of cutting by three common methods. While it is difficult to figure costs except for local conditions, the following comparative

figures may be taken as an approximate average for Ohio. These
figures are made on the assumption that the corn is cut 10 by
10 in., in which case there will be 35 shocks per acre; that
an average hand will cut 1 acre a day by hand; that 2 men
with a sled cutter will cut 105 shocks, or 3 acres; that 7 acres is
an average day's work for a man and team of 3 horses with a
binder, 2 men being required to set the corn up; and, further,
that 30 acres of corn will be cut with the binder each year. The
figures represent the cost of cutting per acre, (1) by hand,
(2) with the sled, and (3) with the binder:

Cutting by hand:

    35 shocks @ 7¢ = $2.45, cost per acre.

Cutting with sled cutter:

2 men @ $2	$4.00
1 horse @ $1	1.00
Interest and depreciation	1.50
Total for 3 acres	$6.50
Cost per acre	2.16

Cutting with binder:

Man and team (3 horses)	$5.00
2 men @ $2	4.00
14 lb. twine @ 10¢	1.40
Oil	.10
Interest and depreciation @ 15 per cent . . .	4.37
Total for 7 acres	$14.87
Cost per acre	2.12

CHAPTER XXV

WAGONS

A wagon is an absolute necessity on the modern farm. Perhaps no other tool is used so many days in the year, and certainly no other tool is called upon to do its work under such varying conditions as the farm wagon. As a rule farmers think that there is very little difference in wagons, and consequently they give but

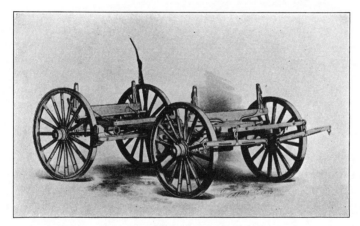

FIG. 405. Wheels with patent hubs

little attention to their construction. A little study of the question, however, will convince anyone that there is a great variation in the types found on the market.

Material. Oak, hickory, and poplar are the materials which enter most largely into the construction of good farm wagons. The best manufacturers insist on having the material air-dried rather than kiln-dried. The air-drying process requires at least three years' time, but results in a more uniform product. Kiln drying is frequently done too rapidly, and the stock is not uniformly cured. Many parts of the best wagons are soaked in linseed oil before being used, a process which makes them less susceptible to the action of the weather.

The wheels. The wheels are without question the vital part of a wagon. The hubs are usually made of oak or of black birch.

FIG. 406. Hub of wagon wheel

The spokes are tapered at the shoulder

It is difficult to say which is the better material, since both are used by standard companies. One firm claims that birch is better, since, because of its yielding nature, it holds the spokes more firmly when they are driven into it.

A patent hub is being used on some wagons (Fig. 405). This hub has some advantages over the compressed hub, but is more severe on fellies and tires and is considered by some smiths to be more difficult to repair.

The spokes are made of oak or of hickory. They should be evenly tapered at the hub tenon, and the shoulder should be cut with some taper also (Fig. 406) in order that the weight may be borne evenly over the entire surface. The mortises in the hub are cut so as to give the wheel the proper dish, that it may hold the tire better and that it may withstand side thrust or extra strain to which it is subjected, as when on sidehills. In addition to these points, dish in a wheel is beneficial in providing for the ex-

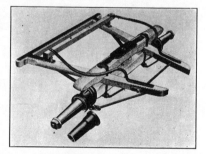

FIG. 407. Front wagon gear

Hickory axles with cast-iron skeins are used. The piece above the axle is called the sand board

pansion and contraction of the tires. The fellies are chiefly of oak, and may be bent or sawed to shape. The two methods seem to be equally good. A rivet through the felly on either side of each spoke is of advantage in preventing splitting. The tires must of course be heavy, and for average farm conditions should not be less than $2\frac{1}{2}$ in. or 3 in. wide. The 4-inch tire is grow-

FIG. 408. Rear wagon gear

The steel skeins are clipped to the axle. Notice the well-braced standards

ing in favor, and experimental evidence shows that the wide tire effects a decided saving in draft.

The height of the wheels varies a great deal. As usually classified, there are three heights, known to the trade as low, medium, and high. A low-wheeled wagon generally has 36-inch front wheels and 44-

inch rear wheels, and a high-wheeled wagon has 44-inch front wheels and 52-inch rear wheels. The medium-wheeled wagon is the class most commonly used by farmers. Where two wagons are needed on a farm, it is a good plan to have one low-wheeled

wagon for ordinary farm teaming. It is, further, very desirable to have at least one wide-tired wagon, with a tire, say, 4 in. wide.

The axles. The axles are generally made of hickory. They may be provided with either cast-iron or steel skeins (Figs. 407, 408, and 409). There does not seem to be much choice between the two types. In either case they should be fastened to the axle by clips rather than by bolts. Other things be-

FIG. 409. The bolster is fastened to the axle by clips

ing equal, that gear is best which has the fewest bolt-holes in the various parts. Many axles are provided with a steel truss, which not only strengthens the axle but holds the skeins in position.

The *skeins* are so constructed and fastened to the axles as to give the wheels what is called gather and what is called pitch, or set. In the attachment of the skein the outer end is given a slight inclination toward the front, an inclination which holds the wheel against the collar and prevents its running against the nut. This is called *gather*; that is, such a setting gathers the front portion of the wheels. The full load on a wagon should be carried upon a plumb spoke, but inasmuch as the wheels are dished, the skeins must be so sloped as to give the proper set to the wheels and at the same time to cause the wheel to run toward the collar rather than toward the nut. This feature of construction is variously termed *pitch, set,* or *bottom gather.* With the proper pitch and gather, a heavily loaded wagon "chucks," as we say; that is, the wheels bear against neither the shoulder of the skein nor the nut with sufficient pressure to hold them in either position, but play back and forth between the two extremes.

FIG. 410. A handy wagon with low steel wheels

Every farm should have a low-wheeled wagon or a set of low steel wheels for the standard wagon

Miscellaneous parts. The gear parts, such as hounds, bolsters, reaches, and poles, are usually made of oak. As said before, the parts should be clipped rather than bolted together. The eveners and the neck yoke are made of hickory. The box, which is made of yellow poplar, should be well ironed and braced, as it generally is one of the first parts of a wagon to wear out. It should have at least three coats of good paint. The brake is now generally attached to the gears, the underslung type being in highest favor.

Size and capacity. The size of a wagon is generally specified by giving the size of skein, the height of wheels, and the width of tire. There are two widths of track — the narrow, or regular, track and the wide track (the former measuring $4\frac{1}{2}$ ft., the latter, 5 ft., from center to center of tires on the ground). The regular track is used almost exclusively in the Northern states.

In Table XXIX are found the size of skein, the weight, and the capacity for the common sizes of general farm wagons.

TABLE XXIX. SIZE OF SKEIN, AND WEIGHT AND CAPACITY OF WAGONS

Size of skein	Weight in pounds	Capacity in pounds
$2\frac{1}{2}'' \times 8''$	1050	2000
$2\frac{3}{4}'' \times 8\frac{1}{2}''$	1100	2500
$3'' \times 9''$	1150	4000
$3\frac{1}{4}'' \times 10''$	1200	4500
$3\frac{1}{2}'' \times 11''$	1300	5500
$3\frac{1}{4}'' \times 12''$	1400	6500
$4'' \times 12''$	1600	7500

The steel wagon. Many of the ordinary farm wagons are equipped with a steel axle, but only a few, except certain low-wheeled farm trucks, have all their gears and wheels of steel. As timber becomes scarcer the steel wagon will probably become more popular. On the other hand, as roads become improved and the hard brick and macadam roads replace the earth road, the weakness of the steel wagon will become more evident, which fact will militate against its use. It is a common observation, that since running gears and wheels of steel are not as yielding under the strain of heavy loads as those of wood, the jar of rough roads will cause the parts to loosen to a greater degree than in an all-wood wagon.

Roller bearings have been used to a limited extent on wagons, but the saving in draft has never been considered sufficient to offset the increased cost of construction. Moreover it becomes impossible to give the skein the proper gather and pitch when the roller bearing is used.

The draft of wagons. The draft of a wagon refers to the number of pounds of pull required to move it. It is measured exactly as a spring balance measures the weight hung upon its hook. The draft depends upon several things, among which are the nature of the roadbed, the weight of the load, the height of the wheels, the width of the tire, and the efficiency of the bearings. All of these may be included in three factors : (1) axle friction, (2) rolling resistance, and (3) grade resistance.

Axle friction is a very small factor in determining the draft of a wagon. Naturally it depends upon the nature of the bearing surface and the state of lubrication as well as upon the ratio of the radius of the wheel to the radius of the axle. If R represents the radius of the wheel, r the radius of the axle, F the force required to move the wheel, and f the frictional resistance, then

$$f \times r = F \times R;$$

whence
$$F = f\,\frac{r}{R},$$

a formula which goes to show that the power required to overcome frictional resistance varies inversely as the radius of the wheel.

Rolling resistance is dependent chiefly upon the nature of the roadbed and the height of the wheels. Drawing a load over a

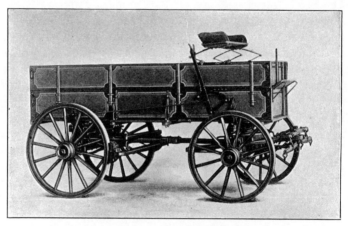

FIG. 411. A stiff-tongue wagon

The underslung brake is the better type. The lever on the bed controls the brake

muddy road is equivalent, in a measure, to pulling the load over an obstruction. A high wheel affords a greater power arm than a low wheel, and hence requires less force to draw it over similar obstructions. Furthermore a small wheel will sink further into a roadbed than will a high wheel under similar conditions.

The following tests compare the draft of a similar load on high, medium, and low wheels on different road surfaces. A load of

2000 lb. was drawn in all cases. The high wheels measured 44 in. in front and 56 in. in rear; the medium, 36 in. in front and 44 in. in rear; the low, 24 in. in front and 28 in. in rear. The wheels were of steel and had tires 6 in. wide. The actual weight of the loaded wagon with each set of wheels was with high wheels, 3762 lb.; with medium wheels, 3580 lb.; with low wheels, 3362 lb.

TABLE XXX.[1] EFFECT OF HEIGHT OF WHEEL ON DRAFT OF WAGONS

KIND OF ROAD	CONDITION OF ROAD	HEIGHT OF WHEELS	DRAFT PER 2000 POUNDS NET LOAD
Gravel	Dry, 1″ sand, small loose stones	High	158.9
		Medium	161.9
		Low	185.3
Macadam	Slightly worn, clean, fair condition	High	108.0
		Medium	108.7
		Low	117.4
Dirt	Frozen solid, ½″ sticky on top	High	189.2
		Medium	213.4
		Low	233.8
	Dry, hard, no dust	High	130.0
		Medium	134.0
		Low	132.0
Timothy-and-blue-grass sod . .	Rather dry and firm, no ruts	High	248.1
		Medium	259.9
		Low	300.6
	Wet and spongy; low wheels cut ruts 3″–4″ deep	High	325.2
		Medium	362.7
		Low	472.6
Freshly plowed ground . . .	Dry and cloddy	High	475.0
		Medium	542.0
		Low	628.0

The results are uniformly in favor of the high wheels, the difference being greatest on grassland and plowed land, where the average farmer does the most of his teaming. It should be said, however, that draft is not the only factor that enters into the choice of height of wheels, and that in general the medium wheels are to be preferred even though the draft is rather more than is the case with the higher wheels.

[1] *Bulletin No. 52*, Missouri Agricultural Experiment Station, Columbia.

The width of the tire is of even greater importance than the height of the wheel, particularly on the farm. The following tests show the influence of width of tire on the draft of wagons on various road surfaces. The net load was 2000 lb. in all cases. The narrow tires were $1\frac{1}{2}$ in. wide; the broad tires, 6 in. wide.

TABLE XXXI.[1] EFFECT OF WIDTH OF TIRE ON DRAFT OF WAGONS

KIND OF ROAD	CONDITION OF ROAD	WIDTH OF TIRE	DRAFT PER 2000 POUNDS NET LOAD
Gravel . . .	Hard surface, no ruts	Narrow	218.4
		Broad	163.8
	Dusty, dry	Narrow	239.1
		Broad	156.7
Dirt	Dry, hard, no ruts or dust	Narrow	137.3
		Broad	104.8
	Surface sticky, firm underneath	Narrow	206.1
		Broad	308.0
Meadow . .	Soft; narrow-tire ruts, 5″–6″ deep; broad-tire ruts, $1\frac{1}{2}$″–2″ deep	Narrow	569.0
		Broad	323.6
	Moist; firm; narrow-tire ruts, $3\frac{1}{2}$″ deep; broad-tire ruts, $\frac{1}{4}$″–1″ deep	Narrow	420.8
		Broad	305.0

The tests show uniformly in favor of broad tires, not only in the decreased draft but in the damage done both roadbeds and fields. In the test on soft and spongy meadowland, for example, the effort that was required to draw the 1-ton net load on narrow tires would have drawn 3517 lb., or a 75.8 per cent greater load on the broad tires. In addition, the ruts cut by the broad tires did no appreciable damage, while those cut by the

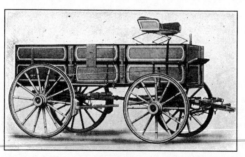

FIG. 412. A drop-tongue wagon with underslung brake

1 *Bulletin No. 39*, Missouri Agricultural Experiment Station, Columbia.

narrow tires were quite damaging. These tests are a forceful argument for broad tires on field and road.

The *grade resistance* is purely a function of the angle of the incline, or of the per cent of grade. A grade is usually expressed as a 5 per cent grade, a 10 per cent grade, etc., the figures meaning that the incline rises at the rate of 5 ft. or 10 ft. vertically for each 100 ft. of horizontal travel. The prob- lem is based upon the in- clined plane. By referring to

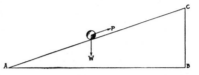

FIG. 413. Illustrating the principle that grade resistance depends upon the angle of the incline

Fig. 413 it may be seen that the grade resistance is the measure of the force P which is required to keep the load from rolling down the plane. If W is the weight of the load, then

$$P \times AC = W \times BC;$$

whence

$$P = W \times \frac{BC}{AC}.$$

In a general way the length of AC is virtually equal to AB, in which case the grade resistance is determined by multiplying the weight of the load by the vertical rise of the grade in each 100 ft. Thus, for a 2500-pound load the grade resistance on a 10 per cent grade is 250 lb.; that is, a force of 250 lb. more is required to draw the load up a 10 per cent grade than to draw it on a level road of the same kind.

CHAPTER XXVI

MISCELLANEOUS TOOLS AND MACHINES

This chapter includes a brief discussion of tools and machines of which some are of importance but, because of lack of space, can be only superficially discussed; others are of interest to but relatively few farmers; and still others, though used to some extent, are not absolutely essential to the average farm. Some machines in the last class, however, should be more commonly used.

ENSILAGE-CUTTERS

The number of silos in the United States has increased at an enormous rate in the last two decades, and as a result the ensilage-cutter has been developed and is now on the market in various forms and sizes.

The cutting-head. There are two types of cutting-heads in common use, the radial-knife cutter and the cylinder, or spiral-knife, cutter. The *radial-knife* cutter, shown in Fig. 414, has the cutting-blades and the blower fans mounted together, as shown in Fig. 415. There may be 2, 3, or 4 knives on the flywheel, the length of cut being con-

FIG. 414. A radial-knife cutter

trolled in part in this way. The *spiral* knife is shown in Fig. 417. The cutting-blades and the fan, or blower, are mounted separately.

There is a difference of opinion as to which is the better type. One company which manufactures both types recommends the radial-knife cutter when a small engine is to be used and the spiral-knife cutter when a steam engine or a large gasoline engine is used. The reason for this is that the radial-knife cutter requires slightly less power than the other type and will not so well stand

the heavy strain to which it is subjected when it is pushed to the limit by a high-power engine. It is probably more difficult in the radial-knife cutter than in the spiral-knife cutter to keep the nice adjustment between the knives and the cutting-bar, which is so desirable. The radial-knife cutter clears the blower well, since the cut feed drops directly upon the fans. In the spiral

FIG. 415. Knives and blower fans of a radial-knife cutter

type the feed must be drawn into the blower-case after it is cut off. The spiral-knife cutter seems to handle alfalfa and similar feeds better than the radial-knife cutter does.

Shredding-heads (Fig. 416) or combined cutting-and-shredding heads are provided for attachment to either type of cutter. The spiral-knife type lends itself to a greater variety of attachments for such purposes than does the radial-knife head.

The blower. Most ensilage-cutters are equipped with a blower for elevating the ensilage into the silo. Although it requires from four to five more horse power to operate the common sizes when equipped with the blower than when the web carrier is used, the former lends itself much better to the proper distribution of the

FIG. 416. A radial-knife head with shredder blades attached

ensilage in the silo. For small silos where a small engine only is available, the web carrier serves the purpose well.

It is essential that the fan and the fan-case should be constructed of the best material and be substantially made in every

416

way, to avoid danger from bursting; otherwise the high speed of the fan and the consequent great pressure created within the fan-case will be very likely to cause the fan-case to burst.

The feed-table and feed-rolls. The corn is carried to the feed-rolls by an endless web (Fig. 418), the speed of which can be

FIG. 417. A spiral knife with fan and belt pulley

varied by changing gears so as to cut the ensilage in different lengths. The length varies from $\frac{1}{4}$ in. to $1\frac{1}{2}$ in., $\frac{1}{2}$ in. being the most common cut. The feed-rolls (Fig. 419) must be positive in their action and must automatically adjust themselves to large and to small bunches.

The upper roll is so arranged that it may be raised at both ends at the same time or at one end at a time. The lever for throwing the feed-carrier out of gear and for reversing the motion should be convenient to the operator.

Speed. In the spiral-knife cutter the cutting-head is driven at from 550 to 650 R. P. M., and the fan at from 650 to 1000 R. P. M. The radial-knife head is driven at a speed of 650 to 1000 R. P. M.

Size, capacity, and power. The size of an ensilage-cutter is nearly always expressed by a

FIG. 418. Looking into the throat of a spiral-knife cutter

number which corresponds to the width of the feed-throat in inches; a No. 15 cutter, for example, has a throat 15 in. wide. The capacity is rated in tons of ensilage per hour and varies from a number of tons equal to about three fourths of the throat width in inches to a maximum capacity which is a number of tons

FIG. 419. Feed-rolls in a radial-knife cutter
The upper roll is free to move up or down

generally equal to the throat width in inches; that is, a No. 12 cutter has a throat 12 in. wide and has a capacity of from 9 to 12 tons per hour. If the cutter is operated by a gasoline engine, the horse power of the engine should equal the capacity in tons per hour. If a steam engine is used, the rated horse power should be equal to about 80 per cent of the capacity in tons; that is, the above cutter, No. 12, would require a gasoline engine of from 9 to 12 H. P. or a steam engine of from 8 to 10 H. P.

General construction. In selecting an ensilage-cutter a thoroughly substantial construction should be secured. The framework must be heavy and well braced; the table-support must be strong, for green corn is very heavy; there must be no projecting corners or pieces to interfere with the free

FIG. 420. A hand feed-cutter of the spiral-knife type

passage of the feed to the feed-rolls, and the entire machine must bear the marks of quality and good workmanship.

HUSKERS AND SHREDDERS

The corn husker and shredder is called upon to perform the combined task of husking the corn and shredding the fodder. The task is more severe than that imposed upon the grain-separator, since the fodder is, as a rule, heavy and frequently not in the best condition.

General construction. The general construction of the husker-shredder is shown in Fig. 421. Corn to be husked is delivered upon

the feed-table, from which it is carried, by means of the feed-carrier, to the snapping-rolls. Passing between these, the ears are snapped off and dropped upon the husking-rolls beneath.

FIG. 421. Sectional view of a husker-shredder

A, feed-table; *B*, feed-carrier; *C*, snapping-rolls; *D*, husking-rolls; *E*, adjusting-arms; *F*, conveyer; *G*, fan; *H*, shredder head; *I*, vibrating rack; *J*, blower

These rolls are placed at an angle with the horizontal and are provided with projecting pegs. As the ears pass down the plane the revolving rolls pick off the husks, which fall through upon the husk-carrier and are conveyed to the blower. The ears of corn fall from the husking-rolls to the elevator, by which they are carried to the wagon or to the crib. The fodder passes from the snapping-rolls into the shredder head and then to the blower. The cleaning-fan separates

FIG. 422. A shredding-cylinder

the husks and dirt from the shelled corn, which it delivers in bags.

The snapping-rolls. The snapping-rolls are of cast iron, and the upper one is free to move up and down to accommodate large or small bundles. The corrugated surface of the rolls takes firm hold of the fodder.

The shredding-cylinder. The shredding-cylinder (Fig. 422) is usually provided with sharp fingers that tear the fodder into shreds. It may be equipped with knives that cut rather than shred. It is claimed that the sharp, sliverlike pieces of the shredded stalks are more injurious to the mouths of the stock that eat the fodder than are the cut stalks. However, the general custom is to shred rather than to cut the feed.

The husking-rolls. The husking-rolls are arranged in pairs. The rolls of each pair revolve toward each other, and the pegs with which they are provided strip off the husks and pass the ears on to the conveyer. They are made of cast iron and are from 30 to 50 in. long. The size of the husker is determined by the number of husking-rolls, there being from 2 to 12 rolls.

Capacity and power. It is very difficult to state the capacity of a husker, since so much depends upon the kind of corn and its condition. Ordinarily one would expect to husk 100 bu. per day for each pair of rolls; that is, a 4-roll husker would husk

FIG. 423. Feed-table, feed-carrier, and snapping-rolls of a husker-shredder

200 bu. per day under average conditions. Where a gasoline engine is used to operate the cutter, about 4 H.P. is required for each pair of rolls. A shredder head requires from 2 to 4 H.P. more than a cutter head.

A small husker. The market offers a small 2-roll husker and shredder designed for the individual farmer. It is inexpensive and requires only a 5-horse-power engine to operate it. It performs the work in a thoroughly satisfactory manner and has a capacity of about 150 bu. per day.

420

FEED-GRINDERS

The individual farmer frequently finds it to his advantage to grind his own grain. Too often is it the custom to haul the feed

FIG. 424. A corn-grinder with disk grinding-plates

to town and pay from 3 to 5 cents per bushel for having it ground, when in the same time it could have been done at home and the cash outlay saved. The common use of small gasoline engines has made the home use of feed mills particularly desirable.

The grinding-plates. The grinding-plates, or burrs, may be divided into two classes, disk grinders and cone grinders. One type of *disk* power grinder is shown in Fig. 424. The burrs in this grinder are supported in a vertical plane and are mounted upon the main shaft of the mill. The middle burr, with a grinding-face on both sides, revolves with

the main shaft, while the two outer burrs are stationary. If ear corn is being ground, the ears are broken up by the upper cutter and the lower crusher and are reduced to a comparatively fine condition before reaching the burrs. The grain is forced into the burrs near the center and is reduced to the proper degree of fineness as it is forced to the edge.

FIG. 425. A corn-grinder with cone grinding-plates

The *cone* grinders are shown in Fig. 425. The movable cone is mounted upon the main shaft with the stationary cone supported in heavy framework around it. Each of the cones is made up of sections which are easily removed for repair. As in the former mill, ear corn is reduced to a fair degree of fineness before it reaches the grinding-plates.

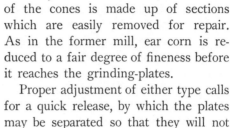

FIG. 426. A sweep mill

Proper adjustment of either type calls for a quick release, by which the plates may be separated so that they will not touch should the hopper become empty. The cone type is probably superior to the disk type in that the cones may be so regulated as not to touch, even when the mill is empty. This is true in a few disk mills also, but not in all. A spring release is usually provided, so that the burrs may spread should any obstruction, such as a nail, pass through.

FIG. 427. Gears of mill shown in Fig. 426

The grinding-plates are usually made of chilled iron. Steel plates are sometimes used, but grain sticks to them and they are not so lasting as good chilled plates. Either type of mill will handle ear corn with the husks on, or ear corn with oats, with barley, or with other small grain.

Capacity and power required. The size of a grinder is determined by the diameter of the burrs, and the capacity depends upon the kind of grain being

FIG. 428. Grinding-plates and gears of mill in Fig. 426

ground, the fineness to which it is ground, and the speed of the grinder. A fair rate seems to be about two or three bushels per hour for each horse power used in driving the machine. The former figure applies to small-sized grinders.

Sacking attachments. Small elevators with belt carriers to facilitate handling the ground grain may be provided at slight cost.

Sweep mills. Fig. 426 shows a sweep mill for use with horse power. Cone grinding-plates are used in this mill, one of them being geared up to a speed from six to twelve times that of the sweep. This mill will grind from four to six bushels per hour with a good team on the sweep. A power attachment is frequently used in connection with the sweep power.

Alfalfa-grinders. There are now on the market a number of mills especially designed for grinding alfalfa, though it is claimed that the mills above described will handle it alone or in connection with other grains.

POTATO MACHINERY

Where potatoes are grown on a large scale, special machinery is absolutely essential for the economical handling of the crop.

FIG. 429. A picker potato-planter

The chief special tools needed are the planter, the digger, and the sprayer.

The planter. There are two general types of potato-planters on the market, the difference in them being in the manner in which the potato pieces are selected and deposited in the ground. They might be designated as the one-man and the two-man planter.

Fig. 429 shows a sectional view of the one-man, or picker, planter. The seed is carried in the hopper, which is usually supplied with an agitator to work the seed down. The revolving shaft is equipped in this particular planter with three arms, on the ends of which are picker points. As these points pass up through the seed-hopper, they pick up pieces, one only to each point, and carry them over to the furrow-opener. At the proper time a stripper forces the pieces off the points and into the bottom of the furrow. This drop works with surprising accuracy.

FIG. 430. A two-man potato-planter

It is seldom that the points fail to pick a piece when traveling through the hopper.

The distance between pieces, or the rate of dropping, is regulated by changing the speed of the revolving arms, or, in some planters, by varying the number of arms. The common distances are 11, 13, and 15 in. At the 11-inch rate, from 12 to 14 bu. are required to seed 1 A.

Fig. 430 shows the two-man potato-planter. A large plate similar to a corn-planter plate, except, of course, that it is larger, revolves beneath the hopper. A portion of it projects beyond the hopper to the rear, as shown. As the plate revolves, each hole

selects a piece of seed, carries it to the shank, and drops it into
the furrow. In order to make sure that each cell will contain a
piece, it is necessary that a man or boy ride just to the rear of

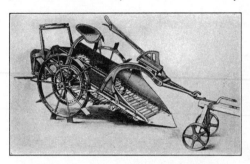

the planter. With this
planter there is abso-
lute certainty that the
pieces will be accu-
rately spaced, while in
the other type there
are certain to be miss-
ing hills.

The furrow-opener,
which is of the shoe
type, must be supported
substantially and must

FIG. 431. A standard elevator potato-digger

have a keen blade, since if the potatoes are properly planted, it
must run from four to five inches deep.

The covering-device, which is essential, may be made up of
disks, one on each side of the row, or it may be composed of
two stationary curved blades, as illustrated in connection with

corn-planters. When the disks
are used for covering, there is
a tendency to run the furrow-
opener too shallow and to depend upon the disks to cover
the seed properly. This results in placing the seed too
close to the surface of the
ground, and much of it becomes completely uncovered
by later working of the soil.
This is not, however, a fault
of the planter but an example of poor judgment in its
operation.

FIG. 432. Rear view of a potato-digger

All planters may be supplied with fertilizer-attachments by
means of which varying amounts of fertilizer may be supplied.
The fertilizer must be so distributed that it will not come in

contact with the seed. Then, too, better results will be secured if it is distributed over a wide space and not dropped in a narrow row.

FIG. 433. A digger with gasoline engine and picking-attachment

The digger is drawn by horses, the engine operating the elevator and picker

The potato-digger. The work of the potato-digger is complicated and difficult. The machine must lift the potatoes with a section of soil about six inches deep and twenty inches wide, in varying states of physical condition, and it must separate the potatoes from this soil and from whatever weeds and trash may be present. A machine capable of accomplishing such work requires the best of material and construction. There is but one standard type of digger, the type shown in Fig. 431.

The plow, or cutting-blade, must be long and keen. For the best work it should be not less than twenty inches wide, the size of the digger being determined by the width of the plow, or (what amounts to the same thing) of the elevator.

FIG. 434. A barrel sprayer

This type of sprayer is suitable for a small acreage and may be used for orchard work as well

The elevator. The rod elevator is the type used in nearly all diggers. The details are fairly well shown in Fig. 431. Each rod with its bent, hooked ends forms a link in the elevator. The upper fold of the elevator runs over two sets of elliptical sprockets

FIG. 435. A stalk-cutter

This tool is used where the cornstalks are left on the ground and plowed under

which (since they serve to jar the load) separate the earth from the potatoes and cause it to drop through the elevator to the ground. Weeds and trash are carried to the rear by means of vibrating arms and are directed to one side so that they will not be deposited upon the potatoes. The fork upon which the potatoes and earth drop as they leave the elevator is given a vibrating motion to assist further in freeing the potatoes of soil, vines, and trash.

General features. The wheels must be strongly built and be provided with strong wide cleats. Some diggers have been deficient in this respect. The elevator and shaker may be driven either

FIG. 436. A beet-seed planter

by gears or by sprockets and chains. The usual arguments may be offered for each method. Perhaps the gear drive affords the more stable construction, but breaks are costly. The fore truck should have quick-turning wheels ; that is, the wheels should turn more sharply than the tongue, this action being of assistance in keeping the digger centered over the row and in turning at the

FIG. 437. A beet-lifter

ends of the rows. All bearings should be easily oiled and as well protected from the dirt as possible.

Potato-sprayers. The most important single feature in a potato-sprayer is the pump. In common with all spray pumps, its cylinder should be of brass and it should be of the double-acting type. A large air-chamber should be provided to equalize the pressure, and it is very convenient to have a valve next to the pump for the purpose of retaining the pressure should it be necessary to stop in the field. The pump should be capable of maintaining a pressure of one hundred pounds. The drive for the pump should be substantial yet simple. It is desirable to have the plunger connection so made that the length of stroke may be changed to regulate the plunger travel to the gait of the team.

The nozzle supports should be adjustable as to both width and height. When the potatoes are small the nozzles should be carried close to the plants; and as the potatoes grow the nozzles must be raised accordingly. The width between the nozzles must of course be regulated according to the width of the rows. In some sprayers the nozzles are supported in front of the sprayer, just behind the horses. In the majority of cases, however, they are placed to the rear of the sprayer. The hose connecting the nozzles to the pump should be wrapped with wire to enable it to withstand the pressure. The barrel should be so located that too great weight will not be thrown on the tongue or shafts. An efficient agitator should be provided to keep the liquid well stirred up.

While many other miscellaneous machines might be discussed in this chapter, it is believed that those given consideration are representative of the ones in which the average farmer is most interested, and the limitations of a work of this kind preclude the mention of others.

CHAPTER XXVII

GASOLINE AND OIL ENGINES

It has long been recognized that human energy is one of the most expensive sources of farm power, and the history and development of modern farm equipment is the result of an effort to reduce man labor to a minimum. The introduction of the gasoline engine has made it possible to economize human labor to a surprising degree, for the tasks on a farm which an engine can be made to perform are numerous. It follows, then, that the widespread use of this important machine makes it imperative that farmers be instructed in the fundamental principles underlying its construction.

The general principle. Gas, gasoline, and oil engines belong to a class known as *internal-combustion* engines, so named because they derive their power from fuel burned inside of the cylinder. In contrast to this type is the steam engine, which might be called an external-combustion engine, because it derives its power from fuel burned outside of the cylinder. An engine operating on the internal-combustion principle has many decided advantages : (1) the energy of the fuel acts directly against the piston ; (2) the engine is ready to start as soon as power is required ; (3) loss of energy is much less than in the steam engine ; (4) the engine does not require constant attention ; (5) the engine can be purchased in small units, as low as one-half horse power. On the other hand, the internal-combustion engine has some evident disadvantages : (1) there is a tendency to unsteady speed because of the intermittent power stroke ; (2) there is no reserve power to meet sudden demands made upon the engine ; (3) high temperature in the cylinder makes lubrication difficult and makes necessary some cooling-device ; (4) a more or less troublesome ignition is required.

General construction. All internal-combustion engines are constructed in essentially the same manner, differing only in certain

429

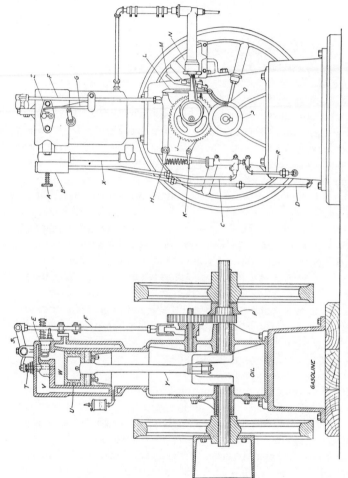

FIG. 438. Sectional and side views of a typical vertical engine

details. Fig. 438 shows a sectional and a side view of a typical vertical engine. The *base* of the engine supports the entire structure and varies in shape, size, and general outline with the style

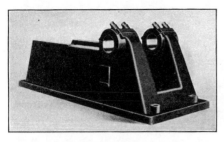

of engine. In Fig. 438 the base contains the fuel-tank, a common arrangement. Figs. 439, 440, 441, and 442 show different types of bases and sub-bases. In the bases for horizontal engines shown in the figures the bearings for the crankshaft are supported at an angle of 45°. This is a very desir-

FIG. 439. A standard type of engine base

Note the angle at which the bearings are placed, the better to take the thrust of the piston

able construction, since the thrust due to the explosions is taken with much less strain on the bearings.

The *crankshaft*-case in the vertical engine shown in Fig. 438 rests upon the base, or the subbase, as it is sometimes called, and contains the crankshaft and the crankshaft bearings; frequently, too, the reducing gears are contained within the case. In the sectional view the plate on the left side of the crank-case is removable, the crankshaft being inserted through this opening. The reducing gears are here shown attached to the side of the crank-case.

FIG. 440. A massive engine base

The *cylinder* is mounted upon the crank-case, being bolted to it, as shown in the side view. The inlet valve (not shown) and the exhaust valve *T* are in the head end of the cylinder. The igniter block *E* pierces the wall of the cylinder, which is cooled by the circulation of water through the jacket *V*.

The *piston* with its piston rings U is connected with the crankshaft by the connecting-rod Y. There are many different types of connecting-rods, some of the more common being shown in Fig. 443, *A*, *B*, *C*, and *D*. The *connecting-rod* is attached to the

FIG. 441. A horizontal-engine base with one of the bearings removed

piston by means of the piston pin shown in the sectional view (Fig. 438). The piston pin is held in place by the two set-screws shown. Several methods of clamping the connecting-rod to the piston pin are shown in Fig. 443, as are the different methods of fastening it to the crankshaft. It should be noted that both ends of the connecting-rod (Fig. 443, *C*) are clamped by the same bolt, which runs through the center of the rod. This makes it easy to adjust the bearings at each end, whereas in the other types it is necessary to remove the piston in order to tighten or loosen the bearing about the piston pin.

The *flywheels* vary a great deal in size and in weight. Their function is to steady the speed and through their momentum enable the engine to meet better the sudden demands made upon it for increased power. The detailed parts shown in

FIG. 442. A subbase for the base shown in Fig. 441

Fig. 438 will be discussed under the operation of the engine.

Fig 448 shows a two-cylinder *opposed* type of engine. The two-cylinder engine makes it possible to secure an impulse, or working stroke, at each revolution of the flywheels, and when the cylinders are opposed the engine is much better balanced.

Types of engines. There are two general classes into which gasoline engines are divided — the 4-stroke cycle engine and the 2-stroke cycle engine. These engines are commonly referred to as 4-cycle and 2-cycle engines respectively, but for the sake of clearness, as well as for accuracy of statement, the terms "4-stroke engine" and "2-stroke engine" will be used. *The four-stroke engine.* The 4-stroke engine is so named since it requires 4 distinct strokes

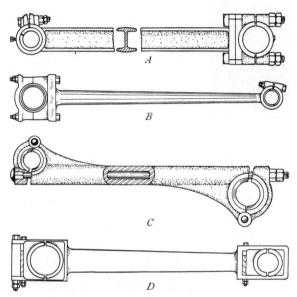

FIG. 443. Several types of connecting-rods

of the piston, or 2 revolutions of the flywheels, to complete a cycle of operation.

Fig. 449 shows a diagrammatic view of the 4 strokes in the cycle and indicates the functions of each. At *A* is shown the suction stroke, during which fuel is drawn into the cylinder, the inlet valve being open. At *B* is shown the compression stroke, during which the gases are compressed to the required degree, both valves being closed. At *C* is shown the expansion stroke, during which the gases, having been ignited, expand and thus exert their full force

FIG. 444. A drop-forged crankshaft

against the piston head. This is the only working stroke in the cycle. At *D* is shown the exhaust stroke, during which the exhaust valve is held open and the burned gases are driven out.

The 2-stroke engine must of necessity take the same steps as does the 4-stroke engine, because none can be omitted; but the

proper mechanism is supplied to make it possible to complete the 4 steps in 2 strokes of the piston.

The two-stroke engine. In the 4-stroke engine there is but 1 gas-tight compartment, the combustion-chamber in the head end of the cylinder. In the 2-stroke engine, shown diagrammatically in Fig. 450,

FIG. 445. A balanced crankshaft
The weights offset the weight of the crank and give a steadier motion

there is the regular combustion-chamber and in addition a secondary compression-chamber which, as shown, is usually the

inclosed crank-chamber, this chamber being connected to the fuel-tank and carburetor through the valve *V*.

Referring now to Fig. 450, the various steps may be explained as follows :

FIG. 446. A crankshaft as it is machined and finished in a lathe

At *A* the piston is shown moving upward, being driven by the momentum of the flywheel. There is a tendency to create a vacuum in the crank-chamber, so that a charge of fuel is drawn

in through valve *V*.

At *B* the piston is moving downward and compressing the charge in the crank-chamber.

At *C* the piston has reached the limit

FIG. 447. A machined crankshaft with chain oilers

of its downward travel and has uncovered the inlet port *I*. The gases in the crank-chamber, having been compressed to a pressure of about ten or twelve pounds per square inch, rush through the inlet port into the combustion-chamber.

At D the piston has moved upward and is compressing the charge in the combustion-chamber. At the same time a new charge is being drawn into the crank-chamber. Just before the piston reaches the end of this stroke the charge is ignited by the spark.

FIG. 448. A two-cylinder opposed air-cooled engine

At E the piston is being driven downward by the force of the expanding gases, and the charge in the crank-chamber is being compressed.

At F the piston has just uncovered the exhaust port X, and the exhaust gases are escaping. It should be noted that the inlet port is not yet uncovered.

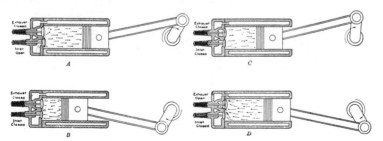

FIG. 449. The four strokes in the cycle of a four-stroke engine

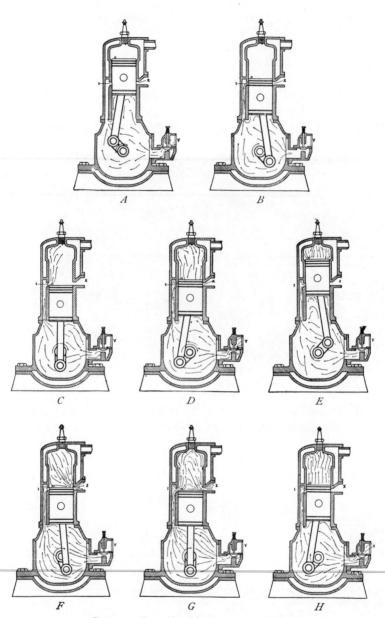

FIG. 450. Operation of a two-stroke engine

At *G* the piston has again reached the limit of its lower travel, and the exhaust gases are seen escaping through the exhaust port, while at the same time a new charge is entering through the inlet port. It should be noted that both inlet and exhaust are uncovered at the same time. The deflector on the face of the piston tends to direct the incoming charge upward so that it assists in expelling the burned charge.

At *H* the piston has moved upward and is compressing a new charge in the combustion-chamber and drawing a new charge from the fuel-tank through the inlet valve *V* into the crank-chamber.

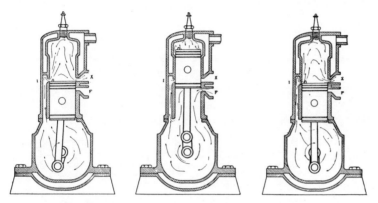

FIG. 451. Operation of a three-port two-stroke engine

The port at *F*, which is covered and uncovered by the piston, takes the place of the valve *V* shown in Fig. 450

Thus, it is seen that at each stroke of the piston *two functions* are performed, so that a cycle of operation is completed at each two strokes, or for each revolution of the flywheels.

A *comparison* of the two types of engine reveals the following essential differences : (1) Since the 4-stroke engine receives an impulse only on every fourth stroke, large flywheels are required to carry the load during the other 3 strokes, and so the engine is of necessity a heavy one. The 2-stroke engine, receiving an impulse every revolution, demands much smaller flywheels and frequently but 1 is used. For this reason the 2-stroke engine is especially desirable for motor boats and other places where space is at a premium and weight a consideration. (2) For reasons noted the 2-stroke engine is wasteful of fuel. The 4-stroke engine is more economical in this respect, using only about 75 per cent as much fuel as the 2-stroke engine, other conditions being similar. (3) The 2-stroke engine has no valves except the one shown at V in the figures, and in the 3-port engine (Fig. 451) even this is eliminated. The 4-stroke engine has 2 valves, which require reducing gears to operate them. (4) The 2-stroke engine maintains a more constant speed than the 4-stroke engine, and for this reason may be better adapted to certain kinds of work. (5) The 2-stroke engine will show the effect of improper fuel adjustment more quickly than the 4-stroke engine.

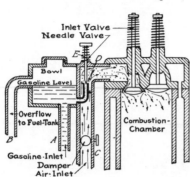

FIG. 452. A pump-feed carburetor

Since the 4-stroke engine is very much the more commonly used for farm work, the remainder of the chapter will deal entirely with this type of engine.

In the successful operation of an internal combustion engine at least four things are absolutely essential: (1) *a proper fuel mixture in the cylinder*; (2) *proper compression of the charge*; (3) *a good spark, properly timed*; (4) *proper valve action*. If each of these four things is accomplished, the engine will run. They will be taken up in their order, and the mechanism required for each step and the principle involved will be briefly discussed.

FIG. 453. A fuel-pump

Carburetors. To secure a good fuel mixture in the cylinder, some form of carburetor is essential. As the name implies, a carburetor is a device for impregnating air with carbon, a thing which is accomplished in this case by passing air over or near the hydrocarbon fuel as it is drawn into the cylinder of the engine. There are three types of carburetors of interest here, and they are classified according to the method used to supply the fuel, as (1) pump-feed carburetors, (2) gravity-feed carburetors, and (3) suction-feed carburetors. All three types belong to the general class of spray car-buretors, since the fuel is injected into the cylinder in the form of a spray.

A *pump-feed* carburetor is illustrated in Fig. 452. The gasoline is fed into the reservoir by a pump (Figs. 453 and 454) which takes the fuel from the base of the engine and forces it up through the feed pipe *A*, the excess returning to the fuel-tank through the overflow-pipe *B*. The pump is operated constantly by the reducing gear on the side of the engine. It may also be operated by hand. The gasoline in the reservoir is kept at a constant level, this level being about one eighth of an inch below the channel leading to the

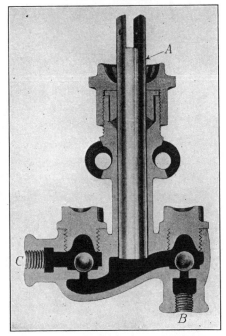

FIG. 454. Sectional view of a fuel-pump

This pump is used with the pump-feed carburetor. *A*, plunger; *B*, pipe from fuel-tank; *C*, pipe to carburetor

inlet valve, this height making it impossible, of course, for the fuel to be forced into the cylinder by the pump. On the suction stroke the inlet valve is opened and air is drawn into the air-inlet pipe *C*. This air rushes with considerable velocity past the mouth of the channel tube *D* and draws in a charge of gasoline, the amount depending upon the size of the opening at the point of the needle valve *E*.

440

In the air-inlet pipe there is usually an air-valve, or damper. This is closed while the engine is in process of starting, to insure a richer mixture being taken into the cylinder. On the

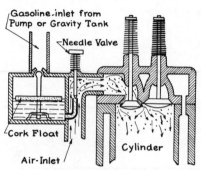

FIG. 455. A gravity-feed carburetor

first two or three explosions it is opened and left open. In the absence of the valve the fingers may be placed over the end of the pipe.

The milled head on the end of the needle valve is usually marked in some manner for a starting position and for a running position. More fuel is admitted while starting than is needed for continued opera-

tion. As the point of the needle becomes worn the markings will not be true, and the operator must use his judgment in setting it.

The *gravity-feed* carburetor is essentially the same in general construction as the pump-feed carburetor. Since the gasoline is fed to the reservoir by gravity, some device must be provided which will feed the fuel down as it is needed. Some form of float valve is used for this purpose, a general type being shown in Fig. 455. When the gasoline in the carburetor chamber has reached the proper level, the float rises and closes the inlet pipe. As fuel is drawn from the chamber into the cylinder the float is lowered and more gasoline is admitted through the inlet, a constant level thus being automatically maintained.

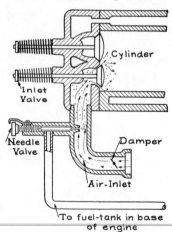

FIG. 456. A suction-feed carburetor

The *suction-feed* carburetor, a type of which is shown in Fig. 456, is essentially the same as the types above mentioned, except that the fuel is drawn from the fuel-tank by suction through the fuel-pipe. A ball check valve is placed in the fuel-pipe, so that the fuel is kept close to the channel tube. This type of carburetor is often called a mixer.

A comparison of these three types shows that the last is the simplest, there being no pump and no float valve. It is, however, very easy to flood the cylinder of an engine using this type of carburetor unless the needle valve is carefully adjusted. The gravity-feed carburetor is satisfactory. One objection may be urged against it, however — the objection that, since the supply tank is above the carburetor, the development of a leak may drain the tank, with dangerous results. There is perhaps less danger of flooding the cylinder of the engine with the pump-feed type, and it gives excellent satis-faction. Of course the gasoline pump may wear out and give trouble, but it is very simple, and little difficulty comes from this source.

FIG. 457. A piston and a piston pin

One piston ring is removed. Note the oil-grooves in the piston

To assist in starting the engine a priming cup is attached to the cylinder, for pouring fuel into the cylinder, so that a complete charge is assured. For small engines a teaspoonful is sufficient; too much is worse than not enough.

Compression. With a proper charge of fuel in the cylinder adequate compression is necessary before the gases can be ignited; it is necessary, at least, before they will explode with the highest efficiency. To secure this compression an air-tight chamber is essential. The piston is a solid piece of metal, working in the cylinder. Even though each is ground and polished to an exact sliding fit, the great changes in temperature inside the cylinder make it impossible to maintain this fit. Consequently the piston is made to slip rather loosely into the cylinder, and piston rings are supplied to make the fit gas-tight. A piston with piston rings is shown in Fig. 457. Grooves are cut in the piston — usually three or four in the smaller engines, more in the larger ones — near the head end, into which are fitted the piston rings. As shown, these rings are not solid, but are cut so that they spring out against the cylinder, making a gas-tight fit. In some engines the rings are fixed so that they cannot turn in the grooves, the joints being broken. In others they are left free to turn. This is some advantage, for while it is possible for all joints to work round to the same position and cause leakage, the rings will foul less if left free to move. They should fit freely in their grooves and should be easily turned about with the fingers.

The compression should be such that it is quite difficult to turn the engine over, when starting it, without releasing the compression in some way, and the piston should rebound with ease when it is forced up against the cushion of air in the chamber. If there is almost no compression, it is useless to attempt to start the engine until the fault is remedied. Poor compression may be due to any one of a number of causes: (1) The piston rings may be sticking. It frequently happens that the rings will stick until the engine warms up, when proper compression will be secured. If the compression is not enough to secure an explosion, a pint of kerosene may be poured into the cylinder and the engine turned over by hand several times. If this does not loosen the rings, it may be necessary to remove the piston. They will frequently be found so completely gummed with oil and carbon deposit as to make it necessary to use a chisel to loosen them. (2) The valves may leak. This may be due to the sticking of a valve stem because of lack of oil or because of a deposit of gummy oil about the stem. More frequently it is due to faulty seating of the valves, particularly of the exhaust valve. (A method of grinding the valves will be discussed in a later paragraph.) (3) The cylinder may be worn out of round or grooved. In horizontal engines there is a tendency to wear both piston and cylinder on the lower side, a tendency which will result in blowing. The position of the defective spot may be detected by holding the hand near the inner end of the cylinder while the engine is running. In unusual cases the cylinder wall may be grooved, as by a projecting piston pin. Remedy in either case can be had only by reboring the cylinder.

Ignition. After the charge has been properly compressed it is necessary to ignite the gas, so that through its expansive power it may drive the piston through the one working stroke of the cycle. Without question, about 90 per cent of all the troubles

with a gasoline engine come from a faulty ignition system. The
following discussion will be simple, yet sufficiently thorough, it

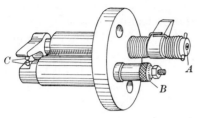

is hoped, to enable the reader
to understand the principles
of construction as well as the
operation of the two common
types of ignition systems —
the make-and-break and the
jump-spark.

FIG. 458. Igniter block for make-and-
break ignition

A, movable electrode; *B*, insulated electrode;
C, igniter points

The *make-and-break* system
of ignition is the simpler of
the two. Fig. 458 shows the
igniter block for this system.
This block fits into the combustion-chamber and contains the
movable electrode and the stationary, insulated electrode. The
insulation on the latter is usually composed
of thin mica washers wrapped around by
thin layers of the same material, which dis-
connects it electrically from the engine
bed. The igniter trip on the valve rod *F*
(Fig. 438) lifts the dog on the movable
electrode during the compression stroke
and brings the two points within the cylinder into contact. At the proper point in
the stroke the dog is released, and a spring
quickly separates the points. These contact points are made of a hard composition
metal to stand the wear and the high heat
caused by the passing of the spark. These
points must fit smoothly and snugly together. In time they become pitted and
rough, when they should be filed or
smoothed with emery cloth.

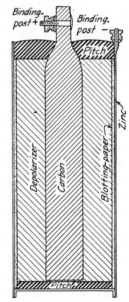

FIG. 459. Section of a
dry cell

A *dry cell* is shown in section in
Fig. 459. This is a common and fairly
satisfactory source of current for gas-engine
ignition. The zinc cup which forms the positive element of the
cell serves as the container for the other materials. A stick of

444

carbon occupies the center of the cup and forms the negative element. Around the carbon is packed a filler (usually granulated carbon containing a good carrier of oxygen), called the depolarizer. Manganese dioxide is sometimes used for this purpose. The filler is then saturated with some solution, usually sal ammoniac, which serves as the electrolyte. Both top and bottom of the cell are covered with a layer of pitch to protect the contents.

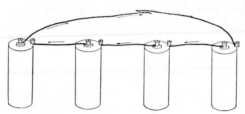

FIG. 460. Dry cells connected in series

As soon as the electrolyte comes in contact with the zinc, chemical action takes place, and the solution is broken up into two parts. The part containing the hydrogen is positively charged and carries its current to the carbon stick; the negative portion combines with the zinc and charges it negatively. If the two poles are now connected outside the cell, as by a wire, a current of electricity will pass from the positive, or carbon, pole to the negative, or zinc, pole.

Certain electrical units are used to measure the flow of this current. The amount of flow is measured in *amperes*, and the force causing the flow is measured in *volts*. The phenomenon is analogous to the flow of water. If a tank several feet in height is filled with water and this water is drawn off through a faucet at the bottom, the flow could be measured in gallons per minute, while the pressure causing the

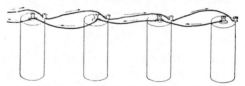

FIG. 461. Dry cells connected in parallel

flow could be measured in pounds per square inch. Amperes, then, correspond to the flow of water in gallons, and volts to the pressure in pounds.

A new cell should show an amperage of from 25 to 30 and a voltage of about $1\frac{1}{2}$. When the amperage falls to 8, the cell should be discarded. This simple description of the construction of a dry cell will serve to make clear some points in regard to its use and care. If the cells get wet, the electrolyte is weakened and chemical action ceases. If they are kept in a very warm, dry place, the electrolyte evaporates and the cell is ruined.

If the poles of the dry cell are connected continuously for an hour or so, action ceases and the cell is dead. It will revive to some extent on standing, but this type of cell is intended to be used only on open circuits; that is, those in which the external circuit is completed for but a short time and then broken, as in gas-engine ignition. It is essential, therefore, that the engine should not be stopped in a position that would complete the circuit. A dead cell may sometimes be revived sufficiently to give some service, by puncturing the zinc cup or the top layer of pitch and soaking it in salt water for a few hours. The service, at best, however, will be short.

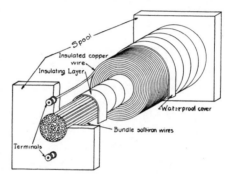

FIG. 462. Construction of a simple spark-coil

This type of coil is used in the make-and-break system of ignition

The cells, as shown in Fig. 460, are connected in *series*; that is, the wiring is taken from the positive pole of one cell to the negative pole of the next. When they are connected in this way, the voltage of the battery is equal to the combined voltage of the single cells, while the amperage of the battery is equal to the amperage of a single cell only. If the cells were connected in *parallel*, that is, with like poles connected, as in Fig. 461, the amperage of the battery would be equal to the combined amperage of the single cells, while the voltage of the battery would be equal to the voltage of a single cell. Since it is high voltage that is required in gas-engine ignition, the cells are always connected in series.

The *simple spark-coil* is included in the circuit to increase further the voltage of the battery. Its construction is shown in Fig. 462. Some insulating-material is first wrapped around a core of soft-iron wires; around this is then wrapped a great many turns of fine insulated copper wire. The action of the coil depends upon the principle that when the circuit is broken there is a tendency for the current to keep on flowing, with the result that an arc is drawn between the separating points, giving a decidedly hot spark.

The *operation* of the make-and-break system is as follows: The wiring, as shown in Fig. 463, is taken from the insulated electrode to the switch; thence through the spark-coil and the battery to the engine bed. The wire leading to the engine bed is frequently called the ground wire. If, when the switch is closed, the points of the igniter block within the cylinder are brought together, the circuit is completed and the current begins to flow. Now, if the points are quickly separated, a long spark is drawn across the gap, the sparking taking place only at the breaking of the circuit. There should be one big blue spark. If a shower of smaller, red sparks appears, either the battery is weak, the contact is imperfect, or the wiring connections are loose. The more rapidly the break is made between the igniter points the hotter will be the spark.

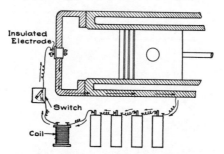

Fig. 463. Diagram of the wiring for a make-and-break system of ignition

It is evident that this system, from the electrical point of view, is very simple. There are only two wires to contend with, and no one need err in connecting these to their proper places. The chief difficulty lies in the fact that there is a moving part piercing the wall of the combustion-chamber. It is also necessary to keep the insulated electrode from electrical contact with the engine — a thing that is not easily done. The insulating-material will frequently become covered with carbon, in which case it is necessary to remove the plug and carefully clean it; it should never be removed unless absolutely necessary. Under all conditions of operation for low-speed engines, however, this system is very satisfactory. It will undoubtedly stand more abuse than the jump-spark system and will give a hotter spark under adverse conditions.

There are a few modified forms of the make-and-break system, one, shown in Fig. 464, is called the *wipe-spark* system, because the electrode points inside the cylinder have a wiping action, one passing across the other. The advantage of this is that the points by their wiping action keep themselves clean. A cam device outside the cylinder revolves the movable electrode. The hammer make-and-break differs from the simple make-and-break in that the movable electrode is struck by a trip hammer just as the spark is wanted; the points, therefore, are separated more quickly than in the simpler type, and the result is a hotter spark.

The *jump-spark* system of ignition is radically different from the make-and-break system. The spark-plug shown in section in Fig. 465 has no moving parts. The plug screws into the combustion-chamber of the engine. The pin

FIG. 464. A wipe-spark device used in the make-and-break system of ignition

running through the center of the plug, with the screw for attaching this battery wire on its outer end, is the insulated electrode. The other pin inside the combustion-chamber is a part of the outer shell of the plug and hence in electrical contact with the engine bed. The ends of the two pins are separated about one thirty-second of an inch.

The battery is made up of the usual dry cells and an *induction coil*. The construction of this coil is shown in Fig. 466. It will be seen that it contains a primary coil similar to the simple coil used in the make-and-break system of ignition, although the core is smaller and made up of finer wires. Around this coil is wrapped some insulating-material, around which are several hundred turns of insulated copper wire finer than that used in the primary coil. This outside coil is the secondary coil, the ends of which terminate in the secondary poles. The induction coil, then, as shown, has two primary and two secondary poles. On the end of the coil-box is the vibrator, or buzzer, the short steel spring of which is shown fastened at one end. On the free end is a disk of steel held directly above the core of the primary coil and a short distance from it.

FIG. 465. Section of a jump-spark plug

A, insulated electrode; B, insulating-material

In wiring this system of ignition the primary wiring must be taken, as shown in Fig. 467, through the battery, the primary poles of the induction coil, the circuit-breaker, and the switch. A wire is then taken from the spark-plug to one of the secondary poles, the other pole being connected to the engine bed or grounded.

The *operation*, then, is as follows : the switch is closed and the engine turned over until the timer completes the primary circuit. The vibrator should then begin to buzz. This buzzing is due to the fact that as soon as the primary circuit is closed the current begins to flow through the primary wires, the core is magnetized, and the steel disk is drawn down to the core. This action breaks the primary circuit. As soon as the current

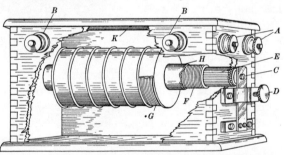

FIG. 466. Sectional view of an induction coil

This type of coil is used in the jump-spark system of ignition. A, primary poles; B, secondary poles; C, buzzer; D, adjusting-screw; E, core of iron wires; F, primary winding; G, secondary winding; H, insulating-material; K, condenser

ceases to flow, the core loses its magnetism, the steel spring draws the steel disk away from it, the primary circuit is again completed, the current begins to flow, the core is magnetized, and the same action is repeated again and again at a very rapid rate.

There is a screw for adjusting the tension of the spring holding the steel disk, by which the frequency of vibration of the spring may be varied. This should be adjusted until the buzzer gives forth a snappy sound. The screw may be turned in so far as to hold the disk down on the core constantly, or it may permit the disk to move so far away that the core when magnetized cannot draw it down. In either case the buzzer will not work.

Sparking at the vibrator points will frequently be noticed. Hence coils are usually supplied with a *condenser*, which, figuratively speaking, serves as a sort of reservoir into which the excess current may flow, and thus decreases the tendency of the current to jump the gap made

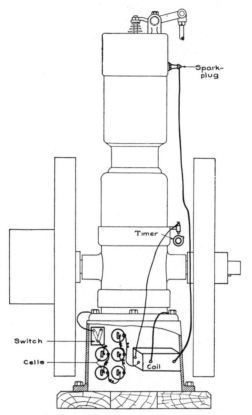

FIG. 467. Diagram of the wiring for a jump-spark system of ignition

by the separation of the vibrator points. This condenser is made up of a number of sheets of tin foil insulated from each other, alternate sheets being connected to one another and the two poles connected to the primary circuit through the parts of the vibrator. The condenser never completely eliminates sparking, however. It is shown in the top of the coil (Fig. 466, *K*).

The current flowing through the primary coil induces a current in the secondary coil. Through this process of induction the voltage is greatly multiplied, the amount being directly proportional to the number of turns in the two windings; and the force of the current is great enough to cause it to jump the gap between the points of the spark-plug, giving a complete circuit from one secondary pole through the plug into the engine bed and back to the other pole. A series of sparks is secured between the points of the plug, one spark in reality appearing for each interruption in the flow of the current through the primary wires. This is due directly to the vibrator.

In the wiring scheme shown there are 4 wires — 2 primaries and 2 secondaries. In many coils there are only 3 poles, one of the secondary poles being omitted. If this is the case there is an inside connection between one of the primary poles and the other end of the secondary winding. Even in coils having the 2 secondary poles this inside connection is often made. Were this true of the coil shown in Fig. 467, the grounded secondary wire could be removed entirely, in which case the secondary circuit would be completed through one of the primary wires.

The jump-spark system may seem to be rather complex electrically, but it is not difficult to keep in order if the parts are understood. There are no moving points in the cylinder, an advantage over the make-and-break; and for high-speed engines, that is, for engines running more than five hundred revolutions per minute, it is more satisfactory. The plugs are cheap and are easily replaced if broken. Another valuable feature is that in testing the spark, the plug may be taken out and laid on the engine; then when the circuit is made one may be absolutely sure that the spark passes. If the plug becomes short-circuited because of a deposit of carbon, as frequently happens, it should be removed, taken apart, and carefully cleaned.

The term " *low-tension* ignition " is often applied to the make-and-break system, since a relatively low voltage is necessary to make a spark. The jump-spark system is often styled *high-tension* ignition, since a relatively high voltage is required.

Sources of current. Thus far the dry cell has been the only source of current mentioned, and in it the electrical energy is the result of chemical action between the elements of the cell. There are several other possible sources of current in which the energy is supplied through mechanical means.

The *magneto* is a form of generator now commonly used. Only the simpler features of the generation of electrical energy through mechanical means will be discussed. It is commonly known that if a loop of wire is rotated between the poles of a permanent magnet, a current of electricity will flow through the wire. An instrument for measuring the intensity and the direction of the current would show that the direction is once reversed during each revolution and twice registers zero. For example, in Fig. 468, *a*, the loop is in a vertical position, and since

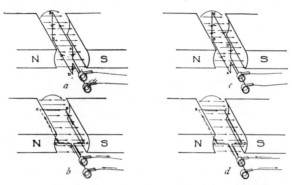

FIG. 468. Diagrams illustrating the principle of a magneto

it is cutting no lines of force, no current will result. In Fig. 468, *b*, the loop has been turned 90° to the right and in this position is cutting the greatest number of lines of force; hence the full intensity of the current is reached and the direction of flow is from *B* to *A*. In Fig. 468, *c*, the loop has passed through 180° and the current is again zero. In Fig. 468, *d*, the loop has passed through 270°, and the full intensity of the current is again reached, while the flow is from *A* to *B*. The current, then, is zero in Fig. 468, *a*, and Fig. 468, *c*, and at its height in Fig. 468, *b*, and Fig. 468, *d*. It flows in one direction while *AB* is moving downward and in the opposite direction while *AB* is moving upward.

If the current generated by this revolving loop is taken by appropriate rings and brushes through an external circuit, as shown, the direction and intensity will vary in this circuit just as they do in the revolving loop. Such a generator is known as an *alternating-current* generator, and the current as an alternating current.

452

If, instead of one loop, a great many loops were wound about a metal core and this core then rotated between the poles of a U-shaped magnet, a simple magneto would result. Fig. 469 shows the outline of such a generator. As the armature revolves,

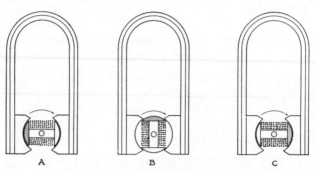

FIG. 469. Diagrammatic section of a magneto
A, no current; *B*, greatest current; *C*, no current

the current varies in intensity and alternates its direction just as in the single loop. If the armature is revolved to the right, the current will flow in one direction, increasing from zero in Fig. 469, *A*, to the full intensity in Fig. 469, *B*, and dropping to zero again in

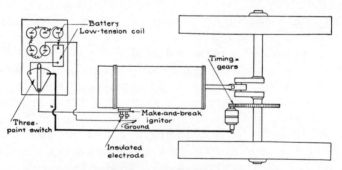

FIG. 470. Diagram of the wiring of a make-and-break system of ignition using dry cells and magneto

Fig. 469, *C*, having passed through 180°. During the second half of the revolution the current will reverse its direction, reaching its full intensity when the shaded head is down and dropping to zero when the original position (Fig. 469, *A*) is reached.

If the external circuit from such a magneto is carried to the spark-plug of an engine, it is evident that the armature must be so driven that the current will be at its height when the spark is needed. The armature therefore must be positively driven and properly timed. It is usually driven through a reducing gear, the armature making one revolution for each two revolutions of the flywheels. Fig. 470 shows such a connection. It would be possible to drive the armature only one fourth as fast as the flywheels, but this is seldom done.

In the type just described, and known as a *rotating* magneto, the armature is revolved continuously. It is necessary to revolve the armature through an angle of approximately 30° only, if, after being given the proper initial position, it is allowed to return at a high speed to its original position. In this case a spark of the highest intensity will be generated, and if the movement is effected at the proper time it will be just as satisfactory as a complete rotation. In Fig. 472 is shown a magneto attached to the igniter block of a make-and-break system of ignition. The armature core is attached directly to the movable electrode. The action of the armature when so connected is shown

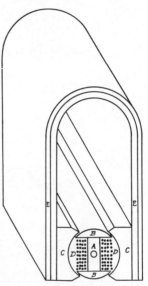

FIG. 471. Parts of a magneto

A and *B*, armature core; *C*, pole shoes; *D*, armature winding; *E*, magnets

in Fig. 474. Just as the igniter points are brought together the armature is turned to the position shown in Fig. 474, *B*. When the points are permitted to separate, the armature springs bring the armature back to its original position, shown in Fig. 474, *A*, generating an intensely hot spark just as the points separate. Such a type is called an *oscillating* magneto.

Magnetos may be driven by means of a friction pulley on the flywheel of the engine. When so driven they cannot, of course, be positively timed to deliver the most intense spark when needed.

FIG. 472. Oscillating magneto attached to a make-and-break igniter block

FIG. 473. Oscillating magneto partially dissembled
Note the laminated core and the stationary winding

454

Because of this friction drive, generators require a spark-coil in the circuit. The speed of the armature is usually about two thousand revolutions per minute, a governor being supplied to draw the friction pulley away from the flywheel if the speed gets too high. A governor is shown in Fig. 475. If the armature is run at too high a speed, the generator will heat and the insulation of the winding is likely to be burned out.

So far, only *low-tension* generators have been referred to, that is, generators which produce a low-voltage current. If such a generator were used with a jump-spark system of ignition, it

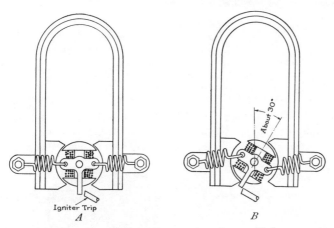

FIG. 474. Diagram to illustrate the operation of an oscillating magneto
A, normal position; *B*, position when spark is required

would be necessary to take the current through an induction coil. It is possible to have two windings, a primary and a secondary, about the armature of the generator, just as there is a primary and a secondary winding in an induction coil. With the condenser, the circuit-breaker, and the timer included in the framework of the generator, a compact and very desirable system of ignition is provided which usually requires no batteries and no extra coils. Such a type is known as a *high-tension* generator.

A magneto should ordinarily give but little trouble. If it fails to ignite the charge, one should look to every other possible source of trouble, such as dirty electrode points, a short circuit in

456

the plug, poor terminal connections, etc., before tampering with the magneto. Never under any circumstances should one attempt to

adjust the magneto unless it is thoroughly understood or unless the company's directions are carefully followed. The armature should never be removed. If it is, demagnetization follows, necessitating the return of the magneto to the makers for repairs. If batteries are used for any purpose, the circuit must not be carried through the magneto or the magneto will be "killed."

FIG. 475. Friction-drive magneto with governor

The governor weights fly out and draw the drive wheel away from the flywheel of the engine

In the care of the magneto one should follow the maker's directions minutely. Oil should be used frequently but sparingly, and the brushes should be kept clean. The armature must not

be allowed to get out of time, and if the oscillating types are used, the armature must be moved through the proper arc. With proper care a magneto should last for years.

Another common form of generator is the *dynamo*. It is made in almost the same way as the magneto except that the armature is rotated between the poles of an

FIG. 476. A low-tension magneto with coil attached

electromagnet rather than between those of a permanent magnet.

The question will naturally arise as to which form of generator is best. A set of dry cells which cost about 25 cents apiece will last from one to six months. If the battery becomes short-circuited, it will run down in an hour or so, but under intermittent use and with proper care it will last for several months. The low-tension magneto, costing from $8 to $15, forms an excellent source of current, and if an engine is used rather steadily, as on a hay-baler, it will undoubtedly pay to invest in one. The high-tension types are more costly, but they do away with the necessity of a separate coil. As a rule the low-tension generators give the less trouble.

FIG. 477. A gear-driven low-tension alternating-current magneto partly dissembled

The *timing* of the spark relates to the proper point in the compression stroke when the spark should occur. In the jump-spark system a special device, previously referred to as the timer, is provided. As explained before, this is found in connection with the primary circuit from the battery, and completes the current each second revolution of the fly-wheels. By altering the position of the timer the spark may be made to pass at different points in the compression stroke.

In the make-and-break system of ignition the timing of the spark is accomplished

FIG. 478. A low-tension direct-current magneto partly dissembled

by varying the time at which the igniter points are permitted to separate. This is usually done by altering the position of the igniter trip or the parts supporting it. A general rule is to have

458

the spark pass when the crank is in advance of center about 6° for each one hundred revolutions of the engine. Another method is to advance the spark until a distinct pound is heard, and then retard it until pounding no longer occurs. The chief trouble with this method is that it requires some skill to detect the point at which

FIG. 479. Parts of a magneto armature

pounding begins. The timer should always be so arranged that the spark may be retarded, or set so late as not to occur until the piston has passed center. This will prevent the engine from kicking back when being started.

Improper timing is certain to result in loss of power. If the spark is too early, the engine will pound; the full force of the explosion meets the incoming piston and a distinct knocking is heard. This not only results in a decrease in power but puts the bearings to an undue strain. If the spark is too late, the full efficiency will not be realized from the fuel, and the engine will heat quickly. This is due to the fact that the gas mixture is not ignited at its highest compression and that when it is ignited it burns and generates heat throughout the stroke, imparting it to

the cylinder walls. A very rich or a very lean mixture will demand a different timing from a normal mixture, since either will burn more slowly than the normal mixture and hence will require an earlier spark. An effort should

FIG. 480. A complete magneto armature

be made, however, to secure a proper mixture instead of adjusting the spark to correspond to a poor mixture.

Preignition refers to the ignition of the charge before the spark occurs. It may be caused by an overheated cylinder, as a result of which the gases are ignited before the proper compression is reached. A small projecting point of metal in the clearance space of the cylinder will frequently become sufficiently hot to cause preignition. One may detect this occurrence by the pounding which usually results.

The valves. In the average farm engine the *inlet valve* is opened by suction. That is to say, when the piston starts on the suction stroke, there is a tendency to create a vacuum within the cylinder, and atmospheric pressure outside the cylinder forces the inlet open. It may be and often is, particularly in the case of high-speed engines, opened by mechanical means. The heavier spring on the exhaust valve prevents any possibility of its being opened on the suction stroke.

The *exhaust valve* is always opened by mechanical means. One device for accomplishing this is shown in Fig. 438. Since it is possible to open the exhaust valve but once for each two revolutions of the flywheels, a reducing gear is necessary, which is shown as the large gear in Fig. 438, *J*. This revolves once every time the flywheels go around twice. On the shaft of this reducing gear is a cam which at the proper time raises the valve rod, and this, through the rocker arm, opens the exhaust. The detent lever which may lock this valve rod up will be discussed under the subject of governors.

There is frequently some device for locking the inlet valve shut while the exhaust valve is open. This may be a positive lock, or it may be some device which increases the compression on the inlet-valve spring while the exhaust is open. In the absence of this device the inlet valve is often opened slightly during the exhaust of the burned gases, they rushing out with such force as momentarily to create a vacuum behind. In such a case fuel would be drawn in only to be exhausted again before being used.

The *timing* of the valves is important. The exhaust valve should open just before the end of the expansion stroke. At this time the expanding gases are under a pressure of from forty to fifty pounds per square inch, and at the opening of the exhaust they rush out, the cylinder being quickly freed of burned gases. The possibility of the piston's being returned against pressure is also prevented. For farm engines the *exhaust **should** open when the crank is in advance of center about 5° for each one*

460

hundred revolutions per minute. The cam which controls the movement of the valve rod is then of such length as to cause the valve to close just about at the end of the exhaust stroke. Some manufacturers give the very simple method of setting the exhaust to close at the end of the exhaust stroke. When so set the length of the cam is usually such as to cause the valve to open at the proper time for the rated speed of the engine. In some engines where the inlet valve is opened mechanically, it is said to be better to open the inlet valve while the exhaust is still open, the argument being that the new charge will start toward the exhaust-valve opening, following the burned gases which are escaping, and thus serving as a sort of scavenger. To reap this benefit to the fullest extent the inlet valve and the exhaust valve should be separated as far as possible (Fig. 481). Such construction, however, is not common in farm engines.

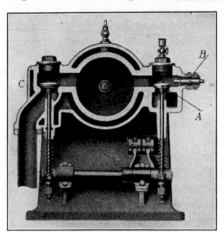

FIG. 481. The valves are located on opposite sides of the cylinder

A, inlet valve; *B*, spark-plug; *C*, exhaust valve

The exhaust valve frequently gives trouble because of the fact that it is exposed to extremely high heat. The valve stem may become warped so that it sticks in its cage; in this case it may seat too slowly or not at all. Some foreign deposit may collect on this valve or on the valve seat, so that leakage results. It sometimes becomes necessary, therefore, to grind the valve to improve its seating, an operation which usually requires the removal of the cylinder head. A slot is generally provided in the valve so that it may be turned about on its seat by means of a screwdriver. A little emery dust, now conveniently furnished in the form of paste, is used while the valve is evenly and regularly turned back and forth on its seat.

The indicator diagram. The best way to understand just what happens within the combustion-chamber during each cycle is to refer to an indicator diagram such as is shown in Fig. 482. Such a diagram is secured by connecting a steam-engine indicator to the combustion-chamber of the engine. The device consists of a small cylinder and a piston behind which is a spring. Since the piston of the indicator is in close connection with the combustion-chamber, the force of the explosion is exerted against the piston, which is raised against the pressure of the spring. Attached to this piston through an arm, or finger, is a pencil point which records on a moving paper the pressure within the cylinder at each and every point of the stroke. On the vertical line is represented in pounds per square inch the pressure inside the cylinder. The horizontal line represents the length of the stroke in inches. The line XY represents atmospheric pressure and is shown at fifteen pounds.

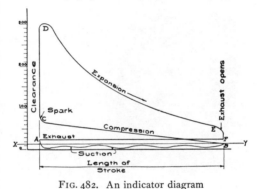

FIG. 482. An indicator diagram

The diagram shows the pressure inside the combustion-chamber at every point in each stroke

Starting now at A, the piston moves out on its suction stroke AB. In the common farm engine the inlet valve is opened by suction, and as the piston moves outward, a part of a charge rushes in. Suction being thus relieved for an instant, the pressure rises nearly to that of the atmosphere, only to be reduced as the piston moves a little further. The suction stroke, then, is represented by a wavy line. At the end of the suction stroke the piston starts back on the compression stroke represented by the line BC. The pressure gradually rises to about 70 lb., a pressure at which the spark is ordinarily produced (point C). This point is reached slightly before the piston has reached the end of its stroke. As soon as the spark passes, the pressure immediately jumps from about 75 to 300 lb. per square inch, and is represented by the line *CD*. The expanding gases then drive the piston on the outward, or expansion, stroke, the pressure gradually falling, as shown by the line *DE*. At *E*, when the gases are still under from 40 to 50 lb. pressure, the exhaust valve is opened, and the pressure drops almost to the line *XY*, as shown at *F*, the end of the stroke. The line *FA* represents the exhaust stroke when the pressure is probably slightly above the atmospheric line.

FIG. 483. Mechanism of a hit-or-miss governor

The flywheel is removed to show the collar which is operated by the movement of the governor weights. Reference to Fig. 438 will help to make this clear

Governors. There are two systems of governors in common use for automatically controlling the speed of engines: (1) the hit-or-miss governor; and (2) the throttling governor.

The *hit-or-miss* governor permits the engine to take a full charge or none at all. Thus the speed is controlled by preventing the engine from taking a charge until a full one is needed. The mechanism for accomplishing this varies, but the principle is always the same. One method is shown in Fig. 483. When the speed of the engine becomes sufficiently high, the weights on the flywheel shaft are thrown outward, and the sleeve on the shaft is drawn out until its flange catches the roller on the short arm of the detent lever, forcing this lever in until it locks the valve rod up. When this rod is up, the exhaust valve is open and no charge can be taken in. As soon as the speed drops, the governor weights will be drawn in by the springs, the sleeve will drop back, the exhaust valve will close, and a new charge will be drawn in on the next suction stroke.

A change in the speed of a hit-or-miss-governed engine is secured in different ways. If the springs connecting the governor weights are tightened, a higher speed will be required to throw them outward. Or, as in the case with many engines, if the short arm of the detent is carried farther from the flange on the sleeve mentioned, the speed will need to be higher in order to throw the detent in. The latter arrangement permits of a change in speed while the engine is running, a feature somewhat desirable.

The *throttling* governor permits the engine to take a full charge or any part of a charge. If the speed drops a little and a slight impulse is needed to bring it back to normal, a small portion of a full charge is admitted. The charge may be controlled as to quantity or as to quality. In the first of these cases the proportion of fuel and air remains the same, the amount of the mixture which is taken in being varied. In the second case the quality of the mixture is varied by controlling the air or the fuel. The former method is more commonly used. In Fig. 484 the wing valve *D* regulates the amount of the mixture that is taken in.

FIG. 484. Sectional view of a hopper-cooled engine with kerosene carburetor

A comparison of the two systems reveals the following differences: (1) The hit-or-miss governor will prove the more economical in fuel, since similar charges are taken in and exploded under similar conditions, whereas the throttling governor, by varying the quantity or the quality of the mixture, alters the conditions under which the charge is exploded. The throttling governor may throttle the charge so much that it does not explode at all. (2) The throttling governor maintains a more steady speed, since the slightest charge is met by a change in fuel conditions, whereas the hit-or-miss governor will not permit the engine to take a charge until the speed has dropped low enough to demand a full charge. (3) The hit-or-miss governor throws a greater strain on the moving parts and on the bearings, because of the greater variation in speed. (4) The hit-or-miss-governed engine is usually supplied with heavier flywheels, a feature which adds considerably to the weight of the engine. When a steady speed is not essential, the hit-or-miss governor is generally to be preferred. For the operation of electric generators, for example, where the lights are run directly from the generator, the throttling-governed engine will prove the more satisfactory.

Cooling systems. There is a vast amount of heat generated within the cylinder of the engine, the temperature at the time of the explosion rising to approximately 2000° F., the melting point of cast iron. A relatively small amount of this total heat energy is converted into useful work — probably, as an average,

FIG. 485. A vertical air-cooled engine
The large tank is used to equalize the pressure when gas is used as fuel

from 15 to 20 per cent; the remainder is carried off through the exhaust and through the cylinder walls. If the walls were not cooled in some way, they would soon become so hot that lubrication would be impossible, the piston would stick, and the engine be ruined. There are two general methods used in cooling gas-engine cylinders: (1) cooling with air and (2) cooling with water or oil.

Air cooling is confined to small-sized engines that are worked intermittently. Fig. 485 shows the usual form. A fan is generally provided to assist in the circulation of air. For an engine used for pumping water or for other outdoor work where it must be exposed to freezing weather, this system has its greatest advantage; it is scarcely efficient, however, for engines larger than five horse power.

FIG. 486. A two-cylinder opposed water-cooled engine
Note the space filled by the water in the sectioned cylinder

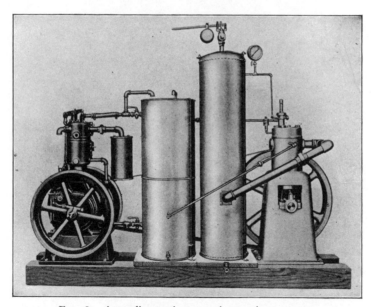

FIG. 487. A gasoline engine operating an air-compressor
The tank next to the engine contains the water for the gravity cooling system. The
air-compressor is used to charge the large air-tank

Water-cooled engines are far more common than any other type. As is seen in Fig. 486, the walls of the cylinder are hollow, and through this space water is circulated by different means. In some engines, as that shown in Fig. 487, the water circulates by gravity. This system is effective, but usually requires a large amount of water, a requirement which is a disadvantage if the tank must be drained in cold weather.

Fig. 488 shows a water cooling system in which the water is circulated by a pump. This system uses a small amount of water,

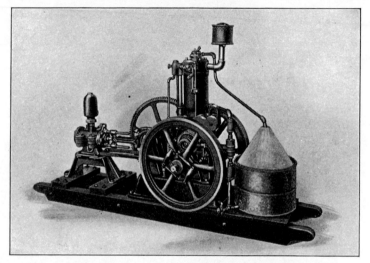

FIG. 488. A vertical water-cooled engine

The water is circulated by a plunger pump. The screen above the tank is for cooling the water; with such a cooler only a small amount of water is required

and in order that this may be kept cool it is distributed over the screen. This is one of the most satisfactory systems now in use. Of course the pump may get out of order, but there is little trouble from this source.

A hopper-cooled engine is shown in Fig. 489. This type has the advantage of requiring a small amount of water and of needing no circulating-device whatever. The water, however, soon becomes very hot, and while there is no great danger to the cylinder if water is always present, it is possible for the cylinder to become too hot under continued use. It will often be noticed that lubrication is difficult in the hopper-cooled engine — a sign that the cylinder is not effectively cooled. Oil instead of water is sometimes used for cooling the cylinder, its use being largely confined to very cold climates, where it is necessary to eliminate the danger of freezing.

The temperature of the cooling water should be about 180° F. It is not advisable to keep it lower than this even when possible, since an engine runs better when the working parts are warm. Whatever system is used, it should always be possible to drain the jacket separately from the tank, if there is a tank. Often a temperature that would be low enough to burst the cylinder if the jacket were left full of water would only freeze the water in the tank slightly.

FIG. 489. A horizontal hopper-cooled engine

Antifreezing mixtures may be used with considerable success when the engine is exposed to freezing weather. A solution of wood alcohol in water makes one of the best mixtures, particularly for a hopper-cooled engine or where the amount of water used is small. The alcohol evaporates rapidly when the water is hot, however, making the mixture rather expensive. The following proportions are recommended for the stated temperatures : a 10 per cent solution for 25° F., a 20 per cent solution for 15° F., a 30 per cent solution for 0° F., a 35 per cent solution for − 10° F.

Commercial calcium chloride dissolved in the water at the rate of $3\frac{1}{2}$ or 4 lb. to the gallon will prevent water from freezing until the temperature drops to − 20° F.; for ordinary temperatures $2\frac{1}{2}$ lb. per gallon of water is sufficient. This material, however, has a tendency to corrode iron and, in time, to form a scale on the jacket walls. This condition is not serious, but it is not desirable.

A 30 per cent solution of glycerin and water will not freeze until the temperature drops to about 10° F., but the solution is rather expensive and is, therefore, not practicable for use in farm engines.

Lubrication. The proper lubrication of a gasoline engine should be carefully attended to at all times. The piston is of course the most difficult part to keep well oiled. The oil used should be good cylinder oil, since this has a high flash point; that is, it will not burn or char at the ordinary temperatures which these parts are likely to reach. Common machine oil should never be used in the cylinder; it burns at too low a temperature and it contains impurities which foul the cylinder and piston parts.

FIG. 490. A horizontal engine with the igniter block in the head end of the cylinder

Note the 2 oil-cups — one for lubricating the piston, the other for the connecting-rod at the crank end

In vertical engines the *splash* system of lubrication is quite generally used. The crank-case contains only enough oil to allow the ends of the bolts or other projecting parts on the connecting-rod just to dip into the oil. The rapid motion of the crank churns the oil into a fine spray. From this source the piston (in part at least), the wrist pin, the crank, and the main bearings are wholly or partly lubricated. The piston is usually provided with a sight-feed oil-cup to lubricate the upper part, including the piston rings. The shaft bearings usually have hard oilers to take care of the outer portions of the bearings. Other minor bearings are oiled by the common hand can.

In horizontal engines the piston is lubricated entirely by a sight-feed cup. There is usually a hole through the upper part of the piston leading to the wrist pin. The crank pin is lubricated by different methods, all of which require more or less constant attention. It will be seen that the vertical engine possesses a distinct advantage in respect to lubrication, as all of the more important parts are reasonably assured of lubrication unless the operator is unnecessarily careless.

Vertical and horizontal engines. The question is certain to arise as to whether one ought to purchase a vertical or a horizontal engine. There are several things to be considered. The vertical engine has the following advantages and disadvantages, as compared with the horizontal engine: (1) it occupies less space on the floor; (2) it is more easily lubricated, since the splash system may be used; (3) the piston wears evenly all around; (6) it is difficult to hold the engine on a foundation unless it is securely fastened. The horizontal engine has the following characteristics in comparison with the vertical engine: (1) all parts are easily accessible; (2) it occupies more floor space; (3) the piston wears out of round; (4) the engine is not so easily lubricated. When everything is considered, the vertical type seems to be most in favor for the smaller engines.

The power of engines. A gasoline or oil engine derives its power from the combustion of fuel inside the cylinder. According to a previous statement only from 15 to 25 per cent of the energy so derived is converted into useful work. The power within the cylinder, then, is quite different from the power delivered at the belt wheel, and this fact gives rise to different kinds of horse power.

Indicated horse power, or cylinder horse power, of engines is the power actually developed within the combustion-chamber of the engine. Although it is not expected that students using this book will have occasion to determine the indicated horse power of engines, the formula for obtaining it is as follows:

$$\text{Indicated horse power} = \frac{PLAN}{33000};$$

in which

$P =$ mean effective pressure on piston in pounds per square inch,

$L =$ length of stroke, in feet,

$A =$ area of piston, in square inches,

$N =$ number of explosions per minute.

The *brake horse power* of an engine is the power which the engine will deliver at the belt. It is obtained by the use of the *Prony brake*, the formula being

$$\text{Brake horse power} = \frac{2\pi \times L \times N \times P}{33000};$$

in which
$L =$ length of brake arm, in feet (Fig. 491),
$N =$ revolutions per minute,
$P =$ net weight on scales.

A common type of Prony brake is shown in Fig. 491. The brake is placed on the belt pulley or on the flywheel of the engine, with the arm resting upon the platform scale as shown. A brake test may be made as follows: After placing the brake in position, as shown, with the nuts perfectly loose, the engine is turned slowly and at uniform speed, first in one direction and then in the other; the weights are recorded, and the mean weight,

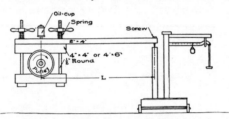

FIG. 491. A common type of Prony brake

which represents the weight of the brake, is secured. After the engine has been started, the wing nuts are tightened, thus increasing the friction and hence the load on the engine. As the load is increased the scalebeam is kept constant, and the wing nuts manipulated in such a way as to keep the scalebeam balanced. While the load is being thus kept constant, the revolutions of the engine per minute are determined. All the data will then be at hand for the solution of the equation for brake horse power (B. H. P.). The solution would be as follows, assuming the following data:

$L = 4$ ft.,
$N = 500$,
$W = 10 =$ weight of brake,
$P' = 30 =$ gross weight on scales, in pounds,
$P = 30 - 10 = 20$.

Then B. H. P. $= \dfrac{2 \times 3.1416 \times 4 \times 500 \times 20}{33000} = 7.6$.

If the brake is to run for a considerable length of time, it is necessary to provide some method for cooling the belt pulley. The oil-cup is provided to prevent sticking and to keep down the temperature, but this is not sufficient for long tests. If the pulley is provided with rims or if wood rims are temporarily attached, a little water may be kept in the pulley and the temperature kept down so that the brake will not stick.

The *approximate horse power* of an engine may be determined if the diameter and stroke of the piston are known. This can only be approximate, however, since fuel conditions vary greatly.

$$\text{Approximate horse power} = \frac{D^2 \times L \times N}{16600};$$

in which
$$D = \text{diameter of piston, in inches,}$$
$$L = \text{length of stroke, in inches,}$$
$$N = \text{revolutions per minute.}$$

If an engine, for example, has a 6 × 8 piston (that is, a piston 6 in. in diameter with an 8-inch stroke) and runs at the rate of 500 revolutions per minute, the formula will apply as follows :

$$\text{Approximate horse power} = \frac{6^2 \times 8 \times 500}{16600} = 8.67.$$

This formula applies to 4-stroke single-cylinder engines only. Since a 2-stroke engine will deliver from one and one-third to one and one-half times as much power as a 4-stroke engine having the same bore and stroke, the following formula may be applied to such engines :

$$\text{Approximate horse power} = \frac{D^2 \times L \times N}{11500}.$$

Applying this formula to a 6 × 8 engine, as used above,

$$\text{Approximate horse power} = \frac{6^2 \times 8 \times 500}{11500} = 11.52.$$

The *rated horse power* of an engine is the size of the engine in terms of horse power as fixed by the manufacturer. It corresponds closely with the brake horse power. Some manufacturers, however, rate their engines low so that they will always deliver the power claimed even when working under adverse conditions, and so that they will show up well in comparative tests. Others rate their engines so high that they will scarcely pull the full load under the most favorable conditions. With reasonable conditions obtaining, however, nearly all engines will develop their full rated horse power.

Engine troubles. When one is examining an engine that is giving trouble, some definite plan or system should be followed. It is useless to crank an engine until one is worn out in a vain effort to get it started; if every part is in working condition, it should start with but little cranking. Carrying out the order of discussion in this chapter, the following plan for the examination of such an engine is recommended:

FIG. 492. An engine connected by gears to a pumping-jack

(1) *The fuel supply should be examined.* There must be good fuel in the tank. Of course it is useless to try to start an engine without fuel in the tank, but this is frequently done. Water may have become mixed with the fuel. By pouring a few drops into the hand and noting the rate of evaporation, one may detect the presence of water. The gasoline should be strained through a chamois skin to remove water. One should make certain, too, that the gasoline pipes leading to the carburetor are not obstructed and that the fuel is supplied in proper quantity. If a pump-feed carburetor is used, the action of the pump is frequently faulty and fuel is not supplied regularly. A speck of dirt in the needle-valve tube will prevent the fuel from entering the cylinder.

(2) *The compression should be tested.* Refer to the discussion on this subject for reasons and remedies for poor compression.

(3) *The ignition system should next be thoroughly tested.* If a make-and-break system with dry cells is used, the wire attached to the insulated plug may be taken off; then, with the switch closed, if the wire is snapped across some clean metal part of the engine bed, a good spark should be obtained. If no spark is obtained the cells are too weak or the connection poor. After battery and connections are tested, the free wire should be snapped across the insulated electrode, care being taken that the igniter points inside the cylinder are not touch-

ing. If a spark is obtained, it proves that the insulation is broken; if no spark results, this electrode is properly insulated. This having been tried, the igniter points should be brought together by raising the dog on the movable electrode. If a spark results, the points are in proper contact; if no spark is obtained, the points do not touch or the contact is imperfect. The igniter block should then be removed and the points made to form a perfect contact. If rough, they

FIG. 493. An air-cooled engine attached to a grain-binder

This is one of the economical uses to which an engine may be put

should be carefully smoothed with emery paper or a fine file.

If a jump-spark system of ignition is used with dry cells as a source of current, the cells and primary circuit should first be tested. After closing the switch, the vibrator on the coil should operate when the circuit is completed by the timer. The vibrator should respond with a snappy sound. If the response is slow and weak the vibrator screw should be adjusted. If there is no improvement, while the trouble may come from a faulty coil, it will usually be found that the cells are weak or the connections poor, and the proper remedy should be applied.

After the primary circuit is found to be properly adjusted, the spark plug should be removed and, with the wire connected, laid on the engine bed. The engine should then be turned over until the timer makes contact. If no sparks appear at the electrode points, the gap may be too wide, the points may be touching, or the plug may be short-circuited. The remedy is to clean the plug thoroughly with gasoline and adjust the points. For remedying imperfect working of the magneto, the reader is referred to the discussion under that subject. After a spark of proper intensity is secured it should be correctly timed according to directions previously given.

(4) *The valves should next be properly timed* according to directions previously given.

(5) *The engine should be generally gone over* to see that all bolts and nuts are tight, that all bearings are properly adjusted, that oil-cups and grease-cups are filled, and that the cooling system is in proper order.

Miscellaneous engine troubles. If an engine is in more or less constant operation but does not seem to be working perfectly, there are certain indications of troubles which a trained eye or ear will discover and remedy without a careful and systematic survey of the whole engine. The following are some of the more common troubles.

Back-firing is usually caused by too lean a mixture. The charge is too weak to explode, but burns slowly; the following charge enters and, coming in contact with this slow-burning mixture, explodes while the inlet is open. A leaking inlet valve may cause back-firing.

An *explosion in the exhaust* is due to the ignition of an accumulation of unburned fuel in the exhaust pipe. This fuel accumulates when so rich a mixture is used that some of it is not burned and is driven out with the exhaust. Moreover, if the engine fails to fire a charge, it will be exhausted before being exploded.

Black smoke at the exhaust is caused by too rich a mixture. Blue smoke at the exhaust is caused by too much lubricating-oil.

Knocking, or pounding, may be due to too early a spark, to loose connections at crank pin or piston pin, or to a broken piston ring.

FIG. 494. Plowing is one of the chief uses to which the farm tractor has thus far been put

FIG. 495. A tractor to be thoroughly practical must be adapted to different kinds of work

Preignition may be caused by an overheated cylinder or by a small projection (as a metal part or a deposit) on the cylinder wall becoming heated to redness.

Overheating is caused by overloading the engine, by failure of the cooling system, or by a late spark.

Misfiring — that is, an occasional miss — may be due to a faulty spark, to a faulty mixture, or to faulty valve action.

Lack of power may be due to a faulty mixture, uncertain ignition, poor lubrication, faulty valve action, an overheated engine, or poor compression.

Farm tractors. The farm-tractor situation is just now in such an unsettled state of affairs that but little space will be given it in this book. At this time, when so many new designs, of such widely different types as to size, weight, and general constructive features, are being put before the farmer, it is almost hopeless to attempt to offer intelligent advice to a prospective purchaser.

Prevailing opinion seems to favor the high-speed, multicylinder, light-weight tractor, weighing from $2\frac{1}{2}$ to 3 tons as representing the type that will appeal most strongly to the small farmer, that is, the farmer tilling from 150 to 400 A. of land. As yet the tractor has not been used extensively for any other field operations than plowing and, in a limited way, the preparing of plowed land for the seed. Attempts have been made to design tractors to be used in cultivating corn, but they have as yet to demonstrate their usefulness.

There are two points of view from which the purchase of a tractor may be considered. It may be expected to replace a certain number of horses on the farm or it may be purchased simply to provide extra power in the busy season — to take care of the peak load. It will seldom be found possible to dispense with any number of horses on the average farm because the full horse power must be available during the seasons of cultivation, of haying, and of harvesting, since few of these operations are now performed with the tractor; it is quite possible that tractors will be used in an increasing way for such operations. That the tractor will find a place in our moderm system of agriculture there is no doubt. It simply remains to be seen what type will be found to be best suited to the average farmer.

CHAPTER XXVIII

ROPE AND ITS USES

Rope is used in so many different ways about the farm that a wider knowledge of various knots, hitches, and splices is very desirable. But few farmers know how to splice a rope, and yet scarcely a haying-season passes but that such knowledge would mean a saving in dollars and cents. The skill necessary to perform the task is easily and quickly acquired if a few simple

FIG. 496. A forest of manila plants

directions are carefully followed, and, once acquired, the process is not readily forgotten. Similarly, an awkward knot, poorly tied, is frequently the cause of much delay and vexation, whereas the proper knot for the place would give perfect satisfaction. It is hoped that this chapter will serve to increase the common knowledge of rope and its uses among both students and farmers.

Material. The greater part of the rope in common use is made from either manila fiber or sisal fiber. *Manila* fiber is a

477

product of the Philippine Islands, being produced from the manila plant (a plant known to the natives as abacá), which in general appearance resembles the banana tree. The work of separating the pulp and skin of the trunk of the plant from the fiber is done entirely by hand. *Sisal* fiber is produced in Yucatan from a plant known as henequen. It is cultivated on a large scale, an acre producing an average of one thousand pounds of fiber annually.

FIG. 497. Cutting manila plants in the Philippine Islands

The manila fiber of the better grades is finer and softer and more pliable than sisal fiber. Sisal fiber, however, is the more uniform in size, length, and quality, and though it makes a somewhat harsher yarn, is now quite

FIG. 498. Cutting leaves from sisal plants in Yucatan

generally used in the manufacture of binder twine, perhaps
90 per cent of our binder twine being made from this fiber. It
is less expensive than manila fiber — another item in its favor.
Manila, however, is much the better fiber for the larger ropes.

FIG. 499. Drying sisal fiber

Making the rope. In the manufacture of rope the fibers are
first twisted into yarns. A number of yarns are then twisted in
the opposite direction, forming a strand. Three or 4 strands —
the number depending on whether a 3-strand or a 4-strand rope is
desired — are then
twisted in the oppo-
site direction to the
twist of the strand
forming the rope.
It is the opposite
twist in each suc-
cessive step that
keeps the rope in its
proper form. The
fact that a new rope
sometimes twists, or
kinks, is due to the

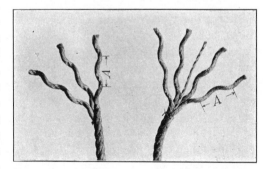

FIG. 500. A three-strand rope (on the left) and a four-
strand rope with a cord in the center

A represents one turn

480

fact that the twists in the elements of the rope do not balance each other. Such kinks may usually be removed by hitching a horse to one end of the rope and letting him drag it over a pasture field.

Three-strand ropes are much more common than four-strand ones. The latter are used in some large sizes and may be made with a straight cord in the center, as shown in Fig. 500.

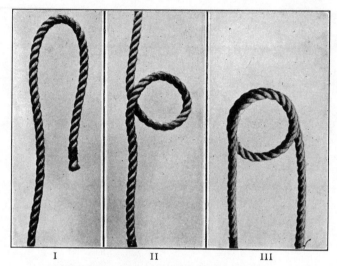

I   II   III

FIG. 501. Terms used in describing knots

I, open bight, or loop; II, bight; III, round turn

Strength of rope. The strength of a rope depends upon several things, but chiefly upon the kind and quality of fiber used. The load which a rope will carry may be specified as the breaking load or as the safe load; the former represents the load which, when steadily applied, will just break the rope; the latter represents the load which the rope will safely carry without danger of breaking. Naturally there is a great variation between the breaking load and the safe load, but the ratio between the two is generally taken as 6 or 7 to 1 ; that is, the safe load is one sixth or one seventh of the breaking load. The factor of safety is the figure which expresses this ratio, which, in the above cases, is 6 or 7.

An approximate rule for determining the breaking strength of a rope as given by Hunt & Miller is as follows: Multiply the square of the diameter in inches by 7200. The results of this rule will vary somewhat from the figures given in Table XXXII, but there is a reasonably close agreement. This table, in addition, gives other information concerning manila rope.

TABLE XXXII. INFORMATION CONCERNING MANILA ROPE

Diameter in inches	Circumference in inches	Weight of 100 ft., in pounds	Number feet per pound	Breaking load in pounds	Safe load in pounds
$\frac{3}{16}$	$\frac{9}{16}$	2	50	230	35
$\frac{1}{4}$	$\frac{3}{4}$	3	$33\frac{1}{3}$	400	55
$\frac{5}{16}$	1	4	25	630	90
$\frac{3}{8}$	$1\frac{1}{8}$	5	20	900	130
$\frac{7}{16}$	$1\frac{1}{4}$	6	16	1,240	175
$\frac{1}{2}$	$1\frac{1}{2}$	$7\frac{2}{3}$	13	1,620	230
$\frac{5}{8}$	2	$13\frac{1}{3}$	7	2,880	410
$\frac{3}{4}$	$2\frac{1}{4}$	$16\frac{1}{3}$	6	3,640	520
$\frac{7}{8}$	$2\frac{3}{4}$	$23\frac{2}{3}$	$4\frac{1}{4}$	5,440	775
1	3	$28\frac{1}{3}$	$3\frac{1}{2}$	6,480	925
$1\frac{1}{8}$	$3\frac{1}{2}$	38	$2\frac{1}{2}$	8,820	1260
$1\frac{1}{4}$	$3\frac{3}{8}$	45	2	10,120	1445
$1\frac{3}{8}$	$4\frac{1}{4}$	58	$1\frac{2}{3}$	13,000	1855
$1\frac{1}{2}$	$4\frac{1}{2}$	65	$1\frac{1}{2}$	14,600	2085
$1\frac{3}{4}$	$5\frac{1}{4}$	97	1	21,500	3070
2	6	113	$\frac{5}{6}$	25,200	3600
3	9	262	$\frac{1}{3}$	56,700	8100

Terms used. As indicated above, when fibers are twisted together, they form a strand. Three or more strands twisted together form a rope. A three-strand rope is sometimes called a hawser. Three hawsers twisted together form a cable. The process of twisting the strands into a rope is called laying the strands. To untwist the strands is to unlay them. One complete passage of a strand around a rope is called a turn (Fig. 500, A). In tying knots a formation such as that shown in Fig. 501, I, is called an open bight, or loop; one such as that in Fig. 501, II, a bight; and one such as that in Fig. 501, III, a round turn.

KNOTS

The following knots are the more common ones, and some of the uses to which each is best adapted are mentioned. In general they are used to form (1) knots in the end of a rope, (2) loops in the end of a rope, (3) loops between the ends of a rope.

I   II

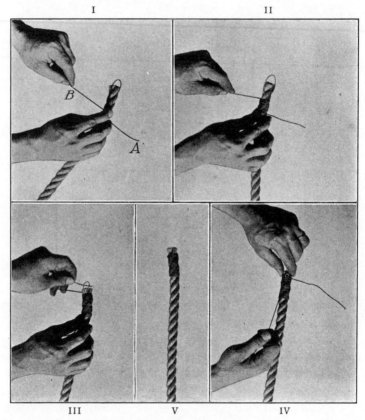

III   V   IV

FIG. 502. Whipping the end of a rope

Whipping. While the process of whipping the end of a rope is not strictly a knot, it is used to prevent the end of a rope from untwisting and takes the place of a knot when the end must not be enlarged, as for passing through the eye of a pulley or other small opening. Form a loop with a strong cord as shown in Fig. 502, I, leaving the short end *A* some 2 or 3 in. long. Wrap the long end *B* toward the end of the rope (Fig. 502, II),

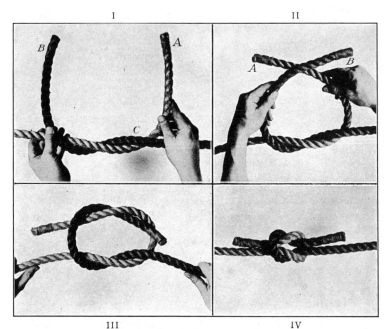

FIG. 503. The square knot

allowing the loop to fall into the groove between 2 strands. When within about ½ in. of the end of the rope pass the long end through the loop (Fig. 502, III), and draw up on the short

FIG. 504. The granny knot

end (Fig. 502, IV) until the loop is drawn well beneath the whipping. The ends should then be trimmed close to the rope, when
the finished job will appear as shown in Fig. 502, V.

Square knot. The square knot is probably used more than any other knot for tying two ends of rope or twine together. It is small and holds well, but draws very tight, and hence is

FIG. 505. The surgeon's knot

hard to untie. It is a good knot to use in tying binder twine.

The knot may be tied by following Fig. 503, I, II, III, and IV. Notice that in the first step end *A* is back of the rope at *C*;

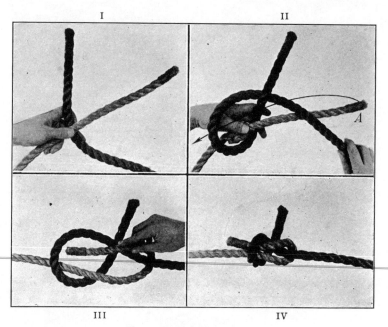

FIG. 506. The weaver's knot

hence in the second step it is placed back of end *B*. In the finished knot note that two perfect loops are secured.

Granny knot. The granny knot is no knot at all and is shown to illustrate how not to make the square knot. Many people do not know the difference between the two, but a comparison of Fig. 504 with Fig. 503, III, and IV, will show that there is a difference.

I   II

FIG. 507. The figure-eight knot

The first step in the granny knot is the same as shown in Fig. 503, I, for the square knot. In the second step end *A* (Fig. 504) is placed in front of end *B*, thus forming the finished knot. This is frequently tied for the square knot, but it will not hold.

Surgeon's knot. This knot (Fig. 505) is tied in much the same manner as the square knot, the only difference being that in the first step the ends are wrapped twice instead of once. The second wrap seems to make the knot more secure.

Weaver's knot. The weaver's knot is generally used by weavers in tying yarn. It is considered by many to be a better knot for

tying binder twine than the square knot. It holds securely and is more easily untied than the square knot. By comparing Figs. 503 and 506 it will be seen that it is very easy to convert the

FIG. 508. The overhand knot

square knot into a weaver's knot. The weaver's knot is tied, however, by a different process. Cross the ends as shown in Fig. 506, I. With the right-hand rope throw a loop around its own end, keeping above the left-hand rope as shown in Fig. 506, II. Pass end *A* back through the loop as indicated by the arrow in Fig. 506, II, and as shown in Fig. 506, III. Draw up the long ends, finishing the knot (Fig. 506, IV). With a little practice this knot is quickly and easily tied.

FIG. 509. The binder knot

Figure-eight knot. The figure-eight knot is used at the end of a rope to keep it from untwisting, to prevent its passing through an opening, or to form a handhold. Form the knot as shown in Fig. 507, I. Draw up for the finished knot (Fig. 507, II).

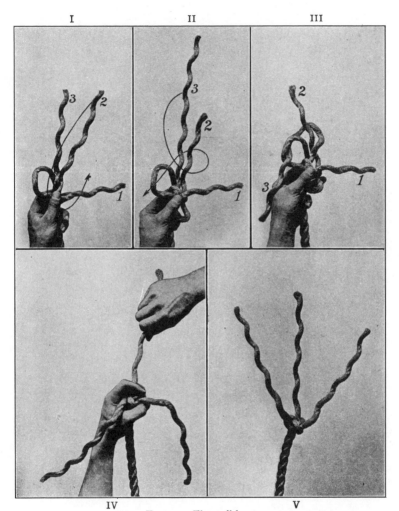

I   II   III

IV   V

FIG. 510. The wall knot

487

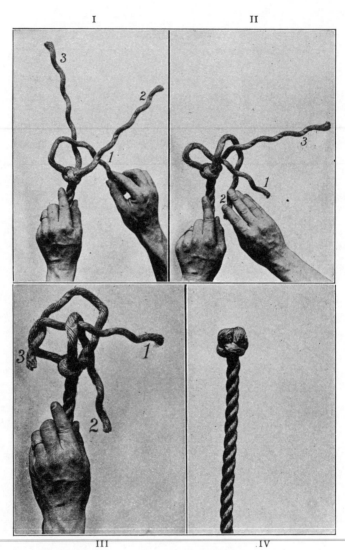

I II III IV

FIG. 511. The wall knot and crown

Overhand knot. This knot is used for much the same purposes as the figure-eight knot. It does not make quite so large a knot. Fig. 508 illustrates the method of tying.

Binder knot. This is the knot tied by grain-binders. It is made by placing two ends of rope together and tying an overhand knot. It is shown in Fig. 509.

Wall knot and crown. The wall knot and crown is used to form a small knot on the end of a rope, as for a handhold, or to

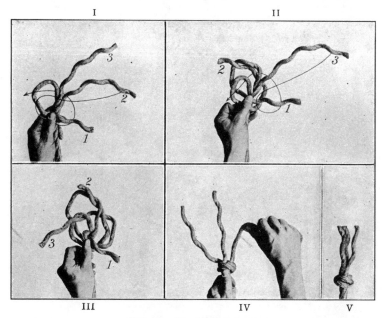

FIG. 512. The Walker knot

keep a rope from untwisting. It is frequently used on the end of a halter rope. It is tied as follows: Unlay the strands four or five turns. Form a bight with strand No. 1 as shown in Fig. 510, 1. Pass the end of No. 2 around the end of No. 1 as indicated by the arrow in Fig. 510, 1, and as completed in Fig. 510, 11. Pass No. 3 to the front of and around No. 2 and through the bight in No. 1 from the rear as indicated by the arrow in Fig. 510, 11, and as completed in Fig. 510, 111. Draw the ends up carefully as shown in Fig. 510, 1v. The wall knot completed is shown in Fig. 510, v.

To begin the crown throw a loop with No. 1 as shown in Fig. 511, I. Pass No. 2 between the loop and No. 3 as shown in Fig. 511, II. Pass No. 3 down through the loop in No. 1 as shown in Fig. 511, III. Draw the ends up evenly and tightly. In Fig. 511, IV, is shown the finished knot. The ends should not be trimmed too closely.

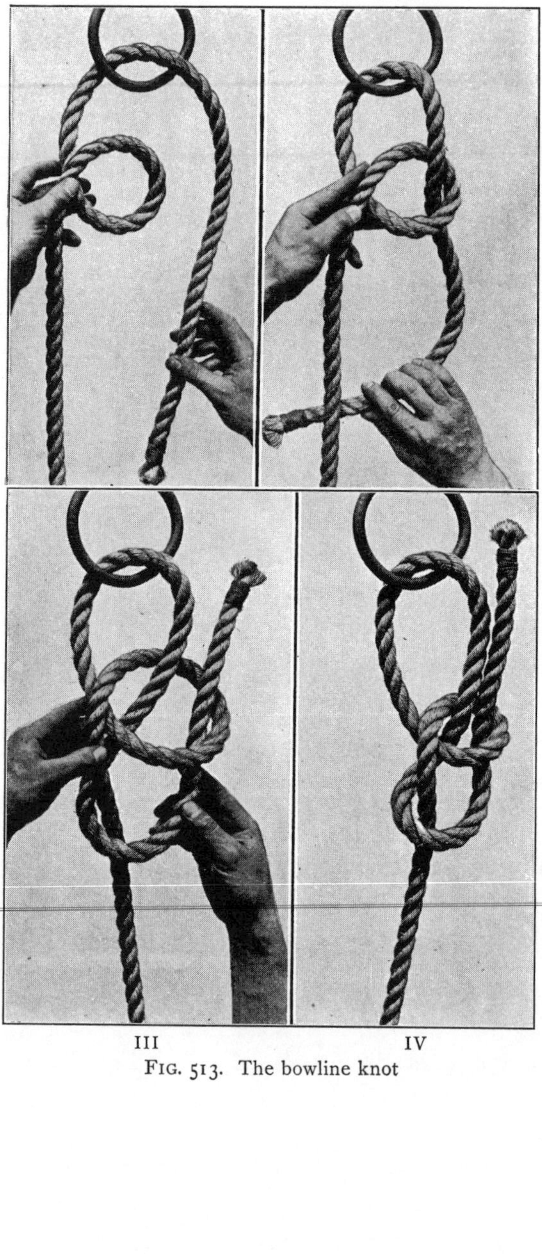

Walker knot. The Walker knot is used for much the same purposes as the wall knot. To tie it, unlay the ends about four turns. Form a bight with No. 1 as shown in Fig. 512, I. Form a bight with No. 2 on top of No. 1, passing the end below No. 1 and through the bight in No. 1 from the rear as indicated by the arrow in Fig. 512, I, and as completed in Fig. 512, II. Bring No. 3 forward, forming a bight around the end of No. 1, and pass the end

I II III IV

FIG. 513. The bowline knot

through the bights in Nos. 1 and 2 from the rear, taking care to pass it beneath the end of No. 1 as shown by the arrow in Fig. 512, II, and as completed in Fig. 512, III. Draw the ends up gradually, as shown in Fig. 512, IV, until the knot is tight. Roll the knot toward the end of the rope with the thumb as shown in Fig. 512, IV. This process gives the finished knot Fig. 512, V, except that the ends should be trimmed.

Bowline knot. The bowline knot is frequently called the king of knots. It is used wherever a loop is needed that will neither

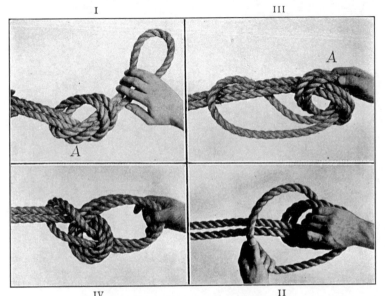

FIG. 514. Bowline in a bight

slip nor draw tight, as, for example, in tying a hay rope to a doubletree clevis. It is tied in several different ways, but the simplest is here given. Form an overhand bight in the long end of the rope as shown in Fig. 513, I. Pass the short end down through this bight, beneath and around the long end, then up through the loop as shown in Figs. 513, II, and 513, III. Tighten the knot by drawing on the long end of the rope Fig. 513, IV. The loop formed by the short end may be drawn up tight or left rather long, as desired.

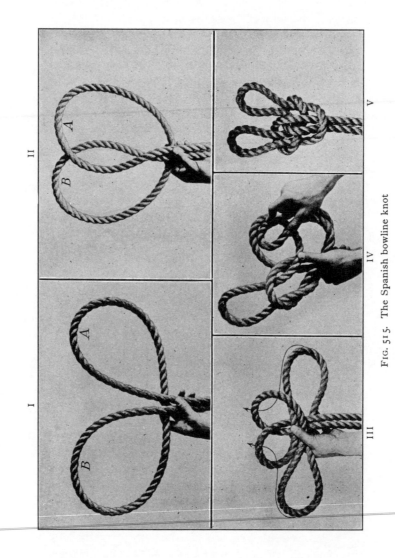

FIG. 515. The Spanish bowline knot

492

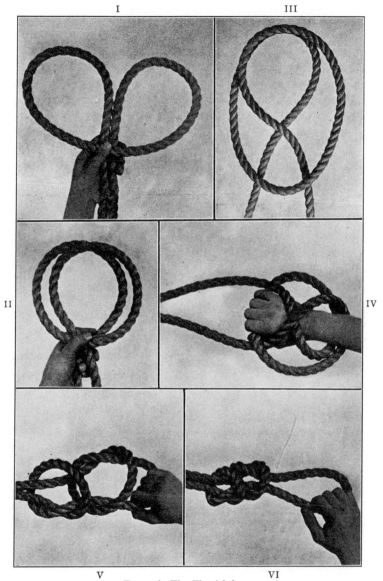

I

III

II

IV

V

VI

FIG. 516. The Flemish loop

493

Bowline in a bight. It is frequently necessary to form a loop in the bight of a rope. For such a purpose the bowline in a bight is very useful. Like the bowline, it is easily untied after a hard pull. The process of tying the knot is as follows: Tie an overhand knot in the bight, as shown in Fig. 514, I. Bend the loop back over the knot as shown in Fig. 514, II. Grasp that part of the knot indicated at *A* (Fig. 514, III) and draw up on the loop end as shown in Fig. 514, IV, thus completing the finished knot.

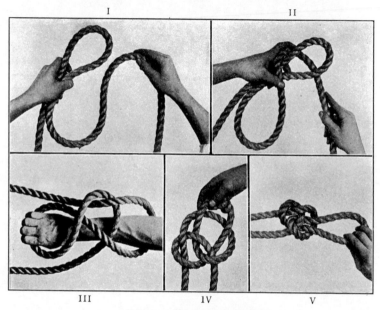

FIG. 517. The harness hitch

Spanish bowline knot. The Spanish bowline knot is used when two loops are wanted in the middle of a rope and when it is necessary to pull on both ends of the rope as well as on the loops. To tie it, form two bights in the rope as shown in Fig. 515, I. Lay *A* over *B* as in Fig. 515, II. Grasp the two bights at the cross between *A* and *B* (Fig. 515, II), and lay them back toward you on top of the rope (Fig. 515, III). Pass the larger loops through the smaller ones from front to rear as shown in Fig. 515, IV. Draw up both loops as shown in Fig. 515, V.

Flemish loop. The Flemish loop is used to form a loop at the end of or in the middle of a rope. It will not slip and forms a permanent knot. The first step in the process of making it is to form two bights in the rope, as shown in Fig. 516, I, and adjust as indicated in Fig. 516, II and III. Insert the right hand and grasp the rope as shown in Fig. 516, IV. Withdraw the hand, pulling the rope through the two bights (Fig. 516, V). Separate the two knots and draw tight as in Fig. 516, VI.

Harness hitch. The harness hitch is used where a loop is wanted in the middle of a rope and when it is necessary to pull on one or both ends of the rope after the loop is made. It is accomplished by first forming a bight in the rope with the left hand as shown in Fig. 517, I. Then, with the right hand, pass the other end of the rope over the bight as shown in Fig. 517, II. Pass the right hand down through the bight first formed, grasping the rope as shown in Fig. 517, III. Draw the rope through the bight as in Fig. 517, IV. Draw up to a finished knot as shown in Fig. 517, V.

Slip knot. The slip knot is used where a loop is wanted that will slip up tight about any object. To tie it, form a bight as shown in Fig. 518, I. Insert your left hand and grasp the long

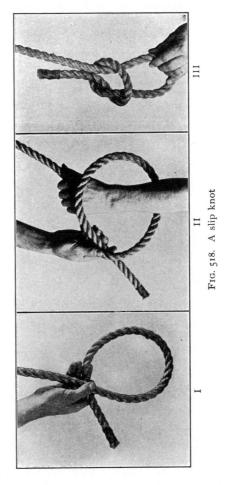

FIG. 518. A slip knot

end of the rope as shown in Fig. 518, ii. Draw the long end back through the bight to make the finished knot (Fig. 518, iii).

Slip knot and half hitch. The short end of the slip knot is frequently secured by giving it a half hitch around the long end of the rope as shown in Fig. 519.

Tomfool's knot. The tomfool's knot is so called because it is a trick knot; and yet it has its uses. The knot forms two slip knots and may be used in ringing hogs, one loop being slipped over the hog's upper jaw and the other used to untie the knot. To tie this knot grasp the rope as shown in Fig. 520, i. Lay the right hand across the left in the manner shown in Fig. 520, ii. Without changing the position of the rope, grasp the rope at A with the left hand and at B with the right hand as shown in Fig. 520, ii and iii. Draw the ropes through the loop as shown in Fig. 520, iv. The finished knot is shown in Fig. 520, v.

FIG. 519. A slip knot and half hitch

Carrick-bend knot. The carrick bend is useful in tying two ropes together when it is necessary to subject them to a heavy pull and still be able to untie the knot easily. It is tied as follows: Throw a bight in the end held in the left hand and a loop in the end held in the right hand as shown in Fig. 521, i. Pass the loop in the right hand over the end in the left hand. Reaching through the bight as shown in Fig. 521, ii, grasp the rope with the right hand, drawing it partly through the bight. With the left hand grasp the end of the rope, bring it under the left-hand rope, and pass it through the bend on top of the bight as shown in Fig. 521, iii. The knot then appears as in Fig. 521, iv. Draw up carefully for the finished knot as shown in Fig. 521, v.

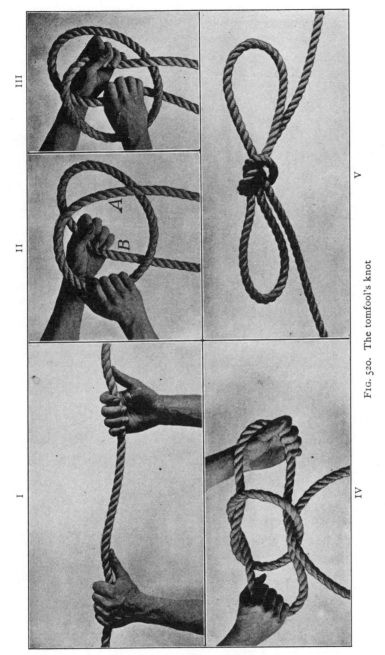

FIG. 520. The tomfool's knot

497

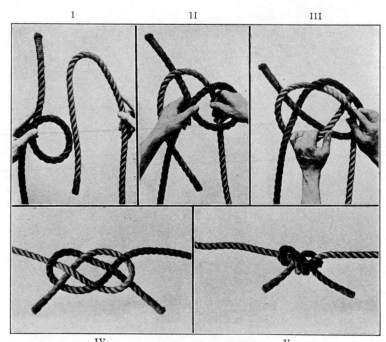

I   II   III

IV   V

FIG. 521. The carrick-bend knot

HITCHES

Half hitch. The half hitch is used to fasten temporarily to some object (as a log, pole, or post) a rope on which there is a steady pull. Its chief use is in lumber camps. After passing the rope around the object, the short end is passed around the long end and tucked under itself as shown in Fig. 522.

Two half hitches. This forms a more secure fastening than the half hitch. After making a half hitch,

FIG. 522. The half hitch

form a second half hitch around the long end of the rope as shown in Fig. 523, I. Care should be taken that the second half hitch is not made as shown in Fig. 523, II, which is incorrect.

I   II

FIG. 523. Two half hitches
I, correct; II, incorrect

I   II

FIG. 524. I, timber hitch; II, timber hitch and half hitch

Timber hitch. The timber hitch is much used in logging-camps. To make it, form a half hitch and then give the short end an additional twist around the rope as shown in Fig. 524, I.

Timber hitch and half hitch. This is a more satisfactory hitch than either the timber hitch or the half hitch separately. It is shown in Fig. 524, II. A half hitch is first made and then a timber hitch is made with the short end of the rope.

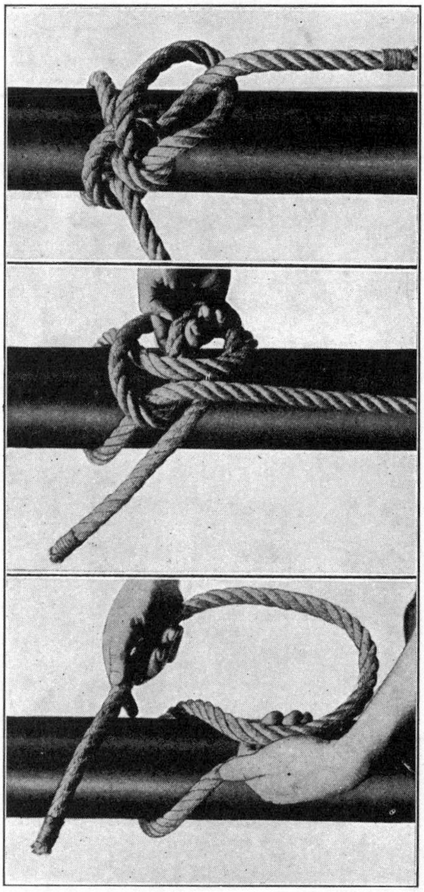

FIG. 525. A halter hitch, first method

Halter hitch. *First method.* The slip knot is most commonly used as a halter hitch, especially when the hitch is made around a pole or tree. To make it, pass the short end around the pole to the right, grasping the rope with the left hand as in Fig. 525, I. Lay the short end across the left hand, forming a bight. Reach through this bight with the right hand, and grasp the short end several inches from its end and draw it through the bight as shown in Fig. 525, II. Draw up tight and pass the end through the loop to prevent its untying (Fig. 525, III).

Second method. Where the rope or strap is tied in a ring or hole in a manger a more secure hitch is obtained as follows: After passing the rope through the ring throw the short end over the long end, grasping each as shown in Fig. 526, I. Be sure to form a decided bend in the long end with the left hand. Pass the short end over the rope and through the bend from the rear as shown in Fig. 526, II. Draw the short end up tight before pulling on the

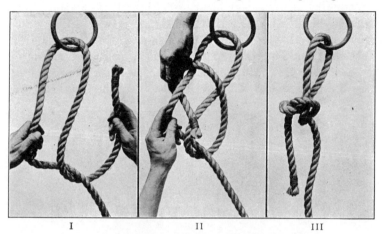

FIG. 526. A halter hitch, second method

long end for the finished knot (Fig. 526, III). This knot will not slip, being thus very useful where a freely slipping loop is required. It is not so likely to come untied as the slip-knot method.

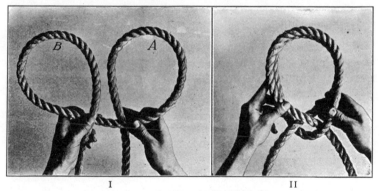

FIG. 527. The clove hitch, first method

Clove hitch. The clove hitch is frequently used by sailors and is, in general, useful for fastening a rope to a post or a pole. It is tied in several ways, the way chosen depending upon conditions.

First method. This method is used where it is possible to form the knot and pass it over the end of the post. To make the hitch, form an overhand bight with the left hand and an underhand bight with the right hand, as shown in Fig. 527, I. Move bight *A* over bight *B* as shown in Fig. 527, II. The hitch is then slipped over a post or a pole and drawn up.

Second method. This method is used when it is necessary to pass the rope around the post or pole. Pass the short end twice

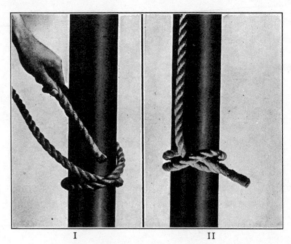

I   II

FIG. 528. The clove hitch, second method

around the pole as shown in Fig. 528, I, bringing the first wrap above the long end. Tuck the short end under itself as shown in Fig. 528, II.

Either method may be used to fasten a rope to a post when there is much of a pull on one end. In the first method the rope is held with the left hand, and the right hand is used in forming first one bight and then the other, placing them over the post as formed. The second method can be used in a similar way except that the short end is passed around the post instead of being looped over the top.

Well-pipe hitch. The well-pipe hitch is used in pulling posts or lifting similar objects, as well pipe. To make it, pass the short end four times around the pipe as shown in Fig. 529, I.

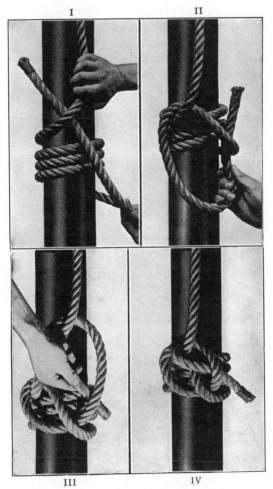

FIG. 529. A well-pipe hitch

Bring the short end beneath the long end and make a half hitch as shown in Fig. 529, II. Then make another half hitch around the long end as shown in Fig. 529, III. Draw up the two half hitches, and the finished hitch will result as shown in Fig. 529, III.

Fisherman's, or anchor, bend. The fisherman's bend is used to fasten a rope permanently to a ring or a hook. The double wrap gives a greater wearing surface. After passing the short end

FIG. 530. The fisherman's bend

twice through the ring it is passed around the long end and through the two turns and half-hitched around the long end as shown in Fig. 530.

Blackwall hitch. This hitch is used to fasten a rope to a hook where the pull is steadily applied. The method of tying is shown in Fig. 531, I and II.

Sheep-shank hitch. The sheep-shank hitch is used to take up slack in a rope, as when a tackle is being used to move a load. It is made thus: Form two open bights, as shown in Fig. 532, I, as long as may be desired. Throw a half hitch over either end as shown in Fig. 532, II and III. If the pull on the rope is not to be steady, a pin should be inserted in each of the loops and tied in place.

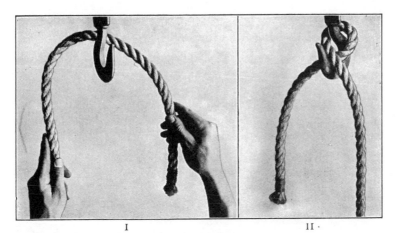

I

II ·

FIG. 531. The Blackwall hitch

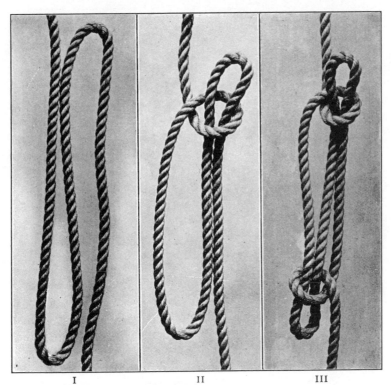

I   II   III

FIG. 532. The sheep-shank hitch

505

506

SPLICES

Splicing is made use of in joining the ends of rope, as well as in making various forms of spliced crowns, spliced eyes, etc. There are two general methods of splicing a rope, known as the short splice and the long splice. Each method has certain advantages.

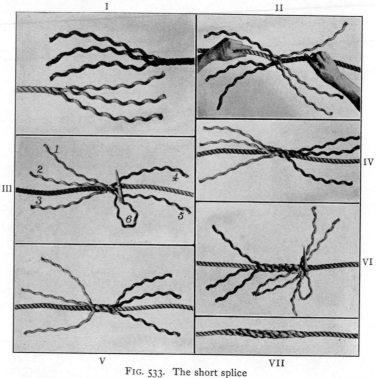

FIG. 533. The short splice

Short splice. The short splice virtually doubles the size of the rope, and hence can be used only where such increase does not interfere with the passage of the rope through pulleys. At times it must be used, if there is but little rope to spare, since the long splice shortens the rope some five or six feet. To make it, unlay the strands about seven turns and tie a cord about the rope as shown in Fig. 533, I. Bring the two ends together as shown in Fig. 533, II, taking care that the strands of one end alternate with those of the other. As the ends are brought together see that the strands are spread as shown in Fig. 534, I, and not as shown in Fig. 534, II. After joining the ends of the rope snugly together tie the strands of one end as shown in Fig. 533, III.

A *marlin spike* is useful in tucking the strands. The spike shown in Fig. 533, III, is a good one. For use with a $\frac{3}{4}$-inch rope the pin should be about 6 in. long and $\frac{7}{8}$ in. in diameter at the large end, tapering to a point at the other end. A $\frac{1}{2}$-inch hole is then bored to a depth of about 1 in. in the larger end. The spike is inserted beneath a strand, and the end of the strand to be tucked is inserted in the hole in the spike. It is thus easily passed beneath the strand as the spike is forced through.

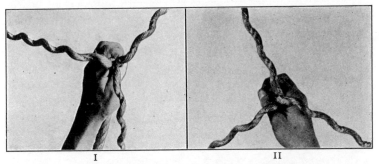

I   II

FIG. 534. Right (at left) and wrong position of strands for splicing

Begin tucking as shown in Fig. 533, III. Take any one of the three strands — No. 6, for example. Tuck it across the rope at right angles to the rope, skipping the strand immediately adjacent (No. 2) and inserting it under the second one from it. Then take No. 4 and No. 5 in order, always skipping the strand next to the one being tucked. Skip one strand only and tuck each strand but once in its turn. Fig. 533, IV, shows the rope with three strands (Nos. 4, 5, and 6) tucked once.

In the same way tuck the other three strands (Nos. 1, 2, and 3) (Fig. 533, V), after removing the cord around them. Draw the strands up tight, making sure that there is no looseness in the rope where the ends are brought together. Proceeding in a similar manner, tuck each strand three times. This completed, divide each of the three strands into two equal parts, untwisting the parts

508

carefully so as not to disarrange the yarns. The three strands to the right in Fig. 533, VI, have been thus divided. Tuck one of each pair of half strands exactly as the full strands were tucked. In choosing the half which is to be tucked take the half which will bind the other close to the rope. After tucking the half strands three times each, cut off the remaining halves close to the rope. The ends of the tucked strands should then be cut off about one-half inch from the rope. The rope may then be smoothed by rolling it under the foot or by pounding it as it is rolled back and forth over a floor or block. After the rope has been pulled for some time the ends of the strands may be trimmed off fairly close to the rope; do not make the

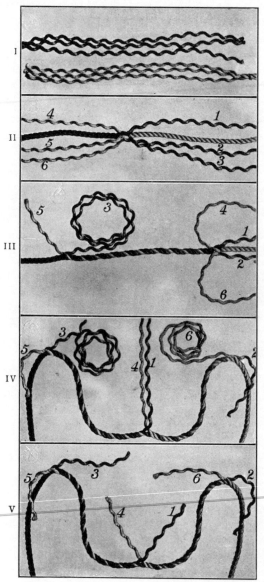

FIG. 535. The long splice, initial steps

mistake of cutting them too close, however, or they are likely to pull out. The finished splice is shown in Fig. 533, VII. This has not been rolled or pressed down in any way.

Long splice. The long splice is used where the size of the rope must not be increased and where a neater and more satisfactory splice than the short splice is desired. The rope is shortened from five to six feet by the process.

In making the splice unlay the strands fifteen turns and tie as shown in Fig. 535, I. Bring the ends together as shown in Fig. 535, II, taking the same precautions as are given under the short splice.

After joining the ends closely together choose two strands that lie adjacent to each other, as Nos. 3 and 5. Unlay strand No. 3 and lay No. 5 in its place as shown in

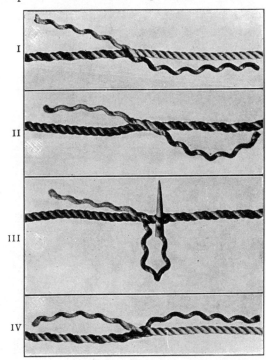

FIG. 536. The long splice (continued)

Fig. 535, III. As soon as No. 3 is unlaid one turn the other should be immediately laid in place ; that is, the one must follow the other up closely. The strand being laid should fit perfectly without much twisting. Proceed as above to within four turns of the end of the strand being laid.

Next choose two (Nos. 2 and 6) of the remaining four strands, taking care that the other two (Nos. 4 and 1) lie adjacent to each other, and proceed to the right as with the first pair. This leaves

510

strands Nos. 1 and 4 at the middle, as shown in Fig. 535, IV. Now cut off the ends of the long strands, leaving each strand about four turns long, as shown in Fig. 535, V. The pairs are now ready to be tucked.

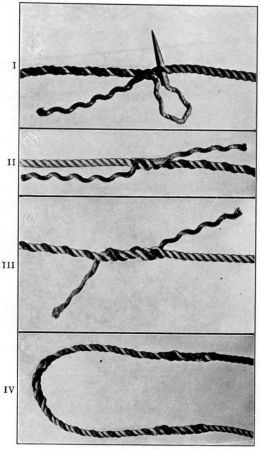

Before starting to tuck see that the strands lie in the position shown in Fig. 536, I, and not as shown in Fig. 536, II. It is in the latter position that the strands are likely to be found at the finish of the laying process. The tucking is done in exactly the same way as in the short splice. Take one end as shown in Fig. 536, III, tuck it over the other end, and draw it up as shown in Fig. 536, IV. Next tuck the other end in a similar manner (Fig. 537, I and II). Tuck each strand three times and cut off one-half inch

FIG. 537. The long splice (continued)

from the rope; the finished splice then appears as in Fig. 537, IV. By rolling the tucks under the foot they may be smoothed out so that the rope is increased in size very little.

Long splice for a four-strand rope. It is sometimes necessary to splice a 4-strand rope. If such a rope has a cord center, cut the cord out and proceed exactly as in a 3-strand rope except that in starting the splice the strands should be unlaid about 20 turns. Then after taking one pair to the left and one to the right as before, leave two pairs instead of one at the middle, Fig. 538, I. It is only necessary to take one pair 5 turns to the right and the

I

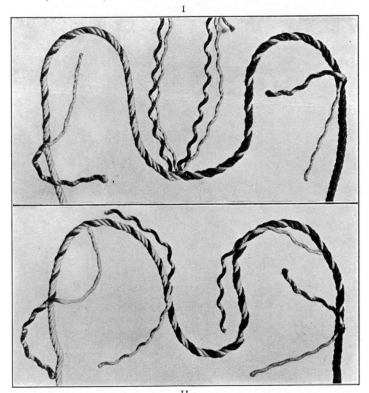

II

FIG. 538. Splicing a four-strand rope

other the same distance to the left (Fig. 538, II), and tuck all pairs as in the long splice.

Mending broken strand. If one strand in a rope breaks, as in Fig. 539, I, unlay each strand about eight turns and secure a strand of sufficient length from the end of the rope or from another rope of the same size and lay it in as shown in Fig. 539, II. Tuck the ends, and the finished work will appear as in Fig. 539, III.

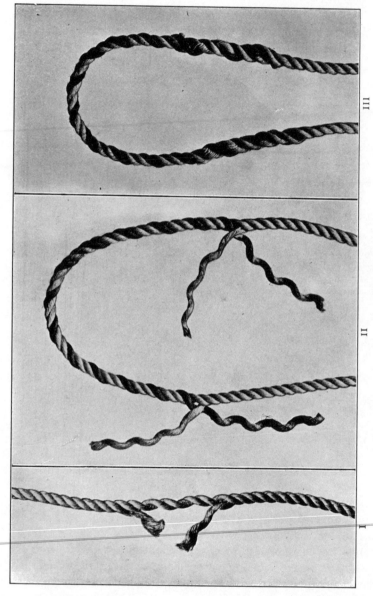

I

II

III

FIG. 539. Mending a broken strand

Spliced crown. The spliced crown is used to prevent the end of a rope from untwisting. It is to be preferred for this purpose to almost any other knot and is particularly desirable where the rope is used for a halter. In making the crown, unlay the strands about five turns. With the middle strand (No. 1) form a bight between the other two as in Fig. 540, I. Lay No. 2 across No. 1 between the bight and No. 3 as shown in Fig. 540, II. Pass No. 3

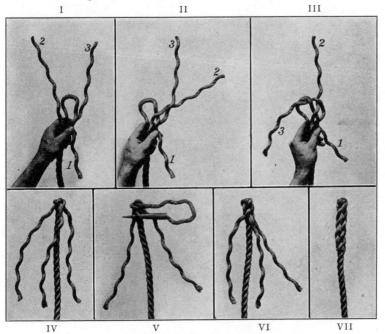

FIG. 540. The spliced crown

down through the bight in No. 1 as shown in Fig. 540, III, and draw up evenly, pulling down on the strands as indicated in Fig. 540, IV. Tuck the ends three times each, beginning as indicated in Fig. 540, V, and proceeding as directed for the short splice. Always tuck the strands in order; that is, tuck all of them once (Fig. 540, VI) before starting on the second tuck. The finished crown is shown in Fig. 540, VII.

If desired after tucking the strands twice, each may be divided as in the short splice, the half strands being tucked once or twice.

Spliced eye. The spliced eye is used where a permanent loop is wanted in the end of a rope, as in fastening a halter rope to the halter. To make the eye, unlay the strands about four turns. Hold the end of the rope in the left hand and form a loop as shown in Fig. 541, I, by bending the rope around towards you, and laying the three strands across the top of the rope. Tuck strand No. I, which is the strand nearest you, under a strand on top of

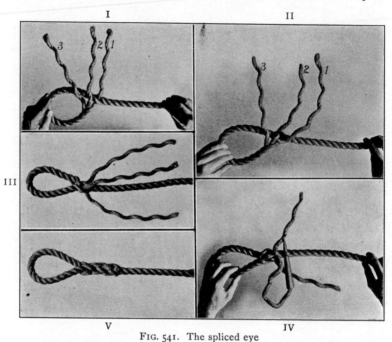

FIG. 541. The spliced eye

the rope as shown in Fig. 541, I. Tuck strand No. 2 under the strand next to the one under which No. I was tucked, as shown in Fig. 541, II. Tuck strand No. 3 under the remaining strand in the rope as shown in Fig. 541, III, and draw the three strands down, making the work as smooth as possible. The last strand tucked will always have a long wrap, but this is not objectionable.

The three ends are now to be tucked three times each as in the case of the spliced crown, the first step being shown in Fig. 541, IV. The finished eye is shown in Fig. 541, v.

Halters

Rope halters as purchased on the market are usually made from an inferior grade of rope. A much better halter will be secured if a good manila rope is purchased and the halter made up in the proper size. As a guide to proper lengths for the halter parts Table XXXIII is given. A better plan is to fit the halter to the animal for which it is being made.

TABLE XXXIII. SIZE AND LENGTHS OF ROPES FOR HALTERS

Animal	Size of Rope in Inches	Total Length in Feet	Length of Parts (Fig. 542, I)			
			A to B	B to C	C to D	D to E
Large horse	$\frac{5}{8}$	15	7	44	10	18
Medium-sized horse .	$\frac{1}{2}$	14	6	40	8	16
Small horse	$\frac{1}{2}$	14	6	36	8	14
Large cattle	$\frac{1}{2}$	12	6	34	7	14
Medium-sized cattle .	$\frac{3}{8}$	12	5	32	6	12

Nonadjustable halter. This is the type of halter most commonly made. After cutting off the proper length of rope, shape the halter as shown in Fig. 542, I, taking care to make all parts the proper length, and mark the points B, E, D, and C by tying cord around the rope.

Now lift a strand in the rope at D and insert the short end of the rope, drawing it through to form the loop as in Fig. 542, II. At point X (Fig. 542, II) raise a strand and insert the long end, drawing it down as shown in Fig. 542, III. This step fixes the size of the loop.

Next unlay the strands in the short end of the rope back to point B (Fig. 542, IV). Now grasp the rope at B and give it two or three reverse twists as indicated by the arrow. This will prevent the headpiece from twisting when the halter is finished. Lift a strand at E and tuck strands No. 1 and No. 2 under it as shown in Fig. 542, V. Now pass strand No. 3 under the rope and tuck it up between Nos. 1 and 2 as shown in Fig. 542, VI.

Finally tuck strand No. 1 along the nosepiece, No. 2 along the long end, and No. 3 up the cheek piece, as shown in

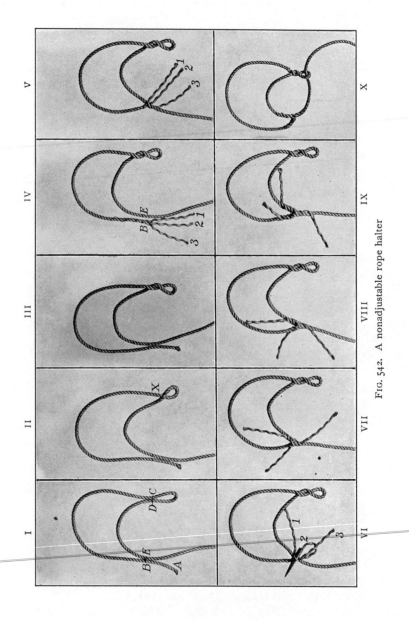

FIG. 542. A nonadjustable rope halter

Fig. 542, VII, VIII, and IX, tucking each three times. Trim off the
ends and insert the long end through the loop as in Fig. 542, X.
The end of the halter rope may be secured by tying any one of
the various knots suitable for that purpose, or the spliced crown
may be used.

Adjustable halter. The adjustable halter is a very convenient
kind of halter to have about the barn, particularly for use on

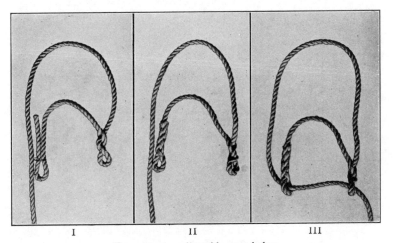

| I | II | III |

FIG. 543. An adjustable rope halter

cattle. It is not so satisfactory for a permanent halter, however,
as the one previously described. In making it, shape the halter
as indicated in Fig. 543, I. Notice that the nosepiece has been
formed with the short end and tucked to form a loop on the
right, as in the first type of halter. Form a spliced eye in the end
(Fig. 543, II), making the eye just a little larger than the rope.
Slip the long end through the two loops as shown in Fig. 543, III.
Only the headpiece, of course, is adjustable, the nosepiece being
fixed in length.

INDEX